BASIC FINANCE

An Introduction to Money and Financial Management

HERBERT B. MAYO
Associate Professor of Finance
Rider College

1978
W. B. SAUNDERS COMPANY
Philadelphia, London, Toronto

W. B. Saunders Company: West Washington Square
Philadelphia, PA   19105

1 St. Anne's Road
Eastbourne, East Sussex BN21 3UN, England

1 Goldthorne Avenue
Toronto, Ontario M8Z 5T9, Canada

Library of Congress Cataloging in Publication Data

Mayo, Herbert B

Basic finance.

Bibliography: p.

Includes index.

1. Finance. 2. Money. 3. Banks and banking. 4. Business
enterprises—Finance. I. Title.

HG173.M394   1978   332   77–84674

ISBN 0–7216–6209–9

Basic Finance:
An Introduction to Money and Financial Management   ISBN   0-7216-6209-9

Last digit is the print number: 9   8   7   6   5   4   3   2   1

DEDICATION

To Pop and Auntie Bea

PREFACE

When I was an undergraduate, I had no real conception of how I would spend my life. I was even uncertain as to my major field of study. And like many students I sampled a variety of subjects for any number of reasons. In retrospect such sampling provided me not only breadth (if not depth) of knowledge but also with a better definition of my likes and dislikes.

Many students have followed a similar pattern of taking a variety of courses, and no doubt many more will continue to do so in the future. Introductory courses and textbooks thus can play an extremely important role in your development, for they expose you to a discipline about which you may have virtually no awareness. Time constraints, of course, mean such courses cannot cover material in depth, but they can whet your appetite for further study in the area.

Even within a general area of study such as business administration or education, you may receive only a brief exposure to particular fields. Most business students receive only a sampling of the various functional areas of business administration. An accounting major, for example, may take just one course in marketing or management, and a marketing major may take only one course in finance. It is for these students that this text is written. Since many aspects of business and business administration involve finance, it is desirable for specialists in the various disciplines of business to have some knowledge of finance institutions and financial decision making. While many students may have only this one exposure to the subject, it should give them a working knowledge of the terms, environment, and mechanics of finance and financial decision making.

Besides introducing the finance student to the world of finance, a major purpose of the text is to entice the non-finance major to do more work in this field. Faculty members naturally want students to pursue their own area of specialty. I want students to take advanced courses in the field, for such advanced work is more stimulating for the instructor. But the fact remains that introductory survey courses are the bread and butter of teaching. Such courses have the largest enrollments and are a main source of demand for the faculty's services. These courses do offer the instructor an excellent opportunity to encourage and entice students to continue studying

v

in the field, and a clearly written and stimulating text can be of considerable help in encouraging students to take additional courses.

The text is divided into the following two distinct parts: money and credit creation, and financial management. Many introductory courses in finance do not cover both areas, but I believe that financial management has much more meaning if the student has background in the area of financial institutions and markets. Of course, if students delay taking a finance course until late in their college career, they may have encountered financial institutions in other courses, and hence parts of the first section of the book may be redundant. But many students survey the field of finance earlier in their college careers and will have had little or no background in financial institutions. It is for these students that this text was primarily written, students who are Sophomores or first semester Juniors. While these students may have had some exposure to business courses (e.g., an accounting course or an economics course), their background is still limited. Introducing them to both financial institutions and financial analysis is a logical extension of their academic development. This approach builds on their foundation and permits them to grow more rapidly in subsequent courses.

The text is constructed with the beginning student in mind. First, the chapters are brief and direct. No attempt is made to pad the text with theoretical subtleties and exceptions. Students will have plenty of opportunity to build on this base if they choose to do so in the future. Second, all the examples in the text are relatively simple, for complex examples are not needed to clarify the points being discussed. The numerical examples employ simple arithmetic, and small numbers are used in these examples. Of course, in the real world a firm will not have sales of $100 or expenses of $80, but this text is seeking not to illustrate the complexity of the real world but to clarify a point in finance. Third, there is a minimum of footnotes and virtually no reference in the text to the academic and professional literature. Students interested in doing further study may consult the reading list at the end of the text.

Finance employs many tools and concepts taught in introductory courses in accounting and economics. Knowledge of certain aspects of economics and accounting is desirable if the student is to have a good grasp of basic finance. However, for the purpose of this text, it is assumed that the student's background in either accounting or economics is minimal. Even though the student may have had a course or courses in either or both subjects, this text will review material pertinent to finance. Thus this text may also be used by the student who wants an introduction to the world of finance but who lacks any formal coursework in economics or accounting.

Besides the text material, each chapter has additional aids for the student. The chapters are preceded by a set of learning objectives. Marginal notes highlight the subject being discussed, and the chapter ends with a list of key words and a set of questions and/or problems. Perhaps the most important of these aids are the learning objectives. Before students read the chapter they should ask what they expect to learn. But that is somewhat contradictory, since, if the student knows what is to be learned, the student probably already knows the material. The learning objectives help to overcome this contradiction by identifying potentially important aspects of the chapter. While these objectives do not cover all facets of the chapter, they do offer a guide to its content.

Since this text serves a general market, there is nothing in it that is original scholarship. The only originality will be in the nature of the presentation (i.e., the order of the material and the choice of examples and words used to convey the material). A book like this evolves and develops over time. I owe a considerable debt to the many students who suffered through classes and tests in which I experimented with examples, questions, and techniques which are incorporated in this text. Their criticisms (often implicit in the looks on their faces) helped me mold my writing style, examples, and questions to better communicate the concepts and tools of financial analysis.

I owe a considerable debt to several people who in one way or another moved the book toward completion. These include my friend and former colleague John Oh (Kansas State) for his initial encouragement to start the project and subsequent interest in its progress. Mary Gamache (formerly a student at Rider College and currently with the Accounting Department of McGraw Hill) gave particular help on the sections concerning accounting and the presentation of accounting statements. Anita Regan, my student assistant for two years, helped in a variety of tasks. Tom Horton (Horton and Daughters) in many ways encouraged and subtly changed the tone of the presentation. My friends Jean and H. Peter Gray took considerable interest and offered encouragement and advice.

I had considerable help from a variety of readers. A warm thank-you is extended to: Anthony J. Curley, Pennsylvania State University; Richard L. Howe, Orange Coast College; William J. Ruckstuhl, The American College; Edward Krohn, Miami-Dade Community College; J. Daniel Williams, University of Akron; Frederick C. Yeager, St. Louis University; Ronald Cerwonka, Providence College; and H. Stephen Grace, Jr., Texas Southern University.

Special thanks, of course, must be given to the people at the W. B. Saunders Company. Wayne Koch, my Editor, could not have been more encouraging and helpful.

Lastly, I must thank my family for tolerating me during the composition and completion of this book. Their understanding is much appreciated.

CONTENTS

Part II   Financial Management

Chapter 1

INTRODUCTION TO THE WORLD OF FINANCE

Learning Objectives

- Contemplate why you are taking this course.
- Recognize the importance of finance to both your career and personal life.
- Understand the purpose and organization of the text.

"Give a man a fish and he eats for a day. Teach a man to fish and he eats for a life time."

Benjamin Franklin

Money, credit. What are they? How are they created? How do individuals and businesses obtain money and credit? How do the stock market and other financial institutions operate? What, if any, investments should an individual or business make?

Business operations and their management are the subject matter of business administration. Money and its management are the contents of finance. Successful business administration requires successful financial management. No matter how small or large the operation, whether it is the corner store or the corporate giant, someone within the firm has to understand finance and answer financial questions. Someone has to make financial plans and financial decisions. Almost anyone can arrive at plans and answers, but poor financial plans can spell financial disaster. Constructing meaningful plans or ascertaining correct answers requires knowing the following two things: (1) the manner in which the financial system functions within the economy and (2) the techniques used by financial managers to reach financial decisions.

FINANCE COURSES

Many colleges and universities offer courses in finance. These courses are designed to teach students how to make financial decisions. The courses will not guarantee financial success, for no course of study can do that. An individual's success will depend on talent, ambition, and willingness to put forth the effort necessary to achieve success. However, by becoming acquainted with the financial environment and educated in the techniques of financial analysis, you should be better able to make the rational financial choices necessary for a successful career, family security, and personal interests.

Finance is both theoretical and descriptive

Finance courses are both theoretical and descriptive. They are theoretical because abstract tools of analysis are necessary to approach and solve financial problems. For example, a firm's management will make more profitable investments in plant and equipment if the financial manager is able to use certain theoretical and analytical tools concerning capital budgeting. This is but one illustration of a theoretical concept that is useful for making decisions. Knowledge and understanding of such theoretical concepts in finance is a prerequisite to successful decision making.

Finance involves institutions and markets

Finance courses are also descriptive and introduce you to financial institutions and markets. You need to know the economic environment in which financial decisions are made. For example, to understand the sources of credit and how money is created, it is necessary to know how the commercial banking system operates. Another illustration of a financial institution is investment banking, for it is through this institution that new securities are sold to the general public. The fiscal policy of the Federal Government, the monetary policy of the Federal Reserve System, and the regulatory activities of the Securities and Exchange Commission are also among the many political and financial institutions that compose the field of finance. The effect of these institutions and the policies they generate are considerations of the subject of finance. Understanding the various institutions and the environment in which financial decisions are made is an integral part of understanding finance.

PURPOSE OF THIS TEXT

The area of finance is broad. No student can acquire during the undergraduate years real expertise in the entire area of finance. That could take a lifetime. So it would be extremely unrealistic to believe that such expertise could be obtained in one brief, introductory course. The course and this book, however, can indicate the breadth of the subject and introduce you to both financial institutions and techniques of financial analysis.

By taking advanced courses, finance majors will develop further the materials presented in this text. It is, however, the author's hope that non-finance majors will be sufficiently fascinated by various aspects of the subject that they, too, will take additional courses in finance. There are many aspects of the subject that are relevent to the general life of the student. All workers earn income, consume part of that income, and save. They must subsequently decide what to do with these savings, and portfolio decisions are an important part of finance. Knowledge of the security markets and the other assets available to savers is part of living in today's world.

This foundation is developed in advanced courses

Finance may be considered as a subset of accounting or economics and may be taught in an accounting or economics department. Finance draws on the analytical tools and information offered by both disciplines. The emphasis, however, usually depends on the background of the author or the instructor. But the subject matter of finance encompasses both accounting and economics and knowledge of both is necessary for a successful career in finance. Additional course work in accounting and economics is important to the finance major. However, since finance may be viewed as a subset of accounting and economics, the student of either of these disciplines should consider taking courses above the introductory level in the area of finance. The importance of finance was well acknowledged by one of the most important of all economists, Lord Keynes. He not only made a fortune in the security markets but also realized that finance is necessary for business to operate. Not all economists, however, acknowledge the crucial role that finance plays and thus frequently assume away the real financial problems that influence the behavior of firms and households.

Finance is related to economics and accounting

Advanced work in finance is particularly useful to accounting majors. Financial analysis often utilizes data generated by accountants, and accountants use many financial techniques. Financial managers and accountants frequently work together to analyze business problems. Awareness of their respective disciplines will increase their ability to work together and communicate. Knowledge of finance is important to accountants, a fact that has been recognized by the National Association of Accountants, which recently instituted the Certificate in Management Accounting (CMA examination). Financial management is an integral part of the examination for CMA certification.

PLAN OF THE TEXT

The text has two parts: (1) the financial environment; (2) financial management

The text is divided into two sections. The first section, which encompasses approximately one third of the text, is devoted to the financial environment. It includes financial institutions, the creation of credit, and policies that affect the creation of credit. This section is similar to material presented in some courses in economics (especially money and banking and macro-economics). Chapter 2 covers money, the circular flow of income, and financial intermediation. Chapters 3 and 4 consider the commercial banking system and how it creates credit. Chapters 5 through 7 consider factors that may affect the ability of commercial banks to lend. These include the Federal Reserve (Chapter 5), fiscal policy (Chapter 6), and international monetary transactions (Chapter 7). Chapters 8 through 10 consider alternative investments available to savers. These include non-commercial bank financial intermediaries (Chapter 8) and the stock market (Chapter 9). Chapter 10 is devoted to the selection of securities. It is a tangent from the general theme of the first section, which is the capacity of commercial banks to create money and credit. The last chapter of the first part is a general overview of the financial environment.

The second part of the text covers financial decision making and the role of financial manager. It includes such topics as financial planning and forecasting, investing in plant and equipment, and managing and financing assets. A chapter breakdown of topics is given in Chapter 12, which serves as an introduction to financial management. In general this part of the text is similar to material covered in courses in financial management or corporate finance. The final chapter seeks to integrate the material presented in the two sections. Financial institutions and government policy affect financial decision making. You need to be aware of this interdependence of financial decision making and the financial environment. This integration thus becomes the final summation of all the material presented in the text.

QUESTIONS FOR THOUGHT AND DISCUSSION

1. Think of several financial decisions you have made. Did you perform any type of financial analysis before making the deci-

sion? If so, what were your sources of information? Did you consider alternative courses of action?

2. Why may a course in finance be important to students majoring in other disciplines? Do you believe this course will aid you to live in a modern, financially-oriented world? If so, how?

	Dollars	Cents
		X X

	Dollars	Cents
NCY		X X

	Dollars	Cents
CURRENCY		X X
COIN		
CHECKS		
List by Bank Number		
Total Deposit		

19____

NUMBER INCLUDING ZEROS

FOR BANK USE ONLY

Part I
THE FINANCIAL ENVIRONMENT

Chapter 2

FINANCIAL INTERMEDIATION

Learning Objectives

- Define money and differentiate it from other assets.
- Trace the flow of resources and payments among the sectors of the economy.
- Explain how savings are transferred into investments.
- Differentiate financial intermediaries from other businesses.

"Neither a borrower nor a lender be."

Shakespeare (Hamlet)

The transfer of resources by borrowing and lending is extremely important to an advanced economy. Without these transfers the level of economic activity could not be sustained and income and employment would fall. Financial intermediaries which stand between borrowers and lenders facilitate this transfer and hence are a crucial component of the nation's financial structure. Actually the nation's financial system contains a variety of financial institutions. Several of these institutions function mainly as financial intermediaries (e.g., commercial banks and savings and loan associations). Other important components of the financial system include financial institutions that are not financial intermediaries, such as the Federal Reserve, the United States Treasury, and the stock exchanges. These financial institutions operate independently of each other, and the roles played by each are discussed in the following chapters.

This chapter lays the foundation for this subsequent discussion by covering in general terms the process of financial intermediation. While this is the most important topic covered, this chapter begins with a discussion of money, its definitions and roles. Then follows a set of flow charts which illustrate the circular flow of resources and payments among the sectors of the economy. Since this flow is facilitated by financial intermediaries, their role and importance are indicated by the circular flow of resources and payments.

Money is anything that is generally accepted in payment for goods and services or for the retirement of debt. This definition has several important words, especially *anything* and *generally accepted*. Anything may perform the role of money, and many different items, including shells, stones, and metals have served as money. During the history of this country a variety of coins and paper moneys have been used. For example, in the past, gold coins served as money in the United States, but today this is no longer the case, for the U.S. Treasury has stopped minting gold coins. Coins are presently made of cheaper metals, such as copper. The value of the metallic content of these coins is less than the value of the coin. For example, the value of the copper contained in a penny is less than the value of the penny. If the copper in a penny were worth more in other uses than as money, people would melt pennies and remove the copper. Copper pennies would cease to exist as money. Then the U.S. Treasury would have to alter the metallic content of the penny.

Since the value of the metal is less than the value of the coin, coins are only "token coins." The extreme case of such token money is paper money, which uses virtually no physical resources. Paper money is cheaper for the government to print and is very convenient to use. Hence it is often employed as a substitute for coins. Perhaps the most convenient form of money is demand deposits in commercial banks. These deposits are readily transferred by check and are generally accepted as a means of payment. Actually the form of money is not really important, for the role of money is not fulfilled by its physical content. As long as an item is generally acceptable for the payment of goods, services, or the retirement of debt, it is money.

The other important words in the above definition of money are *generally accepted*. What serves as money in one place may not be money elsewhere. This fact is readily understood by a person who travels abroad and must convert one currency to another. The paper that serves as money in Great Britain, called pounds, does not serve the role of money in Paris, where French francs are used. Pounds must be converted into francs in order for the holder to buy goods in Paris. The same applies to U.S. dollars because they do not serve as money in other nations. While U.S. dollars may be readily converted into other currencies, they are not generally accepted in other nations and hence are not money.

Demand deposits are money because they are generally accepted. However, a check may be refused. The check itself is not money but is the means for transferring the demand deposit. If the recipient believes there are no funds in the demand deposit, the check will not be accepted. This refusal does not

Money defined

Forms of money

Acceptability of money

invalidate the statement that demand deposits are money, because they are generally accepted as a means of payment.

Power to create money

The power to create money is given by the Constitution to the Federal Government. Congress established a central bank, the Federal Reserve system, and gave it power to control the supply of money and to oversee the commercial banking system. Initially it was not the intent of Congress to create a central bank, for in the Federal Reserve Act of 1913 twelve district banks were established. The Federal Reserve was reorganized by the Banking Acts of 1933 and 1935 to become the central bank known today. The organization of the Federal Reserve and how it controls the supply of money is discussed in Chapter 5.

While the Federal Reserve has control over the supply of money, most of the money supply is created through the process of loan creation by the commercial banking system. (This process of loan creation is explained in Chapter 4.) Thus neither the Federal Reserve nor the Treasury is the prime creator of the nation's supply of money, even though the treasury does mint coins and print currency. Instead, it is primarily the actions of the banking system and the Federal Reserve which expand and contract the nation's supply of money.

The value of money: its purchasing power

Money's value is related to its purchasing power, for money is worth only what it will purchase. Since the country's money supply consists of bank deposits, paper money, and token coins, there are very few real resources in the money itself. Hence the value of money can be related only to the goods it can purchase. As the price of these goods rises, then the value of money declines. Inflation, which is a rise in the general price level of all goods and services, is a devaluation or deterioration in the value of money. As prices of goods and services rise, the price of money falls; its buying power is less.

Sometimes the price of money is stated as the interest rate, but this is incorrect. An interest rate is the price of credit, that is, the price the borrower pays for the use of the lender's money. There are many types of loans (e.g., mortgages, consumer credit, bonds). Thus there are many interest rates which reflect the amount borrowed, the length of time the borrower will have the use of the money, and the credit worthiness of the borrower. There is, however, only one general level of prices, and it is this price level which indicates the value of money.

Definitions of the money supply: (1) M_1; (2) M_2

There are several definitions of the composition of the money supply. The traditional definition has been that the money supply consists of checking accounts in commercial banks (called "demand deposits" because they are payable on demand), plus coins and paper currency. This definition is frequently referred to as M_1.

Some economists argue that the savings accounts in commercial banks should also be considered as part of the money supply. Funds in these accounts may be withdrawn at the option of the depositor; thus the depositor may shift funds between these accounts with relative ease. The distinction between these accounts in commercial banks is therefore blurred. This minority group of economists includes savings accounts in commercial banks as part of the money supply. Hence this definition of the composition of the money supply is M_1 (i.e., demand deposits plus coins plus currency) plus savings accounts in commercial banks. This definition is referred to as M_2.

Actually M_1 and M_2 are not the only possible definitions of the composition of the money supply. For example, savings accounts in other financial intermediaries may be included. It may be argued that funds may be readily transferred among financial intermediaries and that the distinction among types of accounts has diminished. Furthermore legislation is pending that will permit commercial banks to pay interest on checking accounts, and currently some mutual savings banks are permitted to issue checks that may be drawn on savings accounts. The trend in financial intermediaries has been to reduce the distinctions between types of accounts. Thus any definition of the money supply that includes one type of deposit and excludes others may be considered somewhat arbitrary. However, for the purpose of this text, the traditional definition of the composition of the money supply (M_1) is employed.

Demand deposits in commercial banks are the most important component of the money supply. As of December, 1976, the composition of the money supply was as follows:

Composition of M_1

demand deposits: $235.6 billion (74.2%)
currency: $82.2 billion (25.8%)

Demand deposits encompass about 75% of the narrowly defined money supply (M_1). This indicates the important role played by the banking system in the determination of the money supply, for the majority of these deposits are the result of the process of loan creation.

If the broader definition of money supply is used (M_2), the composition of the money supply was

Composition of M_2

demand deposits: $235.6 billion (31.8%)
currency: $82.2 billion (11.1%)
time and savings deposits: $423.7 billion (57.1%)

Time and savings deposits in commercial banks constitute more than half of the money supply when the broader definition is employed. The flow of funds into these accounts then affects not only the capacity of banks to lend and create credit but also the composition of the broadly defined money supply.

Money performs a variety of important roles. It is a medium of exchange and a store of value. It is also a unit of account and a standard of deferred payment. Without money there would be considerably fewer transactions of goods and services, for such transactions would occur only if one party wanted the goods offered by the other party. Such direct transfer of goods and

The functions of money:

(1) medium of exchange

services is called "barter." Barter is an extremely inefficient means of transferring goods, and it should be no surprise to students of finance that money developed as a substitute for bartering. Instead of trading one good for another, individuals sell goods and services for money and then use the money to purchase other goods and services. Money thus facilitates the flow of goods and services by its role as a medium of exchange. An advanced economy could not exist without something performing the role of a medium of exchange. Money then is necessary for the very existence of an advanced economy, and every economically developed nation has a form of money to facilitate the exchange of goods.

(2) store of value

Money may also be used to transfer purchasing power to the future. In this second role money acts as a store of value from one time period to another. Money, however, is only one of many assets that may be used as a store of value. Stocks, bonds, savings accounts, and savings bonds are some of the various assets that savers may use to store value. During periods of inflation the list of potential stores of value increases. Real estate, art works, diamonds, gold and antiques are now included among the many and varied assets that some people use to store value.

A saver's portfolio thus may have a varied mix of assets that perform the role of a store of value. However, all these nonmonetary assets must be converted into money in order for the saver to exercise the purchasing power that has been stored. The ease with which an asset may be converted into money with little loss of value is called "liquidity." Money is, of course, the most liquid of all assets. Other assets may not be readily converted to cash, and investing in them may cause the saver to lose a substantial amount of liquidity. For example, antiques may inflate in value but converting them into money may be a time-consuming and costly process. Hence this type of asset may be very illiquid.

While money is the most liquid of all assets, it earns nothing for the owner. Certain other assets, however, provide their owners a flow of income or services. Bonds and savings accounts pay interest, stocks may pay dividends, and physical goods provide enjoyment. For money to be attractive as a store of value, its liquidity must offset the advantages offered by the other assets. For example, if investors anticipate that security prices will fall, then money may be an attractive, alternative investment. But during periods of high interest rates or rising security prices or inflation, money is a poor store of value, and savers try to minimize the amount of money held as a store of value.

(3) unit of account

Money also performs two other functions. It is a unit of account and a standard of deferred payment. The prices of goods are determined in terms of money instead of in terms of each other. For example, an apple costs $.25 and a bottle of beer costs $.50. The price of the apple is not expressed as the price of half a bottle of beer. Both the prices of the apple and the beer are expressed in terms of money. Money is also the standard for expressing payments over time. For example, loans which are repaid in the future are defined in terms of money. The deterioration of the value of money through inflation illustrates the role of money as a unit of account and a standard of deferred payment. The value of a unit of money and the value of debts repaid in the future are both declining as the price level increases.

In summary, money is crucial to an advanced economy, for it facilitates the transfer of goods and resources. An advanced economy could not exist without something performing the role of money. Since a large proportion of the money supply is demand deposits in commercial banks, the student of finance must understand the banking system. Funds flow into banks through deposits and create for banks the ability to lend. Banks are financial intermediaries that stand between the ultimate lenders, the depositors, and the borrowers. Banks, however, are only one of several types of financial intermediaries. The remainder of this chapter is devoted to a general discussion of the role of financial intermediaries. The following chapters will contain a more detailed discussion of the banking system and how it creates money. Other financial intermediaries are discussed in Chapter 8.

(4) standard of deferred payments

THE FLOW OF RESOURCES AND PAYMENTS

The economy may be divided into the following four sectors: individual households, businesses, government, and foreign trade. Monetary transactions (i.e., payments) and real transactions (i.e., goods and services and resources) flow through the economy to and from each of these four sectors. None of the sectors is isolated from the others for they are all interdependent. However, in an economy like the United States, foreign trade plays a relatively minor role. This is, of course, not true for an economy such as Great Britain where international transactions are a major factor influencing the British economy. Even the United States is not immune from the impact of foreign trade, as was illustrated by the recent oil embargo and the subsequent increases in oil prices. Since the purpose of this chapter is to discuss the role of financial intermediaries, the government and foreign sectors will be omitted from the following discussion. This will help isolate transactions between the general public and business and illustrate the role of financial intermediaries. Thus for the remainder of this chapter there will only be two sectors in the economy: individual households and business firms.

The sectors of an economy

The flow of monetary and real transactions between businesses and households may be illustrated by the flow chart in Figure 2–1. The monetary flows are illustrated in the top half of

The flow of monetary payments and real goods, services, and resources

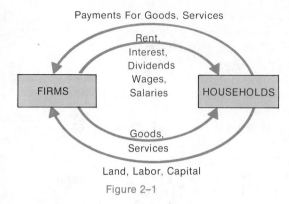

Payments For Goods, Services

Rent,
Interest,
Dividends
Wages,
Salaries

FIRMS   HOUSEHOLDS

Goods,
Services

Land, Labor, Capital

Figure 2-1

Total income: sum of
payments to the
factors of production

Income is either (1)
spent or (2) saved

the chart, and the flows of resources and final goods and services are illustrated in the lower half. Final goods and services flow from the businesses to the general public and real resources (i.e., the factors of production: land, labor, and capital) flow from the general public to businesses. The general public makes monetary payments to businesses for final goods and services. Businesses, in turn, make monetary payments to the general public for the resources. These latter payments are commonly called wages and salaries, interest, rent, and dividends. The sum of these monetary payments to households is called income; thus a person's income is the sum of all the payments to the factors of production that he or she owns. A person may receive wages or a salary, interest, dividends, or rent. Of course, not all individuals receive income from each source. This income represents claims on the final goods and services produced by the economy. The individual can use the income to purchase goods and services. The more income one has, the greater is the command over society's goods and services.

Once the individual has received income, there are two choices: spend the income or save it. Since income represents command over goods and services, the choices are to exercise or not to exercise this command. If the individual chooses to save, then an additional decision must be made: what to do with the savings. The saver must decide where to invest this command over resources that is currently not being used. As was suggested in the previous section, there are many alternative and competing assets in which the saver may invest the savings. In effect, the saver must decide on a portfolio of assets to own. This is an important decision for the individual saver because these assets are the means by which today's purchasing power is transferred to the future. A poor investment decision may destroy this current command over goods and services.

If the value of all the monetary purchases are totalled and all the business payments to the households are totalled, the payments made by businesses will exceed the payments made for goods and services. This is a result of the fact that the general public saves part of its income. Thus some of the flow of payments made to households is lost into individuals' savings. If this savings is not returned to the flow of payments, then the level of income in the country will decline, because there is insufficient aggregate spending to justify continuing the level of production. If production is reduced, then payments to the factors of production will also be reduced.

There are basically two methods for restoring this savings to the flow. One is the direct investment of these savings by the general public into businesses. This occurs when business firms issue securities which are purchased by households or when individuals invest in sole proprietorships or partnerships. The other method for transferring the savings to businesses is through a financial intermediary. A financial intermediary transfers funds that are not currently being used (i.e., saved) to borrowers who currently desire to use those funds. The most important financial intermediary is the commercial banking system, but there are other financial companies, such as savings and loan associations and life insurance companies, that transfer a household's savings to businesses. All these intermediaries perform basically the same function: the transfer of a household's savings to businesses.

This transfer of resources between households to businesses is illustrated by the following flow chart. Figure 2–2 expands the previous flow chart to include savings and their return to the flow.

Payments are made by business to the public for the use of the public's resources. This income either is spent and returned to businesses in the form of payments for goods or services or is saved. This savings is then invested in businesses either directly or indirectly through a financial intermediary. The indirect transfer through the financial intermediary is the more important of the two methods, for most individual households do not invest their savings directly in businesses. Some households do invest

Savings returned to the flow (1) directly or (2) indirectly through a financial intermediary

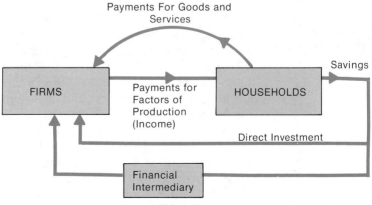

Figure 2–2

money in their own business or partnerships, and firms do issue new securities which are purchased by households. Individual firms, however, issue new securities on an intermittent basis and many years may lapse between issues. Most purchases of securities by households do not transfer savings to businesses, for such purchases transfer securities from one individual owner to another. The primary role of organized security markets is to facilitate this transfer of securities among investors. It is the existence of this secondary market that in part makes securities attractive to investors, thus making it easier for firms to issue additional securities.

In summary, there are flows of resources (land, labor, and capital) to firms. The resources are transformed into goods and services that flow back to households. These flows are "real" because they involve tangible goods, services, and physical resources. In an advanced economy there are also monetary flows as firms pay for the resources and the general public pays for the goods and services. The monetary flows to households generate their income, which must either be spent or saved. If a household chooses to save a part of its income, an additional decision must be made: what form will be used to hold the savings? This portfolio decision is important because it is through it that the command of resources is transferred back to the circular flow. The savings must be returned to businesses in order for the level of income and employment in the economy to be maintained. This transfer may occur in two ways: (1) the savings can directly be invested in or lent to businesses, or (2) the savings can flow through financial intermediaries. These intermediaries, of which the most important is the commercial banking system, stand between savers and borrowers and transfer savers' purchasing power to businesses. Hence financial intermediaries are an extremely important component of the nation's financial system.

FINANCIAL INTERMEDIATION

"T" accounts: abbreviated balance sheets

In general, all financial intermediaries borrow from savers and lend to borrowers. This process may be illustrated by the use of T-accounts, which are abbreviated balance sheets. A balance sheet enumerates (1) the assets a firm or household owns, (2) the liabilities (i.e., what it owes), and (3) its equity or net worth. (The construction of a balance sheet is presented in Part II, Chapter 12.) A T-account simplifies by showing only those assets and liabilities being discussed. All other assets, liabilities, and equity are omitted to ease the explanation. Such accounts are used extensively in the first part of this text.

Simple balance sheet for a financial intermediary

An example of a balance sheet for a financial intermediary such as a commercial bank is as follows:

ASSETS		LIABILITIES AND EQUITY	
Cash	$ 50	Customer Deposits	$440
Loans	300	Other Debt	100
Securities	150	Capital	60
Buildings	100		
	$600		$600

The intermediary has a portfolio of assets which includes not only the loans it has made and securities it has purchased but also any cash and buildings that it may own. Its liabilities include not only the deposits made in the intermediary but also any other debt the intermediary has issued. The equity (i.e., capital) is the owners' investment in the firm. Since the liabilities and equity are the source of funds that purchased the assets, the sum of the assets must equal the sum of the liabilities and equity.

A financial intermediary acquires funds from savers by issuing debt on itself. This process may be illustrated by the following T-accounts:

The deposit

FINANCIAL INTERMEDIARY		SAVER	
Cash ↑	Savings Account ↑	Cash ↓	
		Savings Account ↑	

The financial intermediary acquires the saver's money by issuing a liability on itself or the savings accounts (or in the case of a commercial bank either a savings or a checking account). The saver trades one asset, money, for another asset, the savings account. The intermediary promises to return the money plus interest paid on the savings account in the future.

The financial intermediary then lends the cash to a borrower; when it does, the following transactions occur:

The loan

BORROWER		FINANCIAL INTERMEDIARY	
Cash ↑	Loan ↑	Cash ↓	
		Loan ↑	

The financial intermediary gives up one asset, cash, to acquire another asset, the loan. The borrower acquires the cash by promising to return it in the future and to pay interest while the loan is outstanding. (Of course, cash is rarely used to make loans. Instead the borrower receives a demand deposit. The process of credit creation employing demand deposits is developed in Chapter 4.)

These T-accounts may be combined to illustrate the process of financial intermediation.

Financial intermediation

BORROWER		FINANCIAL INTERMEDIARY		SAVER	
Cash ↑	Loan ↑	Cash ↑↓	Savings Account ↑	Cash ↓	
		Loan ↑		Savings Account↑	

The saver's funds are transferred to the borrower through the financial intermediary. The intermediary in effect transforms the debt of the borrower into debt on itself (the savings account). Savers are more willing to accept this debt than the debt of the ultimate borrower. Through this process of intermediation the borrower is able to acquire the funds because the financial intermediary is able to issue debt that savers will accept. Without the financial intermediary, borrowers and savers would have to transfer the funds directly to each other. However, in advanced economies various types of financial intermediaries have developed that facilitate the transfer of savings to borrowers.

Differences among financial intermediaries involves (1) the types of deposits

All financial intermediaries build a portfolio of assets, and all issue debt to savers. The differences among them are related to the types of liabilities each issues and the types of assets they acquire. For example, the most important feature that differentiates commercial banks from other financial intermediaries is that they can issue demand deposits (checking accounts) as well as savings accounts. Other financial intermediaries such as savings and loan associations cannot issue demand deposits. Demand deposits are used to make payments and are the major component of the nation's money supply. Hence commercial banks are the most important financial intermediary.

NOW accounts

While non-commercial banks cannot offer checking accounts, some states have permitted certain financial intermediaries to issue "negotiable orders of withdrawal." These may be written against certain savings accounts (called NOW accounts). These payment orders permit the transfer of funds through drafts that are very similar to checks. There is pending legislation that would permit more financial intermediaries to offer such accounts. If such legislation becomes law, this distinction between commercial banks and other financial intermediaries will be blurred.

(2) their portfolio of assets

The second major difference among financial intermediaries is the type of assets they acquire. There are a variety of assets available from loans of short duration to long-term loans granted to households, firms, or governments. The differences in the portfolios of financial intermediaries are primarily related to the nature of their business or the legal environment. For example, savings and loan associations specialize in granting mortgages because their depositors tend to leave their money with the savings and loan association for many years. Thus the savings and loan may grant loans that tie up the funds for many years. Commercial banks, however, make a broader spectrum of loans. They stress loans that are rapidly paid off (i.e., mature) primarily because demand deposits turn over more rapidly than deposits in savings and loan associations. Since commercial banks are aware of the need to be able to meet withdrawals from checking accounts, they cannot have a portfolio limited to long-term investments such as mortgages. Their main assets include short-term loans to businesses and the short-term debt of the Federal Government. Long-term loans such as home mortgages compose only a small proportion of the assets of commercial banks.

ADVANTAGES OF FINANCIAL INTERMEDIARIES

What are the advantages of a system of financial intermediaries? Obviously for such a system to exist there has to be advantages to all concerned—borrower, lender, and the financial intermediary. One of the major advantages to the borrower is that the intermediary is able to pool the funds of many people and thus make loans of substantial size. A corporation like General Motors would have a major problem if it continually had to approach individual savers to borrow money. Commercial banks, however, can lend General Motors a significant amount of money, and thus the commercial banks save General Motors the cost of the search for funds. A bank is able to do this because it pools the deposits of many savers and so has larger amounts available to lend.

Advantages of financial intermediation to (1) borrowers

For the saver there are the advantages of income and convenience. Savings accounts pay interest and checking accounts are a convenient means to make payments. These accounts also permit the savers to deposit and withdraw small amounts of money. Other securities like stocks and bonds may not be divisible into such small quantities. If small quantities are available, there is a substantial commission cost for dealing with such small amounts of securities. Hence these securities are not as convenient as savings and checking accounts.

(2) savers

In addition, these accounts are considerably less risky than other investments. There is virtually no risk of loss of funds deposited in a savings or a checking account. This is particularly true with the advent of federal deposit insurance. If a saver places $1000 in a federally insured savings account, the $1000 principal is safe and may be withdrawn at the saver's option. If the saver buys $1000 worth of stock, its value may decline. Such a decline in the principal does not occur with savings and checking accounts. Furthermore, the nature of the intermediary's portfolio reduces the risk of loss to the saver, for the financial intermediary pools its funds and acquires a diversified portfolio of loans, which spreads the risk. Even if the value of some of the intermediary's assets declines, such declines rarely endanger the financial position of the intermediary. In the case in which the financial intermediary does experience financial difficulty, then federal deposit insurance protects the depositors.

While many financial intermediaries do offer federal deposit insurance, it is important to realize that not all offer such insurance. For example, these is no federal insurance program for life insurance companies. A saver's policy is only as strong as the company and the assets it owns. If the company were to fail, the saver stands to lose the funds that have been invested in the life insurance. Hence it is incorrect to assume that savings invested in a financial intermediary are necessarily free from the risk of loss.

(3) the financial intermediary

Besides advantages to borrower and lender, there must also be an advantage to the financial intermediary. It must receive compensation for the service it is providing the lenders and the borrowers. This compensation is the potential for profit. The source of this profit is the difference between what the intermediaries pay depositors and what they charge borrowers. Of course, the lenders and the borrowers could deal directly with each other and share these profits (which they do when stocks and bonds are issued and sold to households). But the advantages offered by financial intermediaries, such as convenience and reduced risk to savers, and the continuous availability of large sources of funds for large corporate borrowers do not exist when the borrowers and lenders deal directly with each other. These advantages offered by the financial intermediaries, however, do require compensation, which is achieved through profits generated by the difference between what the financial intermediary pays its depositors and what it charges its borrowers.

(4) the economy

Financial intermediaries also offer an important advantage to the aggregate economy. Since they facilitate the transfer of funds from savers to firms and households that need funds, financial intermediaries increase the level of income and employment. Because firms are able to acquire funds through the intermediaries, they are able to employ additional labor. This increases the aggregate level of income and employment. These workers would not have been employed if firms had been unable to acquire the necessary funds from the financial intermediaries. Thus all members of the society benefit from the existence of the financial intermediaries. The nation's level of output would be considerably lower if financial intermediaries did not facilitate the transfer of funds from savers to borrowers.

SUMMARY

This chapter introduced the concept of financial intermediaries. These are an extremely important part of the nation's financial structure for they transfer the funds of savers to borrowers. Financial intermediation involves the creation of financial claims. The intermediary creates a claim on itself (e.g., a savings account) when it receives the saver's funds. When it lends the funds, it creates a claim on the borrower. Thus a financial intermediary in effect takes the claim on the borrower and converts it into a claim on itself which the saver is willing to acquire. Savers may directly transfer their savings by purchasing newly issued securities or investing in sole proprietorships and partnerships. However, many savers find financial intermediaries to be the best investments for their funds.

The subsequent chapters will cover various financial intermediaries and financial institutions. The next two chapters discuss the most important financial intermediary, the commercial banking system and its ability to expand the money supply. The following three chapters consider potential influences on commercial banks' ability to lend. Chapter 8 covers non-commercial bank financial intermediaries, and Chapter 9 discusses that well-known and important financial institution, the stock market.

_____ KEY WORDS AND TERMS

money
barter
token money
money supply (M_1, M_2)
demand deposits
price of money
NOW accounts

inflation
portfolio
liquidity
circular flow
financial intermediary
balance sheet

_____ QUESTIONS FOR THOUGHT AND DISCUSSION

1. What is money and why do people need it? Who creates money and in what form? Are there any substitutes for money?

2. What characteristics do all income earning assets possess? Does money also have these characteristics? Why would one hold money as a store of value?

3. What is the circular flow of income? What role does savings play? How may savings be channeled into investment spending? Why is this transfer of savings into investments important in an advanced economy?

4. Since financial intermediaries only transfer title to resources from one economic unit to another, can it be argued that they perform no useful function?

Chapter 3　THE COMMERCIAL BANKING SYSTEM

Learning Objectives

* Enumerate the assets and liabilities of a commercial bank.
* Explain the source of commercial bank profits.
* Isolate sources of risk for commercial banks.
* Identify the purpose of bank regulations.
* Differentiate among commercial banks' total reserves, required reserves, and excess reserves.
* Explain how commercial banks compete.

"A bank is a place where they lend you an umbrella in fair weather and ask for it back again when it begins to rain."

Robert Frost

There are two reasons why the commercial banking system is the most important financial intermediary. First, the size of the banking system and its total deposits are considerably larger than any other financial intermediary. Second, only the commercial banking system has the capacity to create demand deposits. Since demand deposits are a large part of the money supply, the banking system is able to expand (and contract) the nation's supply of money.

This chapter is concerned with commercial banks—the assets they own, the liabilities they have, and the regulations to which they are subjected. These regulations include the required reserves that commercial banks must hold against deposits. As is explained in the following chapter, commercial banks can expand and contract the money supply. This ability to affect the money supply is related to the reserves they must hold against their deposit liabilities. Hence the reserve requirement is an extremely important constraint on commercial banks, for it affects their ability to expand or contract the money supply.

Commercial bank regulation is not limited to the reserve requirements but includes virtually every facet of their operations, affecting not only the interest rates they may pay their depositors but also the manner in which they compete. The last

part of the chapter is devoted to interest rate ceilings and competition among commercial banks.

A COMMERCIAL BANK'S BALANCE SHEET

Commercial banks, like other economic units, have assets,
liabilities, and owners' equity. The balance sheet for a hypothetical commercial bank is given in Table 3–1. For clarity this
balance sheet expresses the entries in dollars and in percentages. The commercial bank owns a varied portfolio of assets.
Since demand deposits may readily be withdrawn, commercial
banks need liquid assets, especially short-term assets that are
readily converted into cash. Loans ($1080 million) constitute the
largest amount of assets, since they are 71 per cent of the
hypothetical bank's total portfolio. The term "loans" is very
broad and covers various types of loans to businesses and consumers. For example, banks are a primary source of short-term
finance for firms and consumers. Such loans earn interest and are
quickly paid off, hence they help meet the bank's need for liquid
assets. While commercial banks tend to stress short-term loans,
they do own some long-term assets such as mortgages. However,
other financial intermediaries, such as savings and loan associations, specialize in mortgage loans, and these financial intermediaries are the major source of mortgage money.

The assets of the bank also include the debt of state and local
governments ($180 million and 11.8 per cent of the total assets),
cash and reserves ($140 million and 9.2 per cent), and various
miscellaneous assets ($90 million and 4.6 per cent). The debts of

TABLE 3–1   A Simple Balance Sheet for a Hypothetical
Commercial Bank (in millions and in percentages)

ASSETS		
Cash and reserves	$ 140.	9.2%
U.S. Government securities	70.	4.6
State and local government securities	180.	11.8
Loans	1080.	71.0
Miscellaneous assets	50.	3.4
	1520.	100
LIABILITIES		
Demand deposits	$ 400.	26.3
Savings accounts	310.	20.4
Corporate and government savings accounts	250.	16.4
Savings certificates (Time deposits)	230.	15.1
Loans from other banks	80.	5.3
Short term borrowing	140.	9.2
STOCKHOLDERS' EQUITY	110.	7.3
	$1520.	100

state and local governments are called "tax exempts" because the interest is exempt from federal income tax. These tax exempt bonds are purchased by the bank in order for the bank to receive tax free income. For a particular bank these bonds will frequently include the issues of local governments served by the bank. Many local governments have excellent working relationships with local banks; they keep their accounts in these banks and borrow from them. Such working relationships between local government and local banks are often important for small communities, for these communities may have difficulty borrowing outside their geographical region.

The cash and reserves are the assets that the bank is required to hold against its deposit liabilities. These assets do not earn interest for the bank, and hence it seeks to minimize the amount of funds tied up in these assets. The miscellaneous assets include such items as the building, plant, and equipment.

Types of deposits

The primary liabilities of the commercial bank are its deposits: checking accounts (demand deposits) and various types of savings and time deposits. These deposits constitute 26.3 per cent and 51.9 per cent, respectively, of the bank's liabilities and equity. Demand deposits are payable on demand, for the owner of a checking account may demand immediate cash. Savings and time deposits are different in that the bank requires notice before paying. For passbook savings accounts this distinction has virtually vanished because funds deposited in a regular savings account may be withdrawn without notice. Time deposits such as certificates of deposits are issued for a set duration. Most time deposits mature in less than two and one half years, but some extend to four or more years. The variety available is illustrated by the following ad for certificates (Fig. 3–1). The annual yields range from 6.27 per cent on the one year certificate to 7.9 per cent on the six year certificate.

These certificates may be redeemed before maturity, but as the small print in the ad says, the owner pays a penalty for withdrawal before maturity. This penalty is loss of interest for ninety days. In addition, the certificate is then considered to be a regular (i.e, passbook) savings account. If the interest previously paid on the certificate is greater than the interest that would have been paid on the regular savings account, the excess must be repaid to the bank.

The remaining liabilities of the hypothetical commercial bank (14.5 per cent of total liabilities and equity) include other borrowings from a variety of sources. For example, commercial banks borrow from each other in a special market referred to as federal funds, and members of the Federal Reserve may borrow from that institution. (Non-member banks cannot borrow from the Federal Reserve but can borrow from other commercial banks in the federal funds market.) The last entry on the hypothetical commercial bank's balance sheet is the equity or

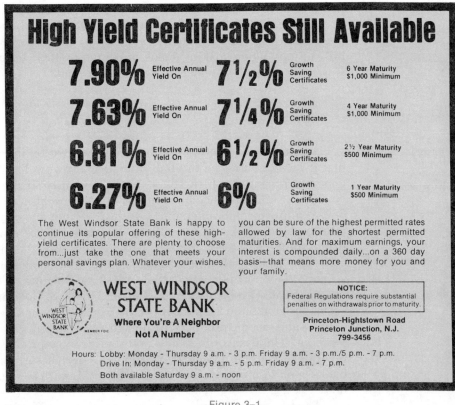

Figure 3–1

the owners' contributions. It is the stockholders' investment in the firm. While this balance sheet illustrates the various sources of funds available to banks, it is obvious that the most important of these is the various types of deposits. For this hypothetical bank the checking and savings accounts are 78 per cent of the firm's liabilities and equity, and hence 78 per cent of the bank's assets are financed by the deposit liabilities.

What is the proportion of the commercial bank's total assets that are financed by debt? As may be seen in the above balance sheet, total deposits greatly exceed the stockholders' equity. The bank has a large amount of debt outstanding when it is realized that the deposits are really loans by households, firms, and governments to the bank. In finance, when a firm uses a substantial amount of debt to acquire assets, the firm is said to have a high degree of financial leverage. As is explained in detail in Part II, Chapter 21, financial leverage may increase the return on the owners' investment but may also increase the degree of risk. If the bank incurs losses the equity of the bank is reduced, and the investors absorb the losses. The liabilities of the bank are not reduced when the bank suffers losses on its investments. Since the bank has only a small amount of equity and a large amount of debt, a small decrease in the value of the assets could eliminate the bank's equity. In this hypothetical case, a 7.3 per cent decline

Commercial banks have a high degree of financial leverage

in the value of the assets from $1520 million to $1410 million will erase the equity. Bankers are aware of this potential risk, and it is one reason why they tend to be very conservative. A bank must be cautious when making loans and investments, because a small amount of loss may cause the bank to fail.

COMMERCIAL BANKS' EARNINGS

Commercial bank's source of profits:
(1) revenues;
(2) expenses

A commercial bank's earnings are generated by the assets that it owns relative to the liabilities that it owes. The assets generate revenues which cover the bank's costs. If the bank generates sufficient revenues, it will operate profitably. Table 3–2, a simple income statement, lists the revenues and expenses of a hypothetical bank. As may be seen from the exhibit, the prime source of the commercial bank's revenues is the interest earned by its loans. Interest charges on the bank's loan portfolio accounted for 86.7 per cent of the bank's total revenues. The tax exempt bonds produced 5.3 per cent, and the U.S. Government securities generated 2.6 per cent of the bank's revenues. Service charges and income produced by the other assets contributed 5.4 per cent. The cash in the vault and the reserves produced no revenue for the commercial bank, and hence it is no surprise that banks seek to minimize the amount of cash and reserves they hold.

The commercial bank's expenses include everyday running expenses, such as wages and salaries and various employee benefits. These accounted for 23.4 per cent of its expenses. The bank pays interest to its creditors who include the holders of time and savings deposits and the various other sources from which the bank has borrowed funds. These interest expenses contributed 55.5 per cent of the bank's total costs. The last expenses are miscellaneous expenses which include insurance, maintenance,

TABLE 3–2   Simplified Income Statement for a Hypothetical
Commercial Bank

REVENUES		
Interest on loans	$144.4 (in millions)	86.7%
Interest on U.S. Government securities	4.4	2.6
Interest on state and local securities	8.8	5.3
Service charges and other income	9.0	5.4
	166.6	100
EXPENSES		
Salaries and employee benefits	36.0	23.4%
Interest on deposits	51.7	33.7
Interest on other borrowings	33.5	21.8
Other expenses	32.2	21.0
	153.4	99.9
PROFIT (before income taxes)	13.2	

and advertising. These accounted for 21.0 per cent of the total cost of operation.

Operations for this hypothetical bank were profitable, for it earned $13.2 million in profits. While the bank's operations were profitable, it took the bank $1520 million in assets to earn the $13.2 million. Thus the bank's return on its total assets was only .86 per cent ($13.2/$1520), which appears to be a meager return. Unless it were able to increase the return on its assets, this return implies that the bank would have to increase its assets by $1162 to earn an additional $10.00. While this profit margin on the bank's assets is small, such a small profit margin on total assets applies to the banking industry. A bank must have a large amount of assets (and correspondingly a large amount of deposits) to generate any significant amount of profit.

Small profit margin

While the profit margin on the total assets is quite modest, the profit earned on the stockholders' investment may be substantial. The owners' (i.e., stockholders') equity for the hypothetical bank is $110 million. This owners' equity represents the stockholders' contributions to the firm. When profits are expressed as a percentage of the stockholders' investment, the resulting quotient gives the return earned by the bank on the stockholders' investment. For the hypothetical bank this return on equity is 12 per cent ($13.2/$110). 12 per cent is considerably better than the .86 per cent earned on total assets. Why are these percentages so different? How is the bank able to earn only .86 per cent on its assets but give the stockholders a return of 12 per cent on their investment? The answer lies in the fact that the bank uses a high degree of financial leverage. The bank is employing a substantial amount of debt to finance its assets. Creditors put up $92.7 of every $100, while the owners only invested $7.3 of the $100. The bank is borrowing funds from one group and paying them interest and lending these funds to other economic units. The interest it is charging on its loans is greater than the interest it is paying, and the profits on these transactions accrue to the stockholders. Thus if the bank only nets $.86 on $100 in assets, the stockholders earn 12 per cent on their investment. The return on the stockholders' investment is magnified by the use of creditors' funds (i.e., the successful use of financial leverage).

Return on stockholders' investment is increased by the use of financial leverage

REGULATION OF COMMERCIAL BANKS

Commercial banks are subject to a considerable amount of government regulation. The purpose of this regulation is to protect the banks' creditors, especially their depositors. The very nature of banking, with its high degree of financial leverage, implies that when a commercial bank fails, substantial losses may be sustained by the bank's depositors. This is exactly what occurred during the Great Depression of the 1930s, when the

Regulation protects depositors

failure of many commercial banks imposed substantial losses on depositors. These losses led to increased regulation of commercial banks and the establishment of federal deposit insurance, all of which are designed to protect depositors. Such protection should in turn promote a viable banking system and ease the flow of savings into investment.

Sources of regulation

The regulation of banks comes from both state and federal banking authorities and the Federal Deposit Insurance Corporation. Banks that have national charters must join the Federal Reserve and are subjected to its regulation as well as examination by the Comptroller of the Currency, which is the federal agency that grants national bank charters. Banks with state charters are regulated by the individual state banking commission. However, any state bank that has joined the Federal Reserve system is also subject to its regulation. These various authorities regulate and supervise such facets of a commercial bank's operations as its geographical location, the number of banks and branches in an area, the types of loans and investments commercial banks may make, and the maximum interest they may pay depositors. This section will discuss several facets of this regulation. Special emphasis is placed on the reserve requirements against commercial banks' deposit liabilities, for, as is explained in detail in the subsequent chapter, the ability of commercial banks to lend is directly related to their reserves.

RESERVES

Reserve requirement against demand deposits

Commercial banks must keep money in reserve against their deposit liabilities. The minimum amount that a bank must maintain as a reserve is determined either by the Federal Reserve or by the state regulatory agencies. This reserve requirement does offer the depositor some degree of safety for deposits, but the prime source of safety for funds deposited in a commercial bank is the Federal Deposit Insurance Corporation (FDIC). While holding reserves against deposit liabilities may increase safety for the deposits, safety is not the prime reason for having reserve requirements. As will be explained in Chapter 5, the reserve requirement is one of the major tools of monetary control. It is the element of control and not safety that is the reason for having a reserve requirement against the deposit liabilities of commercial banks.

Variations in reserve requirements

The amount of the reserve requirements varies with several factors, including the type of deposit, membership in the Federal Reserve system, and the location of the bank. The reserve requirement is set by the Federal Reserve for national banks which must join the Federal Reserve system and state banks that choose to join it. Its reserve requirement is usually higher than the reserve requirement set for state banks that are not members of the Federal Reserve system. State regulatory agencies tend to set lower reserve requirements, which may in part explain why a state bank may choose not to join the Federal Reserve. Even within the Federal Reserve there are different reserve requirements for the same type of account. Banks located in cities, especially financial centers like New York City, have larger reserve requirements. This diversity in reserve requirements is illustrated by the fact that as of April, 1975, the reserve requirement for member banks varied from 12 per cent for demand deposits in small banks to 16.5 per cent for demand deposits in excess of $400 million in large metropolitan banks. While there are different reserve requirements for demand deposits, for the rest of this text the term *reserve requirement* will be used to denote the various reserve requirements, and no attempt will be made to differentiate the various reserve requirements for the same type of account. Thus, for the purpose of discussion, there will be a reserve requirement for time and savings deposits, and a reserve requirement for demand deposits. The potential effects of having different reserve requirements for the same type of account will be ignored.

Commercial banks that are members of the Federal Reserve system may hold their primary reserves in two forms: (1) cash in the vault or (2) deposits with the Federal Reserve. Thus, if the bank's reserve requirement is 15 per cent for demand deposits and the bank receives $100 cash in a checking account, it must hold $15 in reserves against the new demand deposit. The entire $100 in cash is considered part of the bank's total reserves, but the bank must hold only $15 against the deposit liability. The bank may choose to hold $1 of the required reserves in cash in the vault (to meet cash withdrawals) and $14 in the Federal Reserve. The remaining $85 are funds that the bank does not have to hold in reserves, and these will be deposited with the Federal Reserve. This amount ($85) in reserve is called "excess reserves." Excess reserves are the difference between the bank's total reserves and its required reserves. In this example the difference is $100 − $15 = $85. It is a commercial bank's excess reserves that may be lent to borrowers or used for some other purpose such as purchasing government securities. It is the excess reserves that the bank uses to acquire income earning assets. If a commercial bank does not have any excess reserves, it is said to be "fully loaned up." To acquire additional income earning assets such as a government security or a business loan, the bank would have to acquire additional excess reserves.

Excess reserves defined

Commercial banks that are not members of the Federal Reserve may not deposit their reserves in a Federal Reserve bank. Instead they deposit their reserves in other banks called "correspondent banks." Correspondent banks in many cases are large, metropolitan commercial banks. These large correspondent banks frequently provide additional services. For example, they have efficient facilities for the clearing of checks and can facilitate the clearing of checks for the smaller banks.

Role of correspondent banks

The correspondent banks also have research staffs and give management advice and investment counsel. Thus they are extremely important to the well being of the small, local commercial banks. Of course, the reason that the correspondent banks are willing to provide these services is that a small commercial bank's deposits are like any other deposits: they are a source of funds that the larger banks may use. Thus the large commercial banks receive compensation for the services provided to the small banks by being able to use the funds deposited in them by small banks to purchase income earning assets.

Secondary reserves

In addition to the required reserves, commercial banks also hold secondary reserves. These reserves are high-quality, short-term, marketable securities. While regular reserves on deposit at the Federal Reserve do not earn interest, the secondary reserves do earn interest. These short-term securities, such as U.S. government securities (i.e., treasury bills), are also very liquid. Such securities may be readily converted to cash because (1) they may be easily sold or (2) they mature quickly. Thus such securities offer banks both liquidity and a source of interest income.

Importance of the reserve requirement

The importance of reserves and reserve requirements cannot be exaggerated. As is explained in detail in the next chapter, the commercial banking system through the process of loan creation can expand or contract the nation's supply of money. The ability of commercial banks to lend depends on their excess reserves. Thus anything that affects their reserves alters their ability to lend and create money and credit. There are many financial transactions that affect commercial banks' reserves including how the Federal Government finances a deficit or the open market operations of the Federal Reserve. Subsequent chapters will discuss several of these financial transactions and their potential impact on commercial bank reserves.

DEPOSIT INSURANCE

FDIC

Federal Government deposit insurance is one of the positive results of the Great Depression of the 1930s. The large losses sustained by commercial banks' depositors led to the establishment of the FDIC. The establishment of FDIC has significantly increased the general public's confidence in commercial banks. As of this writing, FDIC insures deposits to $40,000. Thus, if a commercial bank should fail, FDIC will reimburse depositors up to the $40,000 limit per account. Since most individuals do not have that much on deposit, these individuals know that their funds are completely safe. (If an individual has more than $40,000, the same degree of safety can be achieved by placing up to $40,000 in different banks.) The $40,000 limit does mean that large depositors, including many corporations, are not fully insured and thus do stand to take losses should a bank fail.

All commercial banks that are members of the Federal Reserve system must be insured by FDIC, and many state banking authorities also require that FDIC insurance be carried by their state non-member banks. However, some state banking authorities do not require federal deposit insurance. Also foreign banks such as Bank Leumi (Israel's largest commercial bank) that are licensed to operate in the United States do not have to carry FDIC insurance.

FDIC insurance is not free, for the commercial banks purchase it from FDIC. Even when the insurance is not required, the majority of commercial banks do carry it. This indicates that the managers as well as the regulators of most state banks recognize the importance to their depositors of the insurance and that the potential benefits more than justify the cost.

Besides offering deposit insurance, FDIC has further increased public confidence in the banking system through its powers of bank examination. By exercising this power to examine banks, FDIC, along with other regulatory agencies, has improved bank practices. The improved bank practices plus the deposit insurance have significantly improved the quality of banking. However, the establishment of FDIC and other regulatory agencies has not eliminated bank failures, for occasionally a bank does fail. The losses, however, are not sustained by the many individuals who have deposited modest sums with these commercial banks. Such deposits are reimbursed by FDIC in full up to the $40,000 limit. Thus, for most individuals, depositing funds in a commercial bank does not subject the funds to risk of loss. Hence the general public's confidence in the banking system is not disturbed by the occasional failure of a particular commercial bank.

FDIC insurance increases public confidence in the commercial banking system

REGULATION Q

One of the most important constraints on commercial banks is Regulation Q, which specifies the maximum rate of interest that commercial banks may pay on savings and time deposits. (Other financial intermediaries such as savings and loan associations are also constrained as to the maximum interest rates they may pay depositors.) The rationale for such maximum interest rates is the belief that interest rate competition may be detrimental to the banking system. It may be argued that if commercial banks paid high rates of interest to depositors, they would have to make riskier loans and charge higher rates of interest to cover the cost of the deposits. Low-quality loans may result in more defaults, and the subsequent bank failures would undermine the soundness of the banking system. While such reasoning may not be true, it is frequently used to justify legal constraints on the maximum interest rates that commercial banks may pay on deposits.

The effect of Regulation Q varies as interest rates vary.

Legal maximum interest rates

When market interest rates on commercial bank deposits are lower than the legal ceiling, Regulation Q is irrelevant and has no effect.

However, when interest rates rise, Regulation Q has a definite impact on commercial banks' ability to lend. As interest rates rise on other short term investments such as treasury bills or the commercial paper issued by corporations, funds are withdrawn from savings deposits in commercial banks and other financial intermediaries. The intermediaries are unable to pay higher amounts of interest and thus cannot compete with the other securities. Since money will tend to flow where returns are the highest, depositors withdraw funds from savings and time deposits and invest in short-term securities, which offer higher yields. Such withdrawals reduce the ability of financial intermediaries including commercial banks to lend. Thus during periods of higher short-term interest rates, Regulation Q acts as a real constraint on banks' ability to lend. For example, during 1974 interest rates on certain short-term funds ranged from 8 to 12 per cent, which is perceptibly higher than the ceiling rates that commercial banks are permitted to pay on regular savings and time deposits. Thus it was not surprising to see commercial banks spending money on advertising and offering bonus prizes as a means to encourage the public to deposit funds. Commercial banks could not offer higher interest rates and thus were forced to find alternative means to attract depositors.

HOW BANKS COMPETE

Banks compete primarily on the basis of product differentiation because price competition is limited. Currently, commercial banks cannot offer customers interest on demand deposits. Obviously, if an individual bank were to make this offer, people would seek to deposit their funds in that bank, but no commercial bank may legally make the offer. Price competition is limited to the interest on savings accounts and service charges on checking accounts and other banking services.

This inability of commercial banks to pay interest on checking accounts partially explains why commercial banks do not want savings institutions to be allowed to have accounts similar to checking accounts. In several states savings institutions may offer depositors accounts that are similar to checking accounts in commercial banks. These accounts (i.e., the NOW accounts discussed in the previous chapter), are savings accounts with a checking account feature. The depositor may use a negotiable order drawn on the savings account to make payment. These accounts are a potential threat to commercial banks, which have lobbied extensively against them.

The banking industry exemplifies competition through

product differentiation. A commercial bank can be differentiated from its competitors by a variety of means. For example, it may offer services: branch offices, Saturday banking hours, free checking, or drive-in tellers. A commercial bank may also offer goods such as watches and blankets as an inducement to depositors. Such devices are a substitute for price competition. If a bank cannot differentiate itself on the basis of price, then it has no choice but to use these alternative means to differentiate itself from other banks.

An important development in the banking industry that has permitted banks to offer customers a wide range of financial services has been the formation of one-bank holding companies. Regulations do not permit commercial banks to enter financially related businesses such as insurance or real estate, and they cannot issue certain types of securities to raise funds. One method to broaden the capacity of banks to raise funds and enter financially related business is for the banks to form a holding company.

Holding companies

Holding companies have been in existence for years, but, with the passage of enabling legislation in 1966, there has been a large increase in the number of commercial banks forming one-bank holding companies. The holding company owns the stock of the commercial bank and the stock of other companies. The public then owns the stock of the holding company. This structure is illustrated in Figure 3–2, a simplified diagram for Citicorp, the holding company for Citibank.

Citicorp is a publicly held company whose stock is traded on the New York Stock Exchange. However, if an investor buys the stock, he is not just buying the stock in a commercial bank. While Citibank is a major component of the total corporation, Citicorp includes a variety of financially related businesses.

Figure 3–2

The reason for adopting this holding company structure is the flexibility it offers Citicorp. While Citibank is subject to the regulations applicable to a commercial bank, Citicorp is not. Instead, it is a holding company which may have non-bank related assets and liabilities. This has permitted Citicorp to enter such fields as credit cards, commercial banking abroad, investment research, and management consulting. Citicorp has become a large, diversified firm than can offer customers not only the traditional banking services but also financially related services. This mix is one means available to Citibank and other commercial banks to differentiate themselves from each other.

SUMMARY

This chapter contained a discussion of the commercial banking system. Emphasis was placed on the sources of bank funds and the use of financial leverage. The very nature of their operation, the borrowing of funds from depositors and the subsequent lending of these funds, implies a substantial degree of risk to their creditors, especially the depositors. This element of risk has led to government regulation at both the federal and state level. Such regulation is designed to increase the safety of deposits and promote a healthy banking system which will facilitate the transfer of funds from savers to borrowers.

While this regulation permeates virtually every facet of commercial banking, emphasis was placed on the reserve requirements. Commercial banks must hold funds in reserve against deposit liabilities. Funds held in excess of the required reserves may be used to acquire income earning assets such as business loans or government securities. Thus commercial banks' ability to lend is directly related to excess reserves. As is shown in the next chapter, the commercial banking system through the process of loan creation is able to expand the supply of money. Hence the reserves of commercial banks and in particular their excess reserves play a crucial role in the commercial banking system's ability to alter the money supply.

KEY WORDS AND TERMS

total reserves
required reserves
excess reserves
tax exempt securities
financial leverage
FDIC
Regulation Q
product differentiation
holding companies

1. What does it mean to say that banks have a high degree of financial leverage? Does this increase the element of risk associated with commercial bank lending? If a bank does fail, who else will suffer a financial loss besides the stockholders? How does FDIC reduce this risk of loss?

2. Why does Regulation Q constrain banks during periods of high interest rates? Why does it not constrain banks during periods of low interest rates? How does Regulation Q reduce competition among banks? In what other ways can they compete?

3. What is the single most important factor that determines whether a commercial bank may make additional loans? How can individuals affect a bank's ability to lend? Why does the shifting of funds from checking to savings accounts alter the ability of commercial banks to lend?

Chapter 4

THE EXPANSION OF MONEY AND CREDIT

Learning Objectives

- Illustrate how commercial banks expand the supply of money and credit.
- Show the importance of commercial banks' reserves in the expansion of money and credit.
- Explain the effect of cash withdrawals when the banking system is expanding.
- Explain the effect of cash withdrawals when the banking system is fully loaned up.
- Show how the supply of credit can expand without an expansion in the money supply.

"If you want to know the value of money, go and try to borrow some."

Benjamin Franklin

How does the commercial banking system expand the money supply and create credit? That is an important question, for commercial banks are the heart of the nation's financial system. They are the primary source of funds for many firms and households. The process by which these funds are created is fascinating and important to the understanding of finance. This ability to create credit comes from the bank's sources of funds: depositors, general creditors, and owners. Money obtained from these sources is the resource that a bank has to lend. This money flows among commercial banks, and, through the system of fractional reserves, the banking system is able to expand the supply of money.

This chapter is concerned with the banking system's ability to expand and contract the supply of money and credit. The first section considers the expansion that may occur when cash is deposited in checking accounts. The second section considers the effect of having a proportion of the cash being withdrawn as the expansion occurs. The third section covers the effect of having cash deposited in a savings account, and the last section covers the effect of a cash withdrawal.

THE MULTIPLE EXPANSION OF COMMERCIAL BANK CREDIT

What is the potential effect of cash being deposited in a checking account? As was explained in Chapter 2, the money supply (M_1) is the sum of demand deposits plus coins and currency in circulation. Cash deposited into checking accounts at commercial banks does not change the money supply. All that is changed is the form of the money from cash to demand deposits. The transactions, however, are extremely important, for they increase the commercial banks' ability to lend. When the commercial banks use this ability and make loans, they increase the supply of money. Commercial banks, by making new loans, cause the supply of money to increase.

Cash deposits increase commercial banks' ability to lend

When an individual makes a $100 cash deposit in a checking account, the balance sheet of the individual and the commercial bank are affected as follows:

INDIVIDUAL		BANK	
Demand Deposit ↑ $100 Cash ↓ $100		Cash ↑ $100	Demand Deposit ↑ $100

The bank incurs a liability, the demand deposit. The deposit is a liability because it is a promise on the part of the bank to pay. There is no specified maturity date, but the individual may demand payment at any time. For incurring the liability, the bank acquires an asset, the cash. The person, however, has only traded one asset for another, for he has exchanged cash for a demand deposit.

Once the cash is deposited in the bank, it is no longer part of the money supply. The cash has been removed from circulation and has been replaced by the demand deposit. The demand deposit is now part of the supply of money. Depositing cash in demand deposits alters the form of money supply from cash to demand deposits but does not alter the total money supply. Depositing the cash, however, does alter the ability of the commercial bank to lend. The act of depositing cash in the checking accounts is very significant, because it creates for that bank excess reserves.

The cash becomes reserves

After the bank receives the $100 cash deposit, this money becomes part of the reserves of the bank. This $100 reserve is divided into two categories: (1) those reserves that must be held against the demand deposit, the required reserves; and (2) those reserves in excess of the reserve requirement which are called excess reserves. If the reserve requirement is 20 per cent, then $20 of the $100 cash reserves are required and $80 are excess reserves. These excess reserves are very important because commercial banks use their excess reserves to acquire income

Reserves are either (1) required or (2) excess

earning assets such as loans and securities. Depositing cash in a commercial bank thus gives it the ability to create loans because the bank obtains a resource that it may lend—excess reserves. Banks do not lend and cannot lend their deposit liabilities. It is the excess reserves that the banks may lend, and any transaction that affects the excess reserves of commercial banks alters their ability to create loans.

If a borrower enters the bank and the bank grants a loan of $80, what effect will this transaction have on (1) the depositor's balance sheet, (2) the bank's balance sheet, and (3) the borrower's balance sheet? Since this transaction does not concern the depositor, it has no effect on the balance sheet. As far as the depositor is concerned, the bank still owes on demand $100. The effect on the borrower and the commercial bank is shown below:

BANK		BORROWER	
Loan ↑ $80	Demand Deposit ↑ $80	Demand Deposit ↑ $80	Loan ↑ $80

The borrower receives an asset—a demand deposit at the bank—and also incurs a liability, the IOU to the bank. The bank acquires an asset, the $80 loan, and the bank incurs a new liability, the $80 demand deposit. This deposit is the money that the borrower receives for the loan.

Why does the commercial bank create a new demand deposit instead of just lending the person the cash? The answer is that the bank does not want the borrower to remove the cash from the bank. The bank wants to keep that cash as long as possible, for it is part of the bank's reserves. The bank does realize that the borrower will spend that money and the reserves will probably be transferred to another bank, but the bank still wants the use of the reserves as long as possible.

Why did the borrower take out the loan? Obviously the borrower does not want to leave the money in the bank and pay interest on the loan but intends to spend it. When the borrower does spend the money, the recipient of the check will either cash it or deposit it in a commercial bank. When the check is deposited the probability of this bank and the borrower's bank being the same is quite small, since there are thousands of commercial banks in the country. When the

check is deposited in the second bank the following transactions occur:

BORROWER		FIRST BANK		SECOND BANK	
Goods ↑	$80	Reserves ↑ $80	Demand Deposit ↓ $80	Reserves ↑ $80	Demand Deposit $80
Demand Deposit ↓ $80					

The borrower has used the checking account to obtain $80 worth of goods and services. The seller of these goods and services deposits the check in an account, and thus the second bank acquires a new checking account. The second bank sends the check to the first bank for payment. The first bank then reduces the checking account of the borrower and transfers $80 worth of reserves (i.e., the cash) to the second bank. This flow of deposits and reserves may be summarized by the following exhibit:

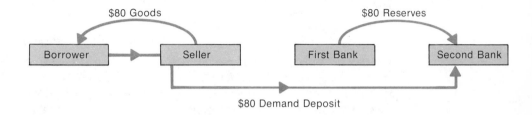

In summary, the loan made possible a purchase by the borrower, and thus a seller has made a sale that may not have occurred without the creation of the loan. Goods have flowed from the seller to the buyer. When the seller deposited the payment in a commercial bank, this caused reserves to flow between the seller's and borrower's banks.

What is the net effect of this transaction on the money supply and amount of credit? Both have increased. There are $180 in demand deposits, the initial $100 deposit in the first bank and the new $80 deposit in the second bank. Thus there has been a net increase in the money supply of $80. This $80 increase came through the process of loan creation, for there is now $80 in new credit. The act of depositing cash in a checking account led to a net increase in the supply of money through the process of loan creation.

The supply of money and credit are increased

The process of loan creation is not limited to the initial expansion of $80, for the second bank now has a new deposit. It must hold reserves against the new checking account. Since the reserve requirement is 20 per cent, the bank must hold in reserve $16 ($80 × .20). It received $80 in reserves from the first bank when the check cleared. Thus $64 of these reserves are excess reserves which the second bank may use to purchase an income earning asset or grant a new loan. If the second bank grants a loan for $64, it creates a new demand deposit of $64. The borrower then purchases goods and services and pays for them with a check drawn on the new demand deposit. The $64 check then is deposited in a third bank and is cleared. This creates for the third bank a new deposit and transfers to it $64 in reserves from the second bank. The third bank divides these reserves into required reserves ($64 × .20 = $12.80) and excess reserves at

The second bank grants a new loan

$51.20. The third bank now has the capacity to acquire income earning assets and create new loans.

The multiple
expansion of money
and credit
This process of lending and passing reserves among banks may continue until there are no more excess reserves. With each new loan there is expansion in the money supply. The net increase in new credit and in demand deposits is many times the initial deposit. This expansion is illustrated in Table 4–1, which continues the multiple expansion for several rounds. As may be seen in the table, each additional loan and new demand deposit (column 1) is smaller, but the sum of the loans (column 2) and new demand deposits rise (column 3). As the total of demand deposits rises, required reserves also rise (column 4). The initial $100 deposited created $100 in reserves. Thus as the required reserves rise, excess reserves must decline (colume 5). Of course, it is this decline in excess reserves that causes each new loan to be smaller. Eventually, if the expansion continues indefinitely, the excess reserves will become zero and all $100 reserves will be required reserves.

If the expansion continues until there are no excess reserves, how much will the money supply increase? What is the increase in new loans? These questions may be answered by the following simple equation:

$$(1) \qquad \frac{\text{Change in excess reserves}}{\text{Reserve requirement}} = \text{Change in credit}$$

Equation 1 gives the increase in new credit and the money supply. In the above example the cash deposit of $100 increased excess reserves by $80. Since the reserve requirement was 20 per cent then the maximum possible expansion in the money supply and new credit is

$$\$80/.2 = \$400.$$

TABLE 4–1   Multiple Expansion of the Supply of Money

INITIAL DEPOSIT = $100   RESERVE REQUIREMENT = 20%

New Demand Deposits	New Credit Created	Cumulative Total Demand Deposits	Cumulative Required Reserves	Excess Reserves
$100.00	$ 0	$100.00	$20.00	$80.00
80.00	80.00	180.00	36.00	64.00
64.00	144.00	244.00	48.80	51.20
51.20	195.20	295.20	59.04	40.96
40.96	236.16	336.16	67.23	32.77
32.77	268.93	368.93	73.79	26.21
26.21	295.14	395.14	79.03	20.97
20.97	316.11	416.11	83.22	16.78
.	.	.	.	.
.	.	.	.	.
.	.	.	.	.
0	400.00	500.00	100.00	0

Depositing $100 in a demand deposit permits an expansion of $400 of new money. Since the new money came through the creation of new credit, then $400 is also the maximum possible increase in new credit. The change in the money supply and the change in credit thus is five times the initial change in the excess reserves.

What is the maximum expansion in demand deposits? This may also be determined by a simple equation. Equation (2) gives the maximum possible expansion in demand deposits

The multiple expansion of demand deposits

(2) $\dfrac{\text{Initial cash deposit}}{\text{Reserve requirement}}$ = Change in demand deposits

Thus, in the above example, the maximum increase in demand deposits would be

$$\frac{\$100}{.2} = \$500$$

The change in demand deposits is five times the initial cash deposit. The difference between the two equations is that the second equation includes the initial deposit. The initial deposit, however, does not change the money supply; it only alters the form of money from cash to demand deposit. While the maximum expansion in demand deposits must include this initial deposit, the increase in the money supply and the new credit does not include the initial deposit. Hence the expansion in new credit and new money is less than the expansion in demand deposits.

For the maximum expansion in money and credit to occur, it is necessary to make several assumptions: (1) the money is always deposited in a checking account and none of the money is withdrawn in the form of cash; (2) banks hold no excess reserves; and (3) there are sufficient borrowers who will borrow all excess reserves. If these assumptions are violated, there are *leakages* which decrease the potential expansion. For example, if each depositor holds 10 per cent of the receipts in the form of cash, then the potential multiple expansion is reduced because this cash withdrawal reduces the excess reserves of the banks. Anything which reduces the bank's excess reserves reduces their ability to create credit and expand the money supply. The potential impact of such cash withdrawals is explained in the next section.

Assumptions

CASH LEAKAGES

In the previous section all the newly created money remains in the banking system in demand deposits. In this section the effects of a cash leakage are considered, for it is assumed that some of the newly created money will be held in the form of cash. For the sake of simplicity it is assumed that for each round of borrowing the public seeks to hold 10 per cent of the money supply in the form of cash.

Some money is held
in the form of cash

As in the previous section, $100 cash is deposited in a demand deposit. This creates for the bank $100 of new reserves, of which 20 per cent is required to be held against the new demand deposits, and $80 are excess reserves that the commercial bank may lend. The commercial bank grants the new loan for $80, and the borrower spends the $80. Up to this point the situation is identical to the previous case, but now the cash leakage enters. The person who received the check deposits $72 in his checking account and holds $8 in cash. This individual has chosen to hold a proportion (10 per cent) of the receipts in the form of cash and not in the form of a demand deposit. Thus the second bank receives a new deposit for $72 instead of $80. The $80 reserves of the first bank are still transferred to the second bank, but $8 of these reserves are used to meet the $8 cash withdrawal. Thus there has been a leakage of cash from the banking system, which destroys some of the reserves of the commercial banks.

Cash leakages
reduce the multiple
expansion

The potential impact of this leakage on the creation of new money and credit may be shown by adjusting equation (1) for the leakage. If the leakage is expressed as a percentage, then the equation becomes

(3)   Change in the money supply $= \dfrac{\text{Change in excess reserves}}{\substack{\text{Reserve requirement plus} \\ \text{the proportion of the} \\ \text{money supply held as} \\ \text{cash}}}$

In the above example the maximum potential change in new money and new credit becomes $266.67. This is determined by substituting the appropriate numbers in the equation:

Change in the money supply = $80/(.20 + .10)
Change in the money supply = $266.67

This $266.67 is perceptibly smaller than the $400 determined in the previous case when there were no cash leakages and all the newly created money remained in demand deposits in commercial banks. The impact of the leakage is to reduce significantly the potential expansion in new credit and money. This general conclusion applies not only to the public's holding cash but also to commercial banks' holding excess reserves. The effect is the same in either case: the multiple expansion in new credit and new money is reduced.

EXPANSION THROUGH SAVINGS ACCOUNTS AND TIME DEPOSITS

In the previous sections, the act of depositing cash in a demand deposit increased the ability of banks to lend because it increased their excess reserves. In this section the cash will be deposited in savings accounts at commercial banks. In both cases there may be expansion of credit, but there is no expansion in the money supply (M_1) if funds are deposited in savings accounts. For the purpose of illustration it will be assumed in this section that (except for proceeds of loans) funds are always deposited in savings accounts in commercial banks. This is an unrealistic assumption, but the example illustrates how credit may be expanded when funds flow into savings accounts as well as when funds flow into checking accounts.

If $100 cash were placed in a savings account, the commercial bank's and the depositor's balance sheets are affected as follows:

Cash is deposited in a savings account

INDIVIDUAL		BANK	
Cash ↓ $100		Reserves (Cash) ↑ $100	Savings Account ↑ $100
Savings Account ↑ $100			

The depositing of cash in the savings account has not changed the saver's assets but altered their form from cash to the savings account. The bank has acquired a new asset (the $100 cash), which becomes reserves for the bank. The money supply (M_1) has decreased when cash (or a demand deposit) is deposited into a savings account because, unlike cash and demand deposits, savings accounts are not considered part of the money supply.

Since the bank has acquired a new $100 savings account, it must hold reserves against that account. If the reserve requirement is 5 per cent, then it must hold $5 against the new deposit liability. Since it also acquired $100 in new reserves, $95 of these are new excess reserves that the bank may use to purchase an income earning asset or lend. If the bank lends these excess reserves, it creates a new loan and a new demand deposit. The balance sheets of the commercial bank and the borrower are affected as follows:

Reserve requirement for savings account

A new loan is created

BANK		BORROWER	
Loan ↑ $95	Demand Deposit ↑ $95	Demand Deposit ↑ $95	Loan ↑ $95

The borrower has a new asset, the demand deposit, and a liability, the note owed the bank. The bank acquires a new asset, the loan, and a new liability, the demand deposit.

The commercial bank realizes that the new deposit will soon be withdrawn, for the borrower will spend the money. Unless the person who sells the goods to the borrower deposits the money back in this bank, the money will flow out of this bank. For illustrative purposes in this section it is assumed that the money is deposited in a savings account in a second commercial bank. The effect of this transaction is shown by the following balance sheets:

FIRST BANK		BORROWER	
Reserves ↓ $95	Demand Deposit ↓ $95	Goods ↑ $95 Demand Deposit ↓ $95	

SECOND BANK		SELLER	
Reserves ↑ $95	Savings Deposits ↑ $95	Goods ↓ $95 Savings Account ↑ $95	

The borrower has used the newly obtained demand deposit to purchase $95 worth of goods. The seller deposits the $95 check in a savings account at the second bank. The second bank sends the check to the first bank for payment and receives $95 in reserves when the check clears. The second bank must hold $4.53 ($95 × .05) in reserve against the new savings account. Since it obtained $95 in reserves, it now has $90.47 in excess reserves. Thus the second bank may now make a new loan, and the process is repeated.

If this process is repeated until there exist no excess reserves, equation (1) may be used to determine the amount of the new credit that will be created. In this example the maximum amount of new credit is

$$\frac{\$95}{.05} = \$1900$$

For this expansion to occur, the funds must always be deposited in savings accounts and the commercial banks must hold no excess reserves. In this case there is no expansion in the money supply, because the funds were always deposited in savings accounts. While there is no new money created, there is the creation of new loans. Thus it is possible to have expansion of credit without expansion of the money supply. The act of depositing cash in the savings account created for the banking system excess reserves that commercial banks may lend. The potential increase in new credit is actually greater in this case because the reserve requirement for savings accounts is smaller and hence the banks have more excess reserves.

Which types of deposit, savings or checking, does the commercial bank prefer? The immediate answer would seem to be that the bank would prefer the savings account because the reserve requirement is lower. However, the commercial bank will have to pay interest on the savings account. Banks by law do not pay interest on checking accounts and may even charge a fee. Thus without knowing the cost of handling the types of accounts, it is impossible to answer the question. The question, however, does illustrate how easy it is to jump to an incorrect conclusion that on the surface appears correct.

CASH WITHDRAWALS

In the previous examples, cash was deposited in accounts which created new excess reserves for the commercial banks. The new excess reserves increased the ability of commercial banks to lend, and through the process of loan creation, the commercial banking system created new money. In this section cash will be withdrawn from commercial banks.

A cash withdrawal is the reversal of a cash deposit and has the following effects on the balance sheets of the commercial bank and the public:

PUBLIC		COMMERCIAL BANK	
Demand Deposit ↓		Cash ↓	Demand Deposit ↓
Cash ↑			

The public has altered the form in which it chooses to hold its money, for the public now holds cash instead of demand deposits. The commercial bank has used an asset, cash in its vaults, to meet the withdrawal. In effect the commercial bank has used an asset to retire (pay off) a liability.

The importance of such cash withdrawals rests on the effect that the withdrawal has on the bank's reserves, for the withdrawal reduces the bank's reserves. If the bank has excess reserves, the withdrawal creates no problems for the bank because it takes the funds out of its excess reserves. After the withdrawal, the bank's total and excess reserves are reduced, but the bank is still maintaining its reserve requirement. All that has really happened is that the bank's ability to make additional loans has been reduced because the bank has lost excess reserves.

Cash withdrawals reduce reserves and may cause the banking system to contract

The situation differs considerably if the bank has no excess reserves. While the bank can meet the withdrawal from its reserves, it now has a major problem: its reserves are insufficient to meet its reserve requirements against its deposit liabilities. The remaining reserves are insufficient to meet its required reserves. Thus the bank must take some action to restore reserves. Where

can the bank get these reserves? It has several choices, including
(1) selling assets, (2) borrowing reserves from other banks, (3)
inducing new deposits into the bank, and (4) borrowing reserves
from the Federal Reserve. (This last option is limited to members of the Federal Reserve system.)

Multiple contraction   If the bank sells assets to increase its reserves, a multiple
contraction will occur unless there are excess reserves in the
banking system. If the bank were to sell some of its assets (e.g.,
government securities), then the buyer will pay for the securities
with a check. That check is drawn on another commercial bank,
and after the check clears, the balance sheets of the two banks are
as follows:

BANK A		BANK B	
Government Securities ↓		Reserves ↓	Demand Deposits ↓
Reserves ↑			

Bank A is now able to meet its reserve requirement, for reserves
were purchased through the sale of securities. These reserves,
however, were transferred from Bank B. If Bank B had no excess
reserves, it is now unable to meet its reserve requirement and
must find reserves. This process of liquidating assets will continue until there has been a multiple contraction in the money
supply. Such a contraction would not occur if Bank B had excess
reserves. The transfer of reserves from Bank B to Bank A that
occurred when the check cleared would have reduced Bank B's
excess reserves but not required that it also contract.

A commercial bank   If Bank A borrows reserves from Bank B, the balance sheets
may borrow reserves   of both banks are altered as follows:

BANK A		BANK B	
Reserves ↑	Loan from Bank B ↑	Loan to Bank A ↑	
		Reserves ↓	

Bank A obtains the reserves by borrowing, and Bank B exchanges one asset (reserves) for another asset. There has been (1)
no change in the total reserves of the banking system, (2) no
change in the deposit liabilities of all commercial banks, and (3)
no change in the required reserves of all banks, because there
has been no change in the deposit liabilities of the commercial
banks. All that has occurred is a change in the location of the
reserves, which does not increase the ability of commercial
banks to lend. However, as a result of this transfer of reserves
between the banks, Bank A is able to meet its reserve requirement. This transfer could not occur unless Bank B had excess
reserves that it could lend. Thus for Bank A to borrow reserves

from another commercial bank, some bank must have sufficient excess reserves to grant the loan.

The market for these reserves is called the *federal funds market*. Federal funds is one of the most well-developed of all short-term credit markets. If a commercial bank lacks sufficient reserves against its deposit liabilities, it is able to borrow reserves from a commercial bank that has excess reserves. If a bank has excess reserves, then it can put these funds to work by lending them in the federal funds market. Thus the bank converts a sterile asset, the excess reserves, into an income earning asset, for it charges the borrowing bank interest for the use of the reserves.

Federal funds market

Since the reserve may be needed for only a very short time period, the loans made in the federal funds market are usually for extremely short periods of time (e.g., a day). Thus any commercial bank that has a temporary surplus of loanable funds may briefly lend them in the federal funds market and earn interest on the funds. Any commercial bank that is temporarily deficient in reserves is able to borrow them for as short a period of time as necessary. The federal funds market illustrates the importance of good management of short-term assets. Since the loans may be for as short a period of time as a day, a bank with excess reserves may put this asset to work for this brief period. Since these loans are of such short duration, the interest rate on federal funds can fluctuate significantly and quickly. When there exists excess reserves in the banking system, the interest rate may fall to nothing, for the quantity supplied of the excess reserves exceeds the quantity demanded. But during periods of excess demand, commercial banks may pay a substantial rate of interest for these loans in order to meet their reserve requirement.

The third way in which Bank A can acquire additional reserves is by inducing the general public to deposit cash back into the bank. Since depositing cash into the bank creates reserves for the bank, such deposits will restore the bank's required reserves. If cash withdrawals are matched by cash deposits, the bank's reserves are unaltered. A commercial bank may try to induce deposits by a variety of advertising and product differentiating techniques. If such actions restore deposits that have been previously withdrawn, the bank will not have to sell assets or borrow from other banks to meet its reserve requirement.

Induce deposits

If Bank A is a member of the Federal Reserve system, it may borrow the reserves from the Federal Reserve Bank. It would not have to sell assets, borrow from other banks, or encourage new deposits. Instead, the Federal Reserve would create for the commercial bank the reserves that the bank needs to meet its reserve requirement. If, however, there were no central bank that could create these reserves, or if the central bank were unwilling to create them, the commercial bank would have to liquidate an asset or borrow the reserves. If there are no excess

Member banks may borrow from the Federal Reserve

reserves in the banking system, or if the general public cannot be induced to increase its holdings of checking or savings accounts, the commercial banking system will have to contract to meet the reserve requirement. The withdrawal of cash from deposits will then cause a multiple contraction of the money supply and multiple contraction of commercial banks' assets. This is precisely what happened during the 1930 depression when there were large withdrawals from commercial banks. Banks had insufficient liquidity to meet these withdrawals. Since the Federal Reserve did not put reserves into the system, many commercial banks were unable to meet the withdrawals and had to close their doors. Thus a major role of the central bank should be to act as a source of reserves and liquidity to commercial banks when all other sources have been drained. The Federal Reserve, by its ability to create bank reserves, is therefore able to create liquidity for banks when such liquidity is needed to meet withdrawals.

SUMMARY

This chapter has examined the process of expanding the supply of money and credit by commercial banks. While the individual commercial bank can only lend funds deposited in it, all commercial banks working together are able to expand the supply of money and credit. This ability to create such expansion is the result of a fractional reserve banking system in which commercial banks must hold only a fraction in reserve against their deposit liabilities. Any reserves in excess of the required reserves may be used by the banks to create loans or buy other income earning assets.

Since banks may lend their excess reserves, anything that affects the reserves of commercial banks alters their ability to lend. There are many monetary transactions that may affect these reserves. These include the monetary policy of the Federal Reserve system, the fiscal policy of the Federal Government, and international monetary transactions. The subsequent chapters consider a variety of financial transactions and their effects on the reserves of commercial banks. Since commercial banks are a primary source of credit for firms, anything that affects the lending capacity of commercial banks has important implications for the financing of business operations.

KEY WORDS AND TERMS

expansion of money
expansion of credit
expansion of deposits

leakages
cash withdrawals
federal funds market

1. Given the following consolidated balance sheet for all commercial banks:

Assets		Liabilities and Capital	
Reserves at Federal Reserve	$400	Demand Deposits	$400
Loans and Government Securities	$700	Time Deposits	$300
Building	$300	Advances from the	
		Federal Reserve	$200
		Capital Stock	$500

The reserve requirement against demand deposits is 20 per cent
and 10 per cent against time deposits.
   (a) If the commercial banks do not sell any assets or in-
       crease their borrowings from the Federal Reserve, what
       is the maximum increase in the money supply that can
       result from this banking system?
   (b) If the commercial banks increased their borrowings
       from the Federal Reserve by $100, what is the maxi-
       mum increase in the money supply that can result from
       this banking system?
   (c) If depositors shift $100 to checking accounts from sav-
       ings accounts, what is the maximum increase in the
       money supply that can result from this banking system?
   (d) Explain your answers to (a), (b), and (c).

2. If a greater proportion of deposits are made in time rather than
   in demand deposits, will the multiple expansion of total deposits and credit be larger? Why? Do you believe that such
   a distinction is desirable?

3. Will an increased use of cash by the public when the banking
   system is not fully loaned up (i.e., when excess reserves exist)
   result in a decline in the amount of credit outstanding? Why
   may the banking system have excess reserves? Would you
   expect excess reserves to exist during a period of tight money
   and high interest rates?

4. If there are no excess reserves in the banking system, will
   new deposits of $2 million create $2 million of excess reserves
   or total reserves? If the reserve requirement against deposits
   is 10 per cent, how much new excess reserves have been

created ? Why would your answer be different if the reserve requirement were lowered to 5 per cent?

Chapters 4 through 9 each contain a set of questions designed to test your understanding of financial transactions and how they affect the capacity of commercial banks to lend. To answer the questions, set up "T accounts." These will aid you in your analysis of the transactions and hence help you answer the question.

5. What is the effect on (1) demand deposits, (2) required reserves, and (3) excess reserves of commercial banks given the following transactions?
   (a) The general public uses money in its checking account to buy bonds issued by corporations.
   (b) Depositors transfer funds in their checking accounts to their savings accounts.
   (c) Savers redeem certificates of deposit and place the funds in checking accounts.
   (d) A commercial bank borrows reserves in the federal funds market.
   (e) Commercial banks make loans to corporations, who use the funds to pay off loans to other creditors such as insurance companies.
   (f) Corporations retire debt owed to commercial banks.

Chapter 5

THE FEDERAL RESERVE SYSTEM

Learning Objectives

* Identify who controls the supply of money.
* Describe the structure of the Federal Reserve.
* Explain the roles performed by the Federal Reserve.
* List the tools of monetary policy.
* Show how open market operations alters the reserves of commercial banks.
* Determine the effect of an increase in the reserve requirement and the discount rate.

"There have been three great inventions since the beginning of time: fire, the wheel and central banking."

Will Rogers

The Federal Reserve system is the country's central bank. In many countries the Treasury and the central bank are one and the same, but in the United States the Treasury and the central bank are independent of each other. Such independence is another example of the checks and balances of the country's political system. While both the Treasury and the Federal Reserve may have the same general economic goals, it does not follow that they pursue the same policies to implement these goals. There have been periods when the two institutions appeared to work at odds with each other and to have followed contradictory economic policies.

This chapter is concerned with the Federal Reserve system. It covers both the role and structure of the Federal Reserve. Attention is given to the tools of monetary policy because it is through these tools that the Federal Reserve is able to alter the supply of money and the reserves of commercial banks. Open market operations, which is the buying or selling of government securities by the Federal Reserve, is the most important tool of monetary policy. Thus special attention is given to open market operations and how it is used to expand and contract the supply of money and reserves of commercial banks.

THE ROLE OF THE FEDERAL RESERVE SYSTEM

Goals of economic
policy

The purpose of the Federal Reserve system is to help achieve full employment, stable prices, and economic growth through the regulation of the supply of credit and money in the economy. Changing the supply of money and credit to achieve these goals is called monetary policy. The Federal Reserve has several tools of monetary policy. The primary ones are the discount rate, the reserve requirements of member banks, and open market operations. The Federal Reserve uses these monetary tools to expand or contract the supply of money to pursue the economic goals of prosperity with full employment and stable prices. When the Federal Reserve seeks to increase the supply of money and credit to help expand the level of income and employment, that is called an "easy" monetary policy. When it seeks to contract the supply of money and credit to help fight inflation, that is referred to as a "tight" monetary policy.

The balance sheet of
the Federal Reserve

While controlling the supply of money and credit is the primary role of the Federal Reserve, it also performs a variety of services and other functions. The many roles that the Federal Reserve system plays are mirrored by the assets and liabilities on its balance sheet. A simplified balance sheet for the Federal Reserve is shown in Table 5–1. The majority of the Federal Reserve's assets are gold certificates and the debt of the United States Government.

Major assets: (1)
Gold Certificates

The gold certificates are warehouse receipts for gold held by the Treasury. Until the Gold Reserve Act of 1934, for every dollar in paper money there had to be a dollar's worth of gold. The gold was held in vaults (e.g., Fort Knox) for safekeeping, and paper

TABLE 5–1   Simplified Federal Reserve Balance Sheet as of
November 30, 1976 (in millions)

ASSETS	
Gold certificates	$ 11,560
U.S. Government securities	91,660
Loans to member banks	40
Cash items in process of collection	8,850
Other assets	12,000
Total assets	$124,110
LIABILITIES	
Federal Reserve notes	$ 83,060
Deposits:	
Member bank reserves	23,300
U.S. Treasury	6,770
Foreign	300
Other liabilities	7,210
CAPITAL	3,470
TOTAL LIABILITIES AND CAPITAL	$124,110

money, which could be converted into gold, was used as a substitute for gold. This monetary system is called a gold standard, for the nation can only have as much paper money as it has in gold. Later the nation changed its monetary system so that the government had to have only a fraction of its paper money backed by gold. The fraction of gold necessary to cover the money supply was established by the Federal Government. Eventually this gold requirement was completely eliminated, and today gold in no way supports the nation's currency. It is the faith of the public in the purchasing power of the money supply that "backs" the currency.

While the Treasury does not have to own gold to support the money supply, it still owns gold. Gold may be used in international transactions, and the Treasury can issue gold certificates to acquire funds from the Federal Reserve. This is illustrated by the following set of T accounts:

TREASURY		FEDERAL RESERVE	
Account at Federal Reserve ↑	Gold certificate ↑	Gold certificate ↑	Treasury account ↑

The Treasury issues a receipt for gold (the gold certificate) and sells the certificate to the Federal Reserve, which increases the Treasury's account. Simultaneously the Federal Reserve's holdings of gold certificates is increased.

Besides issuing gold certificates and selling them to the Federal Reserve, the Treasury could have sold the gold to the general public, for as of January 1, 1975, the general public can legally hold gold. In either case, the issuing of gold certificates or selling the gold to the general public, the gold is a source of funds for the Treasury.

The other major asset of the Federal Reserve is the debt of the Federal Government. As is explained below, this debt is bought and sold by the Federal Reserve through open market operations. These purchases and sales alter the supply of money and the ability of banks to create credit and are the most important tool of monetary policy. The Federal Reserve balance sheet mirrors the importance of this element of monetary policy by the large amount of Treasury debt owned by the central bank. This debt is also a source of revenues to operate the Federal Reserve system, for the debt pays interest. In fact, the Federal Reserve collects sufficient interest to meet its expenses and have a profit. It pays the member banks a modest dividend of 6 per cent on the amount these banks are required to invest in the Federal Reserve. If there is a residual profit after these dividends, the funds are returned to the Treasury.

The remaining assets of the Federal Reserve include cash

(2) Federal Government debt

(3) Cash items in
process

items in process and loans to member banks. The term "cash items" is misleading because it does not involve cash but is concerned with the clearing of checks. This clearing of checks is one of the most important services provided to commercial banks by the Federal Reserve. At a given moment there are always checks being cleared, and they appear on the Federal Reserve's balance sheet as cash items in process. The process is illustrated by the flow chart and T accounts appearing in Exhibit 1. When a check is drawn on an account (e.g., a deposit in Bank A) the funds remain in that bank until the check clears. The second bank that receives the check (Bank B) credits the account in which the check was deposited (i.e., its demand deposits increase). The second bank then processes the check by sending it to the Federal Reserve for clearing. The Federal Reserve subsequently sends the check to Bank A, but for a few days that deposit exists in two banks. Both banks may have the reserves because the Federal Reserve after two days credits the second bank with reserves. In effect the reserves and the deposits are being double

The float

counted. This double counting is called the *float*. If checks take longer to clear, the float increases. This is expansionary because the money is in two places at the same time. Thus changes in the float are important because they affect the reserves of commercial banks and thus alter the ability of these banks to lend and create credit.

EXHIBIT 1

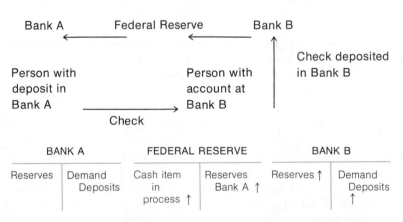

(4) Member bank
loans   •

The Federal Reserve lends reserves to member banks. Thus another of its assets are the promises of commercial banks to repay these loans. As was discussed in the previous chapter, member banks may borrow reserves from the Federal Reserve to meet their reserve requirements. These reserves are not free, and the discount rate, which is the interest rate charged the commercial banks for borrowing from the Federal Reserve, is one of the major tools of monetary policy.

The miscellaneous assets of the Federal Reserve include

foreign currencies. In recent years there has been a large increase in the volume of foreign trade, and such transactions involve foreign currencies. For example, American dollars will flow abroad when Americans travel in foreign countries, when American firms invest abroad, or when the United States Government spends money in or gives aid to a foreign country. These dollars must be exchanged for the local currency, and central banks are the mechanism through which foreign currencies are converted into domestic currencies. Thus the Federal Reserve has holdings of foreign currencies, just as the banks in other countries have holdings of dollars. (The process of exchanging currencies and the effects on domestic banks and their ability to create credit is explained in Chapter 7.)

(5) Miscellaneous assets

The largest liability of the Federal Reserve is the paper currency held by the general public (i.e., Federal Reserve Notes). The Federal Reserve also serves as a depository for commercial banks, the Treasury, and foreign banks. Member banks deposit their reserves in the Federal Reserve, and the Treasury may deposit its funds, such as tax receipts, in the Federal Reserve Banks. The foreign deposits arise as the result of international monetary transactions. Of all the different deposits, the most important is the reserves of commercial banks. By altering these reserves and the amount of Federal Reserve Notes outstanding, the Federal Reserve is able to alter the supply of money and the ability of commercial banks to create loans. It is through the power of the Federal Reserve to create and destroy these liabilities that it eases or tightens credit. Presently there are no constraints on this power of the Federal Reserve to create or destroy these liabilities. Only the goals of public policy, such as price stability or full employment, constrain the central bank, for it is assumed that the Federal Reserve will act to help achieve these economic goals.

The major liabilities
(1) Federal Reserve Notes

(2) Member bank reserves

Congress has also given the Federal Reserve vast supervisory power over individual commercial banks. The purpose of these powers is, of course, to protect the depositors from poor financial management by the bank's management. Such supervision along with the establishment of deposit insurance (FDIC) has increased public confidence in the banking system. The supervisory power of the Federal Reserve includes the enforcement of bank regulations and periodic examination of banks. Periodic reports to the Federal Reserve concerning an individual bank's loans, expenses, and earnings are also required. If the examinations and reports indicate that a bank is following unsound financial policies, then the Federal Reserve can require the bank's management to correct these policies. This ability to force a bank's management to change policy gives the Federal Reserve's supervisory powers real force. The mere existence of this force is sufficient to keep the vast majority of commercial banks pursuing sound financial policies.

Supervisory power of the Federal Reserve

STRUCTURE OF THE FEDERAL RESERVE

(1) Board of
Governors

The power in the Federal Reserve is concentrated in a Board of Governors, consisting of seven people appointed by the President of the United States with the confirmation of the Senate. The appointments are for 14 years, and the terms are staggered so that one new appointment is made every two years. The long terms and the staggering of these terms reduce political pressures and thus contributes to the federal system of checks and balances. The Chairman of the Board of Governors is usually the major spokesman for monetary policy and frequently acts as an advisor to the President on economic policy. The power of the Board of Governors manifests itself in several ways through its power of appointment and control of open market operations.

(2) The District
Banks

The country is divided into 12 districts, with a Federal Reserve bank in each district. Each district bank is managed by nine directors, three of whom are appointed by the Board of Governors. The remaining six directors are elected by member banks and represent the member banks, industry, commerce, and agriculture. By dividing the nation into districts, it is possible to have an individual reserve bank perform specialized financial services pertaining to its region. For example, the financial problems of rural regions may differ from those of urban areas. The decentralizing of the central bank into districts permits a more flexible approach to regional financial problems. Since the city of New York is the financial center of the nation, the district bank in New York is the largest and most important individual reserve bank.

(3) The member
banks

The next component of the Federal Reserve system is the member banks. Commercial banks have either state or national charters. All banks with national charters must join the Federal Reserve system. State banks have the option to join, but many do not do so. The reserve requirements for non-member state banks may be smaller, and the state banking laws may be less strict, which may explain why many state banks do not join the system. The Federal Reserve also permits non-member banks to use its check clearing facilities at no cost. Thus a major service of the Federal Reserve is available to state banks without their joining the system. Membership in the Federal Reserve system does offer a bank several advantages. The primary advantages are the right to borrow reserves from the central bank and the right to deposit funds (i.e., reserves) at the central bank. For some state banks these advantages offset the disadvantages of higher reserve requirements and the more stringent supervision and examination by the central bank.

The member banks are required to invest capital in their district's Federal Reserve Bank. The member banks are the owners of the Federal Reserve system, and for this investment they receive a modest return on their capital from the earnings of the Federal Reserve. As was explained above, the source of these earnings is the interest earned on the U.S. Government debt owned by the Federal Reserve. If the Federal Reserve earns profits that exceed its required dividends to member banks, the excess profits are returned to the Treasury.

The last component of the Federal Reserve is the Federal Open Market Committee, which has control over open market operations. Since open market operations are the most important tool of monetary policy, this committee is a powerful component of the system. The committee consists of the seven members of the Board of Governors and five presidents of the district banks. The president of the New York district bank is a permanent member of the committee, while the four remaining positions rotate among the district bank presidents. Since by voting as a bloc the Board of Governors has a majority on the committee, the board has power over open market operations.

(4) Federal open market committee

In summary, the important components of the Federal Reserve system are (1) the Board of Governors, (2) the district reserve banks, (3) the member banks, and (4) the Federal Open Market Committee. This structure is summarized by Figure 5–1. While the President of the United States appoints the Board of Governors and the member banks own the Federal Reserve, the real power rests with the Board of Governors. It has this power because it (1) appoints three of the nine directors of the district reserve banks, (2) composes a majority of the Federal Open Market Committee, and (3) has regulatory authority over the

Summary of the structure

Structure Of The Federal Reserve

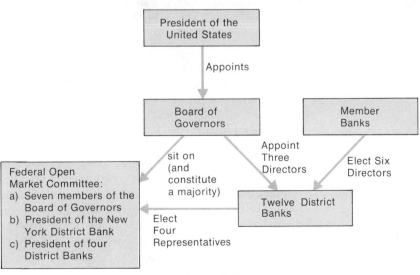

Figure 5–1

Power rests with the
Board of Governors

member banks. Thus the Board of Governors is individually the most important part of the Federal Reserve system.

TOOLS OF MONETARY POLICY

There is a variety of tools that the Federal Reserve may use to affect the supply of money and the availability of credit. These tools are primarily concerned with altering commercial banks' reserves and thereby altering their ability to grant loans and create money. The primary tools of monetary policy are the discount rate, the reserve requirement, and open market operations. There are also selective credit controls concerning real estate and consumer credit. Currently such credit controls apply only to the purchase of securities (i.e., the margin requirement which is discussed in Chapter 9).

Factors affecting
commercial bank
reserves beyond the
control of the
Federal Reserve

While the Federal Reserve is able to affect the ability of commercial banks to lend by affecting their reserves, there are other factors that also affect the reserves of commercial banks and hence alter their ability to lend and create credit. These factors are beyond the control of the Federal Reserve system and increase the difficulty of the Federal Reserve to realize the goals of monetary policy. These factors include (1) the public's desire to hold cash and savings accounts in non-commercial banks, (2) fiscal policy of the Federal Government (i.e., spending, taxation, and debt management), and (3) monetary transactions with foreign countries. Each of these has the potential for affecting banks' reserves and thereby altering their ability to lend. For example, the preceding chapter illustrated how cash withdrawals may cause the commercial banking system to contract. The next two chapters will illustrate how commercial banks' reserves may be affected by fiscal policy and international transactions.

DISCOUNT RATE

(1) Discount rate: the
cost to member
banks of borrowing
from the Federal
Reserve

The discount rate is the interest rate that the Federal Reserve charges member banks when these banks borrow reserves from the Federal Reserve. Member banks borrow reserves from the Federal Reserve to (1) meet their reserve requirements or (2) make advantageous loans when they lack excess reserves. The banks are not borrowing money as such but borrowing reserves which in turn may be used to create credit and demand deposits. A change in the cost of borrowing reserves will alter commercial banks' willingness to borrow from the Federal Reserve. Thus a decrease in the discount rate will stimulate increased borrowing, while an increase in the discount rate will discourage further borrowing and cause banks to retire debt owed the Federal Reserve.

When the commercial bank borrows from the Federal Reserve, the following changes are made in the balance sheet of the commercial bank and the Federal Reserve:

FEDERAL RESERVE BANK		BANK A	
Loan to Bank A ↑	Reserves of Bank A ↑	Reserves ↑	Owed Federal Reserve Bank ↑

The commercial bank acquires a new asset, reserves with the Federal Reserve bank, and assumes a new liability, for it must repay the borrowed reserves. The Federal Reserve bank acquires a new asset, the loan to the commercial bank, and a new liability, the newly created reserves. The new reserves may now be used by the bank to meet its reserve requirement or to grant new loans. If these reserves are used to grant a new loan, the supply of credit and the money supply are increased. Thus, increased use of borrowing from the Federal Reserve system by member banks can lead to an expansion of the money supply and the supply of credit.

While the discount rate may induce behavior on the part of commercial banks, it is a passive tool of monetary policy. The initiative for changes in the level of borrowing rests with the commercial banks. While the Federal Reserve may alter the discount rate, it cannot force banks to borrow or to cease borrowing. An increase in the discount rate does not mean that the banks will cease borrowing and retire their existing borrowings from the Federal Reserve. If the commercial banks are able to pass on to their customers the higher costs of borrowing, then there may be little contraction in the level of credit. Furthermore, not all banks borrow from the Federal Reserve. Only banks that are members of the system are allowed to use this source of reserves, and even then not all member banks borrow from the Federal Reserve. Not only does the Federal Reserve discourage such borrowing, but also some banks prefer to remain free of this obligation. Thus an increase in the discount rate will not affect the lending behavior of these banks.

During the 1960s, the Federal Reserve changed the discount rate infrequently. This is illustrated in Figure 5–2. From 1960 to 1968 the rate was changed only seven times. In the early 1970s there was a rapid increase in the rate, from 5 per cent in 1973 to 8 per cent early in 1974. The rapid increase occurred during a period of inflation and high interest rates when the Federal Reserve sought to fight inflation. As the inflation and interest rates subsided in 1975, the Federal Reserve lowered the discount rate to encourage economic growth and higher levels of employment.

The discount rate is a passive tool of monetary policy. This is illustrated by the fact that a change in the rate often occurs after a change in other rates. For example, when banks increase the rates they charge on loans, they increase the difference between

The discount rate is a passive tool

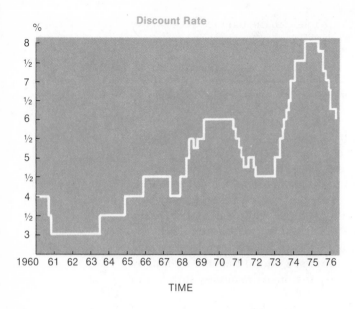

TIME

Source: Federal Reserve Bulletin

September, 1975

Figure 5–2

these rates and the discount rate. This increased difference makes borrowing from the Federal Reserve potentially more profitable. Unless the Federal Reserve wants to encourage such expansion, it will increase the discount rate to decrease the difference between the discount rate and other interest rates. The increase will then discourage the use of borrowed reserves to finance the loans, but such a change in the discount rate followed the increase in other interest rates. Thus the change in the discount rate followed the change in interest rates and did not initiate the change. While the Federal Reserve can seek to tighten the supply of credit by increasing the discount rate and thereby induce banks to increase their interest rates, the Federal Reserve rarely uses the discount rate as an active tool of monetary policy. Instead it employs open market operations because it can achieve its objectives more efficiently.

RESERVE REQUIREMENTS

(2) Reserve requirement—a cumbersome tool

Changes in the reserve requirements against bank deposits is the second major tool of monetary policy. Like the discount rate it is infrequently used as an active tool of monetary policy. Since commercial banks must maintain reserves against their deposit liabilities, any change in these required reserves alter commercial banks' ability to lend. Thus the Federal Reserve can create or destroy the excess reserves of commercial banks by increasing or decreasing the reserve requirement. For example, if the reserve requirement for demand deposits is 12 per cent and is raised to 15 per cent, then each commercial bank that is a member of the Federal Reserve system must increase its required reserves. While they previously had to hold $12 in reserves against every $100 in demand deposits, these banks must now hold $15 in reserves. Therefore, by simply increasing the reserve requirement, the Federal Reserve immediately decreases member banks' capacity to grant loans. A decrease in the reserve requirement is the exact opposite, for it immediately increases commercial banks' ability to lend.

Changing the reserve requirement is a cumbersome tool of monetary policy. When a change in the requirement is made, it produces a large change in the total amount of required reserves. If the reserve requirement were raised from 12 to 15 per cent, then required reserves rise by 25 per cent, which is a large increase in required reserves. Thus if commercial banks' demand deposits were $160 billion and the Federal Reserve were to increase the reserve requirement from 12 to 15 per cent, then required reserves will increase from $19.2 billion to $25 billion. Such an increase in required reserves will have an immediate and far-reaching impact on commercial banks.

Obviously this tool of monetary policy cannot be used to fine-tune the money supply to changing liquidity needs. For example, how could this tool be used to put liquidity into the system for seasonal changes in the demand for currency? The advantages of changing the reserve requirement are (1) the ability to release or absorb large amounts of reserves in one act and (2) an "announcement effect" that serves to indicate the seriousness of a particular policy of the Federal Reserve system.

Since changes in the reserve requirement are unable to produce subtle changes in the money supply, it is rarely used as a tool of monetary policy. The infrequency with which it has been used is illustrated by Figure 5–3, which presents the maximum reserve requirements for demand deposits and savings accounts. As may be seen from this graph, these reserve requirements have been changed infrequently. During 1962–1974 the reserve re-

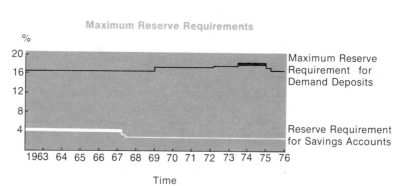

Figure 5–3

quirement against demand deposits was changed only on five occasions, and the reserve requirement for savings accounts was altered only twice.

OPEN MARKET OPERATIONS

(3) Open market operations—the buying and selling of government securities

Of the three major tools of monetary policy, by far the most important is open market operations. Open market operations refers to the purchase and sale of government securities by the Federal Reserve. By buying and selling these securities, the Federal Reserve is able to alter the supply of money in circulation and the reserves of the commercial banking system. The Federal Reserve may buy and sell securities at any time and in any volume. Thus it is able to affect continuously the supply of money and credit. Open market operations then are not only a means of significantly changing the money supply and availability of credit but also of fine-tuning the supply of money on a day-by-day basis.

Role of security dealers

The Federal Reserve does not directly buy and sell securities to the general public or commercial banks. The transactions are negotiated through U.S. Government security dealers who make markets in these securities. The dealers in turn sell the government securities to the general public and commercial banks. Since the sales and purchases are in many millions of dollars, these security dealers must have substantial capital and borrowing capacity to make these markets.

If the Federal Reserve seeks to expand the supply of money, it purchases securities. If it wants to contract the supply of money, securities are sold. After the transactions are negotiated, payments must be made, and it is the act of paying for the securities which alters the money supply and the reserves of the commercial banks. How these transactions and payments are executed and why they affect the supply of money and credit are the subject matter of the next section.

THE MECHANICS OF OPEN MARKET OPERATIONS

EXPANSION

Purchasing securities expands reserves and demand deposits

If the Federal Reserve seeks to increase the supply of money and the reserves of the banking system, it purchases securities. Ownership of the securities is transferred to the Federal Reserve, and the Federal Reserve pays for the securities by writing a check drawn on itself, which the seller deposits in a commercial bank. The bank clears the check and reserves from the Federal Reserve.

These transactions have the following effect on each participant's balance sheet:

FEDERAL RESERVE		COMMERCIAL BANK		GENERAL PUBLIC	
Government Securities ↑	Reserves of Commercial Banks ↑	Reserves ↑	Demand Deposits ↑	Government Securities ↓	
				Demand Deposits ↑	

The general public sold securities and received payment. In effect it traded one asset (the government securities) for another (the demand deposit). The bank, however, has received a new liability (the new checking account) and a new asset (the reserves). The Federal Reserve acquired a new asset (the government securities) and paid for the securities by *creating a new liability* on itself (the reserves of the commercial bank).

The total effect of the transaction has been (1) to increase the supply of money because demand deposits have increased and (2) to increase the reserves of the banking system. The required reserves of the bank rise, for the deposit liabilities of the commercial bank have risen. However, only a fraction of the increase in reserves will be required reserves. Thus the excess reserves of the commercial bank have also risen. This increase in excess reserves means the capacity of the commercial banking system to expand the supply of money and create more credit has risen. Thus, if the reserve requirement against demand deposits is 20 per cent and the Federal Reserve purchases $100 million of government securities from the general public, the reserves of commercial banks increases by $100 million, of which $20 million will be required and $80 million will be excess reserves. The simple equation for expansion (i.e., excess reserves divided by the reserve requirement), now indicates that the potential exists for the commercial banking system to expand the money supply by $400 million ($80 million/.2). The purchasing of $100 million worth of government securities by the Federal Reserve from the general public thus causes not only an increase in the supply of money but also the potential for additional increases in the money supply because the excess reserves of commercial banks are increased.

CONTRACTION

When the Federal Reserve seeks to contract the money supply, it sells government securities. Once again, it is the payment for the purchased securities which alters the money supply and the capacity of commercial banks to lend. If the public buys the securities, it draws down demand deposits, and the money supply and reserves of commercial banks are decreased. The effect of the transaction on the balance sheets of the Federal Reserve, the commercial banks, and the public of the Federal Reserve selling securities is as follows:

Selling securities contracts reserves and demand deposits

FEDERAL RESERVE		COMMERCIAL BANK		GENERAL PUBLIC	
Government Securities ↓	Reserves of Commercial Banks ↓	Reserves ↓	Demand Deposits ↓	Demand Deposits ↓	
				Government Securities ↑	

The general public has traded one asset (the demand deposit) for another (the government security). The commercial bank loses the demand deposit, and, when the check clears and payment is made to the Federal Reserve, reserves of the commercial bank at the Federal Reserve are reduced. The Federal Reserve loses an asset (the government security) and a liability (the reserves). It has, in effect, retired a liability by giving up an asset. The total effect of this transaction has been (1) to decrease the money supply because demand deposits have decreased and (2) to decrease the total reserves of the banking system because commercial banks have fewer reserves on deposit in the Federal Reserve. Since only a percentage of these reserves was required against the deposit liabilities, the excess reserves of the bank are also decreased. Thus, by selling securities in the open market, the Federal Reserve has decreased the supply of money and decreased the excess reserves of the commercial banks. The decrease in excess reserves reduces the ability of the commercial banking system to lend and create credit.

SUMMARY

The Federal Reserve is the nation's central bank. Its purpose is to control the supply of money and credit in the nation. Through this control the Federal Reserve pursues the goals of monetary policy: higher levels of employment, stable prices, and economic growth.

The Federal Reserve has several tools of monetary policy. The primary tools are open market operations, the reserve requirement against member bank deposits, and the discount rate. Open market operations is individually the most important tool of monetary policy. When the Federal Reserve seeks to expand the supply of money and credit, it buys U.S. Government securities. When it seeks to contract the supply of money, it sells these securities. Such purchases and sales affect the reserves of commercial banks and thus alter their ability to lend. By changing the capacity of commercial banks to lend, the Federal Reserve pursues the goals of full employment, price stability, and economic growth.

monetary policy
open market operations
discount rate
reserve requirement
Board of Governors
Federal Open Market Committee
district banks
gold standard
Federal Reserve Notes
gold certificates
float

QUESTIONS FOR THOUGHT AND DISCUSSION

1. Open market operations constitutes the most important tool of monetary policy. Why is it more important than the other tools of monetary policy? How may open market operations be used to contract the supply of money? Notice that it is the act of paying for the securities that causes the contraction.

2. In spring, 1969, the Federal Reserve raised both the discount rate and the reserve requirement. This came in response to increasing rates of inflation and increases in the prime rate (i.e., the rate charged on short-term loans to large borrowers with excellent credit ratings).
   (a) Why, in view of the increase in the prime rate, was the increase in the discount rate to be expected?
   (b) Why would the increase in the reserve requirement have been less expected than the increase in the discount rate?

3. In most countries the central bank is part of the country's Treasury. In the United States the Federal Reserve is owned by commercial banks. May this separation cause friction between the Treasury and the Federal Reserve? Does ownership by commercial banks imply that they control the Federal Reserve?

4. What is the effect on (1) demand deposits, (2) required reserves, and (3) excess reserves of commercial banks given the following transactions?
   (a) The Federal Reserve sells bonds that are purchased by the general public.
   (b) The Federal Reserve sells bonds that are purchased by commercial banks.

(c) The Federal Reserve lowers the discount rate, and commercial banks borrow from the Federal Reserve.

(d) The Federal Reserve lowers the reserve requirement on savings accounts.

(e) The Federal Government sells a new issue of bonds that are purchased by the Federal Reserve. The Treasury deposits the funds in its accounts at commercial banks.

Chapter 6

FISCAL POLICY, GOVERNMENT DEBT, AND THE MONEY SUPPLY

Learning Objectives

- Enumerate the various debt instruments issued by the Federal Government.
- Identify the risks associated with investing in Federal Government debt.
- Differentiate the effects of deficit and surplus budgets on commercial banks' reserves and the money supply.
- Isolate the feature that differentiates state and local municipal debt.

"A national debt, if it is not excessive, will be to us a national blessing."

Alexander Hamilton

Fiscal policy is taxation, expenditures, and debt management by the Federal Government. Like monetary policy, fiscal policy may be used to pursue the economic goals of full employment, price stability, and economic growth. Like monetary policy, fiscal policy can affect the supply of money and the capacity of the commercial banking system to lend.

Taxation or government expenditures by themselves do not affect the money supply. However, when government expenditures exceed revenues, this deficit must be financed. When government revenues exceed expenditures, the government must do something with this surplus. It is the financing of the deficit or disposing of the surplus that may affect the supply of money and the capacity of commercial banks to lend. This chapter is primarily concerned with the effect that fiscal policy may have on the money supply and the reserves of commercial banks.

In the first section special emphasis is placed on the various types of debt issued by the Federal Government. These debt instruments are issued when the Treasury runs a deficit. The second section of this chapter is devoted to the effects of such deficit spending on the money supply and the reserves of commercial banks. The last section considers debt issued by other governments (i.e., state and local municipal debt). Special emphasis is placed on the feature that distinguishes state and local government debt, the exemption of the interest paid by this debt from federal income taxation.

THE VARIETY OF FEDERAL GOVERNMENT DEBT

The Federal Government estimated interest payments of $34.4 billion in 1976 on its debt. This is a substantial payment and was 9.9 per cent of the estimated total expenditures of the Federal Government in 1976. This debt is owned by a variety of investors, including individuals, corporations, and financial institutions. To induce this diverse group of investors to purchase the debt, the Federal Government issues a variety of debt instruments that appeal to the various potential buyers.

Safety is the prime advantage

For investors, the most important advantage offered by the Federal Government's debt is its safety. These debt instruments are the safest of all possible investments, for there is no question that the Treasury is able to pay the interest and repay the principal. The source of this safety is the ability of the Federal Government to create money, which is a constitutional right given only to the Federal Government. Sometimes it is erroneously asserted that the safety comes from taxing power, but the resources of the public are limited. Hence the capacity to tax is limited. There is no such limitation on the Federal Government's capacity to create money. Hence there is no limit on its capacity to pay interest and retire (or at least refinance) the debt.

The various types of Federal Government debt and the amount outstanding of each type differs, as may be seen in Table 6–1.

TABLE 6–1   Types of Federal Government Debt

	LENGTH OF TIME TO MATURITY	$ (IN BILLIONS)	PER CENT OF TOTAL DEBT
Treasury bills	less than one year	$138	32.6%
Intermediate term notes	one to five years	155	36.7%
Long term bonds	over five years	38	9.0%
Savings bonds	various maturities	67	15.8%
Other debt	various maturities	25	5.9%

As may be seen in the exhibit, there has been an emphasis on the use of short and intermediate term financing by the Treasury. This emphasis is partially explained by interest costs. Interest rates on short term debt tend to be lower than interest rates on long term debt. Hence use of short term debt financing reduces the Treasury's interest expense. Furthermore, Congress restricts the interest rate that the Treasury may pay on long term debt. These restrictions do not apply to short term securities. Thus during periods when interest rates are high, the Treasury may not be permitted to sell long term securities even if it desired to issue this type of debt.

Majority of Federal Government debt is short term

SERIES E AND H BONDS

Perhaps the most widely known Federal Government bonds are the Series E and H bonds. The Series E bonds are designed to encourage saving by people of modest means. They are sold in small denominations (e.g., $25, $100, $500 up to $10,000). Thus virtually every person should be able to place modest amounts of savings in these bonds. These bonds do not pay interest in the usual sense but are purchased at a discount (i.e., below their face value). For example, a $25 Series E bond costs $18.75. If the buyer holds the bond until its maturity five years and five months later, the saver receives $25 and has earned 6% on the investment. That is the same return the buyer would earn if $18.75 were placed in a bank that pays 6 per cent a year and left in the bank for five years and five months. The $18.75 grows to $25.00 in either case. There is, however, one major difference between the Series E bond and most other investments, like savings accounts. The interest is not subject to federal income taxation until the Series E bond is redeemed (i.e., cashed in). Interest earned on a savings account, however, is subject to federal income taxation during the year in which it is earned. With Series E bonds the federal income tax may be deferred until the bonds are cashed. The owner of the Series E bond does have the option to have the interest taxed each year. Even though the funds are not received until the bond is redeemed, the owner may report the interest to the Internal Revenue Service on an accrual basis. Most holders of Series E bonds, however, prefer to defer the tax payment until the bonds are redeemed.

Series E bonds are designed for small investors

Income tax may be deferred

H bonds are different than E bonds. They are sold in denominations of $500 and multiples of $500; these bonds mature in ten years and pay 6 per cent interest if held to maturity. The interest is paid every year and does not accumulate, as with Series E bonds. Thus the interest is subject to federal income taxation each year while the interest on Series E bonds may be taxed when the bonds are redeemed. Series H bonds are more attractive to investors who need safe sources of current income. Series E bonds are attractive to people seeking to build up capital who do not need current income.

H bonds offer safe, current income

There is no secondary market in Series E and H bonds. The bonds cannot be sold but may be redeemed at a commercial bank if the owner wants cash. If these bonds are redeemed prior to maturity, the saver loses some interest so that the return is less than 6 per cent. While there is no market in these bonds, the Treasury has issued debt instruments that may be bought and sold in the same way investors buy or sell the stocks and bonds of AT&T. These Treasury debt instruments are not sold on an organized exchange, such as the New York Stock Exchange, but through government security dealers who make a market in these securities. These debt instruments may be classified by the length of time to maturity, which ranges from relatively short term (i.e., Treasury bills) to many years (i.e., Treasury bonds).

TREASURY BILLS

Treasury bills are sold at a discount

Treasury bills are short-term Federal Government debts that are sold in denominations of $10,000 to $1,000,000 and mature in three to twelve months. Treasury bills pay no set amount of interest; instead they are sold at a discount. The Treasury is continually auctioning off these bills, and potential buyers bid for them, with the highest bidders obtaining the bills. Buyers thus bid a price, such as $9700 for a six month $10,000 bill. Such a price yields $300 on an investment of $9700, for the buyer receives $10,000 at maturity. This is a yield of 3.1 per cent (300/9700). Since the investment is a six month bill, the annual simple rate of interest is 6.2 per cent. If the bid price had been higher, the interest cost to the Treasury (and the yield to the buyer) would have been lower.

Active secondary market for bills

Once Treasury bills have been auctioned, there is a secondary market for the bills. They are quoted daily in financial and many city newspapers. For example, the quotes for January 31, 1977, given in the *Wall Street Journal* were:

·U.S. Treasury Bills

DEBT OF MATURITY	BID DISCOUNT	ASK	DEBT OF MATURITY	BID DISCOUNT	ASK
2- 3	4.63	4.41	5-26	4.89	4.81
2- 8	4.63	4.41	5-31	4.91	4.81
2-10	4.59	4.39	6- 2	4.91	4.81
2-17	4.57	4.39	6- 9	4.93	4.85
2-24	4.57	4.39	6-16	4.95	4.85
3- 3	4.58	4.42	6-23	4.97	4.89
3- 8	4.60	4.46	6-28	5.00	4.90
3-10	4.59	4.45	6-30	5.00	4.92
3-17	4.60	4.41	7- 7	5.03	4.95
3-24	4.58	4.44	7-14	5.04	4.96
3-31	4.60	4.48	7-21	5.04	4.98
4- 5	4.68	4.58	7-26	5.04	4.94
4- 7	4.70	4.60	7-28	5.04	5.00
4-14	4.70	4.60	8-23	5.14	5.06
4-21	4.73	4.65	9-20	5.18	5.10
4-28	4.73	4.69	10-18	5.21	5.13
5- 3	4.83	4.75	11-15	5.24	5.16
5- 5	4.82	4.76	12-13	5.26	5.19
5-12	4.83	4.75	1-10	5.23	5.19
5-19	4.87	4.79			

(Reprinted by permission of the *Wall Street Journal.*)

These quotes indicate that for the Treasury bill maturing on October 18, 1977, buyers were willing to bid a price that yielded 5.21 per cent. Sellers, however, were willing to offer the bills at a smaller discount (i.e., higher price) that yielded only 5.13 per cent.

Treasury bills may be purchased not only through brokerage firms but also through commercial banks and the Federal Reserve. These purchases may be new issues or made through the secondary market. One year bills are auctioned once a month. Three and six month bills are auctioned every Monday. If the buyer purchases the bills directly through the Federal Reserve, there are no commissions. Brokers and commercial banks do charge commissions, but the fees are modest (e.g., $25 for $15,000 worth of bills).

Treasury bills are the best short-term investments that stress liquidity and safety. The bills mature quickly, as the above quotes indicate, and there are many issues from which the investor may purchase. Thus the investor may purchase a bill maturing when the principal is needed. Like all Treasury debt, the bills are safe, for there is no question that the Federal Government has the capacity to refund or retire the bills. Treasury bills are purchased by companies with excess cash or commercial banks with excess reserves. Individual savers may also buy Treasury bills, but the large denominations virtually exclude most savers. Since bills are extremely liquid and safe short term debt instruments, they are excellent short term investments for firms and banks. For example, if a firm has to make a payment in four months and currently has the cash, the financial manager can purchase a Treasury bill that matures in four months. The financial manager will earn interest for the firm but assure the firm of having the funds to meet the payment.

Bills offer liquidity and safety

TREASURY NOTES AND BONDS

Treasury notes are intermediate term Federal Government debts that are issued in denominations of $1000 to over $100,000 and mature in one to seven years. Long-term debt is called Treasury bonds. The denominations are $500 to $1,000,000, and they mature in more than five years from date of issue. Since these issues are the safest intermediate and long-term investments available, they are purchased by pension funds, financial institutions, or savers who are primarily concerned with moderate income and safety. Since these debt instruments are so safe, their yields are lower than may be obtained with good quality corporate debt, such as AT&T bonds. For example, in January 1975, AT&T bonds yielded 9 per cent while similar Treasury bonds yielded 6.7 per cent. For many investors this difference is sufficient compensation for the additional risk of owning AT&T bonds.

Long term debt offers moderate income and safety

Potential sources of
loss: (1) Price
fluctuations

While there is no question that the Federal Government can pay the interest and refund its debt, there are ways in which the holder of Treasury notes and bonds can suffer losses. These debt instruments pay a fixed amount of interest which is determined when the notes and bonds are issued. If interest rates later rise, existing issues will not be as attractive, and their market prices will decline. If an investor must sell the debt instrument before it matures, the price will be lower than the amount of the principal (called "par") and the investor will suffer a capital loss.

Interest rates paid by Treasury debt have varied over time. The extent of this variation is illustrated in Figure 6–1, which shows the yields on Treasury bills and Treasury bonds from 1970 to 1976. As may be seen from the chart, the yields on Treasury bonds has ranged from about 5.5 per cent to above 7 per cent. Yields on Treasury bills have fluctuated severely, ranging from a high of 8.7 per cent in August, 1974, to 5.2 per cent only ten months later. The cause for these fluctuations is conditions in the money and bond markets. As the demand and supply vary, so will the yields on all debt instruments including the debt of the Federal Government. Of course, a major factor in the market for Federal Government debt is the Federal Reserve. Through open market operations the Federal Reserve affects not only the supply of money and banks' reserves but also the yields on Treasury debt. These fluctuations in the yields also cause fluctuations in the prices of the debt instruments.

(2) Inflation

The investor may also lose if the rate of inflation exceeds the interest rate being earned. For example, if an investor earns 6 per cent on the government bond and the rate of inflation is 7 per cent, then the investor suffers a loss in purchasing power. The interest is insufficient to compensate for the loss of purchasing power. These two cases illustrate that investing in Federal Government debt, like all types of investing, subjects the investor to risk. Thus while Federal Government debt is among the safest of all investments with regard to interest and principal, some element of risk still exists.

FEDERAL AGENCY DEBT

Safe alternative to
Federal Government
securities

Besides the debt of the Federal Government, certain Federal Government agencies also issue bonds. These agencies include the Federal Home Loan Banks, Federal National Mortgage Association, Bank for Cooperatives, and the World Bank. Like Treasury bonds, these federal agency bonds are traded in the over-the-counter market, and their prices are quoted daily in the financial newspapers. Agency bonds are not issues of the Federal Government, and they have higher yields than Treasury debt. Investors seeking safety and higher yields may find these bonds more interesting than Treasury debt. Agency bonds are extremely safe for they have the backing of the

Federal Government. This backing may be legal, in which case the debt is guaranteed by the Federal Government; or it is a moral obligation, even though the Federal Government does not legally have to support the debt in case of default.

THE STRUCTURE OF INTEREST RATES

Federal Government debt illustrates the relationship between the yields on bonds and the length of time to maturity (i.e., the structure of interest rates). During most periods of history this relationship has been positive, that is, the longer the time to maturity, the higher the rate of interest. This indicates that investors require a higher rate of interest to compensate them for lending their money for the longer time period. Such a relationship is indicated by the yields in Figure 6–2, which plots the yields on Treasury debt as of September 29, 1975. As may be seen in the graph, the bonds that mature further in the future pay a higher rate of interest. For example, short term Treasury bills that mature in six months were yielding 6.8 per cent, but the bonds maturing in 1993 yielded 8.2 per cent.

Positive yield curve

While this structure of interest rates has occurred during most periods of history, there have been periods when the yield curve was negatively sloped or very flat with virtually no slope. One possible explanation of this negative relationship between time and interest rates may be inflation. To fight inflation, the

Negative yield curve

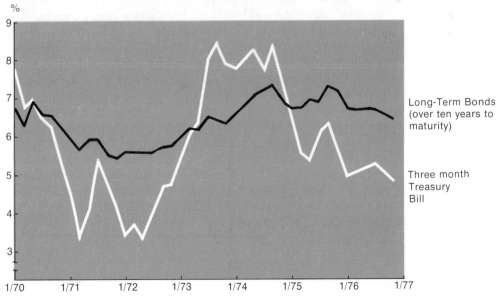

Interest Rates on Treasury
Bills and Bonds 1970–1976

Long-Term Bonds
(over ten years to
maturity)

Three month
Treasury
Bill

Time

Figure 6–1

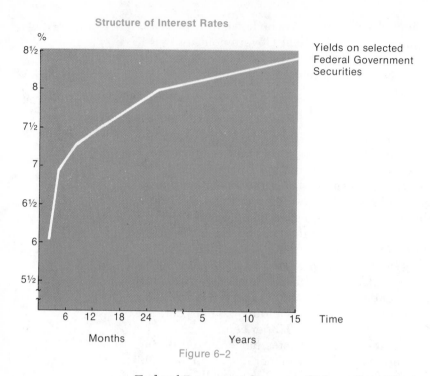

Figure 6–2

Federal Reserve tightens credit by selling Treasury bills, which drives up short-term interest rates. Simultaneously, firms realize that if they sell long-term bonds with the high interest rates, they lock themselves into the high-interest charges. If interest rates subsequently decline, the firms are burdened with the high rates. Hence firms have an incentive to borrow on a short-term basis in anticipation of future declines in the interest rates. This increases the demand for short-term money and drives up short-term relative to long-term interest rates. Investors are also wary of purchasing long-term debt even with relatively high interest rates. If inflation continues and interest rates rise further, then the investors who have purchased the lower yielding debt will suffer losses. The uncertainty concerning the future encourages both issuers and buyers to stress liquidity. Short-term debt not only offers firms a means to finance assets but also returns investors' principal quickly. When such uncertainty occurs, the demand for short-term money may rise sufficiently that short-term interest rates rise above long-term rates, and the yield curve becomes very flat or negatively sloped.

DEFICIT SPENDING

Deficits must be financed

Many financial transactions may affect the reserves of the banking system and hence affect the ability of banks to lend. Deficit spending by the Federal Government is one of these transactions. Deficit spending occurs when the government spends more than it receives in tax revenues. The deficit may be financed from the following three sources: (1) the general public, (2) commercial banks, and (3) the Federal Reserve. The effect on banks' reserves varies with each of these sources of funds, and an example will be used to illustrate the difference among these three sources of funds. In the example the Federal Government raises $70 by taxing the general public. It spends, however, $75, thus creating a deficit of $5 that must be financed from one of the three sources.

1. *Borrowing from the General Public.* When the $70 of taxes are paid, $70 in demand deposits of the general public is transferred from the public's account to the Treasury's account. The Treasury intends to spend $75; so it issues a government security for $5 and sells it to the general public. The public pays for the security, which transfers money from the account of the general public to the Treasury's account. These transactions are summarized by the following T accounts:

Borrowing from the general public does not affect the money supply

PUBLIC		TREASURY	
Demand Deposit ↓ $70 ↑ $5	Taxes owed the Government $70 ↓	Bank Account ↑ $70 ↑ $5	Bonds ↑ $5
Treasury Bonds ↑ $5		Taxes due ↓ $70	

All that has occurred is a transfer of $75 from the public's account at commercial banks to the Treasury's account at commercial banks.

The Treasury now purchases goods or services from the general public for $75. When the Treasury pays for these goods and services, the public's deposits are restored as the funds are transferred from the Treasury account to the general public. This is shown by the following T accounts:

PUBLIC		TREASURY	
Goods ↓ $75		Account ↓ $75	
Demand Deposit ↑ $75		Goods ↑ $75	

What is the change in the money supply and the reserves of the commercial banks as a result of these transactions? There has been no change in the money supply, because there has been no change in demand deposits, currency, and coins. There has also been no change in the reserves of the banking system, and thus there has been no change in banks' ability to lend and create credit. All that has occurred is that the government has obtained $75 worth of resources by taxation and borrowing from the public. By borrowing from the general public to finance a deficit, the

Treasury does not affect the supply of money or the ability of the banks to lend.

2. *Borrowing from the Commercial Banks.* Once again the Treasury taxes $70 from the general public, and the funds are transferred from the general public's account to the Treasury's account. The Treasury then issues a $5 government security and sells it to the commercial banks. The commercial banks pay for the security by crediting funds to the Treasury's account. This set of transactions is summarized by the following set of T accounts:

PUBLIC		BANKS	
Demand Deposit ↓ $70	Taxes owed the Government ↓ $70	Government Security ↑ $5	Demand Deposit of Public ↓ $70
			Demand Deposit of Treasury ↑ $70 ↑ $5

In effect what has happened is that the Treasury has obtained $75 in funds by taxing the general public for $70 and borrowing $5 from the commercial banks. Of course, for the banks to make this loan to the Treasury, the commercial banks had to have excess reserves. At this stage the only difference between this case and the first one is that the purchaser of the government security is the commercial banks instead of the general public. In either case the Treasury acquires the $75 by taxation and issuing new debt.

The Treasury now spends the $75 to purchase goods and services and pays for them by drawing on its checking account. The money is returned to the general public, for they place the $75 in their checking accounts. The bank credits the public's account and debits the Treasury account. This is shown by the following T accounts:

PUBLIC		BANK		TREASURY	
Demand Deposit ↑ $75		Treasury Account ↓ $75		Goods ↑ $75	
Goods & Services ↓ $75		Demand Deposit ↑ $75		Account ↓ $75	

The Treasury still acquires $75 worth of goods and services when it taxes $70 from the general public and borrows $5 from the commercial banks. The question becomes what has happened to the money supply and the ability of the banks to lend.

The money supply has increased because the total demand deposits have increased from $70 to $75. The public started with

$70 in its demand deposits and this has risen to $75. The total reserves of the banking system, however, have not been affected. Since demand deposits have increased, the required reserves of commercial banks must rise. Since total reserves have not increased, the excess reserves of commercial banks have declined. That is exactly what happened because the commercial banks used excess reserves to purchase the debt. There is no difference between banks' granting loans to businesses and banks' purchasing government securities that finance a deficit. In either case the banks use their excess reserves to purchase income earning assets and in both cases the assets are a liability of the borrower. Government securities are liabilities of the government just like the debts of businesses are liabilities of firms. When commercial banks lend to the government by buying the government securities, the money supply is expanded in the same way that the money supply is expanded through the process of lending to individuals and firms. The difference is only the borrower and the type of asset the bank acquires.

3. *Borrowing from the Federal Reserve.* The Treasury may also finance its deficit by borrowing from the Federal Reserve. In this case the $70 in taxes are paid and the general public's demand deposits decline by $70 as the funds are transferred from the general public to the Treasury. Since the Treasury needs $75, the $5 security is issued and in this case is purchased by the Federal Reserve. The Federal Reserve pays for the security by granting the Treasury $5 to its account. The following T accounts summarize these transactions:

Borrowing from the Federal Reserve

PUBLIC		TREASURY		FEDERAL RESERVE	
Demand Deposit ↓ $70	Taxes owed Government ↓ $70	Accounts ↑ $70 ↑ $5	Bonds ↑ $5	Government Securities ↑ $5	Treasury Account ↑ $5
		Taxes due ↓ $70			

The Treasury has funds obtained of $75, $70 by taxing and $5 by borrowing from the Federal Reserve. The difference between this case and the two cases presented above is the source of the borrowed funds. In each case the general public has paid the same amount in taxes ($70) and in each case the government has issued the same amount of debt ($5). In this case, however, the purchaser of the government securities is the Federal Reserve system, not the general public or the commercial banks.

The Treasury now spends the $75 buying $75 worth of goods and services from the general public. It pays for these goods and services by using the funds deposited in its account at the commercial banks ($70) and at the Federal Reserve ($5). This transaction is summarized by the following T accounts:

GENERAL PUBLIC		COMMERCIAL BANKS	

Demand
  Deposit ↑ $75
		Reserves
		  ↑ $5
			Demand
			  Deposits ↑ $75

Goods and
  Services ↓ $70
			Treasury
			  Account ↓ $70

TREASURY		FEDERAL RESERVE	
Accounts ↓ $75			Treasury Account ↓ $5

Goods and
  Services ↑ $75
			Reserves of Banks
			  ↑ $5

The general public has sold $75 worth of goods and services to the government and deposits the check in its checking accounts at the commercial banks. The commercial banks reduce the Treasury account for $70 and request payment from the Federal Reserve for $5. The Federal Reserve makes payment by increasing the reserves of the commercial banks with $5 and decreasing the Treasury account for $5.

Now comes the crucial question: what has happened to the money supply and the ability of banks to lend as a result of the Treasury's running a deficit and financing it by borrowing from the Federal Reserve? Total demand deposits of the public have increased from $70 to $75; thus the money supply has increased. That is no different than when the Treasury borrowed from the commercial banks. The important difference in this third case is that the *reserves* of commercial banks have also increased (by $5). Thus, while required reserves rise to cover the $5 increase in demand deposits, there has also been an increase in total reserves of the banking system. With a fractional reserve system of banking, there is an increase in the excess reserves of the commercial banks. That is, the ability of commercial banks to create further loans and expand the money supply is increased. Thus when the Treasury finances the deficit by selling securities to the Federal Reserve, the money supply and the ability of the banks to lend and further expand the supply of money are both increased. These three cases for financing a government deficit are summarized in Table 6–2.

Expands the money supply and commercial banks' reserves

Effects of borrowing summarized

TABLE 6–2

	CHANGE IN MONEY SUPPLY	CHANGE IN TOTAL RESERVES OF BANKS	CHANGE IN EXCESS RESERVES OF BANKS
Case I—borrowing from general public	None	None	None
Case II—borrowing from commercial banks	Increase	None	Decrease
Case III—borrowing from the Federal Reserve	Increase	Increase	Increase

Of these three cases, the most inflationary is the third case because both the money supply and the ability of banks to lend is increased. There is no increase in the money supply or the ability of banks to lend when the Treasury borrows from the general public. There is an increase in the supply of money when the Treasury borrows from the commercial banks, but this increase uses the excess reserves of commercial banks. Thus, while there is a net increase in the money supply, the commercial banks' ability to lend to businesses and individuals is reduced. Only when the Treasury borrows from the Federal Reserve is there an expansion in both the money supply and the commercial banks' ability to lend.

How the Treasury finances its deficit is important because of the effect on the money supply and on the ability of commercial banks to lend. As was illustrated in the previous chapters, many financial transactions may affect the supply of money and the reserves of commercial banks. How the Federal Government's deficit is financed is another example of a monetary transaction that may have impact on the banking system. Such transactions increase the difficulty of the Federal Reserve to control the supply of money and credit in the nation. Thus these transactions make monetary policy more difficult and decrease the ability of the Federal Reserve to affect the level of income, employment, and prices.

STATE AND LOCAL MUNICIPAL GOVERNMENT DEBT

State and local municipal governments also issue debt. These governments issue debt to finance capital expenditures such as schools. The government then retires the debt as the facilities are used. The funds used to retire the debt may be raised through taxes (e.g., property taxes) or through revenues generated by the facilities themselves. Bonds supported by the taxing authority of the municipal government are called general obligation bonds. Bonds supported by revenues generated by the specific facilities are called revenue bonds. There are various types of revenue bonds, for these have been used to finance such capital investments as roads, hospitals, school dormitories, and pollution control facilities.

Why issue debt

Unlike the Federal Government, state and local governments do not have the power to create money. These governments must raise the funds necessary to pay the interest and retire the debt, but their ability to do so varies. Thus the quality of this state and local debt differs with the financial conditions of each government. Local governments with wealthy residents or valuable property within their boundaries are able to issue debt more readily and at lower interest rates because the debt is safer.

Quality of state and municipal debt varies

The tax base in these communities is larger and can support the debt.

The primary factor that differentiates state and municipal debt from other forms of debt is the tax advantage this debt offers investors. The interest on state and local municipal debt is exempt from federal income taxation. While state and local governments may tax the interest, the Federal Government may not. The rationale for this tax exemption is legal and not financial. The Supreme Court established that the Federal Government does not have the power to tax the interest paid by debt of state and local municipal governments. Since the interest paid by all other debt is subject to federal income taxation, this interest exemption is advantageous to state and local municipal governments, for they are able to issue debt at substantially lower interest costs. The lower interest cost is due to the fact that investors are willing to accept a lower return on state and local municipal debt because the after tax return is equivalent to higher yields on corporate debt. For example, if an investor is in the 50 per cent income tax bracket, the return after taxes is the same for a corporate bond that pays 10 per cent or a state or municipal bond that pays 5 per cent. The investor is willing to accept the lower interest payment on the state or municipal government bond because the after tax yields are the same. The after tax return is 5 per cent in either case.

Investors' willingness to purchase state and local municipal debt instead of corporate and Treasury debt is related to their income tax bracket. As the investor's federal income tax rises, tax exempt bonds become more attractive. If the tax rate is 60 per cent, then a 5 per cent nontaxable municipal bond gives the investor the same yield after taxes as a 12.5 per cent corporate bond whose interest is subject to federal income taxation. The individual investor may determine the equivalent yields on tax exempt bonds and non–tax exempt bonds by the following formula:

interest rate on taxable bonds $\times$ (1 – individual's marginal tax rate) = interest rate on tax exempt bonds.

If the numbers in the previous example are used in this formula, the 12.5 per cent is readily determined by the following formula:

$$X (1 - .6) = .05$$
$$X = \frac{.05}{.04} = 12.5$$

The equivalent yields on taxable and nontaxable bonds for selected taxable incomes is given in Table 6–3. As may be seen in this table, as income rises the marginal tax rate increases. This means that the before tax interest rate must rise to compensate

TABLE 6–3   Equivalent Yields for Taxable and Nontaxable Bonds
at Selected Levels of Taxable Income

SELECTED TAXABLE INCOMES (joint return)	TAX BRACKET (marginal tax rate)	EQUIVALENT TAXABLE YIELDS IF TAX EXEMPT YIELD IS	
		5%	7%
$ 20,000–24,000	32%	7.3%	10.3%
32,000–36,000	42	8.6	12.1
40,000–44,000	48	9.6	13.5
52,000–64,000	53	10.6	14.9
100,000–120,000	62	13.2	18.4

for the additional tax. Thus, if a couple's taxable income rises from the 42 per cent to the 48 per cent joint tax bracket, they must then earn 9.6 per cent on a taxable bond to have the same after tax yield earned by a tax exempt bond paying 5 per cent. If they are in the 62 per cent tax bracket and can earn 7 per cent on a tax exempt bond that is equivalent to 18.4 per cent on the taxable bond. Thus it is not surprising that primary buyers of these bonds are people with high incomes who are in high tax brackets.

The exemption of interest from federal income taxation has been frequently criticized because of the apparent means for the rich to avoid federal income taxation. The exemption does, however, reduce the interest cost for state and municipal governments that issue debt. This reduction in interest cost is in effect a subsidy to state and municipal governments. From an economic viewpoint, the important question becomes—is the exemption the best means to aid or subsidize state and local governments? There are other means, such as federal revenue sharing, that can be used to subsidize state and local expenditures. However, the interest exemption is not an economic question but a political question that results from our federal system of government. Such legal questions are beyond the scope of finance. Changes in the legal structure may in the future alter the tax exemption.

The exemption is a political question

Until the legal structure is changed, the interest on state and municipal debt will remain exempt from federal income taxation. And the implications of this exemption will continue to be (1) that state and local governments can issue debt with interest rates that are lower than individuals and corporations must pay and (2) that these bonds offer the wealthier members of society a means to obtain tax sheltered income.

SUMMARY

This chapter has discussed government debt with emphasis on the debt of the Federal Government. The Federal Government issues a variety of debt instruments that tap the funds of many types of investors. This debt may be for a relatively short duration (e.g., Treasury bills) or it may mature after many years (e.g., Treasury bonds). The denominations of this debt may be very small, such as Savings E bonds that virtually any saver can buy, or the debt may be issued in large denominations that financial institutions like banks find attractive.

The Federal Government's debt comes into existence when the Treasury runs a deficit. When its tax revenues are less than its expenditures, the difference is financed through the issuing of debt. The importance of such deficit spending from the viewpoint of finance is its impact on the supply of money and the reserves of commercial banks. If the deficit is financed through the purchasing of the debt by the Federal Reserve, the supply of money and the reserves of commercial banks are increased. If the nonbank general public purchases the debt, there is no expansion in the money supply and the reserves of commercial banks. The latter case is the least inflationary means for the Treasury to finance its deficits.

Besides the Federal Government, state and local governments issue debt to finance a variety of financial needs. The feature that distinguishes this debt is the interest which is exempt from federal income taxation. This exemption increases the attractiveness of this debt, especially with individuals in high income tax brackets who purchase the bonds for tax exempt income. Since these bonds are attractive, they sell with lower interest rates than comparable corporate debt. Thus state and local municipal governments in effect receive a subsidy through the lower interest rates on their debt.

KEY WORDS AND TERMS

> Treasury bill
> Treasury notes
> Treasury bonds
> principal
> discount
> yield curve
> deficit spending
> tax exempt bond
> general obligation bond
> revenue bond

QUESTIONS FOR THOUGHT AND DISCUSSION

1. If the Federal Government runs a deficit during a period of inflation, is it more desirable for the deficit to be financed by commercial banks or the general public?

2. Why will a Treasury surplus produce a restraint on the economy? How will your answer be influenced by what the Treasury does with the surplus?

3. What does it mean to say that the Federal Reserve "monetizes" debt when it purchases newly issued U.S. Government securities?

4. If the Federal Government runs a deficit, will interest rates rise more if the deficit is financed by borrowing from the general public or from the Federal Reserve?

5. In general, the debt of state and local governments pays less interest than corporate debt. Can one conclude that this debt is less risky than corporate debt?

6. What is the effect on (1) demand deposits, (2) required reserves, and (3) excess reserves of commercial banks given the following transactions?
   (a) The Treasury borrows from commercial banks and uses the funds to retire Treasury bonds held by the Federal Reserve.
   (b) The Treasury borrows from commercial banks and uses the funds to retire debt held by the general public.
   (c) The Treasury issues bonds which are bought by the general public and deposits the funds in the Federal Reserve.
   (d) The Treasury issues bonds which are bought by the general public and deposits the funds in commercial banks.

   What is the important difference between your answers to (a) and (b), and (c) and (d)?

Chapter 7

INTERNATIONAL MONETARY SYSTEM

Learning Objectives

- Distinguish between the sources of supply and demand for foreign currency.
- Be able to construct the current and investment accounts in the balance of payments.
- Illustrate how the balance of trade affects the international flow of currencies.
- Explain devaluation and revaluation, and their effect on the demand for foreign goods.
- Explain the causes of fluctuation in exchange rates.
- Determine the impact of foreign transactions on the money supply and reserves of commercial banks.

"No nation was ever ruined by trade."

Benjamin Franklin

Nations do not live in a vacuum; they are not independent of each other. This applies not only politically but also economically, for a nation such as the United States exports and imports goods, services, and capital from many nations. The importing and exporting of goods, services, and capital can have an impact on the reserves of a country's commercial banking system. This chapter is concerned with that impact. However, to understand the potential impact on reserves of commercial banks, some foundation must be laid. Thus the first section in this chapter covers the demand and supply of currencies and a nation's balance of payments. Next follows a discussion of exchange rates, and the chapter concludes with the potential impact that foreign transactions may have on commercial banks' reserves.

BALANCE OF PAYMENTS

Supply and demand for foreign currency

Demand for foreign goods is also a demand for foreign money. Foreign merchants want payment in their nation's currency, and hence the buyers must acquire that currency. To acquire this money, the buyers use their nation's money. They offer their nation's currency in exchange for the foreign currency. Thus the demand for foreign currency means a supply of domestic currency is being offered in exchange. For example, if Americans want British goods, they must convert U.S. dollars into pounds. Thus they offer (i.e., supply) American dollars in exchange for British pounds. The opposite is true when British citizens seek to buy American goods. To acquire the goods, they must have American dollars, and to obtain these dollars they supply British pounds in exchange for American dollars. Thus, demand for foreign goods, and hence demand for foreign currency, implies supplying the domestic currency.

The market for foreign currencies is called the *foreign exchange market*. Currencies are traded daily, and the prices of major currencies are reported in the financial press. Figure 7–1, a

Foreign exchange market

Foreign Exchange

Friday, January 28, 1977
Selling prices for **bank transfers** in the U.S. for payment abroad, as quoted at 3 p.m. Eastern Time (in dollars).

Country	Friday	Thursday
Argentina (Peso) Finc'l	.0040	.0040
Australia (Dollar)	1.0894	1.0885
Austria (Schilling)	.0582	.0580
Belgium (Franc)		
Commercial rate	.026845	.026875
Financial rate	.026900	.026853
Brazil (Cruzeiro)	.0810	.0810
Britain (Pound)	1.7135	1.7168
30-Day Futures	1.7015	1.7053
90-Day Futures	1.6815	1.6860
180-Day Futures	1.6610	1.6660
Canada (Dollar)	.9795	.9813
China-Taiwan (Dollar)	.0265	.0265
Colombia (Peso)	.028	.028
Denmark (Krone)	.1683	.1687
Ecuador (Sucre)	.0375	.0375
Finland (Markka)	.2614	.2614
France (Franc)	.2011	.2013
Greece (Drachma)	.028	.028
Hong Kong (Dollar)	.2149	.2150
India (Rupee)	.1150	.1150
Iran (Rial)	.0143	.0143
Iraq (Dinar)	3.41	3.41
Israel (Pound)	.1150	.1150
Italy (Lira)	.001134	.001135
Japan (Yen)	.003455	.003464
30-Day Futures	.003454	.003463
90-Day Futures	.003449	.003458
180-Day Futures	.003446	.003455
Lebanon (Pound)	.3450	.3450
Mexico (Peso)	.0470	.0476
Netherlands (Guilder)	.3939	.3935
New Zealand (Dollar)	.9570	.9574
Norway (Krone)	.1874	.1877
Pakistan (Rupee)	.1025	.1025
Peru (Sol)	.01453	.01453
Philippines (Peso)	.1345	.1345
Portugal (Escudo)	.0311	.0310
Saudi Arabia (Riyal)	.2850	.2850
Singapore (Dollar)	.4070	.4068
South Africa (Rand)	1.1535	1.1535
Spain (Peseta)	.01452	.01452
Sweden (Krona)	.2340	.2346
Switzerland (Franc)	.3969	.3967
Thailand (Baht)	.05	.05
Uruguay (New Peso) Finc'l	.2500	.2500
Venezuela (Bolivar)	.2336	.2336
West Germany (Mark)	.4123	.4128
30-Day Futures	.4125	.4130
90-Day Futures	.4130	.4135
180-Day Futures	.4143	.4147

Supplied by Bankers Trust Co., New York.

Figure 7–1

(Reprinted with permission of the *Wall Street Journal*.)

clipping from the *Wall Street Journal*, gives selected currency prices for January 28, 1977. At that time the price of a German mark was $.4130 and a French franc was $.2011. While these prices are subject to change, a person needing marks, francs, or any of the other reported currencies has a reasonable idea as to their price.

The demand for foreign moneys arises in many ways that are not limited to the import of foreign goods and services. Travel abroad requires foreign currency and in effect is no different than importing goods and services. Investing in foreign securities or in plant and equipment in foreign nations also requires foreign funds, as does Federal Government foreign aid or military spending in foreign countries. If one thinks about all the transactions that Americans have with foreign firms, individuals, and governments, it is quite obvious that there is a substantial demand for foreign moneys by Americans. Of course, this large demand may be balanced by foreigners seeking American goods and securities and foreign firms investing in plant and equipment in the United States.

Balance of payments: a summary of currency flows

A summary of all these currency flows is given in the balance of payments. This is essentially a table listing all international transactions such as imports, exports, foreign investments, and government spending abroad. A hypothetical simplified example of a balance of payments statement for the United States is presented in Table 7–1. The first part of the table specifies imports and exports of goods and services during the current year. The value of exported goods was $98.2 billion, and the

Current account

value of imported goods was $106.5 billion. (Since imports result in a currency outflow, parentheses have been placed around the import figures. Such parentheses are used in the table to illustrate currency outflows.) The difference or net figure shows that the value of imports of goods and services exceeded exports by $8.3 billion.

Such a difference is partially explained by large oil imports. However, wheat sales to the Soviet Union would reduce this deficit. Such a reduction in part may explain in some people's minds why the Federal Government encourages such wheat sales. These sales, like all foreign sales, help pay for imported goods.

The next set of entries refers to Federal Government spending abroad. These include military spending ($2.1 billion) and Federal Government grants ($5.4 billion). These grants are basically gifts to foreign countries. The gifts may be unconditional, in which case the country may spend the funds anywhere, or the gifts may be conditional, in which case the country must spend the funds in the United States. These grants may range from flood and disaster relief to military aid. Since military aid is not actual military spending, the two are differentiated in the balance of payments. The total of United States Government spend-

TABLE 7–1   Hypothetical Balance of Payments for the
United States (In Billions of Dollars)
(Adapted from the *Federal Reserve Bulletin,* December, 1976)

CURRENT ACCOUNT		
Exports including travel	$ 98.2	
Imports including travel	(106.5)	
Net difference		$ (8.3)
Military transactions	(2.1)	
U.S. Government spending abroad	(5.4)	
Total U.S. Government spending abroad		(7.5)
Investment income		
U.S. investments abroad	26.1	
Foreign investments in U.S.	(15.9)	
Net difference		10.2
Balance on current account		(5.6)
LONG-TERM CAPITAL		
U.S. investment abroad	(7.2)	
Foreign investment in U.S.	2.2	
Foreign securities bought by U.S.	(1.9)	
U.S. securities purchased by foreigners	.7	
Net difference		(6.2)
BALANCE ON CURRENT ACCOUNT		(11.8)
AND LONG-TERM CAPITAL		

ing abroad was $7.5 billion. While this is considerably less than the $106.5 billion spent on current goods and services, there is no corresponding entry such as exports to help balance this outflow of funds.

Investment income is the current return earned by American investments abroad and the current return earned by foreigners on their investments in the United States. The large amount of investment spending done over the years by Americans abroad produced a currency inflow of $26.1 billion. Foreign investments in the United States generated $15.9 billion in income. These figures indicate that American investments abroad produced a positive net flow of investment income of $10.2 billion. However, income generated by foreign investments in the United States is considerable, and as foreigners continue to invest in the United States, this flow of income should increase over time.

The sum of all these entries gives the balance on the current account. In this case the net balance is a negative $5.5 billion. Thus $5.5 billion flowed out of the United States to pay for items on the current account. It is interesting to note that without the positive investment income the deficit would have been considerably larger. In this case the investment income was sufficient to offset the deficit created by the importing of goods, services, and military spending abroad. The investment income was thus sufficient to pay for all this foreign spending.

Capital account

The long-term capital accounts represent investments of a long-term nature: investment in plant, equipment, and securities. For the year these long-term investments in foreign countries were $7.2 billion, while foreigners invested $2.2 billion in the United States. Americans also bought $1.9 billion worth of foreign securities, and foreigners purchased $.7 billion worth of American securities. The net figure shows that during the year the amount Americans invested abroad exceeded foreign investments in the United States by $6.2 billion. However, while this is an outflow of dollars in the current year, these investments should increase future inflows as they produce income in the future. Thus such investments do create deficits in the current balance of payments, but they should help create surpluses in the future.

Balance of trade

The sum of all the currency flows (i.e., the current account and the long-term capital account) is a negative $11.3 billion. If the nation had spent less or sold more abroad, the nation would have experienced a smaller deficit or even a surplus in its balance of trade. For example, after World War II, the United States consistently ran a surplus in its balance of trade. It exported more goods than it imported, for goods were sold to Europe to rebuild those countries after the war. During some periods of history such a surplus has been viewed as "favorable." Thus one reads that during the seventeenth century the Mercantilists sought a favorable balance of trade. Such a surplus caused gold (the international money of their day) to flow into the country. An inflow of gold was desired by the Mercantilists, who actively pursued policies that encouraged exports and discouraged imports, for these policies caused a "favorable" balance of trade.

Balance of payments must balance

While there may be a surplus or deficit in a nation's balance of trade, the balance of payments must be balanced. There has to be an $11.8 billion entry to balance the currency outflow. Until recently (August 15, 1971) the foreigners holding the $11.8 billion could demand payment in gold. When they bought the gold, the $11.8 billion in currency would return to the United States. Today the dollar is not convertible into gold, and the foreigners must take another course of action. For example, they may hold the dollars, but the dollars do not earn anything. So these funds may be used by foreigners (especially foreign commercial banks and central banks) to purchase short-term Federal Government securities, such as Treasury bills. Such purchases plus any holdings of dollars will balance the currency outflow. Thus the final balance is achieved by the willingness of foreigners to return the money through the purchase of short-term securities or by their willingness to hold the dollars for future use.

A deficit in the nation's balance of trade is primarily the result of goods and investment opportunities in other nations being more attractive than domestically produced goods and investments. Price and quality differentials or the essential nature of a specific good often explain this difference in demand. Some nations are able to produce specific goods cheaper than other nations or they have developed specialized skills which give their goods a reputation for excellence throughout the world. Swiss watches, Japanese cameras, and English bone china are all examples of specialized goods that their respective nations produce either more cheaply or at a higher level of quality than is achieved in other nations. Switzerland, Japan, and Great Britain have an advantage in the production of these goods, and it is not surprising to find other countries importing these specialized quality products. Another example is oil, which is a virtual necessity, and those countries that lack this resource must import it from those nations that have it.

Causes of deficits in the balance of trade

Some countries that can produce particular goods inexpensively or have a resource that is a necessity may consistently export more goods than they import. These countries will run a surplus in their balance of trade while other nations run deficits. This is currently what is happening with the oil-producing Arab nations. They have recently experienced a continuous surplus in their balance of trade. How this money may be recycled into the economies of the nations that are importing the oil has been one of the major economic questions of the 1970s.

One means to alter an imbalance in the balance of trade is to alter the prices of the exporting nation's goods relative to the prices of the importing nation's goods. For example, a country may impose tariffs or import quotas. The former raises the price of the goods and the latter limits the quantities that may be imported. Such tariffs and quotas apply only to specific goods and only in the nation that levies them. A general price change may be achieved by changing the price of one currency relative to all other currencies. Such price changes occur when currencies are devalued or revalued. A devaluation implies that one currency's value is lowered relative to all other currencies. A revaluation is the raising of the price of one nation's currency relative to all other currencies. Under the present international monetary system such price changes occur all the time because the price of a nation's currency varies every day with the demand for and supply of that currency. However, before exploring the present system, it is desirable to show how devaluations and revaluations change the value of one currency relative to other currencies and how this alters the demand and supply of each currency.

Price changes

How devaluation changes the price of one currency relative

Devaluation: lowers
the price of exports
and raises the price
of imports

to all other currencies may be explained by a simple example. For expository purposes let it be assumed that the British pound costs $2.20 in American dollars. Thus if a good is priced at 2.5 pounds, then it costs $5.50 in American money (2.5 times $2.20). If the British were to devalue the pound, then it would take fewer dollars to buy a pound. Thus if the pound were devalued by 5 per cent, it would take 5 per cent fewer dollars to buy a pound. The pound's price in terms of dollars would fall from $2.20 to $2.09. The good will now cost $5.23 because Americans can buy pounds at a lower price. The price of the good in terms of pounds is not reduced. It still costs 2.5 pounds and hence its price to anyone holding pounds is unaltered. However, anyone holding a different currency may purchase pounds at the lower, devalued price. Thus devaluation does not lower prices to the domestic population but lowers the price of domestic goods to foreigners.

Conversely, devaluation also raises all foreign prices to the domestic population. The British now will have to pay more pounds for foreign goods. Before the devaluation, a British pound could purchase $2.20 worth of American goods. If a good cost $3.30, then it cost 1.5 pounds ($3.30/2.2). After the devaluation, the number of pounds necessary to purchase the good is increased to 1.57 ($3.30/2.09) because the value of the pound in terms of dollars is lowered. Thus all foreign goods are more expensive to holders of British pounds because the pound buys smaller amounts of foreign currencies.

Devaluation alters
the quantity
demanded of
imports and exports

Since prices of goods and services have been altered by the devaluation, the quantity demanded will be altered. Holders of British pounds will demand fewer foreign goods because their prices are higher. Simultaneously, since all other currencies can purchase more pounds, the quantity demanded of British goods will increase. This will help erase the deficit in the balance of trade that caused the devaluation. British citizens will import fewer foreign goods, and the rest of the world will buy more British goods. The flow of pounds out of Britain will be reduced, and the country should experience an improvement in its balance of payments.

Revaluation raises
the price of exports
and lowers the price
of imports

The opposite is true for revaluations, which increase the value of one currency relative to another. A revaluation has the effect of raising the price of domestic goods to foreigners and lowering the price of all foreign goods to the domestic population. For example, if the British revalued the pound by 10 per cent, the price of a pound in terms of dollars rises from $2.20 to $2.42. Thus to foreigners the prices of all British goods are increased. Simultaneously, the British pound now buys more foreign money, for a pound purchases $2.42 worth of American goods. The increased prices of British goods should reduce the quantity demanded, while the reduced price of imports will increase the quantity demanded. Thus the revaluation will reduce the demand for domestically produced goods and increase the demand for imports.

Under the current international monetary system such de-valuations and revaluations occur daily, for the prices of curren-cies are permitted to freely fluctuate. If the demand for a particu-lar currency rises so that demand exceeds supply, the price of that currency will rise relative to other currencies. If the supply of the currency exceeds the demand, then the price will fall. Since prices are permitted to fluctuate every day, there are con-tinual devaluations and revaluation as the prices of currencies vary in accordance with supply and demand. That the price of a currency does vary daily is illustrated by Figure 7–2, which plots the price of a pound in dollars during 1975, and 1976. As may be seen in this chart, the pound's price literally varied day by day and experienced a considerable decline in terms of dollars from a high of over $2.40 in March, 1975, to just above $2.00 at the end of 1975, to below $1.70 in 1976.

Freely fluctuating exchange rates means currency prices change daily

While the British pound declined in value during 1976, other currencies rose in value. Figure 7–3 presents the dollar price of the German mark and Swiss franc. Both currencies rose in value against the United States dollar. A German mark cost about $.38 when the year started but rose to over $.42 by the end of the year. The Swiss franc also rose from $.38 to about $.41. Since such price increases are expressed in pennies, they may appear to be small. However, these price increases are about 10 per cent, which means it takes 10 per cent more dollars to buy goods in Germany and Switzerland.

Deterioration in the price of the British pound

The price effect of such revaluations of the German mark and Swiss franc has been made very clear to Americans. German and Swiss products, such as Volkswagens or travel in either

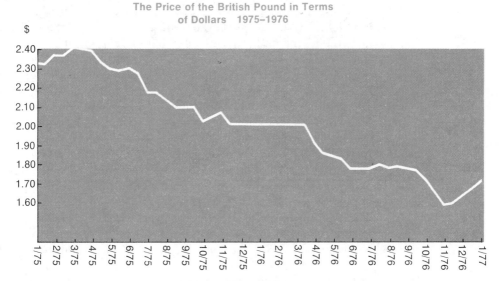

The Price of the British Pound in Terms
of Dollars   1975–1976

Figure 7–2

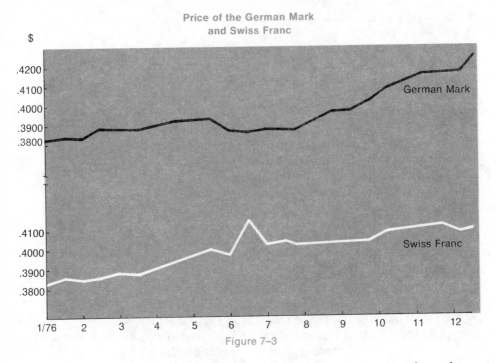

Price of the German Mark
and Swiss Franc

Figure 7–3

country, are considerably more expensive now than when a mark and franc cost about $.25 each. The price increases caused by the currency revaluations no doubt in part explains why Volkswagen's share of the American car market has diminished.

Freely fluctuating currency prices were not always the case, for until March 12, 1973, exchange rates were fixed, and prices of currencies were permitted to move only within a narrow band. For example, in 1967 the dollar cost of the British pound was set at $2.80, and the pound was permitted by central banks to deviate only 2.5 per cent from $2.80 (i.e., to a high of $2.87 and to a low of $2.73). Under this system of fixed exchange rates, it was possible for a country to run a persistent deficit in its balance of trade and have a continual outflow of its currency. If a country's currency was overpriced, then there was no automatic mechanism for reducing its price. Foreign goods would continue to be cheap, and domestically produced goods would continue to be overpriced. Hence imports would continue to exceed exports and money would flow out of the country. For example, Britain has continually experienced problems in its balance of trade because it must import many necessities. During the period of fixed exchange rates, Britain often ran a deficit until eventually the supply of British pounds abroad vastly exceeded the demand. There would then be a monetary crisis which would produce a jolting change in the currency's price. For example, on November 17, 1967, the British devalued the pound from $2.80 to $2.40, for a devaluation of over 14 per cent in one day. Under the current international monetary system, if the supply exceeds the demand, the price of the currency will slowly lose its value over time, as was illustrated in Figure 7–2, by the deterioration in the price of the pound.

Actually under the current international monetary arrangement, no country should have a persistent balance of trade surplus or deficit, for such a surplus or deficit means excess demand or supply of the currency. Such excess demand or supply should be erased by changes in the value of the currency. A persistent balance of trade deficit should be erased as the value of the currency falls, and a surplus should disappear as the value of the currency rises. It is, however, possible that central banks will thwart or at least reduce this adjustment process. For example, if a central bank does not want the value of its currency to fall, it may buy the currency with the assets it owns. Correspondingly, if the bank does not want the value of the currency to rise, it can supply the currency by purchasing the currencies of other nations. Such actions, of course, alter the demand and supply of currencies and hence alter the price of the currency. The importance of such interference becomes more apparent in the next section, which considers the impact of international transactions on the reserves of commercial banks.

Persistent balance of trade deficit should not occur under system of flexible exchange rates

EFFECT ON COMMERCIAL BANKS' RESERVES

As was explained in the first section of this chapter, when purchases are made, a set of international currency flows is established. The effect of these flows may be to alter the ability of domestic and foreign banks to create credit. This effect on commercial banks' ability to create credit may be illustrated by the following example in which United States citizens buy goods in England. When the purchases are made, the Americans acquire goods and pay for them with a check drawn on an American bank. The British merchant deposits the check in a commercial bank and thus obtains a new demand deposit. The T-accounts for the transactions in Britain are as follows:

Foreign currency inflows expand the domestic money supply

BRITISH BANK	
Items in Process ↑	Demand Deposit ↑

BRITISH MERCHANT	
Goods ↓	
Demand Deposit ↑	

The British bank has a new demand deposit and a check drawn on an American bank. The British bank cannot present the check to another British bank for payment, because the check is drawn on an American bank. Thus the check is sent to the British central bank, the Bank of England. This causes the following additional transaction to occur:

BANK OF ENGLAND		BRITISH BANK	
Items in Process ↑	Reserves ↑	Items in Process ↓	
		Reserves ↑	

The British bank receives reserves from the Bank of England, and correspondingly the central bank creates a new liability on itself (the reserves) in payment for the check drawn on the American bank.

Since the check is drawn on an American bank, the Bank of England sends the check to the Federal Reserve, which is the institution through which foreign banking transactions are cleared for payment. This payment from the Federal Reserve can take a variety of forms. For example, the British central bank can request payment in British pounds or American dollars. The British need not take physical delivery of the dollars but can accept an account at the Federal Reserve. Foreign banks may maintain accounts at the Federal Reserve just like the United States Federal Government may keep an account with the Federal Reserve. Such accounts can supply funds to British citizens when they make purchases in the United States. The British bank could request payment in another currency such as German marks. Thus if the Bank of England needs a different currency than American dollars, payment could be made in a third currency. Until recently, the British central bank could have requested and received payment in gold. However, the dollar is no longer convertible into gold, and hence this option is no longer available to the British central bank. It must take either some type of claim on the United States (dollars or a bank deposit) or another currency such as British pounds or German marks.

Currency outflows contract the domestic money supply

If the Bank of England accepts dollars, the following transactions occur. The check is sent to the Federal Reserve for payment in dollars. The Bank of England receives dollars, and the Federal Reserve issues a new claim on itself (the dollars) in payment for the check.

FEDERAL RESERVE		BANK OF ENGLAND	
Items in Process ↑	Dollars ↑	Items in Process ↓	
		Dollars ↑	

The Federal Reserve then clears the check and returns it to the bank on which it is drawn. The Federal Reserve reduces the reserves of the commercial bank in payment for the check, and the bank in turn reduces the individual's checking account. These transactions are illustrated by the following T-accounts:

COMMERCIAL BANK		FEDERAL RESERVE	
Reserves ↓	Demand Deposits ↓	Items in Process ↓	Reserves ↓

As these accounts show, the commercial bank has experienced a decline in both reserves and demand deposits.

This entire transaction may be illustrated by the flow chart presented below. The check goes from the American citizen to the British citizen to pay for goods and services. For the check to clear, it passes through a British commercial bank to the Bank of England to the Federal Reserve to the commercial bank on which it was drawn. The result of this transaction is to set up a series of monetary transactions which were individually illustrated by the above T-accounts. The total transaction is summarized by the following set of T-accounts. The net effect of this set of transactions is to increase demand deposits and commercial bank reserves in Britain but reduce demand deposits and commercial bank reserves in the United States.

Money is transferred from one nation to another

AMERICAN BANK		FEDERAL RESERVE	
Reserve ↓	Demand Deposits ↓		Dollars ↑
			Reserves ↓

BANK OF ENGLAND		FEDERAL RESERVE	
Dollars ↑	Reserves ↑	Reserves ↑	Demand Deposits ↑

There has been a flow of dollars abroad which are lodged in the British banking system and have increased demand deposits and the reserves of the British banks. Since the dollars are abroad,

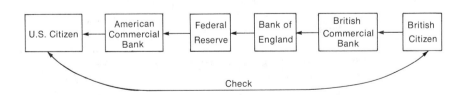

Check

they are no longer part of the United States money supply. Demand deposits and reserves of commercial banks in the United States are reduced. In effect, Americans now have British goods and services, and the British have a claim (the dollars) on American goods and services. The American dollars abroad thus represent claims on American goods that are currently not being exercised.

Foreigners may (1) use the money to increase imports

As was explained in the preceding section, the British now have the following three choices: (1) to exercise this claim and purchase American goods; (2) to trade the dollars for another currency such as German marks; or (3) to hold the dollars. If the British purchase American goods, they may use these American dollars. The money that flowed to Great Britain when the Americans purchased British goods is returned to the United States. Hence, if British people are purchasing American goods and services at approximately the same time and the same value that Americans are buying British goods and services, the currency flows cancel each other. The dollars that go abroad are returned when the British purchase American goods, and there will be no net effect on the commercial banking system.

(2) Sell the money for another currency

The same conclusion holds if the British use the American dollars to buy goods in another country, such as Germany, and if the Germans use the dollars to buy American goods. The only difference is that this is a three-way transaction. Americans sell goods to Britain; Britons use the dollars to buy German goods, and the Germans use the dollars to buy American goods. The dollars that flowed out to purchase English goods are returned to America. There is a balance in the flow of currencies, and the foreign transactions of all three nations are in balance.

(3) Hold the money

If, however, the British do not exercise the claim on American goods or do not pass the claim to a third party who exercises the claim, the balance of trade will not be equal. The value of purchases of goods and services among nations is not equal, and one nation's currency is lodging itself in another nation. The country doing the purchasing has a deficit in its balance of trade, while the other country has a surplus. The deficit nation is losing currency and receiving goods while the surplus nation is losing goods and receiving money. The importance of these transactions on the commercial banking system in each nation is the effect the currency flows have on reserves of commercial banks and each nation's money supply. The reserves of commercial banks and the money supply of the deficit nation are reduced, while the reserves of commercial banks and the money supply of the surplus nation are increased. Thus the potential for commercial banks to expand and create credit is reduced in the deficit nation. But the converse is true in the surplus nation, for the ability of its commercial banks to expand the money supply is increased. Thus a deficit in a nation's balance of trade has serious implications for the supply of credit in both nations.

Persistent deficits in balance of trade result in devaluation

For a short period of time, one nation may run a deficit and soon thereafter run a surplus. In such a case over a period of years the surplus and deficit will tend to cancel each other and there is no net effect on the money supply and the reserves of commercial banks. However, such canceling will not occur if a nation persistently runs a deficit or surplus in its balance of trade.

Under the current international agreements, such a persistent deficit or surplus should not occur. For example, a deficit indicates that a country's prices are too high relative to other countries' prices. As a result, there is excess demand for imports and excess supply of its currency. This excess supply of currency will result in a decline (i.e., devaluation) in the price of that currency on international money markets. Such a price decline will increase the price of imports and reduce the price to foreigners of the country's products. These price changes then should alter the demand for imports and exports. The converse should occur if the country runs a persistent surplus. The value of its currency should rise and discourage the exporting of goods. Thus fluctuations in the value of the currency should tend to stop a persistent balance of payments deficit or surplus.

In reality this mechanism for price changes in currencies may be altered by intervention of central banks. A country may not want the price of its currency to change. For example, a revaluation of the price upwards should result in reduced demand for the country's output, which may in turn result in increased unemployment. Such an increase in unemployment may be politically unacceptable, and hence the central bank seeks to avoid the upward revaluation in the country's currency by supplying the domestic currency the foreigners demand. Thus the nation's central bank permits the expansion in the domestic money supply and commercial banks' reserves and stops the upward pressure on the price of the currency in the world money markets. Therefore, while in theory a deficit or a surplus should be erased by fluctuations in the price of the currency, in practice a central bank can seek to offset the effect of demand and supply on the price of the currency by offering to buy or sell it. Thus it is still possible for a country to have a balance of deficit or surplus for a considerable period of time. This imbalance can then have a significant impact on the reserves of commercial banks and the nation's money supply.

Central banks may intervene to stop currency fluctuations

SUMMARY

This chapter has examined the potential impact of foreign transactions on the reserves of commercial banks. If a country imports more than it exports, there will be a net flow of currency out of the country which will reduce the reserves of its commercial banking system. Conversely, if a country exports more than it imports, there will be a net inflow of money, which will increase the reserves of the commercial banking system. International transactions will have no effect on the money supply or commercial bank reserves if the outflow and inflow of currencies is balanced (i.e., there is no deficit or surplus in the balance of payments).

Under the current international monetary agreements the prices of currencies are permitted to vary in accordance with supply and demand. Thus if a country has a deficit in its balance of trade, the increased supply of the currency will tend to drive down its price and eliminate the deficit. The converse is true for a surplus in the balance of trade, for a shortage in currency will drive up its price and reduce the demand for the currency. Such changes in the price of one currency relative to all other currencies should eliminate the deficit or surplus in a nation's balance of trade.

Achieving equality in the balance of payments is not the only goal of the world's central banks. Full employment and price stability are important economic goals, and they may supersede the balance of payments in the minds of a nation's central bankers. Hence the bankers take actions to affect the price of their nation's currency. These actions may result in a net inflow or outflow of currency and may alter the reserves of commercial banks.

KEY WORDS AND TERMS _____

foreign exchange market
balance of trade
balance of payments
current account
long term capital account
exchange rates
devaluation
revaluation

QUESTIONS FOR THOUGHT AND DISCUSSION _____

1. If the German mark appreciates in value, what effect will this have on foreigners' demand for German goods? What incentive will Germans have to purchase abroad?

2. How may the Federal Reserve offset the impact of foreign currencies flowing into the United States?

3. Why may a country have a persistent balance of payments surplus under a system of fixed exchange rates? Why should

such a problem not occur under a system of flexible exchange rates?

4. What is the effect on (1) demand deposits, (2) required reserves, and (3) excess reserves of American commercial banks given the following transactions?
   (a) Foreigners use funds previously invested in commercial paper to buy stock on the New York Stock Exchange.
   (b) Americans buy American Express Traveler's Checks.
   (c) Americans travel abroad.
   (d) Americans buy stock in South African gold mines on the London Stock Exchange.

Chapter 8

NON-COMMERCIAL BANK FINANCIAL INTERMEDIARIES

Learning Objectives

* Review financial intermediation.
* Differentiate the assets and liabilities of the various financial intermediaries.
* Explain how savings and loan associations affect the supply of mortgage money.
* Show the effect of financial intermediation on commercial banks' reserves and the money supply.
* Explain why some insurance companies and pension plans are not financial intermediaries.

"The savings of many in the hands of one."

Eugene V. Debs

All financial intermediaries have to compete for the funds of savers. Since there are legal limits on the amount of interest that some financial intermediaries can pay depositors, they are frequently forced to compete on a non-price basis by offering services and other features to differentiate their product. If an intermediary can induce savers to deposit funds, then its ability to grant loans is increased. However, if savers view other investments as more attractive, then funds will flow out of financial intermediaries. When funds are withdrawn from these intermediaries, their ability to grant loans is reduced. Thus a flow of funds out of financial intermediaries reduces the available supply of credit.

This chapter is concerned with non-commercial bank financial intermediaries. Emphasis is placed on savings and loan associations, life insurance companies, mutual savings banks, and pension plans. The differences among these financial intermediaries are concentrated in the following two areas: (1) the types of loans and other assets acquired by the intermediary, and (2) the types of debt instruments they issue to savers. As was illustrated in Chapter 3, the types of deposits issued by commercial banks (especially demand deposits) influence the portfolio of assets acquired by these banks. The same principle applies to other financial intermediaries. Thus a flow of funds into (or out of) a particular type of financial intermediary affects the availability of particular types of credit. This is most important in the mortgage market, for non-commercial bank financial intermediaries are a prime source of mortgage financing.

SAVINGS AND LOAN ASSOCIATIONS

Savings and loan associations are just what the name implies: a place for savers to deposit funds which are subsequently lent by the association. Funds deposited in savings and loan associations may be withdrawn with ease, so savers may consider accounts in savings and loan associations as very liquid. These institutions pay interest that tends to be slightly above the rate paid by commercial banks. However, the interest rate may be significantly below other alternative investments, such as short-term corporate debt, because savings and loan associations, like commercial banks, have legal constraints on the maximum rate of interest they may pay. Like commercial banks, savings and loan associations are subject to a substantial amount of regulation. For example, the activities of savings and loan associations are supervised by the Federal Home Loan Bank.

Even though funds deposited in a savings account with a savings and loan may be readily withdrawn, these funds are generally left on deposit for substantial periods of time. This slow turnover of funds permits savings and loan associations to violate one of the cardinal principles of finance by borrowing short and lending long. Borrowing through short-term debt leads to the continual problem of refinancing. If the lenders refuse to continue to grant the short-term credit, the borrower may have to sell the assets at distress prices to pay off the short-term loans. Thus it is not financially prudent to borrow short-term money and use this money to finance long-term investments. But that is exactly what savings and loan associations do. They issue short-term debt, the savings account which may be readily withdrawn, and use the funds to acquire mortgages. Mortgages finance the purchases of real estate, in particular individual homes, and are long-term assets that are paid off over many years.

There are three facts that help savings and loans violate this important financial principle. First, savers tend to leave deposits with savings and loans for a substantial period of time. Second, there has been increased use by savers of savings certificates that mature after a year. These offer higher yields than regular

Savings may be readily withdrawn

passbook savings accounts and now account for over half of savings and loans' deposit liabilities. Third, mortgages are paid off monthly over a period of many years. Thus savings and loans are continually receiving interest and principal repayments. These payments will meet temporary and small withdrawals.

A major source of mortgage money

The importance of savings and loan associations to the mortgage market is illustrated by the aggregate balance sheet (Table 8–1), which gives the amount of mortgages they were financing as of October, 1976. As may be seen from the balance sheet, savings and loans owned $316,073 million in mortgages, which accounted for 82.1 per cent of their assets. They also had $327,778 million in savings accounts outstanding, which accounted for 85.1 per cent of their total liabilities and equity. Hence savings and loan associations are obviously borrowing funds from savers and passing the funds to households and firms in need of mortgage money.

If additional savings were deposited into savings and loans (a process called intermediation), their ability to make additional mortgage loans would be increased. If funds were to flow out of these savings accounts (a process called disintermediation), the ability of savings and loans to grant mortgage loans is reduced. Since they hold such a large proportion of their funds in mortgages, flows of savings into or out of savings and loan associations have considerable impact on the building sector of the economy. The ability to obtain mortgage money influences the demand for construction (especially residential housing). Since the flow of savings into savings and loans alters the ability of potential homeowners to obtain mortgage money, this flow of savings has an important influence on the construction industry.

No effect on the money supply

While the process of intermediation or disintermediation will affect the financing of mortgages, it may have virtually no impact on commercial banks and their ability to lend. This is true because savings and loans (and other non-commercial bank

TABLE 8–1   Balance Sheet for Savings and Loan Associations
as of October, 1976 (in Millions)
(Source: Federal Reserve Bulletin, December, 1976.)

ASSETS		
Mortgages	$316,073	82.1%
Investment in securities and cash	36,538	9.5
Other assets	32,601	8.4
Total assets	$385,212	100.0%
LIABILITIES		
Savings accounts	$327,778	85.1%
Other borrowings	35,770	9.3%
EQUITY	21,664	5.6%
Total liabilities and equity	$385,212	100.0%

financial intermediaries) cannot affect the reserves of commercial banks. If savers withdraw funds from accounts in commercial banks and deposit these funds in savings and loan associations, the following transactions occur:

COMMERCIAL BANK		SAVER		SAVINGS AND LOAN	
Cash ↓	Account ↓	Account at Commercial Bank ↓		Cash ↑	Savings Account ↑
		Account at Savings and Loan ↑			

Initially, deposits at the commercial banks are reduced as the withdrawal occurs. The saver has altered the form in which the savings are held from one type of account to another. The financial intermediary has acquired a new liability, the deposit, and a new asset, the cash.

The question now becomes what will the savings and loan association do with the cash? It will deposit the cash in its checking account at a commercial bank. Thus the complete T-accounts for the transaction are as follows:

Savings and loans use demand deposits

COMMERCIAL BANK		SAVER		SAVINGS AND LOAN	
Cash ↓	Demand Deposit (Saver) ↓	Demand Deposit ↓		Demand Deposit ↑	Savings Account ↑
Cash ↑		Savings Account ↑			
	Demand Deposit (Savings & Loan) ↑				

As these T-accounts indicate, the funds that were initially withdrawn from the commercial banks are now returned to them. The net effect on the commercial bank is nothing unless (1) the funds were initially in a savings account and are now in a checking account, in which case the required reserves of the commercial bank are increased, or (2) if the savings and loan holds the cash, in which case the reserves of the commercial bank are reduced. However, the savings and loan will subsequently lend the funds and will use its checking account. The savings and loan will hold a minimal amount of cash in its vaults to meet cash withdrawals. Thus the entire cash withdrawal should return to the commercial bank. The essence of the entire transaction is (1) that the savings and loan association now has a new asset, a checking account, which it may use to lend and thereby acquire an income earning asset such as a mortgage, and (2) that the commercial bank has not suffered a decline in its reserves or its ability to lend.

When the savings and loan association uses the funds to acquire a mortgage, the following transactions occur:

COMMERCIAL BANK	SAVINGS AND LOAN		BORROWER	
Demand Deposit (Savings & Loan) ↓	Demand Deposit ↓		Demand Deposit ↑	Mortgage ↑
	Mortgage Loan ↑			
Demand Deposit (Borrower) ↑				

The savings and loan employs its checking account to acquire the mortgage. The funds in the checking account are transferred to the borrower in return for the mortgage. The savings and loan thus trades one type of asset, the demand deposit, for another type of asset, the mortgage. The borrower acquires the funds, the demand deposit, by taking out the loan, the mortgage. Again the effect on the commercial bank is to transfer the demand deposit from one depositor, the savings and loan association, to another, the borrower. Presumably the borrower will soon use these funds to pay for the property and thereby transfer the funds to yet another person or business. However, the demand deposit will remain in the commercial banking system unless one of the parties withdraws cash from the commercial bank.

What is the net effect of this transaction? For the saver the net effect is to alter the type of asset being held. Instead of holding an account issued by a commercial bank, the saver is holding an account issued by the savings and loan association. Presumably this account offers the saver some advantage such as a higher interest rate, which induced the transfer of funds from the account at the commercial bank to the account at the savings and loan association. From the viewpoint of the commercial banking system there is no net change. The saver's deposit is transferred to another person or business. Unless there is a cash withdrawal, there is no net change in commercial banks' total deposits. Unless there is a substitution of checking accounts for savings accounts in the commercial bank, the required reserves of the commercial banking system are not altered. Thus the commercial banking system will not have to contract nor will it be able to expand its loans as a result of the funds flowing through the financial intermediary.

Existing money supply turns over more rapidly

For the savings and loan association there has been a net increase in deposits. This increase has permitted it to acquire an income earning asset, the mortgage. Conversely a borrower has been able to obtain funds from the financial intermediary for the purchase of property. Without the deposit, the financial intermediary could not have issued the mortgage, and the borrower could not have acquired the property. Thus the effect of this transaction has been to increase the supply of credit and the total amount of loans outstanding in the economy without affecting the loans of the commercial banking system. In effect, the existing money supply has flowed through the accounts of a variety of individuals (i.e., the saver, the savings and loan association, the borrower, the seller of the property). Funds deposited in commercial banks have turned over more quickly, but since the total amount of deposits in commercial banks has not been altered, the money supply has not been altered. The amount of credit in the economy, however, has increased because there is a new loan in existence (the mortgage), and this loan has financed a new purchase (the property). Thus depositing funds in savings and loan associations will expand their ability to make loans without any corresponding decline in the ability of commercial banks to create credit. Of course, had one of the parties held cash, the ability of commercial banks to create credit would be reduced because their reserves would be reduced. Unless such cash withdrawals occur, the flow of funds into financial intermediaries increases the availability of credit and finance in the economy.

The opposite case (i.e, withdrawals from financial intermediaries) also does not affect the reserves of commercial banks. If funds are withdrawn from a savings and loan, the intermediary must liquidate assets or borrow from the Federal Home Loan Bank to obtain the funds to meet the withdrawal. Liquidating assets does not affect the commercial banking system, as may be seen by the following T-accounts:

Withdrawals also do not affect the commercial banking system

COMMERCIAL BANK		SAVINGS AND LOAN		BUYER	
	Demand Deposit (Buyer) ↓	Mortgages ↓		Mortgages ↑	
	Demand Deposit (Savings and Loan) ↑		Demand Deposit ↑		Demand Deposit ↓

All that occurs is a transfer of income earning assets from the savings and loan association to the buyer in trade for the demand deposit. The ownership of the demand deposit is altered, but from the viewpoint of the commercial bank, total deposits are not altered. The savings and loan now has the money to meet the withdrawal, and it writes a check on its demand deposit. The funds then are transferred from the savings and loan association to the saver making the withdrawal. Only if the saver takes payment in the form of cash will the total deposits of the commercial banking system be altered. Thus disintermediation, like intermediation, does not alter the availability of commercial banks to lend.* It is the withdrawing of cash that alters the reserves of commercial banks and affects their ability to lend. The depositing or withdrawing of funds from financial intermediaries only alters their ability to grant loans. Such deposits and withdrawals do not affect the lending capacity of commercial banks.

OTHER FINANCIAL INTERMEDIARIES

The variety of non-commercial bank financial intermediaries

The major conclusion of the previous section, that a flow of funds in savings and loan associations does not alter commercial banks' ability to lend, also applies to other financial intermediaries. A flow of funds into any non-commercial bank financial intermediary does not alter commercial banks' reserves and hence cannot alter their ability to lend (unless funds flow from savings accounts to checking accounts in commercial banks). The general conclusion applies to the three intermediaries covered in this section.

MUTUAL SAVINGS BANKS

Mutual savings banks are very similar to savings and loan associations. They act as a depository for the funds of savers and in turn lend these savings to households and firms seeking finance. The depositors are the owners of mutual savings banks, but the banks are managed by a board of trustees. While a mutual savings bank may legally view its depositors as owners and not creditors, the owners may readily withdraw their funds. Thus the mutual savings banks are similar to other banks, including savings and loan associations and commercial banks, for they must have sufficient liquidity to meet withdrawals. However, funds that are deposited in these banks turn over slowly, for depositors tend to leave their funds in the mutual savings bank for a substantial length of time. Therefore, mutual savings banks can make loans of long duration.

Mutual savings banks also stress mortgage loans

Table 8–2 presents the assets for all mutual savings banks as of September, 1976. While mutual savings banks do perform the role of a financial intermediary, the total dollar value of their assets indicates that they are a relatively small component of the financial system. The assets of all savings and loan associations are nearly three times the assets of mutual savings banks. This difference in size is partially explained by the fact that less than

---

*There is an exception to this statement if the public buys treasury securities and the treasury deposits the funds in the Federal Reserve. In such a case the reserves of commercial banks are reduced. However, if the treasury deposits the funds in commercial banks, then the reserves of commercial banks are unaltered.

TABLE 8–2   Assets of Mutual Savings Banks as of
September, 1976 (in Millions)
(Source: Federal Reserve Bulletin, December, 1976.)

ASSETS

Mortgages	$ 80,145	62.2%
Corporate securities	32,432	25.1
Other loans	5,478	4.2
U.S. government securities	5,851	4.5
Other assets	5,148	4.0
	$129,054	100.0%

half of the states permit mutual savings banks. By far the most important asset of mutual savings banks is mortgages, which compose 62.2 per cent of their total assets. Mutual banks also own a substantial amount of corporate securities (25.1 per cent of their total assets). These investments in corporate securities differentiate the portfolios of mutual savings banks from savings and loan associations, which are almost entirely composed of mortgages.

LIFE INSURANCE COMPANIES

Life insurance companies also perform the role of a financial intermediary because they receive the funds of savers, create a claim on themselves, and lend the funds to borrowers. However, not all types of insurance companies perform this financial intermediary role, and hence a distinction has to be made between life insurance companies and other types of insurance. Other types of insurance such as property and liability insurance are exclusively services that the individual buys. The price of the insurance is related to the cost of the product, just like the cost of any service such as hotel space or an electrician is related to the cost of producing the service. Of course, the property and liability insurance companies invest the funds they receive from policy holders. However, suppliers of other services will also use the funds they receive. In neither case is there a transfer of savings to borrowers.

The feature that differentiates life insurance companies and makes them a financial intermediary is that they may provide more than insurance against premature death. Ordinary life insurance policies and endowments contain two elements, the insurance and a savings plan. A saver who purchases an ordinary life insurance policy acquires both life insurance and a savings program. The policy's premiums cover both the cost of the insurance and the savings program. As long as the policy is in force, the policy accumulates cash value, which is the savings component of the policy. Many savers find such policies attractive because the periodic payments assure the saver of insurance

Not all types of insurance companies are financial intermediaries

Life insurance policy may include a savings program

plus a periodic savings program. Others find them unattractive because the interest rate paid on the savings is only 2 to 3 per cent. While the interest earned is small compared to savings accounts, the insurance offers unique advantages. For example, the cash value of the policy may be used in the future to make payments on the policy and may be used as collateral for a loan. Many savers borrow against their insurance policies at considerably lower interest rates than they could find elsewhere. (Of course, in effect they are borrowing their own money.)

Insurance companies hold a considerable amount of corporate debt and stock

Life insurance companies use the proceeds of the policies to acquire income earning assets. Table 8–3, which presents the total assets of all life insurance companies, indicates that these companies purchase a varied mix of financial assets. Holdings of corporate debt and stock account for 38 per cent and 10.7 per cent, respectively, of the total assets, while mortgages account for 28.9 per cent. The remaining assets include government securities, real estate, loans to policy holders, and various miscellaneous assets. As the table indicates, life insurance companies are a major source of finance for corporations, for many companies are able to sell a substantial amount of stock and debt to life insurance companies. Therefore, life insurance companies are a major alternative to commercial banks as a source of finance for corporations.

Insurance companies and commercial banks stress different types of corporate loans

While life insurance companies do compete with commercial banks for corporate loans, they serve somewhat different financial markets. First, commercial banks stress liquidity and hence are a primary source of short-term finance. Life insurance companies, however, do not need to stress liquidity. Mortality tables are scientifically constructed and can predict with accuracy the volume of death benefits the life insurance company will have to pay. The company can forecast with a high degree of accuracy the amount of benefits it will have to pay during the year. Thus it is able to construct a portfolio of assets that permits the company to have not only sufficient liquidity but also long-

TABLE 8–3 Assets of Life Insurance Companies as of September, 1976 (in Millions)
(Source: Federal Reserve Bulletin, December, 1976.)

ASSETS		
U.S. government securities	$ 5,150	1.7%
State and local government securities	5,364	1.7
Foreign government securities	6,348	2.0
Corporate bonds	118,706	38.0
Corporate stock	33,419	10.7
Mortgages	90,217	28.9
Real estate	10,175	3.3
Policy loans	25,505	8.2
Other assets	17,160	5.5
Total Assets	$312,044	100.0%

term investments. Since the long-term investments tend to have higher interest rates, a life insurance company will seek to have a substantial amount of its funds in these more profitable assets. Thus the very nature of its financial obligations permits a life insurance company to own more long-term debt than a commercial bank would find prudent to hold.

Secondly, life insurance companies may hold the stock of corporations, while commercial banks may not. Thus life insurance companies participate in a market that is closed to commercial banks. (Commercial banks do manage other people's money in trust accounts and can purchase stock for these accounts.) There are also special tax laws that encourage corporations, including life insurance companies, to make investments in the stock of other corporations. Eighty-five per cent of the dividends received from these investments is exempt from federal income taxation. Thus these companies have an added incentive to purchase the stock of corporations and hence supply corporations with additional equity financing.

PENSION PLANS

The role of a pension plan is to accumulate assets for workers so that they will have funds to live on after retirement. Funds are periodically put in the pension plan by the saver, the employer, or both. The money deposited with the fund then is used to purchase an income earning asset. Thus the saver's funds grow over time as additional funds are paid into the pension plan, and the funds already in the plan earn income.

There are many pension plans in existence, but few of them really serve the function of a financial intermediary. A financial intermediary creates a claim on itself when it receives funds and then subsequently lends the funds to borrowers. Pension plans do create claims on themselves when they receive savers' funds, but not all pension plans in turn invest or lend the money directly to borrowers. Instead they may purchase existing securities, such as the stock of General Motors. For a pension plan to serve as a financial intermediary it must pass the funds directly to a borrower or invest them directly in a firm.

Many pension plans are not financial intermediaries

They purchase existing securities

This distinction between pension plans may be illustrated by the pension plans used by many schools for their employees. Funds may be contributed by both the employer and the employee to the Teachers Insurance and Annuity Association (TIAA) or to the College Retirement Equity Fund (CREF). The actual dollar amount of the contribution varies with the school and the employee's salary. The funds may be contributed by either or may be split between the two plans. CREF purchases existing corporate stock. Money that flows into CREF does not go to the companies that issued the stock. Instead, the money goes to the seller of the stock, who may have purchased the shares many years ago. The only time the company receives the proceeds of a stock sale is when the shares are first issued. All subsequent sales are secondhand transactions with the proceeds flowing from the individual buying the security to the individual selling the security. Funds are not being transferred to the firm. By purchasing the secondhand security, CREF is not performing the role of a financial intermediary.

Other pension plans do perform the role of the financial intermediary

TIAA purchases an entirely different type of portfolio that stresses debt, especially mortgages. In this case funds are transferred from savers to borrowers, and the pension plan is acting as a financial intermediary. It creates a claim on itself when it receives the savers' funds, and it receives a claim from borrowers when the funds are lent to finance purchases. The transfer of purchasing power from saver to borrower by an intermediary that creates claims on itself is the role of a financial intermediary. Hence TIAA is an example of a pension plan that does serve the role of a financial intermediary.

SUMMARY

This chapter has covered several of the many investments available to savers. However, the emphasis was on financial intermediaries and their effect on commercial banks' ability to lend. Non-commercial bank financial intermediaries such as savings and loan associations and mutual savings banks cannot affect the ability of commercial banks to lend. The reason for this general conclusion is that they do not affect the reserves of commercial banks. When funds flow into these financial intermediaries, deposits at commercial banks are not reduced, because the intermediaries use commercial banks as a depository. Hence from the viewpoint of commercial banks there is just a transfer from one account to another. There is no change in total deposits or in total reserves.

The importance of non-commercial bank financial intermediaries is that they permit expansion in credit without a corresponding expansion in the money supply. When funds flow into these intermediaries, they are able to lend, to create credit. There is an expansion in loans but there is no expansion in the supply of money. Since these intermediaries may specialize in types of loans (e.g., mortgages), this ability to expand credit has impact on particular sectors of the economy.

The next two chapters cover one of the most fascinating alternatives available to savers, the stock market. The stock market is not a financial intermediary but a market in second hand (i.e., existing) securities. While it does not create credit, it can have an important impact on all financial institutions. Hence an understanding of the mechanics of security transactions and the role of the stock exchange is an important facet of understanding the nation's financial system.

intermediation
disintermediation
savings and loan association
mutual savings bank
ordinary life insurance
pension plans
mortgage

QUESTIONS FOR THOUGHT AND DISCUSSION

1. Why must virtually all credit transactions involve money but only certain credit transactions result in the creation of new money?

2. Has the growth of non-bank financial intermediaries limited the effectiveness of monetary policy? Should the regulatory power of the Federal Reserve be extended to include these financial intermediaries?

3. What assets do life insurance companies acquire that are not held by savings and loans?

4. What is the effect on (1) demand deposits, (2) required reserves, and (3) excess reserves of commercial banks, given the following transactions?
   (a) Savers deposit in savings and loan associations funds that were previously held in checking accounts.
   (b) The general public withdraws funds from savings and loan associations and uses the funds to buy new bonds issued by corporations.
   (c) People in need of funds borrow money from Household Finance Corporation.
   (d) Savers use funds deposited in savings accounts to buy life insurance.

Chapter 9 THE SECURITY MARKET

Learning Objectives

- Trace the mechanics of a security purchase.
- Explain why the security market is not a financial intermediary.
- Differentiate aggregate measures of security prices.
- Identify the security market's regulatory body and state the purpose of the regulation.
- Explain the effect of security transactions on the money supply and the reserves of commercial banks.

"The stock market is people."

Bernard Baruch

Perhaps the most fascinating and well known financial institution is the stock market. The Dow Jones Averages and the happenings on Wall Street are newsworthy events that are reported here and abroad. But even with all the publicity, the role of security markets is rarely understood. A security market is *not* a financial intermediary, for it does not transfer funds from lenders to borrowers. Instead, it is a secondhand market that transfers securities from sellers to buyers. Firms do not receive the proceeds of the sales. The one and only time that a firm receives proceeds from the sale of securities is when the securities are issued and sold for the first time. (The process of issuing securities is covered in Chapter 24.)

Security markets transfer existing securities from owners who no longer desire to maintain their investments to buyers who wish to increase those specific investments. There is no net change in the number of securities in existence, for there is only a transfer of ownership. The role of security markets is to facilitate this transfer of ownership. This marketability of securities is extremely important, for security holders know that there exists a market in which they may sell their security holdings. This ease with which securities may be sold and converted into cash increases the willingness of people to hold securities and thus increases the ability of firms to issue the securities.

The next two chapters are concerned with security markets and investing. This chapter covers many of the basic elements of investing such as the mechanics of security trading, measures of stock prices, and the regulation of security markets. The last section discusses security markets and their effect on the reserves of commercial banks. The next chapter considers portfolio selection. Profitable investing in securities is not easy, as the declining market of 1973–1974 illustrates. Understanding the basic mechanics of security transactions is only a beginning. Successful investing requires knowledge, patience, foresight, and perhaps a little luck.

SECURITY TRANSACTIONS

MARKET MAKERS

Securities are bought and sold everyday by investors who never meet each other. The market impersonally transfers the securities from the sellers to the buyers. This transfer may occur on an *organized exchange*, such as the New York Stock Exchange, or an unorganized, informal market, called *over the counter*. In both cases there exists a professional security dealer who makes a market in the security. This market maker offers to buy the securities from any seller and to sell the securities to any purchaser. Market makers set a specified price at which they will buy and sell the security. For example, a market maker may be willing to purchase stock at $20 a share and sell at $21; the security is then quoted 20–21, which is the bid and ask. The market maker is willing to purchase (bid) the stock at $20 and to sell (ask) the stock for $21.

The difference between the bid and the ask is the spread, and this spread, like brokerage commissions, is part of the cost of investing. When an investor buys a security, the value of the security is the bid price, but he (or she) pays the ask price. The difference between the bid and the ask thus is a cost to the investor. If there are several market makers in a particular security, this spread will be small. If, however, there are only one or two market makers, then the spread may be quite large (at least as a percentage of the bid price). The spread is also affected by the volume of transactions in the security and the number of securities the firm has outstanding. If there is a large volume of transactions or the number of outstanding securities is large, then there are usually a larger number of market makers. This increased competition reduces the spread between the bid and ask. If the number of outstanding securities is small (i.e., if the issue is thin), then the spread is usually larger.

Organized and informal markets

Difference between bid and ask

The spread

Transactions are either round lots or odd lots. A round lot is the basic unit for a transaction and for stock is usually 100 shares. Smaller transactions like 37 shares are odd lots. For some stocks the round lot is different than 100 shares. For example, for very cheap stocks (sometimes called "cats and dogs") a round lot may be 500 or 1000 shares. For bonds a round lot may be five $1000 bonds (i.e., $5000) or $10,000, or even $100,000 face value of the bonds. Since odd lots are not profitable business for brokerage firms and market makers, the effective cost charged the purchaser is usually higher than the cost of a round lot. This cost may not be explicitly stated but hidden in a higher asking price for the security.

Market makers for securities listed on the New York and American stock exchanges are called specialists. Market makers for over the counter securities are called dealers. Both specialists and dealers quote prices on a bid and ask basis and buy at one price and sell at the other. This spread is one source of their profits as they turn over the securities in their portfolios. These market makers also profit when the prices of the securities rise, for the value of their inventory of securities rises. These profits are a necessary facet of security markets, for the profits induce the market makers to serve the crucial function of buying and selling securities. These market makers guarantee to buy and sell at the prices they announce. Thus an investor knows (1) what the securities are worth at a point in time and (2) that there is a place to sell current security holdings or to purchase additional securities. For this service the market makers must be compensated, and this compensation is generated through the spread between the bid and ask, dividends and interest earned, and profits on the inventory of securities (if their prices rise).

While the bid and ask prices are set by the market makers, the level of these security prices is set by investors. The market maker only guarantees to make *a* transaction at the bid–ask prices. If the market maker sets too low a price for a stock, there will be a large quantity of shares demanded by investors. If the market maker were unable or did not want to satisfy this demand for the stock, this dealer (or specialist) sells one round lot and increases the bid–ask prices. The increase in the price of the stock will (1) induce some holders of the stock to sell their shares, and thereby replenish the market maker's inventory, and (2) induce some investors seeking the stock to drop out of the market.

If the market maker set too high a price for the stock, there would be a large quantity of shares offered for sale. If the market maker is unable or does not want to absorb all these shares, the dealer may purchase a round lot and lower the bid–ask prices. The decline in the price of the stock will (1) induce some potential sellers to hold their stock and (2) induce some investors to enter the market and purchase the shares and thereby reduce any excess buildup of inventory by the market maker.

Thus, while market makers may set the bid and ask prices for a security, they cannot set the general level of security prices.

To set the general price level, market makers must be able to absorb excess securities into their inventory when there exists excess supply and to sell securities from their inventory when there exists excess demand. The buying of these excess securities will require that they pay for them and the selling of securities will require that they deliver the securities sold. No market maker has an infinite well of money or securities. While they may build up or decrease their inventory, they cannot indefinitely support the price by buying, nor can they stop a price increase by sellling. The market maker's function is not to set the level of security prices; all investors do that through buying and selling. The market maker's function is to facilitate the orderly process by which buyers and sellers of securities are brought together.

BROKERS

An investor, after deciding to purchase a security, places a purchase order with a broker. The investor may buy the security at the market price, which is the asking price set by the market maker. The investor, however, may specify a purchase price below the asking price and wait until the price declines to the specified level. This decline may never occur, in which case the investor does not purchase the security. Once the purchase has been made, the broker sends the investor a confirmation statement (Fig. 9-1). This confirmation statement gives the number and type of security purchased (30 shares of St. Joe Minerals Corporation), the per unit price ($34.50), and the total amount due ($1060.81). The amount due includes the price of the securities and transaction fees. The major transaction fee is the brokerage firm's commission, but there may also be state transfer taxes and other miscellaneous fees. The investor has five business days after the date of purchase (8/16/74) to pay the amount due and must make payment by the *settlement date* (8/23/74).

The role of brokers

Brokerage firms establish their own commission schedules, and it may pay the small investor to shop around for the best rates. Large investors are able to negotiate commissions, so that the brokerage costs are generally no more than 1 per cent of the value of the securities. Some brokerage firms offer small investors discount rates that may substantially reduce brokerage fees. However, these firms rarely offer other services such as research and investment advice. For investors who need such services, the discount brokers may be no bargain.

Commissions

The investor may purchase the security on *margin*, which is purchasing the security on credit supplied by the broker. The advantage of using margin is that the investor applies financial

Buying securities with credit (i.e., margin)

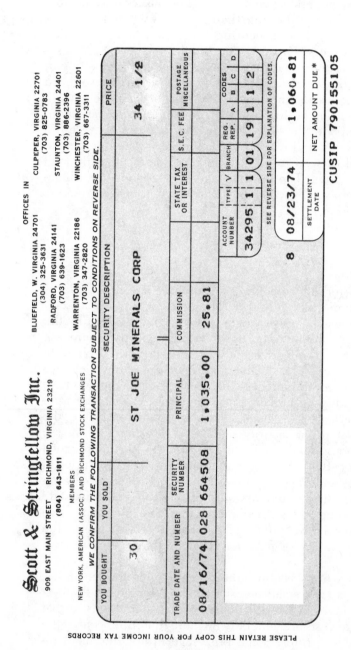

Figure 9–1

leverage to the investment. The potential return on the investment is increased. However, the use of financial leverage also
increases the degree of risk. The margin requirement, the proportion of the total price that the investor must pay, is set by the
Federal Reserve, but individual brokers may require more
margin.

The minimum payment required of the investor is the value
of the securities, times the margin requirement, plus the commission. Thus, if the margin requirement is 60 per cent and the price
plus commission of the 30 shares of St. Joe Minerals is $1060.81,
then the investor must put up $646.81 and borrow $414. The
investor pays interest on $414. The interest rate will depend on
the interest rate that the broker must pay, for the broker borrows
the money from a commercial bank. The investor may avoid the
interest charges by paying the entire $1060.81 and not investing
on margin.

Once the shares have been purchased and paid for, the
investor must decide whether to leave the securities with the
broker or take delivery. If he (or she) leaves them with the
broker, the shares will be registered in the broker's name (i.e.,
in "street" name), and the broker becomes responsible for the
securities. The broker sends the investor a monthly statement of
the investor's security position which indicates the securities
held by the broker, any transactions during the month, and any
dividends and the interest received. Dividends and interest may
be left to accumulate with the broker or may be paid to the investor.

*Leaving securities
with broker*

An example of a monthly statement is given in Figure 9–2.
The statement is divided into two parts. The top half enumerates
all the transactions during the month. According to this monthly
statement, the investor made two purchases (40 shares of Rixon
and 90 shares of Walworth) and one sale (68 shares of Mar-
quardt), received dividend payments from W.R. Grace and
Continental Airlines, and withdrew $82.45 from the account.
The bottom half of the statement enumerates the investor's
security position at the end of the month. In this case the broker
is holding for the customer stock in eleven companies.

The advantage of leaving the securities with the broker is
primarily convenience. The investor does not have to worry
about storing the securities and can readily sell the securities
because they are in the broker's possession. The collection of
interest and dividends may be treated as a kind of forced savings
program, for they may be immediately reinvested before the
investor has an opportunity to spend the money elsewhere. The
monthly statements may be easily stored and are a ready source
of information for tax purposes.

There are, however, a few and important disadvantages of
leaving the securities in the broker's name. If the brokerage firm
fails or becomes insolvent, investors may have difficulty having the securities transferred into their name and even greater

DAVENPORT & CO.
ESTABLISHED 1865

1113 EAST MAIN STREET · RICHMOND , VIRGINIA , 23211

TELEPHONE MILTON 8-1621   TELETYPE RH · 361

MEMBER
NEW YORK STOCK EXCHANGE
AMERICAN STOCK EXCHANGE (ASSOCIATE)
RICHMOND STOCK EXCHANGE

ACCOUNT NO.	T	REP.	DATE MO.	DAY	YR.
4 5 7 9 8	1	2 4	9	3 0	

TYPE OF ACCOUNT

1. CASH   5. SPL. CASH
2. MARGIN   6. SPL. N. P. L.
3. MARGIN #2   7. SPL. SUB.
4. SPL. MISC. 8. WHEN ISSUED
               9. SHORT ACCT.

SETTLEMENT MO. DAY	BOUGHT OR RECEIVED	SOLD OR DELIVERED	DESCRIPTION	PRICE	DEBIT	CREDIT	BALANCE DEBIT UNLESS MARKED CR. * INDICATES NO BALANCE
9 7			BALANCE AUG 31			1 3 2 37	
8			CK DIVD FOR AUG		3 50		
1 1	4 0		CHECK			7 5 0 00	
1 1			RIXON ELECTRONICS	1 9	7 7 2 60		
1 5			24 W R GRACE & CO	D I V		8 40	
2 2			50 CONTL AIRLINES	D I V		5 00	
2 5			CHECK		8 1 60		
2 5			CK RETURNED			8 1 60	
2 7			CHECK		8 2 45		
2 7		6 8	MARQUARDT CORP	1 8 ½		1 2 3 7 84	
2 7	9 0		WALWORTH CO	1 3 ¾	1 2 5 4 88		
							2 0 18 CR
			SECURITY POSITION				
	5 0		CONTINENTL AIRLINES				
	1 9		CUTTER LAB INC A				
	5 0		EASTN STAINLESS STL				
	5 0		ETHYL	2 . 4 0			
	2 4		W R GRACE & CO COM				
	4 0		LAMSON AND SESSIONS				
	2 5		MSL INDUSTRIES				
	3 5		PAN AMER WRLD AIRWY				
	4 0		RIXON ELECTRONICS				
	1 5		SCM CORP				
			WALWORTH CO				

Figure 9–2

difficulty collecting any dividends and interest owed them by the brokerage firm. Second, since the securities are registered in the brokerage firm's name, interim financial statements, annual reports, and other announcements sent by the firm to its security holders are sent to the brokerage firm and not to the investors. The brokerage firm should forward each investor this material but may not. To overcome this, an investor may write the firm and ask to be placed on the firm's mailing list. The firm, however, may choose not to oblige, for it has sent the material to the brokerage firm and may view the additional mailing as an unnecessary expense. Since the shares are held by the broker, the broker votes them at stockholders' meetings. While the broker must seek the stockholders' instructions as to how to vote, this may only be a formality. For example, the broker may send a letter to the stockholder that says, "We intend to vote the shares in the following manner unless otherwise instructed."

Whether the investor ultimately decides to leave the securities with the broker or takes delivery depends on the individual investor. If the securities are purchased on margin, the investor must leave the securities with the broker. If the investor frequently buys and sells securities (i.e., is a trader), then the securities should be left with the broker in order to facilitate the transactions. If the investor is satisfied with the services of the broker and is convinced that the firm is financially secure, then the investor may also decide to have the securities registered in the street name of the broker for reasons of convenience.

If the investor chooses to take delivery of the securities, the investor receives the stock certificates or bonds (Fig. 9–3). The front of the stock certificates identifies the name of the owner, the number of shares, and the name of the transfer agent who transferred the certificates from the seller to the buyer. To transfer ownership the investor must endorse the certificate on the back, just like endorsing a check before depositing or cashing it. Since the certificates may become negotiable if stolen, the investor should take caution to store them in a safe place (e.g., a lock box in a bank). If the certificates are lost or destroyed, they can be replaced, but only at a considerable expense in terms of money and lost time.

The stock certificate

SECURITY EXCHANGES

Companies may seek to have their securities listed on one of the major organized exchanges: the New York or American Stock Exchange. Listing has an element of prestige, for it indicates that the company has grown above local importance and attained a level of size and profitability. Listing may also facilitate future security issues, for investors may be more willing to purchase the securities of companies whose securities are publicly traded on an exchange.

Listed securities

The American Stock Exchange (sometimes referred to as the *curb*) is the smaller of the two major exchanges. The listing requirements for stocks on the American Stock Exchange are as follows:

American Stock Exchange

1. The firm must have 400,000 shares publicly held.
2. The shares must have a market value of $300,000.
3. There must be at least 1,200 stockholders of which 500 must hold 100 to 500 shares.
4. The pre tax income for the previous fiscal year must exceed $750,000.
5. The firm must have tangible assets exceeding $4,000,000.

To be listed, the firm must also conform to certain procedural requirements to publish quarterly reports, solicit proxies, and make public any developments that may affect the value of the securities. Once the securities are listed, the exchange may delist them if the firm is unable to continue to meet the listing requirements, but such delistings are less frequent than listings. For example, the *AMEX Databook* for 1973 indicates that during 1968 to 1972 there were only 118 delistings (i.e., about 20 a year) for failure to meet listing requirements, while 814 stocks were accepted and listed for trading on the American Stock Exchange.

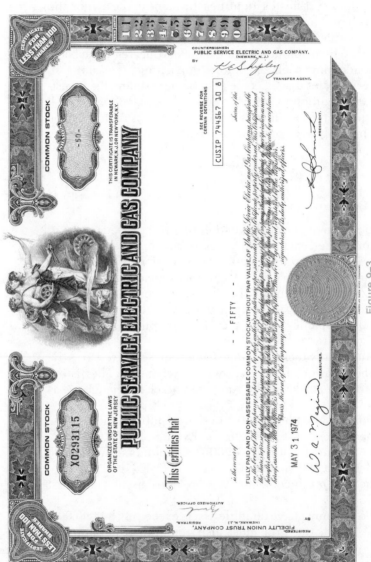

Figure 9–3

The New York Stock Exchange is the larger exchange and lists the securities of companies of national interest that have prospects of maintaining their relative positions in their respective industries. The listing requirements for the New York Stock Exchange are similar to the listing requirements of the American Stock Exchange. The difference in the specific requirements are related to size, as may be seen in the following list: New York Stock Exchange

1. The firm must have 1,000,000 shares held by the general public.

2. At least 2000 stockholders must own 100 or more shares.

3. The firm must have pre tax income of $2,500,000 for the latest fiscal year and pre tax income of $2,000,000 for the preceding two years.

4. The aggregate value of shares publicly held must exceed $16,000,000.

5. The firm must have tangible assets of $16,000,000.

The company is also expected to issue quarterly and annual reports and to announce publicly anything that might affect the value of the shares.

Once the firm's securities have been listed for trading on the exchange, the firm must continue to meet the listing requirements. However, the exchange gives consideration to delisting when (1) the number of shares in the hands of the general public declines to less than 600,000; (2) when the number of stockholders owning at least 100 shares declines to 1200; (3) when the market value of the shares publicly held falls below $5,000,000; and (4) when the value of tangible assets falls below $8,000,000.

Securities that are not traded on an exchange are traded over the counter. While many stocks and some bonds are traded on the New York and American exchanges, the majority of bonds and the stocks of thousands of small companies are bought and sold over the counter. Prices of many of these securities are reported daily in the financial sections of newspapers. There is also an impressive system of communication about price quotations, the National Association of Security Dealers Automated Quotation system (NASDAQ). A broker thus may learn bid–ask prices of many over the counter stocks with ease. If, however, a company experiences financial difficulties and the price of the stock declines to pennies, the price may no longer be quoted. The market makers may also cease to deal in the security, in which case the investor and the broker may have to do a more substantial search in order to sell the security. Over the counter

Actually the distinction between the various exchanges and the over the counter market is slowly being erased. There has already developed a "third market" in which financial institutions negotiate trades in listed securities without the use of a major exchange. The financial papers no longer report New York Stock Exchange transactions. Instead they report the NYSE-Composite transactions, which includes transactions on many The third market regional exchanges (e.g., Midwest Exchange, Pacific Exchange) as well as transactions on the New York Stock Exchange.

National market system is emerging

What is emerging is a national market system for security transactions. New data processing and communication equipment will link all security markets. Brokerage houses will buy and sell actively traded securities from their own inventory without using an exchange. A national market system will include a consolidated system for reporting and clearing security transactions. A composite quotation will give not only firm quotes but also the amount of securities available at those prices.

The trend is obviously in the direction of a national market system. Congress has mandated that a national market system be encouraged. In September, 1975, the Security and Exchange Commission established the National Market Advisory Board to review the current market structure and to recommend appropriate actions to facilitate the establishment of a national market system. There seems to be no question that a national market system will emerge. The only question is how long it will take.

MEASURES OF SECURITY PRICES

Indices of stock prices

Security prices fluctuate daily, and several indices have been developed to measure the price performance of securities. The best known and most widely quoted is the Dow Jones Industrial Average of the following thirty industrial stocks. Dow Jones and Company also computes averages for 15 utility stocks, 20 transportation stocks, and a composite index of all 65 stocks.

These companies that comprise the Dow Jones Industrial Average are among the largest, most well established firms in the nation. Small firms and many firms that have grown into prominence since World War II (e.g., IBM and Johnson and Johnson) are excluded from this average. This has led to criticism of the Dow Jones Industrial Average on the basis that it is too narrow and not representative of the stock market. This criticism has led to the development of other indices such as the Standard and Poor 500 Stock Index and the New York Stock Exchange Index. The Standard and Poor's 500 includes 425 industrials, 25 railroads, and 50 utility stocks. The New York Stock Exchange Common Stock Index includes all listed common stocks. The American Stock Exchange also publishes an index that includes

Allied Chemical	Exxon	Owens-Illinois
Aluminum Co	General Electric	Procter & Gamb
Amer Brands	General Foods	Sears Roebuck
Amer Can	General Motors	Std Oil of Calif
Amer Tel & Tel	Goodyear	Texaco
Bethlehem Steel	Inco	Union Carbide
Chrysler	Inter Harvester	United Technologies
Du Pont	Inter Paper	US Steel
Eastman Kodak	Johns-Manville	Westinghouse El
Esmark Inc	Minnesota M&M	Woolworth

all securities traded on that exchange. These three indices encompass more securities than the Dow Jones Industrials and
therefore may be better indicators of general price movements in
the stock market.

How have stock prices performed? The answer in part
depends upon the time period selected. Figure 9–4 is based on
the year-end closing average of the Dow Jones Industrial Average from 1960 through 1976. As may be seen, this index of
security prices rose during several periods (e.g., 1962–65 and
1969–72). However, there were also periods when security
prices fell. The decline experienced from 1972 to 1974 was particularly severe, for the Dow Jones Industrial Average declined
from 1020 at the end of 1972 to 607 in September, 1974. That is a
40 per cent decline in the average and was the worst setback the
market experienced since the Great Crash in 1929. However, at
the end of 1976 the Dow Jones Industrial Average was again
above 1000 and thus had recouped the losses it suffered in 1974.

These price fluctuations also illustrate the criticism of the
Dow Jones Industrial Average that it is too narrow. Figure 9–5
presents the Standard and Poor's 500 Stock Index and the New
York Stock Exchange Composite Index for 1970–1976. Both
indices show severe declines from 1972 to 1974. However, the
recovery from 1974 through 1976 has not been as large as indicated by the Dow Jones Industrial Average, for neither of these
indices has regained its 1972 high.

Investors who purchased stock during 1974 and held

Stock price movements

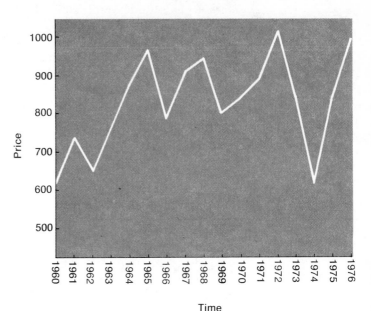

Figure 9–4

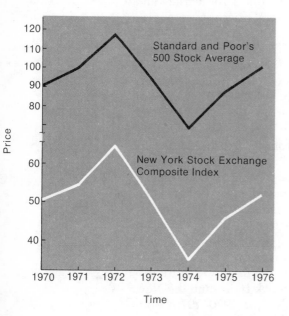

Standard and Poor's 500 Stock Index and the NYSE Composite Index

Figure 9–5

through 1976 probably experienced profits on the investments. However, just because security prices rise, it does not follow that an individual investor experienced profits. The indices are composed of many securities, but the investor must purchase specific securities. An individual's securities may decline in price even though the majority of stock prices rise, but in general the price performance of a diversified portfolio should tend to follow the market. (This tendency of stock prices to move together is further discussed in the next chapter.)

Difference between paper and realized profits

Many security profits are only *paper profits*, for many investors do not sell the securities and *realize* the profits. The tax laws encourage such retention of securities, for the gains are taxed only when realized. Under the Tax Reform Act of 1976 if securities are held for more than a year, any realized profits are taxed as long-term capital gains. Such gains are given more favorable tax treatment than ordinary income. For most individuals the tax rate on long-term capital gains is one-half the tax rate on income. Furthermore, the capital gains tax may be partially avoided if the individual holds the security until death. The security is then taxed as a part of his estate, and that part of the capital gain which occurred prior to January 1, 1977, is not subject to capital gains tax. These tax considerations thus encourage the retention of securities that have risen in price. Unfortunately security prices that have risen may not continue to rise, and many investors who retained securities have watched their paper profits melt away when security prices subsequently declined.

Like many industries, the security industry is subject to a large amount of regulation. Since the vast majority of securities cross state borders, the primary regulation is at the federal level. The purpose of this regulation is to protect the investing public by providing investors with information and preventing fraud and the manipulation of security prices. The regulation in no way assures investors that they will make profits on their investments. The purpose of the regulation is not to protect investors from their own mistakes.

Regulation is (1) primarily at the Federal level

The federal regulation developed as a direct result of the debacle in the security markets during the early 1930s. The first major pieces of legislation were the Securities Act of 1933 and the Securities Act of 1934. These are concerned with issuing and trading securities. The 1933 Act is concerned with new issues of securities, and the 1934 Act is concerned with the trading of existing securities. To administer these acts the Securities and Exchange Commission (commonly called the SEC) was established.

(2) Administered by the SEC

These acts are also referred to as the "full-disclosure-laws," for their intent is to require companies with publicly held securities to inform the public of facts relating to the companies. When firms issue new securities, they must register the securities with the SEC and file a registration statement with the SEC. The SEC will not clear the securities for sale until it has determined if all material facts that may affect the value of the securities have been disclosed. When the securities are sold, the buyer must be given a document (called a *prospectus*) that informs him of the information on file with the SEC. The SEC does not comment on the worthiness of the securities as an investment. It is assumed that the investor who has received the required information will be able to make his own determination of the quality of the securities as an investment.

Purpose: To permit the investor to make an informed decision

Once the securities are in the hands of the general public, the companies are required to keep current the information on file with the SEC. This is achieved by having the firm annually file a report (called the *10-K report*) with the SEC. The 10-K report has a substantial amount of factual information concerning the firm, and this information is usually sent in summary form to the stockholders in the company's annual report. (Companies will upon request also send stockholders without charge a copy of the 10-K report.)

Firms are also required to release during the year any information that may materially affect the value of the securities. Information concerning new discoveries or lawsuits or strikes is disseminated to the general public. The SEC has the power to suspend trading in a firm's securities if the firm does not release this information. This is a drastic act and is seldom used, for most firms continually have news releases that inform the investing public of significant changes affecting the firm. Sometimes the firm itself will ask to have trading in its securities stopped until a news release can be prepared and disseminated.

Disclosure does not mean telling everything

The disclosure requirements do not insist that the firm tell everything about its operations. The firm, of course, has trade secrets that it does not want known by its competitors. The purpose of full disclosure is not to stifle the corporation but (1) to inform the investors so they can make informed decisions and (2) to prevent the firm's employees from using privileged information for personal gain. It should be obvious that employees may have access to information before it reaches the general public. Such information (called *inside information*) may significantly enhance their ability to make profits by buying or selling the company's securities before the announcement is made. Such profiteering from inside information is illegal. Officers and directors of the company must report their holdings and any changes in their holdings of the firm's securities with the SEC. Thus it is possible for the SEC to determine if transactions are made prior to public announcements.

SIPC—protects investors from failures by brokerage firms

One recent change in the regulation of the security markets has been the establishment in 1970 of the Securities Investors Protection Corporation (SIPC). This agency is similar in purpose to FDIC insurance, for SIPC is designed to protect investors from failure by brokerage firms. This insurance applies to those investors who leave securities and cash with brokerage firms. If the firm were to fail, these investors might lose part of their funds and investments. SIPC insurance is designed to protect investors from this type of loss. The insurance, however, is limited to $50,000 per customer. Hence if an investor leaves a substantial amount of securities and cash with a brokerage firm that fails, the investor is not fully protected by the insurance. To increase coverage, some brokerage firms carry additional insurance with private companies to protect their customers.

THE STOCK MARKET AND THE COMMERCIAL BANKING SYSTEM

Stock market is a secondary market and does not affect the commercial banking system

The stock market involves secondhand transfers of securities between individuals. These transactions cannot affect the reserves of the commercial banking system. When an investor uses funds in a demand deposit to buy stock through the New York Stock Exchange, the bank deposit is reduced. But the seller of the security will deposit the funds in an account at a commercial bank. Thus in the aggregate demand deposits, required reserves, and excess reserves of the commercial banking

system are not affected. This transaction is illustrated by the
following set of T-accounts:

BUYER		BANKING SYSTEM	SELLER	
Demand Deposit ↓		Demand Deposits:	Stock ↓	
Stock ↑		Seller ↑ Buyer ↓	Demand Deposit ↑	

The buyer of the securities trades one asset (the demand deposit)
for another (the stock). The seller also trades one asset (the stock)
for another (the demand deposit). The deposits and reserves of
the commercial banking system are not affected by the transaction. All that occurred was a change of ownership of the demand
deposit from the buyer to the seller. Thus security transactions
cannot by themselves alter the money supply or the reserves of
commercial banks.

While security transactions cannot by themselves alter the
money supply and reserves of commercial banks, they may be
part of a transaction that does affect the reserves of commercial
banks. For example, if the buyer uses funds that were deposited
in a savings account to buy the stock and the seller places the
proceeds in a checking account, then the required reserves of
commercial banks are increased. The cause of this increase,
however, is not the security transaction but the fact that the
reserve requirement for the savings account is less than the
reserve requirement for the checking account. The converse
case in which the buyer uses proceeds in a checking account to
buy the stock and the seller places the proceeds in a savings
account could also occur. In this case the required reserves of the
commercial banking system are reduced, which will increase
excess reserves. While these transactions do affect the capacity
of commercial banks to lend, the source of the change in excess
reserves is the difference in reserve requirements and not the
security transaction.

The conclusion—that security transactions between individuals do not affect the money supply and the capacity of commercial banks to lend—also applies when the investors use
borrowed funds (i.e., buying on margin). For example, if an
investor borrows from a commercial bank to buy securities, demand deposits are increased and excess reserves are reduced.
The seller, however, may use the proceeds from the sale to retire
debt owed commercial banks, and thus demand deposits are
reduced and excess reserves are restored. Only if the buyer
borrows from commercial banks and the seller does not use the
proceeds to retire debt owed commercial banks are excess reserves reduced. However, it could just as easily be assumed that
the buyer uses existing funds and the seller retires debt. Under
this assumption demand deposits are reduced and excess re-

serves are increased. Hence, if special assumptions are made, demand deposits and excess reserves are affected by security transactions. But the effect is the result of the special assumptions, and the general conclusion that security transactions do not affect the money supply and the reserves of commercial banks still holds. Security transactions on organized exchanges or in the over the counter markets between individuals cannot by themselves alter the money supply or the capacity of commercial banks to lend.

SUMMARY

This chapter has covered security markets. These markets are primarily second-hand markets that transfer securities among investors. Security markets cannot by themselves affect the supply of money or the capacity of commercial banks to lend. These markets are, however, an important part of the structure of the financial system. Second-hand markets increase the liquidity and marketability of securities and thus make it possible for firms and governments to issue securities to the general public. The issuing of securities is a major source of funds for corporations, along with financial intermediaries and retained earnings. Without second-hand security markets, the ability of firms and governments to raise outside capital would be severely reduced.

Purchasing securities in the second-hand market may be done with ease, for there has developed a sophisticated system of brokers and security dealers. An investor may readily purchase or sell securities, but such ease of transactions need not produce investment profits. Profitable investing requires knowledge, skill, and patience. An introduction to these skills is presented in the next chapter. While a few investors may have made millions in the stock market, this is not true for all investors. The typical investor may find that the returns offered by security markets are not significantly different than other financial institutions. If an investor enters this market with the intention of getting rich quickly, this investor may take undue risks and lose a substantial amount of capital.

KEY WORDS AND TERMS

organized exchange
American Stock Exchange
New York Stock Exchange
over the counter market
NASDAQ
Security and Exchange Commission (SEC)
Dow Jones Industrial Average

Standard and Poor's 500 Stock Index
SIPC
prospectus
margin

Chapter 9 also includes a considerable amount of jargon used by the investment community. This jargon includes:

market maker	settlement date
bid and ask	street name
spread	third market
brokerage commissions	trader
specialists	transfer agent
dealers	paper profits
round and odd lots	inside information
confirmation statement	thin issue

_____ QUESTIONS FOR THOUGHT AND DISCUSSION

1. Why are the organized exchanges second hand markets? Why do they not perform the role of a financial intermediary?

2. Securities are purchased through brokers and dealers who "make markets." What does it mean to make a market? How does the market maker earn profits? Is this role socially desirable?

3. The security industry like the banking industry is regulated. What is the purpose of this regulation? How is it different from the purpose of banking regulation?

4. Stock prices do fluctuate. From the library obtain the high–low prices for IBM from 1966 to 1977. During this period, what was the trend and how much did the high–low prices deviate from this trend? How does the price performance of IBM compare with the Dow Jones Industrial Average during this time period?

5. What is the effect on (1) demand deposits, (2) required reserves, and (3) excess reserves of commercial banks, given the following transactions?
    (a) An investor buys AT&T stock on the New York Stock Exchange.
    (b) An investor purchases a stock on margin. The broker obtains the funds from a commercial bank.
    (c) AT&T issues new shares and they are purchased by existing stockholders.
    (d) A saver removes funds from a savings account in a commercial bank and buys the stock from IBM.

Chapter 10

THE SELECTION OF SECURITIES

Learning Objectives

* Identify sources of readily available information.
* Differentiate between fundamental and technical analysis.
* Explain how beta coefficients may be used to help select securities.
* Describe the main elements of the random walk hypothesis.
* Differentiate between closed end and open end investment companies.
* List the advantages and disadvantages of investing in investment companies.

"Take calculated risks. That is quite different from being rash."

George Patton

The preceding chapters have been concerned with financial institutions and their potential effect on the supply of money and credit. This chapter is a tangent because it discusses security selection from the viewpoint of the individual investor.

The chapter begins with sources of information that may be used to help select securities. Next follows a brief discussion of two techniques of security selection: fundamental and technical analysis. Risk and beta coefficients and the random walk hypothesis close the first part of the chapter. The final part of the chapter discusses an alternative to selecting one's own portfolio, the investment company. The different types of investment companies and their advantages and costs to the investor end this chapter on security selection.

SOURCES OF INFORMATION FOR THE INVESTOR

There are many investment advisory services available to the investor. Many brokerage firms have research departments that analyze a firm's financial position and place within its industry. These services are frequently offered free to investors, who cover the cost of this research in commissions. Merrill Lynch, Pierce, Fenner, and Smith, Inc. and several other brokerage firms also publish material that is purely informational and is available to the public without charge. Merrill Lynch is by far the largest supplier of this complimentary literature. Its publications include the following items:

"How to Read a Financial Report"
"How Over-the-Counter Securities are Traded"
"Investing for Tax-Free Income"
"How to Buy and Sell Commodities"
"What is Margin?"
"The Bond Book"

There are also publications that an investor may purchase, such as financial newspapers and specialized investment advisory services. Table 10–1 is a representative list of sources of information for the investor.

Many brokerage firms carry these publications, and the investor may also find them at the local library. While none of the publications can consistently predict the future (and the investor should be skeptical of any publication that claims the subscriber may make a fortune), investors do need to be well informed. Diverse reading of financial information is an excellent means to keep abreast of events in the financial markets. Thus the investor should be aware of these general sources of financial information.

Besides sources of general information, there are trade and professional publications devoted to specific industries. The *Oil and Gas Journal* and *Public Utilities Fortnightly,* which cover oil and gas and utilities, respectively, are but two of the many publications specializing in particular industries. Such material may be very specialized and technical but very useful to the

TABLE 10–1

NAME OF PUBLICATION	FREQUENCY OF PUBLICATION
Barron's	Weekly newspaper
Business Week	Weekly magazine
Financial Analysts Journal	Professional journal; published six times a year
Forbes	Twice monthly magazine
Fortune	Monthly magazine
Moody's Industrial Manual	Annual
Moody's Transportation Manual	Annual
Moody's Public Utility Manual	Annual
Standard and Poor's Corporate Records	Six times a year
Value Line Investment Survey	Weekly coverage of selected firms
Wall Street Journal	Daily newspaper

investor seeking knowledge in specific fields. For example, an investor seeking information concerning location of oil exploration and known reserves to help choose among selected oil drilling and exploration firms may find the *Oil and Gas Journal* a particularly useful publication.

No shortage of information

Actually there is no shortage of readily available information. The problem for the investor is separating the wheat from the chaff and processing it into useful information from which to infer conclusions. Even if the investor relies solely on the advice of others, such as a broker or an investment survey, the investor still must select among the alternatives suggested. For example, the Value Line Investment Survey recommends 100 stocks that it believes will outperform the market during the next 12 months. Obviously the investor will not buy the entire list but select among these stocks. Some tools that may be used to aid in the selection process are the subject matter of the next sections of this chapter.

FUNDAMENTAL APPROACH

Stresses financial position and earnings capacity

There are two methods used by investors (other than random choice or "hot tips" from a variety of sources) to select securities: the fundamental approach and the technical approach. The fundamental approach stresses such fundamentals of finance as the firm's earning capacity, its growth potential, and its sources of finance. The fundamental approach compares firms within an industry to identify those with the greatest potential. Emphasis is placed on the firm's economic performance and its potential to improve its position within its industry. Ratios, financial data, and astute observation are the primary tools of fundamental analysis.

PE ratio

One particularly important ratio used in fundamental analysis is the ratio of stock price to the firm's per share earnings. This ratio is commonly referred to as the PE ratio for price/earnings. The PE ratio indicates what the market is willing to pay for each $1.00 of earnings. A PE of 12 thus shows the stock is selling for 12 times the firm's earnings. There is also the implication that if the firm's earnings increase by $1.00, the price of the stock will rise by $12.00.

Firms in the same industry tend to have similar price/earnings ratios. However, if a firm has an excellent record of earnings growth and the security market anticipates this rapid growth will continue, the PE ratio tends to be higher. Thus IBM's stock tends to have a higher PE than most common stocks because it has consistently achieved excellent growth in earnings and dividends. If a firm is viewed as being riskier than typical firms, the PE ratio tends to be lower. The price/earnings ratio of Ethyl Corporation tends to be relatively low because

Ethyl is a primary manufacturer of lead additives for gasoline. With the current concern for pollution control, and since lead additives are a source of pollution, the market views Ethyl as being risky. Even though the firm has been diversifying its operation, the dependence on lead additives as a major source of profits has resulted in a lower PE than achieved by other chemical companies.

Fundamental analysis is not limited to a comparison of PE ratios but encompasses financial, industrial, and economic information. Central to all the analysis is a belief in the growth of the economy and the industry. Selecting the industry is particularly important because most firms grow as the industry grows. Rarely does a firm in a declining industry offer an excellent investment opportunity. After the investor has identified the industries that one believes will offer excellent growth opportunities, one then considers the firms within the industry. This process may be illustrated by the following simple example. An investor believes that energy related stocks have excellent potential for growth. Since President Carter has stressed the development of coal resources, this investor decides that coal companies may be the best way to invest in the energy industry.

There are many ways to approach investing in coal. For example, several large coal companies are owned by non-coal companies. Exxon, Continental Oil, Ethyl Corporation, and Gulf and Western all have interests in the coal industry. Exxon and Continental Oil offer the investor a package of energy-related interests. Ethyl is primarily a chemical company and Gulf and Western is a conglomeration of products that include not only natural resources but also Paramount Pictures, Consolidated Cigar, and automotive replacement parts. While coal contributes to these firms' earnings, it is not their primary source of earnings; hence the investor may look elsewhere for a coal-related investment.

Example: coal industry

Another means to invest in the potential growth of coal is to purchase coal-related securities, such as railroads that haul coal or companies that make equipment which mines coal. Thus the investor may consider such railroads as the Chessie System or Norfolk and Western or such machinery and equipment manufacturers as Ingersoll-Rand or Harnischfeger Corporation. These firms may prosper if the nation establishes an energy policy that stresses the development of coal resources. These examples illustrate some of the possibilities available to the investor.

If the investor wants a firm whose primary business is coal mining, then none of these previously mentioned firms meet this criterion. Such an investor would isolate firms whose primary sources of profit are mining coal. Four such firms are presented in Table 10–2. Then the investor will seek to identify the best coal producing company by comparing several measures of each firm's performance. These may include the dividend yield

TABLE 10–2   Selected Ratios for Four Coal Companies
(Source: *Business Week,* December 27, 1976, and *Forbes,*
January 1, 1977.)

	DIVI-DEND YIELD	PRICE/ EARN-INGS	RETURN ON EQUITY (5 YEAR AVERAGE)	ANNUAL GROWTH (5 YEAR AVERAGE) SALES	EARNINGS
Eastern Gas and Fuel	3.0%	8	18.4%	15.8%	22.0%
Pittston	3.0	.8	32.2	18.4	33.9
St. Joe Minerals	3.3	11	22.9	26.5	14.8
Westmoreland	3.0	8	32.4	20.9	46.3

(cash dividend divided by the price of the stock), the PE ratio, the return earned on the firm's equity and various growth rates. These factors do not exhaust all the possible variables the investor may consider. Chapter 15 discusses many additional ratios the investor may compute to help identify the best investment.

As is frequently the case, the best investment may not be obvious from the analysis. Companies in a particular industry tend to have similar valuations unless there are specific reasons for higher or lower valuations. For these four coal firms the valuations are quite similar. For example, the dividend yield (per share dividend divided by the price of the stock) is virtually the same (3 per cent) for all four companies. Their PE ratios are similar. Only St. Joe Minerals is commanding a somewhat higher ratio (11 versus 8). St. Joe also has the highest five year average growth rate of sales, but its five year average rate of earnings was the lowest of the four firms. On the basis of earnings growth Westmoreland is the best performer, and it also has the highest return on equity. These last two ratios may argue for purchase of Westmoreland. However, Pittston's data are almost comparable. The choice may depend on other considerations such as the investor's perception of the quality of the management of each firm.

From the individual investor's viewpoint, there may be little real basis for selecting among any of the four coal companies. In the section presented later in this chapter on random walk hypothesis, the implication is that it probably does not really matter which of the four coal companies is selected as part of a diversified portfolio. Furthermore, fundamental analysis offers little insight into the timing of the purchase. Technical analysis may offer some guidance on the timing and is covered in the next section.

TECHNICAL APPROACH

While the fundamental approach is built upon the firm's financial condition and earning capacity, the technical approach is based on the market performance of the firm's securities. It attempts to identify superior investments by analyzing the past price performance of the firm's stock. This type of analysis emphasizes price trends and deviations from these trends. For example, if the price of a stock has risen significantly above the price trend, technical analysis asserts that the price will decline and return to the trend. Graphs and charts are a primary tool of technical analysis, and investors who use this type of analysis are frequently referred to as *chartists*.

Past price performance may indicate future price movements

While both methods seek to identify securities for purchase, the two approaches are significantly different. Fundamental analysis suggests that real factors such as the firm's productivity and profitability will ultimately rule the stock's price. The stock of IBM and Johnson and Johnson have been superior price performers because of the superior fundamentals of the firm's superb managements, superior earnings growth, and strong balance sheets. Technical analysis, however, stresses factors such as price trends and volume of transactions. Stocks that are rising in price will continue to do so. When the chartist perceives that this trend is not continuing, it is time to liquidate that security even if the firm has superior management, excellent growth potential, and a strong balance sheet.

Such a situation is illustrated by Figure 10–1, which plots a hypothetical company's stock price over time. As is shown by line (1), there is a definite positive trend in the price of the stock. This line may also indicate "support." If the price of the stock approaches the line, chartists believe that investors will consider this a buying opportunity. This buying supports the price of the stock which should not fall below this trend line. If the price does fall ("penetrate") below this support line, chartists consider such penetration to be a sell signal.

HYPOTHETICAL STOCK'S PRICE PERFORMANCE

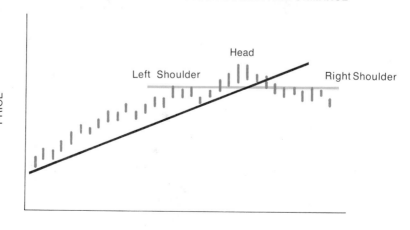

Figure 10–1

This pattern of stock prices also illustrates another configuration that is important to chartists. While there is a trend in this stock's price, the rate of growth in the stock's price slows down and forms a pattern called "head and shoulders." Line (2) shows the left and right shoulders with the "head" protruding above this line. For chartists such a formation is also a "sell signal." They believe that the stock should be sold because the right shoulder is considered to be evidence that the upward trend in the stock's price has stopped.

Trend lines and head and shoulders are not the only patterns followed by chartists. There are many configurations of stock prices that users of technical analysis believe are indicators of future stock prices. The accuracy of such predictions, however, is open to question, and academic research has never demonstrated that charting techniques result in superior investment results. In fact, since charting may result in more trading of securities, it is quite possible that the technical approach will produce inferior results when the broker's commissions are considered.

Both approaches
may help in selecting
securities

While some investors believe in either the fundamental or technical approach to the exclusion of the other, an investor should be aware of both. Wise investing is difficult, and both approaches do offer insights into market performance. Over long periods of time, security prices are related to real economic variables such as economic growth, but, in the short run, there can be large fluctuations in security prices. The technical approach then may aid in the timing of security purchases. There is, however, a body of knowledge which questions the usefulness of either approach. This is the random walk hypothesis.

RANDOM WALK HYPOTHESIS

The previous discussion of sources of information and investment techniques indicates that the investor may become inundated by the material available to help select securities. The random walk hypothesis casts skepticism on the effectiveness of this material in aiding the selection process.

Random walk
assumes
competitive, efficient
security markets

The random walk hypothesis is built upon sophisticated analysis of the competitiveness of security markets and the efficiency with which these markets react to new information. This hypothesis asserts that changes in security prices are random. Tomorrow's price is not related to (i.e., is independent of) today's price. This implies that past information offers little predictive power of future price performance. Just because a stock has recently risen is no indication that it will continue to rise. Such beliefs are in contradiction to the technical approach which asserts that past price performance is a guide to future price movements.

The random walk hypothesis is also not admired by believers in fundamental analysis. Fundamental analysis implies that if the analyst identifies the best firms, the selections should outperform the market. The random walk hypothesis denies this. It suggests that financial analysts have the same information (e.g., annual reports) to work with, and they use similar tools of analysis. If a new piece of information becomes known, it is readily disseminated and the market reacts. For example, if an oil firm discovers new oil reserves, the information is released and the stock price adjusts accordingly. Unless an analyst knew the facts before the general public, there would be insufficient opportunity to profit. Of course, if the analyst anticipated the discovery and purchased the security before the announcement, profits would result. However, the random walk theory believes that few, if any, financial analysts have the capacity to anticipate consistently such events. Thus, in general, financial analysts will not outperform the market.

Has little support from advocates of fundamental and technical analysis

The exception to this conclusion concerns the use of inside information (i.e., knowledge of facts before they are released to the general public). A financial analyst who learns of a discovery before it is made public can react accordingly. However, a person who uses inside knowledge for personal gain has violated the security laws and is subject to prosecution. A famous case on the use of inside information concerned several executives of Texas Gulf Sulfur. This case illustrates that insiders can and sometimes do use inside information for personal gain. These executives bought the company's stock after learning that the firm had discovered large sulfur deposits but before this information was released to the general public. When the news was released, the price of the stock rose, which obviously generated profits for the holders of the stock. However, in this case the violators were successfully prosecuted.

Use of inside information

The random walk hypothesis suggests that in the absence of inside information a portfolio of securities will tend to move with the market. Over a period of years this portfolio will tend neither to outperform nor underperform the market. It suggests that the best strategy may be to buy a diversified portfolio and hold it. Such a portfolio will minimize the brokerage costs and should give the investor a return consistent with the return earned by an index of stock prices.

A possible strategy: buy and hold

RISK AND BETA COEFFICIENTS

Investing in securities involves risk. The firm may deteriorate or even fail, causing the value of its securities to decline. Also the market may decline, causing the value of a financially strong firm's securities to fall.

If one purchases a security, one has no assurance that its

price will rise or even remain stable. Of course, the investor may seek to reduce risk by using various analytical techniques, such as ratio analysis. However, such techniques cannot erase risk, and it is naive to believe they can.

A saver or investor can reduce the risk of loss by holding money in a savings account. However, the return on money is nonexistent and even negative during periods of inflation, when the purchasing power of money declines. The return earned by a regular passbook account at a savings and loan association cannot exceed 5.25 per cent. The attraction of securities is the anticipation of a return that exceeds the modest return earned on savings accounts. Of course, it is unrealistic to expect security prices to double overnight or every year. But a return of 9 per cent annually, which may be achieved by investing in securities, will double the value of one's investment every eight years.

In the literature on portfolio theory, there are two sources of risk. These are often referred to as unsystematic and systematic risk. Unsystematic risk refers to characteristics unique to the firm. Systematic risk is the result of the general movement in security prices.

The usual way to handle unsystematic risk is to accumulate a diversified portfolio. Such diversification is achieved by holding securities in firms in different industries. For example, a diversified portfolio may consist of stocks of firms in such industries as banking, electric utilities, energy, housing, office equipment, steel, drugs, and cosmetics. A portfolio of ten utility companies is not diversified, because what happens to one firm tends to happen to all. For example, if energy costs rise for Public Service Electric and Gas, these costs are probably rising for Detroit Edison. Diversification is achieved by a mixture of firms and industries so that events in one industry may have no bearing on or may even be beneficial to the other industries. For example, increased energy costs and lower profits for electric utilities may result in higher earnings for coal and oil companies.

While diversification will reduce and may even eliminate unsystematic risk, systematic risk still remains. Security prices tend to move together. However, while all security prices fluctuate, some fluctuate more than others. Some types of securities are riskier; for example, common stocks are riskier than bonds. Price movements in common stocks tend to be greater than movements in bond prices. Also within a class of securities, some issues are riskier than others. For example, AT&T's bonds are less risky than the bonds of smaller telephone companies.

One measure of risk is the volatility of a security's price relative to the market. This is called a "beta coefficient." While this name may seem formidable, the concept is not, for a beta coefficient is a simple measure of systematic risk. It is a measure of the responsiveness of the price of a particular security to the market as a whole. This measure may be achieved by dividing the percentage change in the price of the stock by the percentage change in the price of the market. Thus a beta coefficient for a specific firm is

$$\frac{\% \text{ change in the price of a stock}}{\% \text{ change in a price index of the market}}$$

When security prices rise, some rise more rapidly. Such stocks will have beta coefficients greater than 1. For example, a beta coefficient of 1.2 indicates that if the market rises by 10 per cent this particular stock will rise by 12 per cent. The converse is also true. When the market as a whole declines, the security price will fall more rapidly than the market. In this case a 10 per cent decline in the market produces a 12 per cent decline in the price of the specific stock.

How beta coefficients may be computed for specific firms is illustrated by the following examples. At the beginning of 1976 the Dow Jones Industrials were 852 and closed the year at 1004 for a 17.8 per cent gain. The year-end closing price of Teledyne was 69½, up from 22⅛, and the price of Coca-Cola closed at 76, down from 82¼. During 1976, Teledyne outperformed the market, but Coca-Cola underperformed the market. For Teledyne the beta coefficient is

$$\frac{214.1 \text{ percentage change}}{17.8 \text{ percentage change}} = 12.0$$

For Coca-Cola the beta coefficient is

$$\frac{-8.2\%}{17.8\%} = -.46$$

These coefficients indicated that a 10 per cent increase in the market produced a 120 per cent increase in the price of Teledyne but a 4.6 per cent decrease in the price of Coca-Cola.

Using only one observation (as in the above examples) would be most misleading. Instead, beta coefficients should be computed by averaging many of these individual calculations. Obviously, if one were to compute percentage changes daily and average the results for a period of years, one would have to perform an immense number of calculations. Fortunately this may be avoided, for the beta coefficients of many securities are readily available. The Value Line Investment Survey publishes beta coefficients for over 1500 stocks traded on the New York and American Stock Exchanges. This investment survey is available in libraries and brokerage firms or may be purchased from its publisher. Hence one may learn the beta coefficient for many stocks without computing them. For example, as of December, 1976, Value Line reported that Disney Productions' beta coefficient was 1.50, and for Jantzen it was .80. This indicates that if the market rises by 10 per cent, the price of Disney should increase by 15 per cent and the price of Jantzen should increase by 8 per cent.

While beta coefficients are a measure of price volatility, the investor should remember that they are based on past price performance, which may not be indicative of future price performance. Securities that were in favor in the 1960s and were volatile then may not be as volatile today. Conversely, a firm whose stock price has been relatively stable may become more volatile. For example, in June, 1975, the beta coefficients reported by Value Line for Disney and Jantzen were 1.45 and .85, respectively. Disney has thus become more volatile, for the coefficient has risen to 1.50. Jantzen has become less volatile, for its beta coefficient has fallen to .80.

What beta coefficients do indicate is a measure of the systematic risk associated with investing in particular securities. An individual investor who seeks higher returns may invest in securities with higher betas, for during periods of rising security prices these securities have historically outperformed the market as a whole. An investor who is less willing to bear risk may select securities with low beta coefficients, for during periods of declining security prices these securities have outperformed the market. Beta coefficients thus become another tool available to investors to help them select securities consistent with their investment goals.

INVESTMENT COMPANIES

Many savers and investors find managing their own portfolios to be difficult or time consuming. Instead of doing their own investing, they purchase shares in investment companies. Investment companies are not financial intermediaries, because they primarily invest in second-hand assets. They do, however, compete for investors' funds with financial intermediaries. They have been popular vehicles for savers and play a significant role in security markets.

Investment companies purchase securities on the open market (that is, they buy existing securities that are being offered for sale). Occasionally they may buy new securities issued by corporations, in which case the investment company is serving the function of a financial intermediary. In this case it is channeling the funds of savers to firms that may use the money to purchase plant and equipment. But investment companies primarily stress investments in second-hand assets, that is, stocks and bonds that were previously issued.

There are two general types of investment companies: closed end and open end. The open end investment company is commonly referred to as a "mutual fund." The difference between the open end and closed end investment company is the nature of their capital structure. The closed end mutual fund has a set capital structure, such as all stock or a combination of stock and debt. For example, there is a specified number of shares and dollar amount of debt that the company may issue. In an open end company the number of shares varies as investors put in and take out funds from the mutual fund. Since the closed end investment company has a specified number of shares, an investor who wants to invest in a particular company must purchase existing shares from current stockholders; any investor who owns shares and wishes to liquidate the position must sell the shares. The shares in closed end investment companies are bought and sold in the open market just as the shares of stock in companies are bought and sold.

The closed end has a fixed capital structure

With an open end investment company, an investor who wants a position in a particular fund purchases shares directly from the company. The mutual fund issues new shares after receiving the money and purchases assets with the newly acquired money. If an investor who owns shares in the fund wants to liquidate his position, he sells his shares back to the company. The shares are *redeemed,* and the fund pays the investor from its cash holdings. If the fund lacks sufficient cash, it will sell some of the assets it owns to raise the cash to redeem the shares.

The open end has a variable capital structure

The shares of an investment company have a net asset value which is their proportional share of the company's net assets. The net asset value of the investment company is the sum of the value of the stocks, bonds, cash, and other assets minus any liabilities of the company. The net value of any share of stock in the investment company is the net asset value of the fund divided by the number of shares outstanding. The market price of a closed end company, however, need not be the fund's net asset value. Instead, the market price may be above or below the net asset value of the shares. If the market price is below the net asset value of the shares, the shares are said to be selling for a discount. If the market price is above the net asset value, the shares are selling for a premium.

Net asset value

Investing in closed end investment companies involves several costs which the saver does not incur when funds are deposited in financial intermediaries. First, since the shares are purchased on the open market, there is the brokerage commission for the purchase and for any subsequent sale. Second, the management of the company charges a fee to manage the fund, and this fee is subtracted from any income that the fund's assets earn. These management fees range from 0.1 to 2.0 per cent of the fund's net asset value and generally average about 0.5 per cent of the fund's net asset value. Third, when the company buys or sells securities, it also has to pay brokerage fees. Thus investing in closed end investment companies involves three costs that the investor must bear. Other alternative investments such as savings accounts do not involve these costs.

Cost of investing in closed end investment company

Source of profits

Investors in closed end investment companies may make profits in a variety of ways. First, the company may pay dividends from its sources of income. If it collects dividends and interest on its portfolio of assets, this income is distributed to the fund's stockholders as dividend income. Second, if the value of the fund's assets rises, the fund may sell the assets and realize the profits. These profits then are distributed as capital gains to the investment company's stockholders. Third, the net asset value of the portfolio may increase and cause the market price of the company's stock to rise. In this case the investor may sell the shares on the market and realize capital gains. Fourth, the market price of the shares may rise relative to the fund's net asset value.

These differences between the investment company's net asset value and the stock price is illustrated by the quotes presented below for closed end funds, taken from the *Wall Street Jounal.* Virtually all the quoted closed end funds were selling for a discount, and in several cases the discount exceeded 30 per cent of the net asset value of the shares.

Some investors view the market price relative to the net asset value as a guide to buying and selling the shares of a closed end investment company. If the shares are selling for a sufficient discount, the shares are considered a buy. If the shares are selling for a sufficient premium, the shares are considered for selling. Of course, determining a sufficient amount of premium to justify the sale or sufficient amount of discount to justify the purchase is not simple. The amount of discount and premium does vary. That is, the market price of the shares may sell for a lower discount or a larger premium relative to the shares' net asset value. Hence it is also possible for the market price of the fund to fluctuate even if the net asset value is stable. If the market price does rise relative to the net asset value, an investor may be

Closed-End Funds

Friday, January 28, 1977

Following is a weekly listing of unaudited net asset values of closed-end investment fund shares, reported by the companies as of Friday's close. Also shown is the closing listed market price or a dealer-to-dealer asked price of each fund's shares, with the percentage of difference.

	N.A. Value	Stk Price	% Diff		N.A. Value	Stk Price	% Diff
Diversified Funds	**Common**		**Stock**	BancrftCv	22.53	16⅝	−26.2
				Castle	24.19	18⅛	−25.1
AdmExp	14.70	11⅞	−19.2	ChaseCvB	11.56	8⅞	−23.2
BakerFen	56.40	35½	−37.1	CLIC	(−8.00)	....	.....
Carriers	17.21	14⅝	−15.0	Diebold	9.35	6½	−30.5
CentSec	8.55	6¼	−26.9	Japan	12.74	9⅝	−24.5
GenAInv	12.50	10⅜	−17.0	KeysnOTC	9.92	7⅝	−23.1
Lehman	13.07	11⅜	−13.0	NatlAvia	22.95	15¾	−31.4
Madison	16.98	12⅛	−28.6	NewAmFd	18.02	14	−22.3
NiagaraSh	13.45	11⅞	−11.7	PetroCp	25.13	25½	+ 1.5
OseasSec	4.63	3⅛	−32.5	RETIncC	2.82	2¼	−20.2
aTri-Contl	25.17	20¾	−17.6	S-GSecInc	1.80	1½	−16.7
United	11.70	10⅜	−11.3	Source	17.25	13	−24.6
US&For	22.01	16¾	−23.9	StdSh	41.87	26⅝	−36.4
Specialized Equity and Convertible Funds				ValueLn	4.21	2¼	−46.6
AmUtilS	15.32	12¼	−20.0				
bASA	15.20	19½	+28.3				

a-Ex-Dividend. b-As of Thursday's close. z-Not quoted.

(Reprinted by permission of the *Wall Street Journal.*)

able to sell the shares for a profit. However the investor is subjected to risk of loss, for the value of the investment may decline if the value of the assets decline or if the shares sell for a larger disount from their net asset value.

Open end investment companies, "mutual funds," are very similar to closed end investment companies, but there are several important differences. One important difference pertains to the cost of investing, which arises when the investor purchases the shares. Mutual funds continuously offer to sell new shares, and these existing shares are sold at their net asset value plus a sales fee commonly called the "loading charge." (Shares are redeemed at their net asset value and there is no additional fee.) The loading fee may range from nothing for "no load funds" to 6 to 9.3 per cent for "load funds," with the average fee being 8 per cent.

Mutual funds

Which funds are "no load" funds is immediately apparent by the way in which mutual fund prices are quoted. The exhibit on page 144 from the *Wall Street Journal's* quotation of mutual fund prices illustrates this difference. The paper reports the net asset value (NAV) and the offer price, and any change in the net asset value from the previous day. If the offer price and net asset value are the same (i.e., if the fund has "no loading" charge), N.L. is given in the offer price column. Thus the Aetna Income Shares with a net asset value of $13.02 per share and an offer price of $14.23 is not a no load fund. The buyer pays $1.21 ($14.23 − 13.02) to purchase a share worth $13.02. Such a charge is 8.5 per cent of the asking price. The Alpha Fund has a net asset value of $10.92. It is a no load fund; hence its shares may be bought and sold from the company at $10.92.

No load funds

Investors in mutual funds also have to pay management fees which are deducted from the income of the fund and commission costs when the fund buys and sells securities. Thus the cost of investing in mutual funds may be substantial when the total costs (the loading charge, management fees, and brokerage) are considered. Of course, for no load mutual funds the cost of investing is substantially reduced.

The second difference between closed end and open end investment companies is the source of profits. As with closed end investment companies, investors may profit from investments in mutual funds from several sources. Any income from the fund's assets is distributed as dividends, and if the fund's assets appreciate in value and the fund realizes these gains, the gains are distributed as capital gains. If the net asset value of the shares appreciates, the investor may redeem the shares at the appreciated price. Thus, in general, the open end mutual fund offers investors the same means for making profits as the closed end investment company, excepting the possibility that the market price of the closed end may rise relative to the net asset value of the shares. The possibility of a declining discount or increased premium is a potential source of profits that are available only

Mutual Funds

Friday, January 28, 1977

Price ranges for investment companies, as quoted by the National Association of Securities Dealers. NAV stands for net asset value per share; the offering includes net asset value plus maximum sales charge, if any.

	NAV	Offer NAV Price Chg.
Acorn Fnd	14.67	N.L.+ .01
Adv Invest	10.06	N.L.+ .01
Aetna Fnd	7.46	8.15+ .02
Aetna InSh	13.02	14.23+ .01
Afuture Fd	9.24	N.L.- .01
AGE Fund	5.48	5.59- .04
Allstate	8.60	9.25+ .02
Alpha Fnd	10.92	N.l..+ .05
Am Birthrt	9.78	10.69+ .02
Am Equity	5.16	5.65+ .01
American Funds Group:		
Am Bal	8.13	8.89+ .02
Amcap F	5.58	6.10+ .01
Am Mutl	9.80	10.71- .01
Bnd FdA	15.23	16.64+ .01
Cap FdA	6.37	6.96+ .01
Gth FdA	4.64	5.07 ...
IncF Am	16.44	17.97 ...
I C A	14.06	15.37+ .02
Nw Prsp	15.93	17.41+ .01
Wash Mt	7.14	7.80+ .01
American General Group:		
A GenBd	8.99	9.83 ...
A GC Gr	4.11	4.49 ...
A Gn Inc	6.50	7.10- .01
A GnVen	11.57	12.64- .06
Eqty Gth	6.66	7.28- .01
Fd Amer	6.58	7.19 ...
Prov Inc	3.94	4.25- .01
Am Grwth	5.68	6.12+ .03
Am Ins Ind	(z)	(z) (z)
Am Invest	5.34	N.L.+ .02
AmInv Inc	12.34	N.L.+ .04
AmNat Gw	2.81	3.07- .02
Anchor Group:		
Daily Inc	1.00	N.L. ...
Growth	6.53	7.04 ...
Income	7.47	8.05+ .02
Spectm	4.51	4.86- .02
Fund Inv	6.82	7.35 ...
Wa Natl	9.97	10.75+ .01

	NAV	Offer NAV Price Chg.
Income	10.66	11.65+ .02
Resrch	14.98	16.37+ .02
Lifelns Inv	7.25	7.92- .01
Lincoln National Funds:		
Selct Am	7.08	N.L.+ .01
Selct Spl	12.91	N.L.- .02
Loomis Sayles Funds:		
Cap Dev	10.18	N.L. ...
Mutual	12.96	N.L.- .01
Lord Abbett:		
Affilatd	8.29	8.95- .01
Bond Deb	11.33	12.38 ...
Income	3.57	3.86 ...
Lutheran Brotherhd Fds:		
Broth Fd	10.58	11.56 ...
Broth Inc	9.23	10.09+ .01
Bro MBd	10.08	11.02+ .01
Broth US	9.88	10.80 ...
Mass Company:		
Freedm	8.08	8.83 ...
Indep Fd	7.11	7.77 ...
Mass Fd	10.58	11.56- .01
Mass Financial Svcs:		
MIT	10.66	11.49+ .05
MIG	8.52	9.19+ .04
MID	14.60	15.74- .01
MFD	11.85	12.78+ .04
MCD	12.81	13.81- .04
MFB	15.81	17.05+ .01
Mather Fd	13.28	N.L.+ .01
ML CapFd	12.92	13.82 ...
ML RdyAs	1.00	N.L. ...
Mid Amer	(z)	(z) (z)
Money Mkt	1.00	N.L. ...
MONY Fd	9.19	10.04- .12
MSB Fund	14.58	N.L.+ .01
Mutl BnFd	9.04	9.88+ .03
M I F Fd	(z)	(z) (z)
M I F Gro	(z)	(z) (z)
Mutual of Omaha Funds:		
Amer	11.69	11.87 ...
	4.09	4.45

(Reprinted by permission of the *Wall Street Journal*.)

Portfolio can be varied or specialized

through the closed end investment company and not through a mutual fund.

The portfolios of investment companies may be varied or very specialized. In general, the companies may be classified into one of the following four types: income, growth, special situations, and balanced. The names of the classes are descriptive of the types of assets the companies own. Income funds stress assets that produce income; they buy assets that produce generous dividends or interest income. Growth funds stress the growth of the value of the assets with little emphasis given to current income. Investment companies stressing special situations tend to specialize in more speculative securities that under the special situation may yield large returns, and balanced funds have a mixture of securities that sample the attributes of the assets of the more specialized companies. Investment companies may also specialize in other ways. For example, a company may be limited to investments in the securities of a particular industry such as airlines (e.g., National Aviation) or gold (e.g., ASA Ltd.). There are also funds that specialize in securities in a particular country (e.g., the Japan Fund, which invests in

Japanese securities) or a particular type of security, such as bonds (e.g., American General Bond Fund).

There are several advantages to investing in investment companies. The small investor receives the advantage of diversification and the spreading of risk. Small investors may lack the resources to construct a diversified portfolio, but by investing in an investment company, they are able to own a portion of a diversified portfolio. Second, the portfolio is professionally managed and under continuous supervision. Investors rarely have the time and expertise to manage their own portfolios, and (except in cases of large portfolios) they lack the resources to purchase professional management. By investing in an investment company, the small investors buy the services of professional management which may increase the investor's return. Third, the administrative detail and the custodial aspects of the portfolio (e.g., the physical handling of securities) is done by the management of the company. Fourth, most investment companies offer dividend reinvestment plans in which the dividends and capital gains are retained by the fund and used to purchase additional shares. The investor receives no cash income but instead receives additional shares. Since no cash has been received, no cash can be spent by the investor. Instead the earnings of the fund may be immediately reinvested to earn more income and profits for the investor. Fifth, mutual funds permit investors to make small monthly investments.

Advantages of purchasing investment company shares

While there are advantages of investing through investment companies, there are also disadvantages. Several of the advantages offered by investment companies are not unique to them alone. First, even though these companies offer professional management, they cannot guarantee to outperform the market. While a particular fund may do well in any given year, it may do very poorly in subsequent years. This is probably the greatest source of criticism of these funds. Their managements have not consistently been able to outperform the market. In some cases a randomly selected portfolio has done better than the securities selected by the funds.

Disadvantages of purchasing investment company shares

Second, the services offered by the investment company may be obtained elsewhere. For example, the trust department of a commercial bank offers custodial services. Even leaving securities in the broker's name relieves the investor of keeping the securities and reduces record keeping. In addition, dividend reinvestment programs are not unique to investment companies. They are offered by many companies such as AT&T, Sperry Rand, and Union Carbide.

Third, the individual investor may acquire a diversified portfolio with only a modest amount of capital. Diversification does not require 100 different stocks. A diversified portfolio can be achieved with five to ten different securities. If the investor has $10,000, then $1250 invested in the stock of eight companies in different industries produces a diversified portfolio. Diversification is available to modest as well as to large investors. Neither has to purchase shares in investment companies to get the advantage of diversification. Such individual investments also avoid the management fees charged by the investment companies.

While mutuals have been a popular investment vehicle, their popularity has diminished. No doubt the mediocre performance of many funds partially explains this decline in popularity. Also, investors have found alternative investments that offer attractive yields, such as higher yielding certificates of deposit or quality bonds. During 1972 and 1973, many funds experienced more redemptions of shares than sales. While sales exceeded redemptions in 1974, redemptions again started to exceed sales in 1975.* Such net redemptions mean investors are removing funds from investment companies and indicates their importance has diminished.

SUMMARY

Selecting securities can be a difficult, even baffling experience for investors. But many Americans do own stock, and many others indirectly have interests in the stock market through investments in investment companies, life insurance, and pension plans. Many people probably do not realize the extent to which their financial resources may be related to the security markets.

This chapter has considered several factors an investor may use to aid in the selection of securities. There is a wealth of published material available for investors to use. Actually the investor may be overwhelmed by the excessive amount of published material on investments.

The investor may use a variety of techniques to select securities. These range from "hot tips" to fundamental analysis of a firm's financial position to technical analysis of the price performance of the stock. However, according to the random walk hypothesis, outperforming the market may be impossible to achieve, and a portfolio of diversified securities will tend to achieve a return consistent with the market as a whole. Such a diversified portfolio reduces the risk of investing in securities, because there is less reliance on the performance of a particular security. The risk associated with a particular stock is reduced. One firm can fall on hard times without destroying the value of the diversified portfolio. The risk that remains is the tendency for security prices to move together systematically. Thus, while a diversified portfolio reduces the unsystematic risk, it cannot erase the systematic risk associated with general movements in security prices.

---

*In 1976 net redemptions were the highest in history.

Some investors have turned to another means of achieving diversification by purchasing shares of investment companies. There are two types: the closed end investment company and the mutual fund. The closed end investment company has fixed capital structure. The investor buys shares in a closed end investor in the same way that shares are purchased in individual companies. The open end investment company (i.e., the mutual fund) issues new shares to the investor and purchases the shares back should the investor desire to liquidate his position. Buying the stock of investment companies may reduce the investor's need to manage money, but such companies cannot guarantee success. The investor still bears the risk of loss even if others manage the assets.

_____ KEY WORDS AND TERMS

fundamental approach   beta coefficient
technical approach   closed end investment company
PE ratio   mutual fund
chartist   no load fund
systematic and unsystematic risk   net asset value
random walk hypothesis   inside information

_____ QUESTIONS FOR THOUGHT AND DISCUSSION

1. Two investors are considering two stocks for possible investment. The beta coefficients for the two stocks are 1.25 and .65. How may this information help the two investors choose between the two securities?

2. Why does the random walk hypothesis find little support among financial analysts and users of technical analysis?

3. What are the sources of potential profit (and loss) and the costs of purchasing the shares of investment companies?

4. What sources of information useful for making investment decisions are readily available to you?

5. If an investor owns the stock of four telephone companies, three steel producers, and three automobile manufacturers, does the investor possess a diversified portfolio? To achieve more diversification, what should the investor do?

Chapter 11   OVERVIEW OF THE FINANCIAL SYSTEM

Learning Objectives

* Review financial intermediation and its importance to an advanced economy.
* Review commercial banks' reserves: total reserves, required reserves, excess reserves.
* Review the process of expansion and contraction of the money supply and the supply of credit.
* Review non-commercial bank financial intermediaries.
* Review the tools of monetary policy and how they affect the supply of money and credit.

"A 'generalist' is a specialist who can relate his own small area to the universe of knowledge."

Peter Drucker

The financial structure of the nation is amazingly complex and encompasses a variety of financial institutions. The primary function of this structure is to facilitate the transfer of resources from savers to borrowers. People may save for a variety of reasons, ranging from greed to uncertainty concerning the future. However, all savings represent current command over goods that the saver is not using. This command over resources must be used in order for the economy to maintain the level of income and employment. It is the primary role of financial institutions to facilitate this transfer of purchasing power from those who are currently not using it, savers, to those who currently need it, borrowers.

This transfer of resources from the saver to the borrower may occur directly when a firm issues securities that are bought by the general public or when individuals invest in sole proprietorships or partnerships. However, many of the nation's largest firms have not sold new securities to the general public for several years, and others only issue securities on an intermittent basis. Thus, in many cases, resources are transferred indirectly through a system of financial intermediaries. These intermediaries stand between the borrowers and the ultimate lenders (i.e., savers) and facilitate the transfer of resources. Financial intermediation thus occurs whenever a firm (e.g., a bank) receives funds and issues a claim on itself (e.g., a savings account) and then uses the funds to lend to another economic unit. In effect, the claim on the final user of the resources is converted into a claim on the financial intermediary, which savers are willing to own.

While there are a variety of financial intermediaries, by far the most important intermediary is the commercial banking system. Not only is the volume of bank deposits greater than the funds available to other financial intermediaries, but also commercial banks are the only financial intermediary that may issue demand deposits. Demand deposits are part of the nation's money supply. Thus when commercial banks lend, they alter the supply of money as well as the supply of credit. While other financial intermediaries may affect the nation's supply of credit, they cannot affect its supply of money.

The ability of commercial banks to lend and expand the supply of money is related to their reserves. Commercial banks must hold funds in reserve against their deposit liabilities. The amount of the reserve requirement is set either by the various state banking authorities or by the Federal Reserve. Since the majority of bank deposits are in national banks, the reserve requirements set by the Federal Reserve have the greatest impact on the commercial banking system's reserves. Funds tied up in reserves do not earn income for the commercial banks; thus there is an obvious incentive to minimize the holdings of reserves. Hence, when commercial banks do have excess reserves, they will seek to use them to acquire income earning assets. When commercial banks do lend their excess reserves, new demand deposits are created. These demand deposits are new money. Thus by granting loans and expanding their deposit liabilities, commercial banks alter the nation's supply of money. Therefore any factor that affects their reserves and in particular their excess reserves has the capacity to affect the nation's money supply.

The most important influence on commercial banks' reserves is the Federal Reserve, which is the nation's central bank. The Federal Reserve system is composed of the member banks, the 12 district Federal Reserve Banks, the Federal Open Market Committee, and the Board of Governors. The role of the Federal Reserve is to alter the money supply in such a way as to pursue certain economic goals, which include price stability, full employment, and economic growth (i.e., a higher standard of living). These general goals are pursued by a variety of means, including not only the fiscal policy of the Federal Government but also the monetary policy of the Federal Reserve. The Federal Reserve has several tools to achieve monetary policy. These tools (the discount rate, the reserve requirements, and open market operations) work by affecting commercial banks' reserves. The most important of these tools is open market operations, which is the buying and selling of securities by the Federal Reserve. By buying Federal Government securities, the Federal Reserve is able to expand the supply of money and commercial banks' reserves. By selling securities, it is able to contract the supply of money and reserves. By altering the total reserves of commercial banks, the Federal Reserve is able to affect their excess reserves and induce behavior on the part of commercial banks which affects both the supply of money and credit in the economy.

The Federal Reserve is not the only economic unit that can affect the excess reserves of commercial banks. By their decision to hold a particular type of bank deposit, depositors also affect the excess reserves of commercial banks. Since there are different reserve requirements for different types of accounts, a shift of funds from one account to another (e.g., a shift from checking to savings accounts) alters commercial banks' excess reserves. Furthermore, depositors can affect the total reserves of commercial banks. The decision to hold cash instead of deposits directly affects commercial bank reserves because cash is part of their reserves. The act of depositing cash expands commercial banks' lending capacity, but the converse is also true, for cash withdrawals reduce the reserves of commercial banks. Cash withdrawals destroy their capacity to expand the supply of money and credit. Hence the general public can have a substantial impact on commercial banks' ability to lend by altering their holdings of cash relative to commercial bank deposits.

The general public can also affect commercial bank reserves by choosing to purchase foreign goods instead of domestically produced goods. Such purchases cause money to flow abroad and out of domestic banks, thus reducing the domestic money supply and the reserves of domestic commercial banks. If foreigners buy goods here, the opposite is also true, for the domestic money supply and the reserves of domestic commercial banks are increased. Of course, the commercial banks and the Federal Reserve cannot control these purchases. The Federal Government may discourage foreign purchases through import taxes and quotas; however, as long as there is free choice, individuals may purchase foreign goods. Such purchases cause international flows of currency that affect the domestic money supply and the reserves of commercial banks.

The fiscal policy of the Federal Government may also affect the reserves of commercial banks. Fiscal policy is represented by taxation and spending by the Federal Government and the management of its debt. The Federal Government virtually never has a balanced budget in which expenditures are exactly matched by tax revenues. In recent times the budget has generally run at a deficit, and expenditures have exceeded tax revenues. This deficit must be financed, and the Federal Government may borrow the funds from a variety of sources (the general public, commercial banks, or the Federal Reserve). The source of the funds used to finance the deficit can have an impact on the reserves of commercial banks. When the Federal Government borrows from the Federal Reserve, the effect is to increase the supply of money and the reserves of the banking system. Funds borrowed by the Federal Government in this case are really no different than if the government had printed and spent newly issued money. The deficit is in effect "monetized," and this expansion in money will result in the creation of new reserves for commercial banks, which they can use to expand the supply of money further.

While the above financial transactions do affect the reserves of commercial banks, there are many financial transactions that do not. When individuals borrow from each other, new loans and credit are created, but there is no effect on the supply of money and the reserves of commercial banks. The money is transferred from one individual to another, and the transferring of money between individuals does not alter the money supply. This same general principle applies to financial transactions among noncommercial bank financial intermediaries and borrowers. For example, savings and loan associations, life insurance companies, and mutual savings banks are not able to expand the supply of money or to alter the commercial banks' ability to expand the supply of money. They do not have the capacity to create demand deposits, nor do they have the power to affect commercial banks' reserves. When funds flow into (and out of) non-commercial bank financial intermediaries, only the ownership of the existing supply of money is changed. However, these flows do alter these other financial intermediaries' ability to grant loans. Thus the available supply of credit is altered even though there is no change in the supply of money or the ability of commercial banks to lend.

This same principle holds with regard to the security markets. The stock exchanges and over the counter markets involve transactions between individuals, and these transactions cannot affect the supply of money or the reserves of commercial banks. Security markets offer investors a means to facilitate transferring ownership from one investor to another. The firm that issued the securities does not receive the proceeds from the sale. The only time that a firm receives the proceeds is when the securities are initially issued. Hence the vast majority of security transactions are between different investors and not between investors and firms. The existence of these security markets does mean that a person who buys a security knows that there is a market in which the security may be sold. This increased marketability of securities makes stocks and bonds more attractive and hence makes it easier for firms to issue additional securities. Of course, when the firms do issue securities, funds flow from investors to the firms, which in turn use these funds to purchase additional assets or to retire debt. But even the issuing of new securities does not affect the money supply or the reserves of commercial banks, because all that is occurring is a transfer of existing money from one individual, the investor, to the firm issuing the securities.

When many financial transactions do not affect the supply of money or the ability of commercial banks to lend, they do alter the ability of firms to finance their operations. Finance is a necessary condition for a firm to operate, and inability to obtain this finance is a frequent cause of business failure. While commercial banks are a primary source of funds, they are only one of many, and each firm uses a variety of sources of finance. While there may be many sources of finance, there is only a given amount of money in the system at any one moment. Of all the financial intermediaries, only commercial banks are able to increase (or decrease) this supply of money. Hence, while a firm may borrow funds from sources other than commercial banks, these sources cannot be a limitless pool of finance. Ultimately the source of all credit is related to the supply of money and the ability of commercial banks to lend. The final control over that supply of money and the reserves of commercial banks rests with the Federal Reserve. Hence the power of the Federal Reserve to affect the reserves of commercial banks and money supply has an impact on other sources of credit. Therefore, when the Federal Reserve tightens credit, firms have difficulty obtaining credit because all sources are squeezed. By constraining commercial banks, the Federal Reserve is able to tighten all sources of credit.

After understanding the financial environment, the student may proceed to the study of financial management. Financial management encompasses many facets of a firm's operations including (1) planning and control, (2) deciding which assets to acquire, and (3) finding sources of funds to finance the assets. Part II of this text is an introduction to financial management. The viewpoint of Part II is from the role of the financial manager, which is described in the next chapter. The subsequent chapters explain the many facets of the financial manager's job and introduce the analytical tools that are used by financial managers. The intent is to introduce all students to many diverse fields, such as marketing, organizational development, or economics, to the world of financial management. Students of financial management will have to pursue the subject in greater depth, but all students should be aware of the content of financial management.

financial intermediation
commercial bank reserves
goals of economic policy
Federal Reserve
monetary policy

REVIEW QUESTIONS FOR THOUGHT AND DISCUSSION

1. What is a financial intermediary and what significant role does it play in an advanced economy?

2. The commercial banking system is the most important financial intermediary. What distinguishes commercial banks from other intermediaries? What affects their capacity to lend?

3. Why is the Federal Reserve such an important financial institution? How can it alter the supply of money and credit?

4. What is deficit spending by the Federal Government? How may it affect the capacity of commercial banks to lend?

			Quarterly									Annual
		Actual						Forecast				Actual
1975:1	1975:2	1975:3	1975:4	1976:1	1976:2	1976:3	1976:4	1977:1	1977:2	1977:3	1977:4	1974
1446.2	1482.3	1548.7	1588.2	1636.2	1675.2	1717.6	1762.3	1809.7	1858.4	1909.7	1964	
1468.4	1512.3	1550.6	1592.5	1621.4	1659.2	1700.1	1744.5	1791.2	1838.8	1888.7		
933.2	960.3	987.3	1012.0	1043.6	1064.7	1089.5	1118.0	1148.6	1175.9			
122.1	127.0	136.0	141.8	151.4	155.0	158.9	164.0	169.6				
394.4	405.8	414.6	421.6	429.1	434.8	443.6	454.0					
416.7	427.4	436.7	448.6	463.2	474.9	487.0	50					
172.4	164.4	196.7	201.4	229.6	239.2	25						
148.0	145.8	146.1	148.7	153.4	157							
94.9	94.6	94.3	96.6	100.3								
53.1	51.2	51.8	52.1									
46.6	48.6	52.6										
(22.2)	(30.0)											
325.6												

CONSOLIDATED BALANCE SHEETS
S Inc. and subsidiaries
(llars in thousands)

ASSETS

Current assets:

Cash and cash equivalents

Notes and accounts receivable, le
doubtful accounts, returns and
1976, $73,608; 1975, $71,493

Inventories

Program rights

Prepaid expenses

Total current assets

Investments

Property, plant and e

Land

Buildings

Machinery and equipme

Leasehold improvements

Less accumulated deprec

Net property, plant and e

Excess of cost over net as
acquired, less amortizati

Other assets

FORM - 4

Date _____

$ _____

Payee _____

Remarks _____

_____

_____

TUCKER TOY STO
Comparative Income S
For the Years Ended December

1978

$3

Sales
Less: Sales Returns and Allowances
Net Sales
Cost of Goods Sold:
Inventory, January 1
Purchases
Goods Available for Sale
Inventory, December 31
Cost of Goods Sold

Gross Margin
Operating Expenses:
Selling Expenses
Administrative Expenses
Total Operating Expenses

Operating Income
Financial Expense
Income before Income Taxes
Estimated Income Tax Expense
Net Income

+(Less than 1 percent)
Not applicable. Since the am
rcentage increase.

Part II
FINANCIAL
MANAGEMENT

Chapter 12

THE ROLE OF THE FINANCIAL MANAGER

Learning Objectives

- Isolate the goal of management.
- Describe the financial manager's various tasks.
- Enumerate the differences and similarities among the types of businesses.
- Differentiate among progressive, proportional, and regressive taxes.
- Explain how differences in taxes on income, dividends, and corporate earnings affect the decision to incorporate.

"Labor can do nothing without capital, capital nothing without labor and neither labor nor capital can do anything without the guiding genius of management."

W. L. MacKenzie King

All firms employ someone who performs the role of the financial manager. This role involves a variety of tasks that range from planning and control to maintaining the firm's ability to pay its bills. For the sole proprietorship, the financial manager is the owner who makes all the substantive decisions concerning the firm. As the firm expands, it is able to employ people with some degree of specialization, and the financial manager's role develops into a specialized position. If the firm is sufficiently large, the job may be performed by a staff that reports to a vice president in charge of finance. Since large firms have specialized staffs, more emphasis can be placed on the role of the financial manager. The tasks of the financial manager, however, are basically the same for small and large firms, and someone must perform these tasks. Unfortunately, small firms frequently lack the resources to perform adequately the role of the financial manager.

This chapter is concerned with the role of the financial manager. It introduces the topics that will be developed in greater detail in subsequent chapters. This chapter also includes a discussion of the differences among proprietorships, partnerships, and corporations. Since a major source of the difference is the result of taxes, the chapter concludes with a section on personal and corporate federal income taxation and how these taxes affect the decision to incorporate.

MAXIMIZATION OF THE VALUE OF THE FIRM

What is the goal of management? Management must have some basis for judging its performance. For example, the goal of management in a capitalistic economic system may be the maximization of profits by the firm. This goal may be of little use for a financial manager, for it omits the elements of time and uncertainty. Maximum profits when? Maximum profits at what risk? Time and risk are important elements of finance, for decisions are made in the present that will affect the firm over a period of time, and success is definitely not certain.

The goal that is generally accepted as the principal focus in finance is the maximization of the value of the firm. Management should make decisions that maximize the present worth or present value of the firm. Thus decisions made by management that affect the firm's well-being over time are judged by their effect on the present worth of the firm. It is this present value that management seeks to maximize. This value may be readily measured if the company has shares of ownership (stock) that are held by the general public, for the market price of the stock is indicative of the value of the company. While security prices are subject to fluctuations, firms that have consistently grown and prospered have seen the value of their stock (and hence the value of the company) increase. For these companies management has consistently made decisions that increased the value of the company. The price of the company's stock then is indicative of management performance.

Goal of management: maximize present value of the firm

Smaller firms or firms whose stock is not owned by the general public (and these are by far the largest number of firms in existence) do not have market prices for their stock. Hence owners and managers may not be able to ascertain readily the value of the firm. The only time that the value of the firm is determined is when the firm is liquidated or sold, for at that time the value of the firm is its liquidation value or sale price. Since such liquidation and sales occur only once, in general the owners and managers do not know what the true value of the firm might be. They may use the value of their firm's equity as shown on the accounting statements as some indication of the firm's worth, but management cannot be certain of the firm's true value.

While maximization of the value of the firm may not be more operational than the maximization of profit, it does bring to the foreground the importance that the finance discipline places on

Emphasis on present worth of the firm

present value. Present value is related to future events, and it is the current decisions by management that affect these future events. Management should seek to make those decisions that increase the value of the firm over time but should achieve this increased value without sustaining excessive risk. The financial manager, by increasing the firm's profitability and decreasing the element of risk or uncertainty, contributes to the maximization of the value of the firm.

The increasing of profits and reduction of risk resulting in higher present values is perhaps best explained by examples. A firm may diversify operations to increase profits and reduce risk. St. Joe Minerals Corporation recently acquired a coal operation. This acquisition diversified its product lines and increased profits. In addition, the coal operation reduced the firm's dependence on lead and zinc. The firm's profits are now less responsive to changes in lead and zinc prices; hence the firm may be viewed by some investors as being less risky. The increase in profits and the decrease in risk should increase the present value (i.e., the present price of the stock) of the firm. In the case of St. Joe Minerals, the price of the stock at the end of 1976 was near its historic high and more than double its price in 1970.

Not all decisions result in increased profits or reduced risks. For example, the merger of the Pennsylvania and New York Central Railroads led to the collapse of both. The merger did not result in the reduced costs and increased profits that were anticipated. The Penn Central merger is an example of a decision that did not increase profits. Debt financing by real estate investment trusts is an example of a decision that increased risk. The excessive use of debt financing by real estate investment trusts significantly increased the risk associated with their investing in real estate. Many of these trusts found themselves unable to meet their obligations and the value of their own stock plummeted. Thus decisions that fail to increase profitability or that increase risk result in a decline in the value of a firm and may result in bankruptcy.

THE ROLE OF THE FINANCIAL MANAGER

The tasks of the financial manager

One of the most important jobs of the financial manager is to assure that the firm meets its financial obligations as they come due. The financial manager must make sure that the firm has sufficient cash to pay the firm's bills as they come due. Such liquidity is also a prerequisite to the acquisition of additional external finance. Outsiders will not be willing to lend or invest their funds in the firm if they believe that the firm will be unable to meet its obligations as they come due. Maintaining sufficient

(1) Maintain liquidity

liquidity then is a necessary condition to successful business. But such maintenance of liquidity is not free, for if the firm holds cash, then it is not holding an income earning asset. While the firm is able to pay its bills as they come due, this liquidity is reducing the firm's profitability. If the cash were invested in income earning assets, the firm's profits would be increased. That is the essence of the financial manager's dilemma: the safety of cash versus the profitability of other assets.

Besides anticipating the firm's cash needs and then assuring that the money is available when it is needed, the financial manager should invest any excess funds profitably. By investing this excess in short-term assets, the financial manager is able to earn interest but maintain a degree of liquidity. Investing excess cash requires knowledge of the money market. The financial manager needs to know the various types of assets that can be purchased and the potential returns and risks associated with each type of investment. These short-term assets include certificates of deposits issued by commercial banks, commercial paper sold by large corporations, and treasury bills. Once the financial manager knows the different types of investments and the timing of the firm's cash needs, then excess cash may be invested in the best short-term assets that increase the firm's profitability.

And (2) invest excess cash

Requires knowledge of the money market

Estimating when the firm will need cash and when it will receive cash is an important facet of maintaining the firm's solvency. Some cash flows into and out of the firm on a regular basis, but other cash flows occur intermittently. For example, cash sales and collections for some items occur continuously over time, while there may be seasonal bulges or cyclical peaks and troughs for other items. Many cash outflows are on a continuous basis, as the firm pays wages and salaries and its suppliers for raw materials and inventory. Many payments, however, are intermittent. For example, taxes may be paid quarterly and debt retirement payments may be made annually. The financial manager needs to know when all these cash inflows and cash outflows are to occur so that the firm's liquidity needs may be balanced by its sources of payment.

There are a variety of tools available to help the financial manager perform these jobs. These tools are discussed in the next seven chapters. They include analysis of financial statements, budgeting (especially the cash budget), forecasting, and working capital management. Chapter 13 considers the construction of financial statements; Chapter 14 discusses the expansion of fixed assets and how long-term assets are depreciated. Financial statements provide the sources of data for ratio analysis (Chapter 15). There are a variety of financial ratios that may be compared with the ratios of other firms in the industry. Such comparisons will permit the financial manager to see if the firm is at least performing at the industry's norm.

Tools available to maintain liquidity

Planning includes the determination of level of output necessary to break even (Chapter 16), various forecasting techniques, and the cash budget (Chapter 17). These techniques help the financial manager anticipate the level of sales, the amount of assets necessary to obtain those sales, and any deficiencies in the firm's cash position. The last chapters in this section consider the management of these current assets (Chapter 18) and their financing (Chapter 19). In summary, Chapters 13 to 19 provide the financial manager with tools to help manage current operations, especially maintaining the firm's solvency and increasing its profitability.

Long-term investment decisions

The financial manager's job is not just limited to the management of short-term assets and liabilities, emphasizing meeting the firm's financial obligations as they come due. The financial manager also plays a role in the decision to invest in long-term assets (e.g., plant and equipment), and how to finance these investments. The investment decision is the general theme of Chapters 20 to 23. Financing long-term investments is the focus of Chapters 24 to 26.

There are many alternative long-term investments that a firm may make, and the financial manager helps allocate long-term capital within the firm. This choosing among competing long-term investments is called capital budgeting. Capital budgeting encompasses the entire operation of the firm. Different divisions within the firm compete for its resources, and the financial manager must help allocate resources within the firm. This allocation decision is similar to all economic decisions, for economics is the allocating of scarce resources among competing alternative uses. The financial manager performs the same function by allocating scarce financial resources among alternative uses within the firm. A capitalist economic system allocates on the basis of price, but the financial manager has no such simple means to allocate resources within a firm. The different departments within a firm do not bid for the resources, so the financial manager must use other techniques to allocate the firm's scarce resources. These techniques are discussed in Chapter 23; the financial manager needs knowledge of these methods of capital budgeting in order to allocate long-term capital within the firm.

Requires knowing cost of funds

Before the financial manager can allocate scarce long-term capital, there must be some criterion by which to judge possible investments. This is the firm's cost of capital (i.e., cost of funds necessary to finance the assets). To determine the cost of funds, the financial manager must understand the possible gains and risks associated with debt and equity financing. (These are covered in Chapter 21, Financial Leverage). Financial leverage may increase the investors' return on their money, but the use of financial leverage also increases the element of risk as the firm

And firm's capital structure

becomes obligated to pay interest and repay the principal. The increase in risk may decrease the attractiveness of the firm to investors and creditors. To compensate the investors and creditors for the increase in risk, the return to investors and rate of interest paid to creditors will increase.

The financial manager must determine the firm's optimal capital structure, that is, the best combination of debt and equity financing. This optimal capital structure minimizes the combined cost of debt and equity capital and is covered in Chapter 22. The cost of capital is a crucial component of capital budgeting because it is the criterion by which investments are judged. Thus the financial manager, in order to perform the role as the allocator of the firm's scarce capital, must also determine the firm's best combination of sources of finance. Hence the discussion of financial leverage (Chapter 21) and the firm's optimal capital structure (Chapter 22) precedes the discussion of capital budgeting (Chapter 23).

Chapters 24 to 26 consider the various sources of funds available to finance long-term investments. A firm may obtain finance from a variety of sources that range from creditors such as insurance companies to equity investors. The financial manager needs to be aware of the relative merits and costs associated with each source in order to match the particular source and the asset being acquired. In general, long-term assets should not be acquired with short-term liabilities, for such liabilities must be continually refinanced. Instead, long-term assets should be acquired by using long-term sources. While short-term sources are considered in Chapter 19 as part of the management of current operations, long-term sources are discussed in Chapters 24 through 26. Chapter 24 covers issuing securities, and Chapters 25 and 26 cover long-term debt and equity, respectively. Chapter 27 contains special topics (mergers, multinational operations, and bankruptcy). These topics are particular applications of the general principles covered earlier in the text. For example, the decision to merge or open a foreign operation employs capital budgeting concepts. The last chapter gives a general overview of financial management.

Obtaining long-term finance

In summary, the financial manager has a multifaceted, complex job. The financial manager is responsible for (1) assuring that the firm has sufficient liquidity and that excess funds are profitably invested, (2) participating in financial planning and control, (3) determining the firm's optimal capital structure, and (4) allocating scarce resources among the competing uses for the resources. That is an amazing job description, for it encompasses many elements of a firm's operation. It is not surprising to learn that large corporations have staffs that perform that financial manager's function. Unfortunately, small corporations, partnerships, and sole proprietorships frequently lack the resources to perform the financial manager's job adequately. The job, however, does not disappear. Financial decision making must still be performed, but it is frequently performed by a manager who lacks the training, the time, or the staff to do the job well. This inadequate performance can be costly, for financial problems are among the biggest causes of business failure.

TYPES OF BUSINESSES

Most business may be classified into one of three types: sole proprietorships, partnerships, and corporations. Other types of business include syndications, trusts, and joint stock companies. By far the largest in number is the sole proprietorship, but corporations own the majority of the nation's productive capacity, generate most of the sales, and earn most of the profits. Sole proprietorships are primarily "ma and pa" operations that are limited to small operations like the corner store. However, many large corporations had such modest beginnings, and American business is filled with stories of a talented person building a small business into an industrial leader.

(1) The sole proprietorship

A sole proprietorship, as the name implies, has one owner. The firm may employ other people and may borrow money, but the sole proprietor bears the risk of ownership and reaps the profits if they are earned. These are important elements of a sole proprietorship, for the firm has no existence without its proprietor. The firm is not a legal entity that can be held responsible for its action. The sole proprietor is responsible for the firm's actions and thus is legally liable for the firm's debts. Sole proprietors bear the risk of ownership, and this risk is not limited to their personal investments. They can lose more than the money invested in their businesses because the sole proprietor can be held liable for the debts incurred to operate the business. However, since the sole proprietorship is not a legal entity, the firm pays no income taxes. Any profits are considered to be income for the sole proprietor and thus are subject only to personal income taxation.

(2) Partnerships

A partnership is very similar to a proprietorship except that there are at least two owners (i.e., partners) of the business. While a partnership may have as few as two owners, there is no limit to the number of partners. A partnership has no life without its partners. The partners are the owners, and they reap the rewards and bear the risk of ownership. Each of the partners contributes something to the firm, and this contribution need not be money. For example, several partners may contribute money while others contribute expertise.

When a partnership is formed, the rights and obligations of the partners are established. The most important of these are the partner's shares of profits and the extent of the liability of the partners. In the simplest case, each partner contributes some percentage of the money necessary to run the business and receives this percentage of the profits. However, not all partnership agreements are this simple. For example, if one partner contributes cash and the other contributes expertise, the division of profits may not be 50–50. Instead, the distribution will be mutually established by the partners.

In general all the partners bear the risk of enterprise. Each partner is liable for the total debt of the firm. Thus the individual partner's liability is not limited to his contribution to the firm. While creditors initially seek settlement of claims from the firm, they can sue the partners for payment if the firm fails to meet the claims. If one partner is unable to pay the prorated share of these obligations, the other partners are liable for these debts. In addition, a partner's share may be seized to settle personal debts. The partner's creditors must initially sue the individual for personal obligations, but if these cannot be met, the creditors then have a claim on the partnership. While these claims and counter claims may be complex, the general order is that personal creditors have an initial claim on the partner's personal assets, and the firm's creditors have the initial claim on the partnership's assets. If personal assets are insufficient to meet the individual's obligations, then creditors may make a claim against that partner's share of the partnership. If the firm's assets are insufficient, then the partnership's creditors may make claims against the individual partners.

There is a type of partnership that grants limited liability to certain partners. These partnerships are called "limited partnerships;" in these the "limited partners" are liable only for their contributions. While these partners have limited liability, they have no control over the operation of the firm. Such control rests with the remaining (or general) partners who are subject to unlimited liability. This form of partnership is popular for very risky types of enterprises. For example, most Broadway shows are limited partnerships. There are two types of partners: the investors who finance the production and the producer who arranges for the production. The investors (who are called "angels") are limited partners who share the profits with the producer. These investors have limited liability, for the maximum amount that they can lose is their monetary contribution. The producers, however, have unlimited liability. The producers generally do not invest their own funds but instead stage the work with the limited partners' money. If, however, the producer incurs liabilities in excess of the money invested by the limited partners, then the producer becomes liable.

Limited partnerships are also common in mining and prospecting, in which case the limited partners invest the money and the unlimited partners prospect for the natural resource (e.g., gold or oil). Such limited partnerships protect the investors from unscrupulous people who might incur enormous expenses and leave the bills to fall on the other partners. The prime advantage of such partnerships is taxation, for any losses accrue to the individual partners, and the tax loss may be used to good

Limited partnerships

advantage by the individual partners. Such tax advantages (called "tax shelters"), however, were significantly reduced by the 1976 Tax Reform Law.

(3) The corporation

A corporation is an artificial, legal economic unit established by a state. Every corporation must be incorporated in a state. There is much variation in the individual state laws that establish corporations, and this variation has resulted in some states being more popular than others in which to form a corporation. Under the state laws, the firm is issued a certificate of incorporation that states the name of the corporation, the location of the corporation's principal office, the purpose of the corporation, and the number of shares of stock (shares of ownership) that are authorized (i.e., the number of shares that the firm may issue). In addition to the certificate of incorporation, the firm receives a charter that specifies the relationship between the corporation and the state. At the initial meeting of stockholders, bylaws are established that set the rules by which the firm is governed (e.g., the voting rights of the stockholders).

A legal entity

In the eyes of the law a corporation is a legal entity that is separate from its owners. It may enter contracts and is legally responsible for its obligations. This significantly differentiates corporations from sole proprietorships and partnerships. Once a firm incorporates, the owners of the corporation are liable only for the amount of their investment in the company. Owners of corporations have "limited liability," and this limited liability is a major advantage of incorporation. Creditors may sue the corporation for payment if the corporation defaults on its obligations, but the creditors cannot sue the stockholders. For many small corporations, however, limited liability may not exist. Creditors may ask that the stockholders pledge their personal assets to secure a small corporation's loans. Thus if the corporation defaults, the creditors may seize assets that the shareholders have pledged. If this should occur, then the liability of the shareholders was not limited to their initial investment. Limited liability does apply in substance to large corporations that have assets to pledge or sufficient credit ratings to receive unsecured loans. Thus an investor knows that upon purchasing the stock in a company such as General Motors, the maximum amount that can be lost is the amount of the investment. If the firm were to go bankrupt, then the creditors cannot seize the assets of the stockholders. Such limited liability is a major advantage of incorporating a firm, for occasionally a large corporation (e.g., Penn Central) does go bankrupt.

Ease of transferring ownership

A second potential advantage of incorporation is the ease with which title of ownership may be transferred from one investor to another. All that is necessary for such transfer is for the investor to sell the shares of stock (which are evidence of ownership) and have the name of the new owner(s) recorded on the corporation's record of stockholders. Such transfers occur daily through organized security exchanges like the New York Stock

Exchange. This transfer of ownership, however, may be considerably more difficult for small corporations or corporations that are owned by just a few stockholders. For the ease of transfer to occur, there must exist a ready market for the stock. For small corporations there is no ready market in their stock, and hence the owners may have difficulty transferring the title to their shares. Finding a buyer for stock in a small corporation may be a very difficult task. Thus, while the ease of transferring ownership is an advantage of incorporating, this advantage does not apply to all corporations.

A third advantage of incorporating is permanence. Since the corporation is established by the laws of the state, it is permanent until dissolved by the state. Proprietorships and partnerships cease when one of the owners dies or goes bankrupt and must be re-formed in order to continue to operate. Corporations, however, continue to exist when one of the owners dies. The stock becomes part of the deceased owner's estate and is transferred to the heirs. The company continues to operate, and a new corporation is not formed. Permanence offers a major advantage for incorporating if the owners envision the firm's growing in size and operating for many years, since the expense of re-forming the relationship among the owners is avoided.

Permanence

Perhaps the most important advantage of incorporating is taxation. Corporations and partnerships and sole proprietorships are taxed differently. In some cases this difference argues in favor of incorporating; under other circumstances the difference favors partnerships and sole proprietorships. Since the issue of taxation is so important, the remainder of this chapter will be devoted to it and its influence on the decision to incorporate.

Differences in taxes

TAXES AND THE DECISION TO INCORPORATE

Taxes play an extremely important role in financial decision making. Most of the decisions involving taxes stress minimizing the amount of taxes that the firm or individual has to pay. The diversity and complexities of tax laws that affect financial decision making are staggering and require tax expertise. Unfortunately, few individual businessmen can obtain this expertise and still perform their other roles. Hence some lawyers and accountants have become tax experts and sell their services to individuals and managers of firms.

Taxes are levied by governments at all levels. The sole proprietor through the manager of the largest corporations will find a variety of tax laws that affect the business. These taxes include corporate income taxes, capital gains taxes, state and local taxes on property such as real estate, plant and equipment, and inventory. Within this country there are thousands of governmental units ranging from small localities to the federal government. It is beyond the scope of this introductory text to discuss all the tax laws and government regulations that affect the decision making of a firm. However, reference to many of these laws is made throughout the text as the laws are appropriate to the particular topic being discussed. The purpose of this section is to illustrate how the differences in federal corporate and personal income taxation affect the decision to incorporate a business. However, before the question of incorporation can be approached, it is necessary to consider the important difference between the personal and corporate income taxes that affects the decision to incorporate. This difference revolves around the progressivity of the two taxes.

PROGRESSIVITY OF TAXES

The Federal Government's personal income tax is progressive. Other taxes, such as property taxes or sales taxes, are not progressive but are regressive or proportional. What do the terms progressive, regressive, or proportional imply?

Progressivity depends on the tax rate

Progressivity and regressivity are determined by the taxes paid relative to some tax base such as an individual's income or a corporation's profits. An income tax is progressive if, as the individual's income rises, the tax *rate* increases. It is not sufficient for the absolute amount of taxes paid to increase with the increases in income. For a tax to be regressive, the tax rate declines as the tax base increases. If the tax rate remains constant as income increases, then the tax is proportionate.

The difference between the progressive, regressive, and proportionate taxes is illustrated in Table 12–1. The first column gives an individual's income. The second and third columns illustrate a progressive tax, for the tax rate increases with the increases in income. The fourth and fifth columns illustrate a regressive tax, for the tax rate declines as incomes rise. The last two columns illustrate a proportionate tax, for the rate remains constant as income changes. As may be seen in this table, the absolute amount of tax paid increases in each case. However, the

TABLE 12–1   Differences in Taxes Paid Under Hypothetical Progressive, Regressive, and Proportional Tax Rates

INCOME	PRO-GRESSIVE TAX RATE	TOTAL TAX PAID	RE-GRESSIVE TAX RATE	TOTAL TAX PAID	PROPOR-TIONAL TAX RATE	TOTAL TAX PAID
$10,000	10%	$ 1000	10%	$1000	20%	$ 2000
20,000	15	3000	9	1800	20	4000
30,000	20	6000	8	2400	20	6000
40,000	25	10,000	7	2800	20	8000
50,000	30	15,000	6	3000	20	10,000

effect of the higher tax rates on the total amount of taxes is considerable as the income rises from $10,000 to $50,000. With the regressive tax structure, the tax rises from $1000 to $3000. With the progressive tax, the amount paid in taxes rises to $15,000.

Many people believe that taxes should be progressive because individuals with higher income are not only more able to pay but also should bear a larger proportion of the cost of the government. It is on this basis that many regressive taxes (especially the property tax) are criticized. Regressive taxes place a larger share of the cost of government on those individuals with the least ability to afford the burden. Arguments for progressive taxes, however, are primarily based on ethical or normative beliefs. It is a moral judgment that people with higher income should pay a proportionately higher amount of tax.

Progressivity is a moral issue

The federal personal income tax is progressive, for as the individual's income rises, the tax rate increases. As the individual reaches higher income tax brackets, the rate at which additional income is taxed rises. The tax rate on this marginal income is referred to as the individual's marginal tax rate. That the federal income tax is progressive is illustrated by Table 12–2, which gives the federal income tax for a married couple filing a

Federal personal income tax is progressive

TABLE 12–2   Marginal and Average Federal Income Tax Rates for a Married Couple Filing a Joint Return

TAXABLE INCOME	MARGINAL TAX RATE	TOTAL TAXES PAID	AVERAGE TAX RATE
$ 1,000	15%	$ 140	14.0%
2,000	16	290	14.5
3,000	17	450	15.0
4,000	19	620	15.5
8,000	22	1,380	17.25
12,000	25	2,260	18.83
16,000	28	3,260	20.38
20,000	32	4,380	21.9
24,000	36	5,660	23.58
28,000	39	7,100	25.36
32,000	42	8,660	27.06
36,000	45	10,340	28.72
40,000	48	12,140	31.03
44,000	50	14,060	31.95
52,000	53	18,060	34.73
64,000	55	24,420	38.15
76,000	58	31,020	40.82
88,000	60	37,980	43.16
100,000	62	45,180	45.18
120,000	64	57,580	47.98
140,000	66	70,380	50.27
160,000	68	83,580	52.24
180,000	69	97,180	53.98
200,000	70	110,980	55.49

joint return. The first column gives their taxable income (i.e., their income after they have reduced their gross income by any appropriate deductions and exemptions). The second column gives the tax rate on income earned in that tax bracket (i.e., the marginal tax rate). The third column gives the total taxes paid on the income, and the fourth column gives the average tax rate paid by the family on its taxable income (i.e., the total taxes paid divided by the level of income). As may be seen in the second and fourth columns, the marginal and average tax rates increase with income, which indicates that the federal income tax rate is progressive. However, the second and fourth columns also indicate there is a difference between an individual's tax on additional income (i.e., the marginal tax bracket) and the tax on the entire income. It is the marginal tax rate that affects an individual's behavior. For example, it is this marginal tax rate that influences the decision to purchase certain securities such as tax exempt state and municipal bonds.

Federal corporate income tax

The federal corporate income tax is a combination of progressive and proportionate taxes. The reason for this is that there are only three tax brackets. The first $25,000 of corporate income (profits) are taxed at the rate of 20 per cent. The next $25,000 are taxed at 25 per cent, and additional profits are taxed at a rate of 48 per cent. Thus the tax rate on additional profit is either 25 or 48 per cent. Since the total tax structure combines three steps, the average corporate tax is progressive. This is illustrated in Table 12–3, which shows different levels of corporate income and federal income taxes. The first column gives the corporation's taxable income; the second column gives the marginal tax rate. The third column presents the total tax that the corporation must pay, and the last column gives the average tax rate (i.e., the total taxes divided by the corporation's earnings). Thus, while the marginal tax rate is either 20, 25, or 48 per cent, the tax rate on the total corporate income starts at 20 per cent and approaches 48 per cent as the level of corporate income rises.

TABLE 12–3   Marginal and Average Federal Corporate Income Tax Rates

PROFITS	MARGINAL TAX RATE	TOTAL TAXES PAID	AVERAGE TAX RATE
$ 10,000	20%	$ 2,000	20.0%
25,000	20	5,000	20.0
40,000	25	8,750	21.8
60,000	48	16,050	26.8
100,000	48	35,250	35.3
150,000	48	59,250	39.5
200,000	48	83,250	41.6
500,000	48	227,250	45.5
1,000,000	48	467,250	46.7

Since the tax rate does rise with the increase in corporate profits, the corporate income tax is progressive, but this progressivity is simply the result of the first $50,000 being taxed at the lower rates.

The differences in the structure of the personal and corporate federal income taxes are illustrated by Figure 12–1, which plots the average and marginal personal and corporate income tax rates given in Tables 12–2 and 12–3. As may be seen from Figure 12–1, except at low levels of income, the corporate marginal tax rate is less than the personal marginal. For a single person the marginal tax rate rises even more rapidly than the joint marginal tax rate. As we will examine in the following section, this difference in the tax rates is a major reason for a sole proprietor to incorporate the business, for incorporating may reduce taxes.

Differences in personal and corporate income taxes

THE DIFFERENCES IN TAX RATES AND THE DECISION TO INCORPORATE

The effect of taxes on the decision to incorporate is illustrated by Table 12–4. This table shows the disposable income an individual will have with a single proprietorship or with a corporation. The table is divided into two cases. In the first example there is no reinvestment of funds in the business. In the second example an equal amount for the proprietor and the corporation is reinvested in the firm. Both sections of the table start with $50,000 of earnings. Taxes are then subtracted from these earnings to determine the individual's disposable income. Since the proprietorship pays no in-

Marginal and Average Tax Rates
(Federal Personal and Corporate Income Tax)

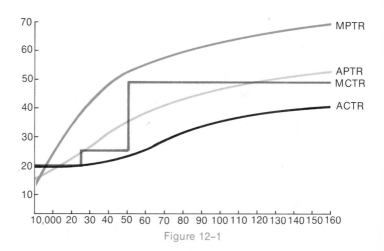

Figure 12–1

come taxes, in both cases the entire $50,000 becomes the income of the owner. In the first case the corporation pays $11,250 in corporate income tax, and the net earnings ($38,750) are distributed as dividends to the owner. The owner then pays personal income tax ($17,060 on the proprietorship's income and $11,478 on the corporation's dividends). The residual is disposable income. As may be seen in the last row of the first example, the disposable income is greater for the proprietorship ($32,940 versus $27,272). Why is it larger? The answer lies in the fact that for the corporation the $50,000 was taxed twice, once at the corporate level ($11,250) and once at the personal level ($11,478).

Reinvestment
argues for corporate
form

The second example in Table 12–4 illustrates a different situation in which funds are reinvested in the company. Once again, both the sole proprietorship and corporation earn $50,000. The corporation pays the owner and manager a $20,000 salary and has a net profit of $30,000. It then pays $6250 in corporate income tax and retains $23,750 in earnings which may be reinvested. The proprietorship, however, cannot retain earnings but must distribute its earnings to the owner. Thus, in the case of the proprietorship, the owner receives $50,000 but receives only $20,000 from the corporation. The owner then pays personal income tax of $17,060 and $4380, respectively, leaving a net income of $32,940 and $15,620. If the proprietor now invests $23,750 in the firm (as was done in the case of the corporation), the individual's disposable income is reduced to $9190, which is

TABLE 12–4   Comparison of Total Federal Income Tax
     for a Sole Proprietorship and a Corporation

CASE 1—NO RETENTION OF EARNINGS	Proprietorship	Corporation
Profits	$50,000	$50,000
Corporate income tax	—	11,250
Net profits	50,000	38,750
Earnings distributed	50,000	38,750
Personal income tax married filing a joint return excluding deductions and exemption	17,060	11,478
Disposable income	32,940	27,272

CASE 2—RETENTION OF EARNINGS		
Profit (before salary)	$50,000	$50,000
Salary	—	20,000
Corporate profits	—	30,000
Corporate taxes	—	6,250
Net available for reinvestment	—	23,750
Personal taxable income	50,000	20,000
Personal income tax	17,060	4,380
Disposable income	32,940	15,620
Personal reinvestment	23,750	—
Net disposable income	9,190	15,620

smaller than the $15,620 the owner obtained through the corporation. In this example the corporate form of enterprise resulted in total taxes of $10,620 but the proprietorship resulted in $17,060.

This tax saving is the result of how the corporation's funds were distributed. Corporations may pay salaries to managers who are also stockholders and treat these payments as expenses. Salaries to the sole proprietor are not permitted, and all profits are income to the owner. Thus it is the splitting of funds between the corporation and the owners which permits the corporate structure to take advantage of the lower tax rates. If the firm needs additional funds, then the ability to pay the salaries and retain earnings strongly argues for the corporate form of enterprise.

However, if the firm pays low salaries and distributes earnings as cash dividends, the argument is reversed. Cash dividends are subject to "double taxation" because they are paid from after tax earnings and are taxed again as part of the individual recipient's personal income. Such double taxation argues against incorporation. Thus the decision to incorporate is strongly influenced by (1) the amount of profits earned, (2) the tax rates on the firm's profits and the owners' income tax bracket, (3) the firm's need to retain earnings, and (4) the owners' need for income. These variables will, of course, differ for various cases; hence there is no clear-cut answer to the question to incorporate. However, if the sole proprietor intends to reinvest earnings and have the firm grow, it will probably be advantageous to incorporate.

OTHER TAX CONSIDERATIONS THAT ENCOURAGE INCORPORATION

Besides differences in the tax treatment given personal and corporate incomes, there are other elements in the tax laws that encourage incorporation. Two areas are particularly important: fringe benefits and capital gains. Income tax is levied when income is received, but a corporation may be able to increase its employees' benefits without increasing their taxes through the granting of fringe benefits. How employees' benefits can be increased without raising their taxes may be illustrated by the case of medical insurance. Virtually every person can use medical protection. If the insurance costs $300 a year, a person in the 25 per cent income tax bracket will have to earn $400 before taxes in order to have $300 after taxes to buy medical insurance. A corporation, however, may participate in a group insurance plan that covers the firm's employees. The employees do not receive monetary income but instead receive free medical insurance. The receipt of medical insurance is not treated as income for the purpose of personal

Fringe benefits and capital gains receive favorable tax treatment

income taxation. Such a fringe benefit is untaxed income. The firm still has the expense, but instead of paying the employees and having the income taxes, the firm buys the insurance and the employees receive the benefit of the firm's expenditures.

Fringe benefits have been a popular means of increasing the wages and salaries of many employees. Many large corporations have been willing to grant such fringes instead of increased wages because the cost of the fringes is less than the increase in wages that would be necessary for the workers to purchase the goods for themselves. Employees also realize the potential tax savings of fringe benefits, so these benefits may be an important reason for working for corporations. Many large corporations offer fringe benefits such as medical insurance, paid sick leave, and retirement programs. In many cases these benefits escape or defer income taxation. For example, retirement programs postpone the tax until the employee has retired. At that time the employee may have a lower level of income and thus be in a lower tax bracket.

Another tax reason for incorporating is the possibility of taking advantage of the lower tax rates on long-term capital gains. If an investor owns stock in a company for more than 12 months and sells the stock for a profit, the gain is taxed at the lower of 25 per cent of the gain or one half of the individual's income tax bracket. Thus, if the investor is in the 40 per cent tax bracket, the long-term capital gain will be taxed at 20 per cent. This tax law means that if a proprietor incorporates the business and subsequently sells it for a long-term capital gain, the profit from this sale will receive more favorable tax treatment.

Capital gains taxation, the handling of fringe benefits, and the differences in federal tax rates on personal and corporate income are important factors that must be considered when a proprietor or partners are considering to incorporate the business. The decision is not an easy one, for there may not be a clear-cut answer. However, if the owners aspire to have the firm grow in size, it is usually advantageous to incorporate. With the exception of selected types of partnerships that are given special tax treatment, firms of any substantial size are corporations.

SUMMARY

This chapter has considered (1) the many-faceted role of the financial manager, (2) forms of business, and (3) the effect of taxes on the decision to incorporate. The remainder of the text will develop the role of the financial manager. This role encompasses many vital aspects of the firm, from maintaining sufficient liquidity to meet bills as they come due to deciding which of the many competing investments the firm should make. The job includes planning, forecasting, analyzing financial statements, and budgeting. It is an important job that must be performed by all firms, whether they are small single proprietorships or large corporations. Managers and owners of small firms, however, rarely have the time and skills to perform the financial manager's many tasks well. Unfortunately many business failures may be attributed to this failure to perform well the roles of the financial manager.

The subsequent chapters will develop the various aspects of the financial manager's job. Part II of the text has four subdivisions. The first is the management and control of current operations. This encompasses preparation of financial statements, ratio analysis, planning and forecasting, and working capital management. The second part considers long-term investment decisions and covers financial leverage, cost of funds, and capital budgeting. These investments must be financed. The third section discusses the various sources: issuing new securities, long-term debt, and equity. The last section considers special topics such as growth through mergers, international investments, and bankruptcy. The final chapter gives an overview of financial management.

_____ KEY WORDS AND TERMS

profit maximization   transfer of title
wealth maximization   permanence
liquidity versus profitability   progressivity
sole proprietorship   regressivity
partnership   reinvested earnings
limited partners   fringe benefits
limited liability   capital gains
corporation

QUESTIONS AND PROBLEMS FOR THOUGHT
_____ AND DISCUSSION

1. If you buy stock in IBM, you have limited liability. What does that mean? If you start your own corporation, why may you not have limited liability?

2. One of the major advantages of incorporating may be the ease of transferring ownership in the corporation. Why is this more true for large than for small corporations? Why is this not true for partnerships?

3. It is often asserted that the property tax is regressive. Does

that mean homeowners with more valuable homes pay less property tax? Do you feel that taxes should be progressive?

4. Examine the federal income taxes paid on taxable income of $20,000 for a married couple filing a joint return and a single person. What is the difference? Do you believe that the difference is justifiable?

5. A firm has income (before interest, dividends, and taxes) of $200,000. Interest expense is $10,000, and preferred dividend payments are $30,000. What is the federal corporate income tax bill? Would the answer be different if the firm paid $40,000 in interest and no preferred dividend?

Chapter 13

ACCOUNTING STATEMENTS

Learning Objectives

- Construct a simple balance sheet.
- Construct a simple income statement.
- Calculate earnings per share.
- Differentiate between the time dimension of the income statement and the balance sheet.
- Illustrate how the statement of retained earnings shows the distribution of earnings.
- Differentiate a use from a source.
- List the weaknesses in accounting data.

"Annual income twenty pounds, annual expenditure nineteen nineteen six, result happiness. Annual income twenty pounds, annual expenditure twenty pounds ought and six, result misery."

Charles Dickens (David Copperfield)

The basic data for much financial analysis may be found in accounting statements. Managers, financial analysts, and investors use accounting statements to help them make decisions. Thus an understanding of accounting statements is crucial to the study of finance. Unfortunately it is not possible to cover in this chapter all the subtleties and theories of accounting relevant to the construction of these statements. This chapter does present the basic components of these financial statements and gives a foundation for understanding them, which is a basic requirement for managers, investors, and anyone else making financial decisions.

The statements covered in the chapter are the balance sheet, the income statement, the statement of retained earnings, and the statement of changes in financial position. This chapter is primarily descriptive and concentrates on the construction of the balance sheet and income statements. The use of the information presented on these statements will be covered in subsequent chapters.

THE BALANCE SHEET

Book value: assets
minus liabilities

What is a business worth? One method of answering this question is to enumerate what a business has, what is owed, and then calculate the difference. This difference is called the "book value" and may be indicative of what the business is worth. A balance sheet indicates a firm's book value because it lists the firm's assets and liabilities; the difference between these assets and liabilities is the firm's equity (i.e., the owners' investment in the firm). An example of a balance sheet for a hypothetical firm is given in Table 13–1. On the left hand side of the balance sheet are listed the firm's assets; the liabilities and net worth are listed on the right hand side of the balance sheet. A balance sheet need not necessarily be constructed in this form with the assets on the left and the liabilities and equity on the right. However, this particular form is frequently used, for it clearly illustrates the assets, liabilities, and net worth of the firm.

For a firm to operate it must have assets, and these assets are divided into the following three groups: (1) current assets, which are expected to be used or converted into cash within a year; (2) long-term assets, whose life span exceeds a year; and (3) investments.

Long-term assets

Long-term assets are the firm's plant, equipment, and land. These assets are used for many years in conjunction with the firm's current assets and employees to create the product or service that the firm offers for sale. The type and amount or long-term assets that a firm uses varies with the industry. Some industries like utilities or transportation require large amounts of plant and equipment. Firms in these industries must have large investments in long-term assets in order to operate. Not all firms choose to purchase these long-term assets. Instead the firm may choose to rent, and the renting of these assets is called leasing. In either case, leasing or owning, the firm utilizes primarily long-term assets to produce its output.

Depreciation
allocates the cost of
long-term assets

The hypothetical firm has substantial investments in long-term assets. The balance sheet indicates that the firm initially invested $800,000 in plant and equipment. This plant and equipment has been depreciated by $200,000 and is currently being carried on the books at $600,000. This depreciation is important because it is the process of allocating the cost of the equipment over its useful life. Thus the book value of the asset is reduced as it is used by the firm. (The methods of depreciation and their effects on the firm's earnings are discussed in Chapter 14.)

The firm also owns land worth $200,000. Land does not depreciate with use, and hence the book value of the land is the purchase price unless the value of the land has been restated to indicate a price change. For example, as a result of inflation, the value of the land may have risen, in which case the accountants

TABLE 13-1 Hypothetical Firm Balance Sheet as of December 31, 1976

ASSETS

Current Assets:

Cash and cash equivalents		$ 100,000
Accounts receivable ($310,000 less allowance of $10,000 for doubtful accounts)		300,000
Inventory		
Finished goods	300,000	
Work in process	250,000	
Raw materials	150,000	700,000
TOTAL CURRENT ASSETS		1,100,000

Plant and Equipment

($800,000 less accumulated depreciation of $200,000)		600,000
Land		200,000
		800,000
Investments		200,000
TOTAL ASSETS		$2,100,000

LIABILITIES AND STOCKHOLDERS' EQUITY

Current Liabilities:

Accounts payable		
Trade account	200,000	
Accrued wages	50,000	$ 250,000
Bank notes and current portion of long-term debt		100,000
Accrued interest		10,000
Taxes		40,000
TOTAL CURRENT LIABILITIES		400,000

Long-Term Debt:

Mortgage		400,000
5% bonds due 1999		200,000
TOTAL LONG-TERM DEBT		600,000
TOTAL LIABILITIES		1,000,000

Stockholders' Equity

Common stock ($2 par value; 200,000 shares authorized; 100,000 shares outstanding)		200,000
Additional paid-in capital		150,000
Retained earnings		750,000
TOTAL LIABILITIES AND STOCK-HOLDERS' EQUITY		$2,100,000

may have increased the land's value on the books. However, this revaluation rarely happens, and hence many firms have "hidden assets" such as land whose market value is understated.

Inventory: raw materials to finished goods

Firms must have goods and/or services to sell. These are the firm's inventory. Not all inventory is ready for sale, for some of the goods may be unfinished (goods in process), and there may also be inventories of raw materials. For the hypothetical firm the inventory is $700,000. This is subdivided into three classes: finished goods ($300,000), work in process ($250,000), and raw materials ($150,000). Only finished items are available for sale, and it may take a considerable amount of time to process raw materials into finished goods. Thus much of a firm's inventory may not be very salable and cannot be readily converted into cash.

Sales: cash or accounts receivable

When the goods or services are sold, the firm receives either cash or a promise for payment in the future. This credit sale generates for the firm an accounts receivable which the firm intends to collect during the fiscal year. For the hypothetical firm there is $300,000 in receivables. This is a net figure obtained by subtracting doubtful accounts ($10,000) from the total amount of receivables ($310,000). Since a firm may not collect all its accounts receivable, it is necessary to make an allowance for the doubtful accounts and enter only the net realizable figure in the tabulation of the firm's assets.

A cash sale generates for the firm the asset cash. Since holding cash will earn nothing for the firm, some of the cash may be invested in short-term money instruments (e.g., Treasury bills). Cash and short-term money instruments may be combined under a classification called cash and cash equivalents. For the hypothetical firm, cash and marketable securities are $100,000. This money is available to meet the firm's immediate financial obligations.

The summation ($1,100,000) of the cash and cash equivalents ($100,000), the accounts receivable ($300,000), and the inventory ($700,000) constitute the firm's current assets on December 31, 1976. It is the current assets that flow through the firm during its fiscal year. They are used to meet the firm's financial obligations which must be paid during the year. Thus the size and quality of the current assets are important in determining the firm's ability to meet its current obligations.

Assets other than those used in operations

The remaining entry on the asset side of the balance sheet is other investments. These investments are primarily securities such as stock in other companies. Since these securities may be readily sold and converted into cash, such assets may be treated as part of the firm's current assets. However, if the firm purchased the securities with the intention of holding them for several years as an investment, the securities may be treated as a separate category on the balance sheet. For the hypothetical firm, $200,000 is tied up in such investments. The summation of the short-term assets ($1,100,000), long-term assets ($800,000), and investments ($200,000) is the total assets ($2,100,000) owned by the firm. These assets are financed by the other side of the balance sheet, its liabilities and equity.

　　The firm's liabilities are divided into two groups: (1) current liabilities, which must be paid during the fiscal year, and (2) long-term liabilities, which are due after a year. Short-term liabilities are primarily its accounts payable and short-term loans. As the firm may sell goods on credit, so it may also purchase goods and raw materials on credit. This trade credit is short-term and is retired as the goods are produced and sold. Accounts payable also include wages and salaries that have been earned but not paid. For the hypothetical firm the total of these accounts payable is $150,000. Besides accounts payable the firm has other short-term debt which must be paid during the fiscal year. This includes short-term notes for funds the firm has borrowed from commercial banks or other lending institutions and that portion of its long-term debt that must be retired this year. For the hypothetical firm, these items are $120,000. The remaining current obligations are interest owed (accrued interest) and taxes that must be paid during the year. For the hypothetical firm, these are $10,000 and $40,000, respectively. The sum of all these current liabilities is $400,000. The financial manager must anticipate having sufficient cash to meet these current obligations as they fall due during the firm's fiscal year.

　　The firm has long-term obligations which are retired after the current fiscal year. These represent part of the permanent financing because these funds are committed to financing the business for a long period of time. Short-term liabilities cannot be considered part of the firm's permanent finance, since these liabilities must be paid relatively quickly. For the hypothetical firm the long-term liabilities consist of the mortgage on its plant and equipment ($400,000) and an issue of long-term debt ($200,000). The mortgage and long-term debt are periodically retired, and, as was indicated above, that portion of these long-term liabilities that is due in the current fiscal year is classified as a short-term liability.

　　In most balance sheets the firm's equity is given after the liabilities. There are three essential entries: the stock outstanding, additional paid in capital, and the earnings that have been retained. The stock outstanding and the paid in capital represent the cost of the stock when it was initially sold to investors. This cost is the sum of the par value ($2.00 in this case) times the number of shares outstanding (100,000) plus the additional paid in capital of $150,000. Thus, for the hypothetical firm, the investors paid $350,000 ($3.50 × 100,000) for the 100,000 shares. The retained earnings ($750,000) represent the accumulated earnings of the firm that have not been distributed (i.e., paid out) to stockholders in the form of dividends. If the firm has con-

Debt: long- and short-term

Short-term debt is retired during the fiscal year

Long-term debt is retired after the fiscal year

Equity is the owners' investment in the firm

sistently operated at a loss, then the retained earnings will be negative, indicating the accumulated losses of the firm. The retained earnings, like the common stock and paid in surplus, represent the investment by stockholders in the firm. Since they would receive the earnings if they were distributed, retained earnings become part of the stockholders' contribution to the financing of the firm. The distribution of the current year's earnings between cash dividends and retained earnings is shown in the statement of retained earnings presented below.

The sum of stock outstanding, additional paid in capital, and retained earnings is the net worth or book value of the firm. For the hypothetical firm the book value is $1,100,000. If the firm should cease operations and the assets were sold and the liabilities were paid off, then the owners would receive their investment in the firm. If the assets and liabilities are accurately measured by the dollar values on the balance sheet, then the book value is the amount the owners will receive in the liquidation. Thus, from an accounting viewpoint, the net worth is the value of the firm. However, for reasons that are discussed subsequently, the book value of the firm may be misleading.

Permanent capital: long-term debt and equity

Equity, like long-term debt, is part of the permanent capital of the firm, for it is not retired during the fiscal year. The sum of the long-term debt and equity is the permanent capital of the firm, for they are long-term commitments of funds to the firm. Such financing is the backbone of the firm's financial structure and should be used for financing all long-term assets. Short-term liabilities should not be used to finance long-term assets, because such liabilities must be continuously refinanced. Permanent capital, however, is long-term financing and may be used to finance both long- and short-term assets.

The construction of a balance sheet gives management an indication of the firm's financial position. For the hypothetical firm the balance sheet indicates that the firm owns assets valued at $2,100,000, owes liabilities of $1,000,000, and has equity of $1,100,000. The sum of the liabilities and equity must equal the sum of all the assets, for it is the liabilities and equity that are financing the assets. The assets could not be acquired if creditors and owners did not put up the funds. Hence the sum of the sources of funds (i.e., the liabilities and equity) must equal the sum of the assets. For the hypothetical firm, the balance sheet indicates that liabilities are financing 47.6 per cent ($1,000,000/$2,100,000), and the equity is financing 52.4 per cent ($1,100,000/$2,100,000) of the total assets. Therefore, the balance sheet indicates the proportion of the assets that are financed with debt and with equity.

Constructed at a point in time

Two additional points need to be made about balance sheets. First, a balance sheet is constructed at a specific time (e.g., the end of the fiscal year). It indicates the value of the assets, liabilities, and net worth at that moment and only at that moment. Since financial transactions occur continuously, a balance sheet may rapidly become out of date. Second, the values placed on the assets need not mirror their market value. Instead, the values of the assets may be over- or understated. For example, the firm owns accounts receivable and not all of these accounts may be paid. Therefore, the value of the firm's accounts receivable may be overstated. Also, the value of the firm's inventory may be overstated if, for example, it has to be sold at a loss to remove it from the shelves. As was explained earlier, the firm will set up a reserve against these potential losses. Allowances will be made for doubtful accounts and obsolete inventory in an effort to make the balance sheet entries more accurate. However, the allowances may be insufficient, and thus the value of the assets will be overstated. Conversely, the value of other assets may be understated. For example, the land on which the plant is built may have increased in value. The firm may continue to carry the land on its books at the cost of the land. This, of course, understates the value of the land if it has appreciated in value.

Book values are not market prices

For the book value of the firm to be a true indication of the value of the firm, the value of all the assets on the balance sheet should be stated at their market prices. However, the value of the assets stated on the balance sheet need not necessarily be their current market prices. Accountants suggest that assets should be valued conservatively at the lower of (1) cost of the asset or (2) market value. Such conservatism is prudent but may result in assets having hidden or understated value if any appreciation is not recognized. Under these circumstances the equity or net worth of a firm need not be a good measure of the value of the firm.

THE INCOME STATEMENT

The income statement tells investors how much the company earned during the fiscal year. It is a summary of receipts and expenses and hence indicates the firm's profits or losses. Table 13–2 is a simple income statement for a hypothetical firm. The statement starts with a summary of the firm's sources of revenue: sales ($1,000,000). Next follows a summary of cost of goods sold ($750,000), and the difference between sales and cost of goods sold, which is the gross profit ($250,000). After the gross profit is determined, selling and administrative expenses ($100,000) and interest charges ($40,000) are subtracted to determine the net profit on the sales ($110,000). If the firm had other sources of income, such as interest income ($10,000), this is added to the net profit on sales to give the firm's income before taxes ($120,000). Since there are federal and state corporate income taxes, to obtain the net income available to stockholders the corporate income tax ($50,000) must be subtracted from the profit

TABLE 13–2   Hypothetical Firm Income Statement for
            the Year Ended December 31, 1976

Revenue from sales	$1,000,000
Cost of goods sold	750,000
Gross profit on sales	$ 250,000
Selling and administrative expenses	100,000
Earnings before interest and taxes	$ 150,000
Interest expense	40,000
Interest income	10,000
Earnings before taxes	$ 120,000
Taxes	50,000
Earnings available for stockholders	$ 70,000
Number of shares outstanding	100,000
Earnings per share	$ .70

before taxes to obtain the net profit ($70,000). Stockholders are
generally not concerned with total earnings but with earning per
share. Thus the bottom line of the income statement is total
earnings divided by the number of shares (100,000). This is
referred to as earnings per share (EPS = $.70), which is the
amount of earnings available to each share of common stock.

Earnings: revenues minus expenses

After the firm earns profits, management must decide what
to do with these earnings. There are two choices: (1) pay out
some or all of these profits to stockholders in the form of cash
dividends or (2) retain the earnings. Retained earnings may be
used to purchase assets or retire liabilities. As was explained in
the previous section, the retained earnings on the balance sheet
are the sum of all the firm's profits that have accumulated during
the firm's life. These retained earnings have been put to use to

Earnings are either retained or distributed

finance the purchase of assets or to retire debt. How this year's
earnings were used does not appear on the income statement. All
that the income statement does is summarize the revenues and
expenses of the firm during the fiscal year and indicate whether
the firm produced a net profit or loss. To learn how the earnings
were employed and if there were changes in the firm's sources of
finance during the fiscal year, it is necessary to consult the state-

Retained earnings are used by the firm

ment of retained earnings and the statement of changes in financial position.

STATEMENT OF RETAINED EARNINGS

The statement of retained earnings indicates the amount of
the firm's current earnings that is added to the firm's previously
retained earnings. It shows the division of earnings between

those distributed to the stockholders and those retained to finance additional assets. The statement of retained earnings for the hypothetical firm is given in Table 13–3. The statement indicates that the firm had previously retained $700,000 of its earnings. In 1976, the firm earned $70,000 and distributed cash dividends of $20,000. Thus the firm retained $50,000 of its earnings and will enter its 1977 fiscal year with retained earnings of $750,000. This $750,000 represents the accumulation of earnings over the firm's life. These earnings are part of the stockholders' investment in the firm because they represent a claim on the firm's assets. Therefore, the $750,000 must also appear in the equity section on the firm's 1976 balance sheet.

There is a common misconception that if a firm has retained earnings, it has cash and can pay cash dividends. Retained earnings are not cash. After the firm earned these profits, it used them to purchase income-earning assets or retire outstanding debt. Thus they are used to increase the firm's profitability and are not held in the form of cash. How these earnings and the firm's other sources of finance were employed during the year is revealed by the statement of changes in financial position.

Retained earnings are not cash

STATEMENT OF CHANGES IN FINANCIAL POSITION

The statement of changes in financial position illustrates yearly changes in the firm's sources of finance and how these sources were employed. Formerly this statement was called the statement of sources and uses of funds and was also referred to as the "funds statement." This statement shows the various sources of finance and explains how the sources were utilized. Hence it gives a good indication of where the firm is going. For example, it will show if the firm had a large expansion in a particular asset such as plant and equipment. Furthermore, the statement of changes in financial position will identify recent changes in the firm's financing decisions. The importance of this statement has been recognized, for it is now required by the SEC in the annual reports issued by publicly held corporations. This section is designed to illustrate the importance of isolating how funds were acquired and used and not to develop the statement of the changes in financial position.

TABLE 13–3 Statement of Retained Earnings

Accumulated retained earnings 1975		$700,000
Earnings 1976	$70,000	
Dividends	20,000	
Increase in retained earnings		50,000
Accumulated retained earnings 1976		$750,000

The importance of the statement of changes in financial position may be illustrated by the following example. This statement brings to the foreground the distinction between income and cash. A firm with profits may not have cash, or a firm may have plenty of cash and not be earning profits. For example, a firm may sell output on credit for a profit. Although the firm has made a profitable sale, it has not received cash but has accepted an accounts receivable. This illustrates that a firm's earnings and cash position are two distinct things. The statement of changes in financial position, by indicating (1) the funds acquired by the firm and (2) where the funds were spent, helps fill the gap between the firm's reported earnings and its cash position.

Funds are used (1) to acquire an asset, (2) to pay off a liability, or are (3) distributed as cash dividends. Thus the acquisition of an asset or the reduction of a liability is a *use* of funds. Funds are acquired when an asset is sold, when a new liability is incurred, or when equity is increased. Disposing of an asset, issuing new debt, or income are all *sources* of funds. Thus the statement of changes in the financial position will indicate that increased debt is a source and that the increased plant and equipment is a use. By constructing such a statement of sources and uses of funds, it is possible to discern how the firm obtained funds during the year and how they were employed.

Changes in a firm's financing may be shown by comparing a firm's balance sheet for two consecutive years. Any asset that has decreased, any liability that has increased, or any increase in equity is a source of finance. Any asset that has increased or any liability that has decreased is a use of funds. This is illustrated for the hypothetical firm in Table 13–4, which gives the firm's balance sheets for 1975 and 1976. In order to illustrate the sources and uses, the 1975 and 1976 balance sheets have been laid out vertically with the liabilities and the capital placed below the assets. To the right of the balance sheets are two columns that give the change in the balance sheets from one year to the next. The first of these columns gives the uses of funds, and the second column gives the sources of funds acquired by the firm during the year.

This exhibit indicates that the firm's total uses of funds were $240,000, and these uses must be balanced by corresponding sources of finance. The exhibit also indicates the specific uses of the funds. For the hypothetical firm the important uses were an increase in inventory of $70,000 and a reduction in short-term debt owed the bank of $100,000. There were also increases in cash ($20,000) and accounts receivable ($25,000), and funds were used to reduce interest owed ($2,000), taxes payable ($3,000), and the mortgage ($20,000).

The firm's primary sources of funds were an increase in long-term bonds ($150,000) and the retention of earnings ($50,000). A reduction of $20,000 in plant and equipment also provided funds for the firm. Since the firm is carrying less plant

TABLE 13-4   1975 and 1976 Balance Sheets for a
Hypothetical Firm

	BALANCE SHEET DECEMBER 31, 1975	BALANCE SHEET DECEMBER 31, 1976	USES	SOURCES
Cash and cash equivalents	$ 80,000	$100,000	$ 20,000	
Accounts receivable	275,000	300,000	25,000	
Inventory	630,000	700,000	70,000	
Plant and equipment	620,000	600,000		$ 20,000
Land	200,000	200,000	—	
Investments	200,000	200,000	—	
Accounts payable	230,000	250,000		20,000
Bank notes	200,000	100,000	100,000	
Accrued interest	12,000	10,000	2,000	
Taxes	43,000	40,000	3,000	
Mortgage	420,000	400,000	20,000	
Bonds	50,000	200,000		150,000
Common stock	200,000	200,000		—
Paid in surplus	150,000	150,000		—
Retained earnings	700,000	750,000		50,000
			240,000	240,000

and equipment, this releases finance for other purposes. The remaining source of funds was an increase in accounts payable ($20,000). The sum of all these sources is $240,000 which financed the $240,000 uses of funds.

What has the isolating of sources and uses added to the financial manager's knowledge? By providing a more detailed breakdown of changes in specific assets and liabilities, it brings to the foreground changes in the firm's financial position. For the hypothetical firm there was an increase in long-term financing indicated by the increase in bonds and retained earnings. This has replaced a substantial amount of short-term financing, the bank loan. Thus there has been a substitution of more permanent financing for short-term debt. There has also been a substantial increase in inventory which may indicate that the firm is planning an increase in sales. However, this increase would also alert the analyst to the possibility of excess inventory which may cause future losses if sales fail to materialize. By isolating year-to-year changes in the firm's financial position, the analyst has a better indication of recent changes in the firm's operations and financial position than can be obtained from a single balance sheet.

Highlights significant changes in financial position

LIMITATIONS OF ACCOUNTING DATA

There are several weaknesses inherent in accounting statements, but they do not justify avoiding the financial analysis that employs accounting data. The financial analyst needs to be aware of the weaknesses so that analysis may be interpreted in light of any weaknesses in the accounting data.

(1) Nonmeasurable items

First, accounting data does not show nonmeasurable items such as the quality of the research department or the marketing performance of the firm. Performance is measured solely in terms of money, and the implication of accounting data is that if the firm consistently leads its industry (or is at least above average), its management and divisions are qualitatively superior to its competitors. There probably does exist a relationship between performance and superior financial statements, and IBM's strong financial statements mirror the quality of its management, research staff, and marketing ability. However, many a firm may be able to improve temporarily its financial position and achieve superior performance that cannot be maintained.

(2) Auditing weaknesses

Second, accounting data may not be sufficiently challenged by auditors. While accounting statements are audited, the auditors may lack knowledge of specific areas germane to the firm's accounting statements. For example, the auditors may accept the estimates of the firm's engineers because the auditors lack the specialized knowledge necessary to challenge the estimates. This is not meant to suggest that the auditors are incompetent but that they lack specific knowledge to verify the authenticity of some of the data used by the firm's accountants.

(3) Problem of aggregation

Third, accounting statements available to the public are aggregates. While the management of the firm has access to more detailed data, individual investors or security analysts, who use accounting statements as a basis for their analysis, may not have sufficiently detailed information. For example, a firm may not give its sales data by product lines. Aggregate sales data do not inform the public which of the company's products are its primary sources of revenue. Aggregate numbers on the firm's income statements and balance sheets may hide important information that the investor or security analyst could use in the study of the company. The accounting professional certainly is aware of this weakness, and there has been a trend to increase disclosure of information in financial statements.

(4) Valuation problems

Fourth, accounting data may be biased. For example, the valuation of assets by the lower of cost or market value may result in biased information if the value of the assets has significantly risen (as they may during periods of inflation). Such increases in value are hidden by the use of the historical cost, and thus the accounting statements are not giving a true indication of the value of the firm's assets. If the value of the assets has risen and this is not recognized by the accounting data, then the rate of return earned by the firm on its assets is biased upwards. If the true value of the assets were used to determine the rate of return that the firm is earning on its assets, the rate would be lower. In this case the use of historical cost instead of market value will result in inaccurate measures of the firm's performance.

A fifth problem with accounting data has developed within the last decade because of inflation. This makes comparisons of accounting data from 1966, 1971, and 1976 tenuous. Items purchased in 1966 cannot currently be replaced at 1966 prices. As the firm's plant and equipment wear out, these assets will have to be replaced at higher costs. For the firm to maintain its current capacity, additional financing will be required to cover the higher costs.

(5) Inflation

Accounting for periods of inflation poses one of the biggest problems facing accountants. The SEC requires that firms disclose what it would currently cost to replace inventory and plant and equipment used in operations. A charge sufficient to cover replacing the assets would be made during the accounting period. Thus, using this replacement cost accounting would reduce current earnings. However, without such adjustments the deterioration of the value of money is not indicated by accounting data.

Replacement accounting

The above discussion illustrates some limitations and weaknesses in accounting data. The data, however, do offer a means to analyze a company. While problems may exist with the data, that is not sufficient reason to avoid performing financial analysis that employs accounting data. As long as the analyst is aware of the potential weaknesses, the results of the analysis may be interpreted in the light of the weaknesses in the data being used.

SUMMARY

This chapter has covered the four basic accounting statements: the balance sheet, the income statement, the statement of retained earnings, and the statement of changes in financial position. The discussion has been descriptive. Certainly the theory and actual construction of the statements deserve further study by students of finance. This chapter can only serve as a brief introduction to these complex accounting statements.

Accounting statements are one of the basic sources of information used by financial analysts. The subsequent chapters will employ and develop data presented on these statements. Chapter 15 is devoted to ratio analysis which combines information on the various statements in order to perceive trends and to compare firms. In Chapters 21 and 22 the question of debt versus equity financing is covered. Later in the text all the various sources of funds are covered in detail.

KEY WORDS AND TERMS

current assets
inventory

> plant and equipment
> current liabilities
> accounts receivable
> long-term debt
> net worth
> retained earnings
> book value
> earnings per share
> source and use

QUESTIONS AND PROBLEMS FOR THOUGHT AND DISCUSSION

1. What is the time dimension of the four major accounting statements? Do you think the time dimension reduces the reliability of the balance sheet?

2. Investors frequently only glance at a firm's income statement. What are they looking for? Why may they be deceiving themselves?

3. The statement of changes in financial position has become increasingly important. What information does it give to the financial analyst?

4. From the following information construct a simple income statement and a balance sheet.

Sales	$1,000,000
Finished goods	200,000
Long-term debt	300,000
Raw materials	100,000
Cash	50,000
Cost of goods sold	600,000
Accounts receivable	250,000
Plant and equipment	400,000
Interest expense	80,000
Number of shares outstanding	100,000
Earnings before taxes	220,000
Taxes	100,000
Accounts payable	200,000
Other current liabilities	50,000
Other expenses	100,000
Equity	450,000

Chapter 14   DEPRECIATION

Learning Objectives

- Differentiate between assets that automatically vary with sales and fixed assets.
- Define depreciation and explain how accelerated depreciation allocates the cost of an asset more rapidly.
- Differentiate among the types of depreciation.
- Determine how depreciation is a source of funds.
- Explain why accelerated depreciation and investment tax credits stimulate investment spending.

"A reasonable allowance for the exhaustion, wear, and tear."

Federal Tax Code

Depreciation is the allocation of the cost of the fixed asset over its useful life. Depreciation reduces the value of the asset to allow for the deterioration that occurs as the asset is used. The bulk of this chapter is devoted to explaining and comparing the different methods of depreciation.

The first section considers the expansion of fixed assets as the firm expands. The second section is devoted to a general discussion of depreciation. The third section covers different methods for accelerated depreciation. The various methods are then compared in the next section of the chapter. The final section contains a brief discussion of tax credits.

EXPANSION OF FIXED ASSETS

As a firm grows, it will use more assets. Such expansion in assets is part of the firm's growing. Some assets automatically expand with the level of sales. For example, the level of inventory automatically expands as the firm grows because the firm must carry more inventory to meet the higher volume of sales. Other assets, especially long-term assets such as plant and equipment, will not automatically expand with the level of out-

Difference between automatic and periodic expansion of assets

put. Instead the plant and equipment will be used more intensely. The number of shifts using the plant may be increased, or employees may work overtime. However, if the expansion of sales continues and appears to be a permanent instead of a temporary increase in sales, management will expand the level of plant and equipment.

This difference between assets that automatically expand with the level of output and assets that increase only after a considerable rise in the level of output is illustrated in Figure 14–1. The left hand side illustrates those assets that increase with output. This relationship is shown by the steadily increasing line AA that represents the level of these assets at each level of sales. The right hand side illustrates the relationship between those assets that are increased only after the higher level of sales has been achieved. Thus from zero sales to sales of S_1, the level of plant and equipment remains constant, at A_1. After the level S_1 has been obtained, further increases in the level of output require expansion in the plant and equipment. Thus the level of assets rises from A_1 to A_2. This higher level of assets is maintained until sales rise from S_1 to S_2 when the plant and equipment must be further expanded. The level of fixed assets then rises to A_3.

Decision to expand should employ capital budgeting techniques

The decision to expand the level of operations is like any other investment decision and should be made with the help of the capital budgeting techniques presented in Chapter 23. These long-term assets, like all assets, must be financed. Since they are long-term assets, they should be purchased with long-term sources of finance. These sources are the topics of Chapters 25 and 26, which cover long-term debt and equity financing. Management of long-term assets is not limited to purchasing and financing but also includes depreciation and replacement. Long-term assets do not wear out in a single year but are used over a period of years. Depreciation is the process of allocating the cost of these assets over their useful lives. Long-term assets

Relationships Between Sales and Various Assets

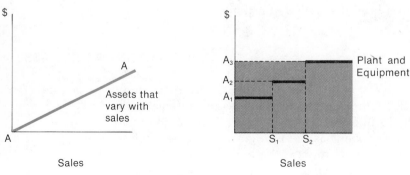

Figure 14–1

must eventually be replaced. This replacement may occur after the assets have been fully depreciated, that is, after the asset has been fully used. The replacement may also occur before the asset is fully used up if a newer, more efficient asset becomes available. The choice of the method of depreciation and the decision when to replace plant and equipment are important decisions in the management of long-term assets, and the remainder of this chapter is devoted to depreciation. The replacement decision is discussed as an example of capital budgeting in Chapter 23.

DEPRECIATION

One expense that requires special attention is depreciation. Depreciation is difficult because it represents a non-cash expense. It is the allocation of the cost of long-term assets like plant and equipment over their useful lives. This allocation of the costs may be in an even dollar amount each year, which is called straight line depreciation. The allocation may, however, be in larger dollar amounts during the initial years of the asset's life and smaller amounts during the last years of the asset's life. This is called accelerated depreciation. Accelerated depreciation may be achieved by either of two methods: sum of the years digits or double declining balance. As will be illustrated below, the advantage of accelerated depreciation is that it allocates the cost of the asset faster and thus initially decreases the firm's income taxes.

The allocation of the cost of an asset over its useful life

Depreciation expense arises in the following way. A firm has the following balance sheet:

ASSETS	LIABILITIES AND EQUITY
Cash $1000	Debt $500
	Equity $500

It currently only has cash that it acquired from investors (the equity) and from creditors (the debt). In order to produce some product, the firm uses the cash to acquire equipment. After the purchase the balance sheet becomes as follows:

ASSETS	LIABILITIES AND EQUITY
Cash $600	Debt $500
Equipment $400	Equity $500

The $400 cash was spent when the equipment was acquired, and thus the firm no longer has these funds. In effect it has traded one asset for another.

Applies to long-term
assets

The firm purchased the equipment to produce output to sell and anticipates that the equipment will operate for several years. For example, the firm may anticipate that the equipment may last four years, after which time it will have to be junked and replaced. If the firm anticipates that the $400 machine will have a useful life of four years, then the firm may depreciate the machine on a straight line basis for $100 a year. This is determined by using the following formula:

$$\text{Annual depreciation} = \frac{\text{cost}}{\text{anticipated useful life in years}}$$

In this case annual depreciation is:

$$\frac{\$400}{4} = \$100$$

Salvage value

In effect the firm is saying the $100 worth of the machine is depreciated or consumed each year and that at the end of four years the machine is totally consumed and valueless.

If the equipment can be sold after four years, then it has a salvage value. Salvage is important, for the anticipated salvage value must be subtracted from the cost of the equipment to determine the cost that may be depreciated. If the anticipated salvage value for the $400 piece of equipment is $100, then only $300 ($400 − $100) may be depreciated. Thus the annual depreciation expense would be $75 ($300/4) instead of the annual depreciation charge of $100, which is used when there exists no salvage value. Thus salvage value reduces the amount of the annual depreciation expense.

Why depreciation is
important

Depreciation is important for two reasons. First, since it is an expense, it alters the firm's profits and taxes. Second, since depreciation is a non-cash expense, it is treated in finance as a source of funds for the firm. Both these points are discussed below and are illustrated by the depreciation expense on the above firm's $400 piece of equipment. To simplify the illustration, straight line depreciation is used, and there is no salvage value. The annual depreciation expense is thus $100.

Effect on profits and
taxes

The importance of depreciation expense on profit and corporate income tax is illustrated as follows. If the output produced by the firm's machine is sold for $800, and if, after operating and administrative expenses of $500, the firm has a profit of $300, is the $300 a true statement of the profit? The answer is no, because no allowance has been made for the $100 of the machine's value that has been consumed to produce the output. The true profit is not $300 but $200, which is $300 gross profit minus the $100 depreciation expense. The firm now pays corporate income tax on its profit of $200 and not on the profit before the depreciation expense. If the corporate income tax rate is 25%, then the firm pays $50 (.25 × $200) in taxes instead of $75 (.25 × $300) which it would have to pay if the depreciation expense were omitted. Since the depreciation expense reduces the firm's profits, it also reduces its income taxes.

Since the firm bought the equipment in the first year, it may be suggested to add the entire cost of the equipment to the firm's expenses for that year. Would the firm have a true statement of its profits? Once again, the answer is no, because the firm's costs are incorrectly stated. The firm's expenses would be $900, which includes the $500 operating expense and the $400 cost of the equipment. The firm would be operating at a loss of $100 ($800 revenues minus $900 expenses). This understates the profits because the entire equipment was not consumed during the year. Only one fourth of the equipment's value was consumed during the first year. Hence, only one fourth of the equipment's value should be charged (i.e., "expensed") against the firm's annual revenues. Overstating depreciation, like understating depreciation, alters the firm's profits.

The second important feature of depreciation is that it is a source of funds. In the above example, the $100 depreciation expense did not involve an outlay of cash. The operating and administrative expenses required that the firm make an outlay of money, but the depreciation expense did not involve the expenditure of money. The outlay of cash occurred when the machine was initially purchased and not while it was being used. Depreciation is a non-cash expense item that allocates the initial cash outlay (i.e., the purchase price of the equipment) over its useful life. Since no cash is expended by the firm as a result of the depreciation expense, depreciation is thus said to be a source of funds because it is recouping the original outlay for the machine. Hence depreciation increases the flow of cash in the firm.

This seemingly contradictory statement (that an expense will increase the firm's cash flow) may be illustrated by the above example. A simple income statement for the firm is as follows:

Depreciation expense is added back to income and becomes a source of funds

Sales	$800
Operating Expenses	500
	300
Depreciation	100
Gross profit	200
Taxes	50
Net profit	$150

Only the operating expenses ($500) and the tax ($50) required a disbursement of cash. The firm has $250 ($800−$550) left. This is the $150 profit and the $100 depreciation expense which is added back to get the cash flow generated by operations. Thus cash flow is the profit (after taxes) plus depreciation expense.

The firm has $250 that it may use and $100 of those funds is the result of the depreciation expense. Hence depreciation expense is said to be a source of funds for the firm. The firm must now decide what to do with the $100 generated by the depreciated asset. For example, it may restore the depreciated asset, purchase a different asset, retire outstanding debt, or make payments to stockholders. Each of these acts is, of course, a use for the funds generated by the non-cash expenditure, depreciation.

ACCELERATED DEPRECIATION

Conceptually, accelerated depreciation is no different than straight line depreciation except that a greater proportion of the asset's purchase price is depreciated in the early years of the asset's life. Depreciation charges thus are larger when the plant and equipment are new and smaller than when the plant and equipment are old. This variation in the expense, of course, alters the firm's profits. When the depreciation charge is larger, the firm's profits and corporate income taxes are smaller. By using accelerated depreciation the firm is able initially to decrease its profits and taxes but increase its cash flow.

Sum of the digits

There are two methods of accelerated depreciation: the sum of the years digits and the declining balance. The sum of the digits adds the number of years that the asset will be depreciated and uses the sum as a base. Thus if the estimated life of a machine is four years, then the following numbers are added: $1 + 2 + 3 + 4 = 10$. This number, 10, is employed as the denominator in a ratio that is used to determine the proportion of the asset's value that may be depreciated each year. The numerator in this ratio is the number of years left in the useful life of the asset. Thus for an asset that has four years of useful life the amount depreciated in the fourth year (i.e., one year left in the asset's useful life) is 1/10 of the asset's cost. For the $400 piece of equipment used in the example in the previous section the amount that would be depreciated in each of the equipment's four years of useful life is as follows:

YEAR	DEPRECIATION FACTOR	ANNUAL DEPRECIATION EXPENSE	BOOK VALUE OF THE ASSET
1	4/10	.4 × 400 = $160	$240
2	3/10	.3 × 400 = 120	120
3	2/10	.2 × 400 = 80	40
4	1/10	.1 × 400 = 40	0

Double declining balance

The double declining balance method of depreciation uses a constant rate instead of a constant dollar amount, as is used in the straight line method. The value of the asset is depreciated at some constant percentage, like 33.3 per cent or 50 per cent. The title "double declining balance" implies that the rate to be used is double the rate employed in the first year under the straight line method of depreciation. Thus, if a piece of equipment is to be depreciated at the rate of 10 per cent of its total cost for 10 years, then under the double declining balance method the value of the asset would be reduced by 20 per cent each year.

How the method is applied may be illustrated with the $400 piece of equipment used in the previous section. If straight line depreciation is used, it is depreciated over four years at $100 a year. Thus the initial depreciation rate was 25 per cent ($100/400 = .25). With the double declining balance method of depreciation this rate is doubled to 50 per cent, and the asset's value is reduced by 50 per cent each year. Thus depreciation in the first year is .50 × $400 = $200, and the depreciation schedule for the four years becomes:

YEAR	ANNUAL DEPRECIATION EXPENSE	BOOK VALUE OF ASSET AFTER DEPRECIATION
1	$200	$400 − $200 = $200
2	100	200 − 100 = 100
3	50	100 − 50 = 50
4	25	50 − 25 = 25

The value of the asset (i.e., the third column) is reduced by 50 per cent each year to determine each year's depreciation expense. For example, the value of the asset is $200 after the first year. The depreciation expense in the second year is $200 × .5 = $100, and the value of the asset is reduced to $100 (i.e., $200 − $100). After four years the machine has been depreciated by $375, and $25 of the value remains. With the double declining balance method of depreciation the total value is never completely depreciated (i.e., the book value of the asset never reaches zero). As is illustrated by the third column, the book value of the asset declined each year by the same percentage, but the absolute dollar amount of the decline is less each year. While the depreciation expense was $200 in the first year, it is only $25 in the fourth year. The fixed percentage (i.e., the 50 per cent) is being taken of a smaller value each year. Thus the total amount of depreciation approaches the initial value of the asset but does not equal it.

To avoid this problem, firms that use the double declining balance method of depreciation switch to straight line depreciation whenever the amount of depreciation by the double declining balance method is less than that obtained by straight line. The remaining value of the asset then is depreciated on a straight line basis for the rest of the asset's life. By making this switch the problem of the asset having a residual value that is not depreciated is avoided. This technique is illustrated by the following schedules:

YEAR	ANNUAL DEPRECIATION EXPENSE	BOOK VALUE OF ASSET AFTER DEPRECIATION
1	$200	$200
2	100	100
3	50	50
4	50	0

For the first two years the accelerated method is used, which reduces the value of the asset to $100 after two years. The $100 value then is spread evenly over the remaining two years of the asset's life so that after four years the asset is fully depreciated.

METHODS OF DEPRECIATION COMPARED

Differences revolve around their effect on earnings, taxes, and cash flow

All three methods of depreciation allocate the cost of plant and equipment over their useful lives. The differences among them are related to their effect on the firm's profits and thus to their effects on the firm's taxes and cash flow. These methods are summarized in Table 14–1, which compares the methods. The table is divided into three sections. The first section illustrates straight line depreciation, while the second and third sections illustrate accelerated depreciation (sum of the digits and double

TABLE 14–1   Comparison of Straight Line and Accelerated Depreciation

YEAR	OPER-ATING REVENUES	DEPRE-CIATION EXPENSE	INCOME BEFORE TAXES	INCOME TAXES	NET INCOME AFTER TAXES	CASH FLOW
Straight Line Depreciation						
1	$300	$100	$200	$50	$150	$ 250
2	300	100	200	50	150	250
3	300	100	200	50	150	250
4	300	100	200	50	150	250
Totals		400		200	· 600	1,000
Accelerated Depreciation (Sum of the Digits)						
1	300	160	140	35	105	265
2	300	120	180	45	135	255
3	300	80	220	55	165	245
4	300	40	260	65	195	235
Totals		400		200	600	1,000
Accelerated Depreciation (Double Declining Balance)						
1	300	200	100	25	75.00	275.00
2	300	100	200	50	150.00	250.00
3	300	50	250	62.50	187.50	237.50
4	300	50	250	62.50	187.50	237.50
Totals		400		200	600	1,000

declining balance, respectively). The first column gives the year, and the second column gives the firm's operating revenues after all expenses except depreciation. The third column gives the depreciation expense for each of the methods. The remaining four columns illustrate the effects of depreciation expense. The fourth column presents the firm's taxable income; the fifth column gives the income taxes, and the sixth column gives the net income or profit after the taxes. The seventh column gives the firm's cash flow, which is the sum of its earnings after taxes plus its depreciation expense. As may be seen in the table, the accelerated methods of depreciation initially (1) reduce the firm's taxable income, which reduces its taxes, and (2) increase the firm's cash flow.

The table, however, also illustrates that the accelerated methods of depreciation increase the firm's income and taxes and reduce its cash flow in the later years of the asset's life. Actually the total depreciation expense, net income after taxes, taxes, and cash flow over the asset's life are the same for all three methods of depreciation. This can be seen by adding the depreciation expense, taxes, net income, and cash flow columns. The sums are equal for all three methods of depreciation. If accelerated depreciation does not ultimately reduce the firm's taxes and increase its cash flow over the life of the asset, what then is the advantage of accelerated depreciation? The answer to this question is the timing of the taxes and the cash flows. Accelerated depreciation increases the firm's cash flow during the early years of the asset's life and delays the payment of the taxes to the latter years of the asset's life. Accelerated depreciation increases the cash flow now, and thus the firm has the funds to reinvest now and thus earn more profits. By deferring the taxes, the firm is receiving a current loan from the Federal Government. And what is equally important, this loan has no interest cost. In effect the Federal Government, by permitting accelerated depreciation, is granting firms interest-free loans that may be used to earn more profits. Accelerated depreciation is another of those devices that the Federal Government uses to induce behavior. By granting accelerated depreciation, the Federal Government encourages investment in plant and equipment, for firms want to take advantage of the delayed taxes and the initial increased cash flow. By encouraging such investment, the Federal Government is inducing firms to increase the productive capacity of the nation and to increase the level of employment, for workers must build the plant and equipment and operate it after it has been installed.

Accelerated depreciation initially reduces profits and increases cash flow

THE TAX CREDIT

An alternative means available to the Federal Government to induce spending on plant and equipment is the tax credit. A

Tax credit reduces taxes payable

tax credit is the ability to reduce taxes by some amount (i.e., it is a credit against one's tax liabilities). For example, the Federal Government may permit firms that invest in equipment to reduce their taxes by 10 per cent of the cost of the equipment. Thus, if equipment costs $1 million, the firm may then reduce its federal income taxes by $100,000 (.10 × $1,000,000). Such a reduction in taxes increases the cash flow from the equipment, which in turn stimulates investment spending.

Tax credits may also be given to individuals as well as firms. For example, purchases of certain homes earned credits for individuals against their 1975 federal income tax. This particular tax credit was designed to stimulate the homebuilding industry by encouraging buyers to invest in newly built homes. Purchases of secondhand homes were not eligible for the credit. Thus the credit specifically encouraged purchases of new homes (perhaps at the expense of old homes) as a means to relieve the building industry's economic slump.

Tax credits have also been suggested as a means to encourage the installation of energy-saving equipment. For example, President Carter's energy proposals include tax credits for the installation of home insulation. The tax savings would be some proportion of the cost of installation. This would have the effect of reducing the cost by the amount of tax savings. This reduction in cost should increase the quantity demanded. Thus, by offering the tax credits, the Federal Government is encouraging (even inducing) homeowners to install the energy-saving insulation.

The tax credit is a flexible policy tool

Tax credits can be a very flexible policy tool. The credit may be changed from year to year to be consistent with the Federal Government's current policy. For example, in 1975 the investment tax credit was 10 per cent, while previously it had been 7 per cent. Such variation was, of course, designed to stimulate more investment spending in 1975 to help fight unemployment. During periods of high levels of employment and rising prices, the Federal Government reduces or eliminates the credit to reduce investment spending as one means to fight the inflation. The reverse would apply during periods of higher unemployment, for the tax credit can be used to stimulate the economy. This flexibility offered by tax credits is desirable because the Federal Government can use these credits to affect spending behavior without changing the structure of the tax system.

SUMMARY

This chapter has considered the allocation of the cost of long-term investments over their useful life. This allocation of cost is called depreciation. There are two classes of depreciation, straight line and accelerated. Under straight line depreciation the same dollar amount is subtracted each year from the value of the investment. Under accelerated depreciation the initial cost of the investment is reduced more rapidly, for larger dollar amounts are subtracted during the early years of the asset's life. Thus accelerated depreciation permits the cost of the investment to be written off faster, which initially reduces the firm's profits and income taxes. Since depreciation is a noncash expense, accelerated depreciation initially increases the cash flow from the investment. This increased cash flow may be reinvested to increase the profitability of the firm.

Rules for the use of depreciation are established by Congress and the Internal Revenue Service. Since accelerated depreciation writes off an investment more rapidly and increases the cash flow generated by the investment, it encourages capital spending. Tax credits which reduce taxes payable also encourage spending. Both accelerated depreciation and tax credits are used by the Federal Government as tools of economic policy. By altering firms' ability to use accelerated depreciation and tax credits, the Federal Government induces behavior consistent with the economic goals of full employment, stable prices, and economic growth.

KEY WORDS AND TERMS

straight line depreciation
salvage value
cash flow
double declining balance
sums of the digits
tax credit

QUESTIONS AND PROBLEMS FOR THOUGHT
AND DISCUSSION

1. If a firm uses accelerated instead of straight line depreciation, can the firm depreciate an asset by a larger amount over the asset's useful life? If a firm uses accelerated instead of straight line depreciation, what effect will this have on the cash flow from an investment in plant and equipment?

2. The right to use accelerated depreciation is granted by the Federal Government. Why does the Federal Government permit the use of accelerated depreciation? What purpose does it serve? What other alternatives are available to the Federal Government to achieve the same goals?

3. Since a tax credit increases profits but accelerated deprecia-

tion reduces profits, does the former encourage and the latter discourage investment spending?

4. Can all assets be depreciated? Why are current assets such as accounts receivable not depreciated?

5. A firm has earnings of $12,000 before interest, depreciation, and taxes. A new piece of equipment with an expected life of five years is installed at a cost of $10,000. The equipment has no anticipated salvage value, and the firm pays 25 per cent of its earnings in taxes. What are the earnings and cash flow in years one and five for the firm using the three methods of depreciation discussed in the chapter? What is the source of the differences in earnings and cash flows?

Chapter 15   RATIO ANALYSIS

"Mathematics is the science which
draws necessary conclusions."

Benjamin Pierce

Perhaps the most frequently used tool to analyze a company is ratio analysis. This tool is popular because it is readily understood, and ratios can be computed with ease. They are used by a firm's management, creditors, and investors, for ratio analysis facilitates comparisons. Management may use ratio analysis as (1) a planning device, (2) a tool for control, or (3) a means of identifying weaknesses within the firm. This type of analysis is particularly useful for isolating problems within the firm. After identifying these weaknesses, the financial manager can take remedial action to correct the problem. Failure to take a positive course of action will result in further deterioration, which will reduce the value of the firm.

Besides management, ratio analysis may be employed by creditors and investors. Creditors may employ it to establish the ability of the borrower to pay interest and retire debt. Investors may use ratios to compare firms in an industry for the purpose of selecting superior securities for investments. The data used in ratio analysis are easy to obtain, for many ratios employ numbers available in a firm's annual report. Thus ratio analysis is a simple, convenient means to obtain an indication of a firm's performance.

While a variety of people use ratio analysis, they need not compute the same ratios. There is a large number of ratios that may be computed. The individual should select those ratios that are best suited to the individual purpose. For example, a bond holder is concerned about the firm's ability to pay the interest and repay the principal and is less concerned with the rate at which the firm's inventory is sold. While the rate at which inventory turnover may affect the ability of the company to pay the interest and principal, the bondholder is more concerned with a more aggregate picture of the firm's financial position than just the inventory turnover. Thus while bondholders may compute any number of ratios, they should reduce the number of ratios and compute those that are relevant to their needs.

TYPES OF RATIOS

Ratio classifications

While there are a large number of possible ratios, they may be classified under one of the following groups: (1) liquidity, (2) activity, (3) profitability, (4) leverage. Liquidity ratios give an indication of the cash position of the firm. They indicate the ability of the firm to pay its bills as they come due. Activity ratios are concerned with the speed that non-cash current assets such as inventory turnover. These ratios indicate how rapidly inventory and receivables flow through the firm and how rapidly they convert to cash. Profitability ratios are a measure of the performance of the firm; they answer such questions as how much the firm is earning on its equity. Leverage ratios are concerned with the extent that debt is used to finance the firm's assets.

Time series and cross section analysis

These ratios may be computed and interpreted from two viewpoints. They may be compiled for a period of years to perceive trends; this is *time series analysis*. The ratios may be computed at the same time for several firms within an industry; this is *cross sectional analysis*. Time series and cross sectional analysis may be used together. Rarely will all the ratios indicate the same general tendency. When they are taken as a group, the ratios should give the investigator an indication of the direction in which the firm is moving and how it compares with other firms in its industry.

In the sections that follow, several ratios are discussed and illustrated. These ratios do not exhaust all the possible ratios, and certainly the analyst may find that in a specific occupation additional ratios or more sophisticated versions of some of the ratios presented below are needed. The purpose of this chapter is only to serve as an introduction to ratio analysis and to indicate how ratios are compiled, interpreted, and used. To illustrate the ratios, the balance sheet (Table 15-1) and income statement (Table 15-2) of a hypothetical firm will be used.

Liquidity Ratios

Liquidity = ease of conversion to cash without loss

Liquidity is the ease with which assets may be converted into cash without loss. If a firm is liquid, it will be able to meet its

TABLE 15-1 Hypothetical Balance Sheet

ASSETS		LIABILITIES AND STOCKHOLDERS' EQUITY	
Current Assets		Current Liabilities	
Cash	$ 2,000	Accounts payable	$13,500
Short-term investments	200	Other current expenses	4,200
Accounts receivables	21,000	Taxes due	4,100
Inventory	24,000	Total Current Liabilities	21,800
Total Current Assets	47,200	Long Term Debt	15,600
Plant and Equipment		Stockholders' Equity	
Land	1,500	Common stock	5,000
Buildings	12,600	Retained earnings	38,900
Machinery	20,000	Total Liabilities and	
Total Assets	$81,300	Stockholders' Equity	$81,300

bills as they come due. Thus liquidity ratios are useful not only to short term creditors of the firm who are concerned with being paid but also to the firm's management who must make the payments. The ratios are called "liquidity ratios" because they give an indication of the degree of liquidity or "money-ness" of the current assets of the company.

THE CURRENT RATIO

The current ratio is the ratio of current assets to current liabilities.

Current ratio = Current assets/Current liabilities

It indicates how well the current liabilities, which must be paid within a year, are "covered." For the hypothetical firm the current assets are $47,200 and the current liabilities are $21,800; thus the current ratio is

$$\frac{\$47,200}{\$21,800} = 2.17,$$

which indicates that for every dollar that the firm must pay

TABLE 15-2 Hypothetical Income Statement

Sales		$100,000
Credit sales	$84,000	
Cash sales	16,000	
Cost of goods		80,000
Gross profit		20,000
Interest expense		1300
Income tax		9200
Net profit		$ 9500

within the year, there is $2.17 in an asset that is either cash or should become cash during the year.

For most industries it is desirable to have more current assets than current liabilities. It is sometimes asserted that it is desirable to have at least $2 in current assets for every dollar in current liabilities (i.e., a current ratio of at least 2:1). If the current ratio is 2:1, then the firm's current assets could deteriorate in value by 50 per cent and the firm is still able to meet its short-term liabilities. While such rules of thumb are convenient, they need not apply to all industries. For example, electric utilities usually have current liabilities that exceed their current assets. Does this worry short-term creditors? No, because the short-term assets are of high quality (accounts receivable from electric users). Should a person fail to pay the electric bill, the company will cut off service, and this threat is usually sufficient to induce payment. The higher the quality of the current assets (i.e., the higher the probability that these assets can be converted to cash at their stated value), the smaller the need for the current ratio to exceed 1:1. The reason for selecting such a rule of thumb as a current ratio of 2:1 is that creditors frequently believe that not all current assets will in fact be converted into cash, and to protect themselves the creditors want a current ratio of at least 2:1.

While management also wants to know if the firm has sufficient liquid assets to meet its bills, the current ratio may have an additional use to management. A low current ratio is undesirable because it indicates financial weakness. A high current ratio may also be undesirable, for it may imply that the firm is not using funds economically. For example, the firm may have issued long-term debt and used it to finance too much inventory or accounts receivable. The high current ratio may also indicate that the firm is not taking advantage of available short-term financing. Since short-term debt tends to be cheaper than long-term debt, failure to use short-term debt may reduce profitability. Thus a high or low numerical value for the current ratio may be a signal that the management of short-term assets and liabilities needs changing.

WEAKNESSES IN THE CURRENT RATIO

While the current ratio gives an indication of the ability of the firm to meet its current liabilities as they come due, the ratio does have weaknesses. The current ratio may be readily changed, and it is an aggregate measure of liquidity that does not differentiate the degree of liquidity of the different current assets. The current assets may be cash or inventory, and the current ratio does not distinguish between them. The following section considers these disadvantages of the current ratio and suggests alternative measures of liquidity that give a better picture of the liquidity position of the firm.

That the current ratio may be affected with ease may be shown by the following which gives a very simplified balance sheet for a firm.

ASSETS		LIABILITIES AND CAPITAL	
cash	$1000	accounts payable	$3000
inventory	4000	short-term notes	3000
accounts receivable	5000	long-term debt	5000
plant and equipment	5000	equity	4000

The current ratio of this firm is 1.67 ($10,000/$6000). The management of the firm may increase the current ratio by any one of the following ways. First, management may sell plant and equipment for cash, which will increase the current assets while holding constant the current liabilities, and thus the current ratio rises. While this does increase the degree of liquidity, it may be detrimental to the firm, for the firm may need plant and equipment in order to produce. Thus liquidity has been bought at the expense of productive capacity.

Management may also sell plant and equipment for cash and use the cash to retire current liabilities (such as the short-term note or the accounts payable). This certainly increases the current ratio because the firm is reducing the denominator (current liabilities) in the ratio. For example, if the firm sold $1000 in long-term equipment and retired $1000 of the accounts payable, the current ratio for the firm would rise from 1.67 to 1.8. While the degree of liquidity has been increased, it may have again been bought at the expense of productive capacity. From the viewpoint of the current ratio, however, the firm is more liquid and therefore is better able to meet its current bills as they come due.

Management may issue more long-term debt and use the acquired cash to increase the current assets or to pay off short-term liabilities. This will increase the current ratio, but the increase is achieved by obligating the firm to pay interest over several years and to generate enough money to retire at some future date this long-term debt. Thus, while the firm may be increasing its liquidity now, it may be doing so at the expense of future liquidity.

The management of the firm may issue more stock and increase the equity base of the firm. The money acquired by issuing the stock may be used to increase current assets or to pay off current liabilities. Either of these will increase the current ratio, and the firm will be more liquid. However, the increased liquidity has been purchased by issuing more shares which may reduce the return to the current stockholders (i.e., dilute the current stock) or may decrease management's ability to control the company since there are now more shares in existence.

Management may retire current liabilities by paying them off with cash. This also will increase the current ratio (as long as the ratio exceeds one), but a firm needs cash to work with. Paying off short-term liabilities solely to improve the current ratio may be detrimental, for the firm has less cash even though by the current ratio the firm appears to be more liquid.

Is an aggregation

The second type of problem with the current ratio is that it is an aggregation of all current assets and does not differentiate among current assets with regard to their degree of liquidity. The ratio considers inventory which may be sold after three months on credit which in turn may not be paid for several additional months as no different than cash or a short-term government security. This failure to distinguish among the degrees of liquidity has led to the development of ratios that explicitly consider the relative liquidity of the current assets.

THE ACID TEST

Acid test removes inventory

It may take many months before inventory is sold and turned into cash. Inventory is not a very liquid current asset, so a variation on the current ratio is the ratio of all current assets except inventory divided by current liabilities. This ratio is called the *acid test* or *quick ratio* (both terms are used for this ratio) and is expressed as follows:

$$\text{Acid test} = \frac{\text{Current assets} - \text{Inventory}}{\text{Current liabilities}}$$

For the hypothetical firm the acid test is

$$\frac{\$47,200 - \$24,000}{\$21,800} = 1.06,$$

which is perceptibly lower than the current ratio of 2.17 determined in the previous section. The difference is, of course, the large amount of inventory that the company is carrying. This lower acid test or quick ratio indicates that the firm may have difficulty meeting its bills as they come due if it must rely on converting its inventory into cash to meet these current liabilities. The acid test, however, does not indicate that the firm will fail to pay its bills. The ability to pay the bills will be influenced by such factors as (1) how quickly cash flows into the firm, (2) the firm's ability to raise additional capital, (3) how rapidly the bills come due, and (4) the relationship the company has with its suppliers and their willingness to extend credit. The acid test just indicates how well the current liabilities are covered by money and assets that may be converted into cash relatively quickly. In effect, the acid test considers that not all current assets are equally liquid, and hence this test is a more stringent measure of liquidity.

THE COMPONENTS OF THE CURRENT ASSETS

Another approach to this problem is to rank the current assets with regard to the degree of liquidity and determine each one's proportion of total current assets. The most liquid current asset is cash. Next is marketable securities like treasury bills or certificates of deposit. Then comes accounts receivable, and last is inventory. For the hypothetical firm the proportion of each amount to the total current assets is as follows:

Current assets as a proportion

CURRENT ASSET	PROPORTION OF TOTAL CURRENT ASSETS
Cash	4.2%
Short-term investments	.1
Accounts receivable	44.9
Inventory	50.8

Since this technique ranks the current assets from the most liquid to the least liquid, it gives an indication of the degree of liquidity of the firm's total current assets. If a large proportion of the total current assets is inventory, the firm is not very liquid. This ranking takes into consideration that the degree of liquidity varies with the type of asset, and it recognizes that not all current assets are readily convertible into cash. The decomposing of the current assets according to their degree of liquidity along with the acid test gives management, creditors, and investors a better measure than the current ratio of the ability of the firm to meet its current liabilities as they come due. These ratios then are a basic supplement to the current ratio and should be used to analyze the liquidity of any firm that carries a significant amount of inventory in its operations.

Activity Ratios

Activity ratios indicate how rapidly the firm is turning its inventory and accounts receivable into cash. The two activity ratios most frequently encountered are inventory turnover and receivables turnover. The more rapidly the firm turns over its inventory and receivables, the more rapidly it is acquiring cash. Hence high turnover indicates that the firm is rapidly receiving cash and is more able to pay its liabilities as they come due. Such high turnover, however, need not imply that the firm is maximizing profits. For example, high inventory turnover may indicate that the firm is selling items for too low a price in order to induce quicker sales. A high receivables turnover may be an indication that the firm is too stringent with extending credit to buyers, and this may reduce all sales and result in lower profits. A high turnover is not desirable by itself. Comparisons must be made

Activity ratios measure how rapidly assets turn into cash

with industry averages in order to have some basis for making assertions that the turnovers are too slow or too rapid.

INVENTORY TURNOVER

Definition of
inventory turnover

Inventory turnover is defined as annual sales divided by inventory. Thus inventory turnover is as follows:

$$\text{Inventory turnover} = \frac{\text{Sales}}{\text{Inventory}}$$

Since all assets must be financed, the more rapidly the inventory turns over, the less are the financing needs of the firm. For the hypothetical firm the inventory turnover is as follows:

$$\frac{\text{Sales}}{\text{Inventory}} = \frac{\$100,000}{\$24,000} = 4.17$$

This indicates that annual sales are 4.17 times the level of inventory. Inventory thus turns over 4.17 times a year or every 2.9 months (12/4.17 = 2.9). For the hypothetical firm management can anticipate that an average item will be held for three months, and hence the firm will need financing for that period to carry the item.

Inventory turnover may also be defined as cost of goods sold divided by the inventory. In particular, accountants may prefer to use cost of goods sold because accounting places much emphasis on the determination of cost. Financial managers may prefer sales in order to stress how rapidly the inventory flows into sales. In addition Dun and Bradstreet uses sales instead of costs in its "Key Business Ratios." Hence analysts must use sales to inventory if they are comparing a specific firm with the Dun and Bradstreet industry averages.

Either definition, however, may be acceptable provided that the user is consistent. If the cost of goods sold is used instead of annual sales, then all inventory turnover ratios used as a basis of comparison must also use cost of goods sold instead of annual sales. This points out the need for the person doing ratio analysis to be aware of the definitions being used and to apply the definitions consistently. Otherwise the analysis may be biased.

RECEIVABLES TURNOVER

Definitions of
receivables turnover

Receivables turnover is defined as annual credit sales divided by receivables. Thus the receivables turnover is as follows:

$$\text{Receivables turnover} = \frac{\text{Annual credit sales}}{\text{Accounts receivables}}$$

An alternative definition substitutes annual sales for annual credit sales. That is

$$\text{Receivables turnover} = \frac{\text{Annual sales}}{\text{Accounts receivables}}$$

Either definition is acceptable as long as it is applied consistently. While management may use either definition, investors, however, may be limited to the data provided by the firm. If annual credit sales are not reported by the firm, then the investor will have no choice but to use annual sales.

For the hypothetical firm the income statement indicates annual credit sales of $84,000. Thus the first definition may be used; so the receivables turnover is

$$\text{Receivables turnover} = \frac{\$84,000}{\$21,000} = 4$$

This indicates that annual credit sales are four times the receivables. The larger the ratio, the more rapidly the firm is turning its credit sales into cash. For the hypothetical firm the receivables turnover is four times a year, and this indicates that they are paid off on the average of every three months.

An alternative means to measure receivables turnover is the average collection period, which is expressed by the following equation:

$$\text{Average collection period} = \frac{\text{Receivables}}{\text{Credit sales per day}}$$

For the hypothetical firm credit sales per day are $230 ($84,000/365). Thus the average collection period is

$$\frac{\$21,000}{\$230} = 91 \text{ days}$$

This implies that when the firm makes a credit sale instead of a cash sale, on the average it can expect payment in 91 days. This is essentially the same information derived by the receivables turnover ratio. If it takes the firm 90 days to collect the receivables, then they are turning over four times a year. This is the same answer given above by the ratio of annual credit sales to accounts receivable. However, by stressing the number of days necessary to collect the receivables, the average collection period may be easier to interpret and hence be preferred by some analysts.

Turnover ratios need to be interpreted very cautiously, especially if these simple versions are used. These ratios are

Turnover ratios may be biased

dealing with dynamic events, since they are concerned with how long it takes an event to occur. This problem of time implies that these turnover ratios may be significantly biased if the firm has (1) seasonal sales, (2) sales that are lumpy and do not occur evenly during the fiscal year, or (3) growth in inventory and sales during the fiscal year. Under these circumstances the use of year end figures may produce ratios that are significantly biased.

The potential bias may be seen in the following example, which presents the monthly inventory of a firm that has a seasonal type of business. During the year inventory is accumulated in anticipation of large sales during the season, which in this case is the Christmas season.

MONTH	INVENTORY AT END OF MONTH	SALES DURING THE MONTH
January	$ 100	$ 50
February	100	50
March	200	50
April	200	50
May	300	50
June	400	50
July	500	50
August	700	50
September	1000	400
October	1000	1300
November	1200	2000
December	300	1200
		$6300

If year end figures for inventory and yearly sales figures are employed, the inventory turnover is 21 ($6300/$300), which indicates that inventory is turning over almost every two weeks. This, however, is very misleading because it fails to consider the large build-up of inventory that occurred during the middle of the year. In this case the use of year end inventory figures significantly increases the inventory turnover. The inventory turnover appears to be more rapid than it was.

Averaging will increase accuracy

There are several means to help alleviate this problem. For example, the average of the monthly inventories may be used instead of the year end inventory. The monthly average inventory is $500 (total inventory acquired during the year divided by 12). When this figure is used with the annual sales, the turnover is 12.6, or about once a month. This is much lower than the turnover indicated when the year end inventory figure was used.

Other methods for removing the potential bias may be to construct monthly turnover averages or use moving averages. The point is, however, that turnover ratios may be subject to bias and hence may be misleading. In order for these ratios to be helpful, users of these ratios need to recognize the potential bias and take steps to remove it. This increases the reliability of the ratios and makes them a more useful financial tool.

Profitability ratios are measures of performance that indicate what the firm is earning on its sales or assets or equity. The gross profit margin is earnings before interest and taxes divided by sales, and the net profit margin is the ratio of profits after taxes to sales.

$$\text{Gross profit margin} = \frac{\text{Profits before interest and taxes}}{\text{Sales}}$$

$$\text{Net profit margin} = \frac{\text{Profits after taxes}}{\text{Sales}}$$

Computing both these ratios may appear unnecessary, but by computing both management can see the effect of changes in interest expense and taxes on profitability. If the management only computed the net profit margin, then an increase in tax rates or interest rates will decrease the profit margin even though there has been no internal deterioration in the profitability of the firm. For the hypothetical firm the gross profit margin is

$$\text{Gross profit margin} = \frac{\$20,000}{\$100,000} = 20\%$$

and the net profit margin is

$$\text{Net profit margin} = \frac{\$9,500}{\$100,000} = 9.5\%$$

These indicate that the company earns 20 cents before interest and taxes for every dollar of sales and 9.5 cents after interest and taxes for every dollar of sales.

Other profitability ratios measure the return on assets and the return on equity. The return on assets is earnings divided by assets.

$$\text{Return on assets} = \frac{\text{Profits after taxes}}{\text{Total assets}}$$

The return on equity is earnings divided by the equity or the net worth of the firm

$$\text{Return on equity} = \frac{\text{Profits after taxes}}{\text{Equity}}$$

Equity is defined as the sum of the common stock, the additional paid in capital (if any), and the retained earnings (if any). Return on equity measures the return the firm is earning on its stockholders' investment. If the company has any preferred stock, the ratio must be adjusted by subtracting the dividends paid the preferred stockholder from the earnings and the par value of the preferred from the equity. Since the common stockholders are interested in the return on their investment, the preferred stock should not be included in determining the return on the common stock equity. For the hypothetical firm the return on total assets is

$$\text{Return on total assets} = \frac{\$9,500}{\$81,300} = 11.7\%$$

The return on the equity is

$$\text{Return on equity} = \frac{\$9,500}{\$43,900} = 21.6\%$$

This indicates that the firm returns \$.117 for every dollar invested in assets and \$.216 for every dollar invested by the common stockholders.

Some ratios may be used together to analyze a company. One such technique is the DuPont system, which is also referred to as a measure of the earning power of the firm. This system combines profit margin and turnover ratios to give the return on the firm's investments. That is,

$$\text{Return on investment} = \frac{\text{Earnings}}{\text{Sales}} \times \frac{\text{Sales}}{\text{Assets}}$$

Since sales cancel out, the return on investment reduces to

$$\text{Return on investment} = \frac{\text{Earnings}}{\text{Assets}}$$

This is basically the same as the return on assets presented above. What then does the DuPont system add? The advantage of the system is that it permits the decomposition of each of the ratios into its component parts. This decomposition is illustrated in the following chart.

Return on investment = Profit margin × Total assets turnover

$$\frac{\text{Profit}}{\text{margin}} = \frac{\text{Profits}}{\text{Sales}} = \frac{\text{Revenues} - \text{Cost of goods sold} - \text{Administrative expense} - \text{Interest} - \text{Taxes}}{\text{Sales}}$$

$$\frac{\text{Total assets}}{\text{turnover}} = \frac{\text{Sales}}{\text{Total assets}} = \frac{\text{Sales}}{\text{Cash} + \text{Accounts receivable} + \text{Inventory} + \text{Plant and equipment}}$$

By decomposing the ratios into their component parts, management may be able to isolate sources of the firm's problems.

DuPont system facilitates comparisons

Combining turnover and profitability ratios facilitates not only comparisons of firms in the same industry but also comparisons of firms in different industries. Some industries like grocery stores have rapid turnover but small profit margins. These low profit margins may appear to indicate that the industry is not very profitable. Other industries may have large profit margins but very slow turnover, for example, furniture stores. If profit margins are considered in a vacuum, this industry appears to be very profitable. If this were true, owners of grocery stores should convert to furniture stores. The answer is that the return on investment may be similar in both cases when the turnover and the profit margins are both considered. A furniture store may turn over its inventory twice a year and thus has to have large profit margins to compensate for the slow turnover. The grocery store, however, may earn less than a penny on a dollar of sales but turns over its inventory rapidly and thus earns many pennies as the result of the high turnover. Both industries may be equally profitable when the profit margins and turnover are taken together. Sales volume, profit margins, and inventory turnover should not be considered alone but in conjunction with each other, and the DuPont system brings all three together.

Leverage Ratios

THE DEBT RATIO

Measures of the use of debt financing

One of the more frequently computed types of ratios is the leverage ratio. While few investors bother to consider a firm's turnover, many investors are concerned with a firm's degree of financial leverage. The reason for this concern is discussed in detail in Chapter 21. This section is devoted only to measuring financial leverage.

Definitions of debt ratio

The two most commonly used ratios to measure financial leverage are (1) debt to equity and (2) debt to total assets. The latter is commonly referred to as the "debt ratio." These ratios are as follows:

(1)
$$\frac{\text{Debt}}{\text{Equity}}$$

(2)
$$\frac{\text{Debt}}{\text{Total assets}}$$

For the hypothetical firm the values of these ratios are respectively

(1)
$$\frac{\text{Debt}}{\text{Equity}} = \frac{\$37,400}{\$43,900} = 85.2\%$$

(2)
$$\frac{\text{Debt}}{\text{Total assets}} = \frac{\$37,400}{\$81,300} = 46.0\%$$

The debt-to-equity ratio indicates that there is $.852 debt for every dollar of equity. The debt ratio indicates that debt is financing 46 per cent of the firm's assets.

Leverage ratios are aggregate ratios. They both use total debt and hence do not differentiate between short-term and long-term debt. The debt-to-equity ratio uses total equity and hence does not differentiate between preferred and common stock financing. The debt-to-total assets ratio uses total assets and hence does not differentiate between current and long-term assets.

Debt financing is associated with risk

This aggregation is not a problem, for these ratios are measuring the proportion of the total assets that creditors (both short- and long-term) are financing. The smaller the proportion of total assets that creditors are financing, the larger the decline in value of the assets that may occur without threatening the creditors' position. Leverage ratios thus give an indication of risk. Firms that have high leverage ratios are considered riskier because there is less cushion to protect creditors if the value of the assets deteriorates. For example, the debt ratio for the hypothetical firm is 46.0 per cent. This indicates that the value of the assets may decline by 54 per cent (100%−46%) before the equity is destroyed, leaving only enough assets to pay off the debt. If the debt ratio had been 70%, then only a 30% decline in the value of the assets will endanger the creditors' position.

Leverage ratios are not only an indication of risks to creditors but also a measure of risk to investors, for firms that are highly financially leveraged are riskier investments. If the value of the assets declines or if the firm should experience declining sales and losses, the equity is wiped out more quickly for financially leveraged firms than for unleveraged firms. Hence the degree of financial leverage is an important measure of risk for investors as well as for creditors.

Variation in firms' use of debt financing

Leverage ratios differ significantly among firms. In Table 15–3 the debt ratios for several large industrial firms are presented. Table 15–4 presents the debt ratio for selected telephone companies. The tables have been arranged in descending order from the highest debt ratio to the lowest. As may be seen from

TABLE 15–3   Debt Ratios for Selected Industrial Firms
(Source: 1975 Annual Reports.)

Lockheed	95.2%
Gulf and Western	65.4
Philip Morris	59.7
Miles Labs	56.7
Union Carbide	46.1
Texaco	45.6
Coca Cola	26.7
IBM	24.3

TABLE 15–4   Debt Ratios for Selected Telephone Companies
(Source: Value Line Investment Survey; February 4, 1977.)

FIRM	DEBT RATIO
Mid-Continental Telephone	64.0%
Continental Telephone	62.5
United Telecommunications	61.0
Central Telephone	58.0
General Telephone and Electronics	56.0
Rochester Telephone	51.5
Pacific Telephone and Telegraph	49.0
AT&T	48.0
New England Telephone	47.0
Mountain States Telephone and Telegraph	46.5

both tables the proportion of a firm's total assets financed by debt varies not only across industries but also within an industry. The telephone companies' debt ratios do have less variation than the debt ratios of the selected industrial firms. While the range for the industrial firms is from 95.2 to 24.3 per cent, the range for the phone companies is 64 to 46.5 per cent.

Within an industry there is an optimal combination of debt to total assets. Finding this optimal capital structure of debt and equity financing is important to maximizing the value of a firm, and Chapter 22 is devoted to the optimal capital structure of a firm. It is sufficient for now to suggest that finding the optimal degree of financial leverage may significantly benefit the common stockholder by increasing the earnings of the company and permitting faster growth and larger dividends. If, however, the firm is too financially leveraged or *under capitalized*, creditors may require a higher interest rate to compensate them for the increased risk, and investors may also be less willing to invest their money in a highly financially leveraged corporation. Thus leverage ratios, which measure the degree of financial leverage used by the firm, may be among the most important ratios that managers, creditors, and investors may calculate.

COVERAGE RATIOS

Leverage ratios also include measures of the ability of a firm to service its debt, that is, to pay the interest and retire the principal. Coverage ratios indicate to creditors and management how many times the earnings of the company exceed the interest, and hence these ratios are called "times-interest-earned." Times-interest-earned is the ratio of earnings available to pay the interest divided by the amount of interest. That is

Measures of ability to pay interest (i.e., coverage)

$$\text{Times-interest-earned} = \frac{\text{Earnings before interest and taxes}}{\text{Annual interest charges}}$$

A ratio of 2 indicates that the firm has $2 after meeting other expenses to pay $1 of interest charges. The larger the times-interest-earned, the safer is the interest payment. For the hypothetical firm the times-interest-earned is $\dfrac{\$20,000}{\$1,300} = 15.4$ and that indicates the firm is more than earning its interest expense, because for every dollar in interest expense the firm is earning $15.40.

Ability to cover interest expense is important, for failure to meet interest payments as they come due may throw the firm into bankruptcy. Deterioriation in the times-interest-earned ratio may give an early warning to creditors and investors as well as management of a deteriorating financial position and an increased probability of default of interest payments.

Coverage varies with subordination

In the above form the times-interest-earned ratio is an aggregate ratio that lumps together all interest payments. Some debt issues may be subordinate to other debt issues and therefore paid only after the senior debt is paid. Thus it is possible that the senior debt is paid in full but nothing is left to pay the interest on the subordinate debt. When this subordination exists, the times-interest-earned ratio may be altered to acknowledge this subordination. For example, consider a firm with $1000 in earnings before interest and taxes with $10,000 in debt consisting of two issues. Issue A is $8000 and carries an interest rate of 5 per cent. Issue B is $2000 and carries an interest rate of 7 per cent and is subordinate to issue A. The subordination may explain why the second issue has the higher interest rate, for the creditor demands the higher rate in return for accepting the riskier debt issue.

The times-interest-earned for each debt issue is computed as follows. A firm has two debt issues (A and B) and $1000 earnings before interest and taxes. The interest on issue A is $400 and on issue B is $140. For issue A there is $1000 available to pay the $400 interest and thus the coverage ratio is

$$\frac{\$1000}{\$400} = 2.50$$

For issue B there is $1000 to cover the interest on A and B. Thus for issue B the coverage ratio is

$$\frac{\$1000}{\$400 + \$140} = 1.85$$

It would be misleading to suggest that the coverage for issue B is the amount available *after* issue A was paid. In such a case that would indicate coverage of

$$\frac{\$600}{\$140} = 4.29$$

This is clearly misleading. Issue B would have the higher coverage ratio and thus appear to be safer than the senior debt. The proper way to adjust for subordination is to add the interest charges to the denominator and not subtract the interest paid the senior issue from the numerator. Successive issues of subordinated debt would have their interest payments added to the denominator. Since the total amount of earnings available before taxes to pay the interest is spread over ever increasing interest payments, the coverage ratio declines and hence gives a truer indication of the actual coverage of the subordinated debt.

Coverage ratios have also been developed to include the repayment of principal, preferred stock dividends, and rental and lease payments. However, such ratios are beyond the scope of this introductory text. The above discussion indicates desirability of computing coverage ratios and how they may be computed and interpreted. These ratios are a measure of the safety of interest payments, for they indicate earnings available to cover the interest payments.

SUMMARY

This chapter has been concerned with ratio analysis. Ratios have several advantages for they are easily computed and readily permit comparisons. Since publicly held corporations must give stockholders pertinent financial information, ratio analysis may be employed not only by management and creditors but also investors.

Many ratios may be computed, and only a selected few were presented in this chapter. These ratios are summarized below. They do not exhaust all the possible ratios an analyst may compute. Furthermore, definitions of several of these ratios vary, as different analysts refine specific ratios to meet specific needs. Thus it is very important that the analyst be aware of the definitions being employed so that the analysis is consistent. Without such consistency, ratio analysis can be very misleading.

While the analyst may compute all the ratios, it is preferable to identify those ratios most relevant to the goals of the analysis. Blindly computing all the ratios may produce irrelevant information and confuse the analytical work. Once the pertinent ratios have been selected, the results of the analysis give a measure of a firm's performance. This may be compared with other firms in the industry or traced over time to learn if trends have developed. Industry averages tend to be stable over time. Hence if the firm is significantly different from the industry average, there should be an explanation. Ratio analysis then is a convenient tool to aid management perceive (1) the firm's position within the industry and (2) trends that have developed. With this information in hand management may plan future courses of action to correct weaknesses identified by the ratio analysis.

KEY WORDS AND TERMS _____

> liquidity
> time series
> cross sectional
> acid test
> quick ratio
> turnover
> profitability
> return
> leverage
> coverage
> DuPont system

QUESTIONS AND PROBLEMS FOR THOUGHT
AND DISCUSSION _____

1. Company A sells furniture, and its current ratio recently rose. Can you conclude that the firm is more liquid? What other test of liquidity would you suggest? If this firm increased its inventory near the end of its fiscal year, why may the inventory turnover be a poor measure of activity?

2. What is the effect on the current ratio and the acid ratio if
   (a) a firm buys inventory for cash?
   (b) a firm buys inventory on credit?
   (c) In which case does the firm appear to be more liquid?
   (d) What is the source of funds used in (a) and (b)?

3. Why may turnover ratios be biased? How can this bias be reduced? Why is this reduction in bias important?

4. Why would you expect different debt ratios for different industries? Why may there also be considerable difference in debt ratios for firms within the same industry?

5. Company A has three debt issues of $3000 each. The interest rate on issue A is 4 per cent; on issue B the rate is 6 per cent; on issue C the interest rate is 8 per cent. The firm, which sold 150 units of output at $6 each, has variable costs of $3 per unit and fixed costs of $50. Compute the "times-interest-earned" for issue C. What does your answer imply? Does this mean the interest will not be paid?

6. You are a loan officer. A firm needs a short-term loan to finance inventory and accounts receivable. You perform a ratio analysis and receive the following results:

	1974	1975	1976	INDUSTRY AVERAGE
Current ratio	2.1	2.2	2.4	2.5
Acid ratio	1.4	1.0	1.7	1.0
Inventory turnover	3X	3.5X	4X	2.5X
Receivables turnover	2X	2.1X	2X	2.1X
Net profit margin	7%	6.8%	6%	7%
Return on equity	10%	9%	8.5%	10%
Debt ratio	30%	31%	30%	35%

Which ratios are the most important to your analysis? What important weakness do the ratios indicate? What strengths are indicated by the ratios? Would you grant the loan?

SUMMARY OF RATIO DEFINITIONS

I. Liquidity Ratios
    a. Current Ratio
        (1) $\dfrac{\text{current assets}}{\text{current liabilities}}$
    b. Acid Test
        (2) $\dfrac{\text{current assets} - \text{inventory}}{\text{current liabilities}}$
II. Activity Ratios
    a. Inventory Turnover
        (3) $\dfrac{\text{sales}}{\text{inventory}}$
      or
        (4) $\dfrac{\text{cost of goods sold}}{\text{inventory}}$
    b. Receivables Turnover
        (5) $\dfrac{\text{annual credit sales}}{\text{accounts receivable}}$
      or
        (6) $\dfrac{\text{annual sales}}{\text{accounts receivable}}$
      or
        (7) average collection period
            $\dfrac{\text{receivables}}{\text{credit sales per day}}$
III. Profitability Ratios
    a. Gross Profit Margin
        (8) $\dfrac{\text{profits before interest and taxes}}{\text{sales}}$

b. Net Profit Margin

$$(9) \ \frac{\text{profits after taxes}}{\text{sales}}$$

c. Return on Assets

$$(10) \ \frac{\text{profits after taxes}}{\text{total assets}}$$

d. Return on Equity

$$(11) \ \frac{\text{profits after taxes}}{\text{equity}}$$

e. Return on Investments (DuPont System)

$$(12) \ \frac{\text{earnings}}{\text{sales}} \times \frac{\text{sales}}{\text{assets}}$$

IV. Leverage Ratios

a. Debt Ratios

$$(13) \ \frac{\text{debt}}{\text{equity}}$$

or

$$(14) \ \frac{\text{debt}}{\text{total assets}}$$

b. Coverage Ratios

$$(15) \ \frac{\text{earnings before interest and taxes}}{\text{annual interest expense}}$$

Chapter 16

PLANNING: BREAKEVEN ANALYSIS AND OPERATING LEVERAGE

Learning Objectives

- Calculate the breakeven level of output.
- Illustrate several uses for breakeven analysis.
- Differentiate between linear and non-linear breakeven analysis.
- State the meaning of operating leverage.
- Determine the effect of shifting variable costs to fixed costs.
- Explain how an increase in operating leverage increases risk.

"Forewarned—forearmed"

Cervantes (Don Quixote)

Planning is crucial to a firm's health, for a firm cannot survive without forethought by its management. Planning is essentially anticipating the future in order to take action presently. Since the future is unknown, or at least uncertain, planning is difficult. Such difficulty, however, is not sufficient reason to avoid making plans.

All planning has a time dimension. Some planning is intended for the immediate future. These include such plans as the level of inventory that the firm will carry and when short-term financing will be necessary to carry that inventory. Other plans involve longer time spans. The expansion of the plant or the firm's entry into a new product line are examples of managerial decisions that will affect the firm for many years. This element of time is similar to economists' distinction between the short and the long run. While economists are not precisely referring to calendar time, they are suggesting that some changes in a firm's operation may be made relatively quickly, while other changes require longer time periods. The decision to expand production and carry more inventory is a short run decision. Increasing the plant and the scale of operation is a long run decision.

There are a variety of tools available to management to aid in planning operations. The material in the previous chapters may be used as aids in planning. This chapter and the one that follows add several tools to help management plan the firm's operations. Breakeven analysis and the degree of operating leverage are covered in this chapter. The subsequent chapter covers forecasting and budgeting.

BREAKEVEN ANALYSIS

Breakeven: neither profits nor losses

Breakeven analysis is a frequently used tool in financial planning. Breakeven analysis seeks to determine that level of sales which generates neither profits nor losses and hence causes the firm to "breakeven." Breakeven analysis also permits management to see the effects on the level of profits of (1) fluctuations in sales, (2) fluctuations in costs, and (3) changes in fixed costs relative to variable costs. Breakeven analysis is based on the following three mathematical relationships: the relationship between (1) output and total revenues (i.e., sales), (2) output and variable costs of production, and (3) output and fixed costs of production.

Total revenue: price times quantity

The relationship between output and total revenues (TR) is the number of units sold (Q) times the price (P) for each unit. This may be expressed as a simple equation. Total revenue equals price times quantity sold. In symbolic form this equation is expressed as follows:

(1) $$TR = P \times Q$$

The larger the number of units that are sold at a given price, the larger the firm's total revenue. This relationship is illustrated in the first three columns of Table 16–1, which presents the cost and revenue of a firm used in breakeven analysis. The first

Revenues expand with sales

column gives the price of the product and the second column the quantity sold. By multiplying these together, the total revenue in the third column is obtained. Since the per unit price is $2.00, then the total revenue for a level of sales of 1000 units is $2000.

In Figure 16–1 total revenue is illustrated as a straight line that runs through the origin, for at zero units of output there can be no revenues. As output is increased, total revenue increases. The rate at which total revenue increases (i.e., the slope of the line) is the price of the output. This rate is constant, for each additional unit of output is assumed to be sold at the given price.

Costs: fixed and variable

Costs of production are divided into two of the following classes: (1) costs that vary with production, such as labor expense; and (2) costs that do not vary with output, such as adminis-

TABLE 16–1   Relationships Between Output and Revenues,
Output and Cost, and Output and Profits

(1) P	(2) Q	(3) TR	(4) FC	(5) b	(6) VC	(7) TC	(8) PROFITS
$2	$ 0	$ 0	$1,000	$1	$ 0	$1,000	($1,000)
2	200	400	1,000	1	200	1,200	(800)
2	400	800	1,000	1	400	1,400	(600)
2	600	1,200	1,000	1	600	1,600	(400)
2	800	1,600	1,000	1	800	1,800	(200)
2	1,000	2,000	1,000	1	1,000	2,000	0
2	1,200	2,400	1,000	1	1,200	2,200	200
2	1,400	2,800	1,000	1	1,400	2,400	400
2	1,600	3,200	1,000	1	1,600	2,600	600

trative expense or interest charges. This classification of cost is
somewhat arbitrary, for fixed costs may become varied and variable costs may become fixed. For example, a company may
refinance its debt and change its *fixed* interest expense or may
change its management personnel and change its *fixed* administrative expense. Union contracts may convert some variable
costs into fixed costs. For example, a union contract may require

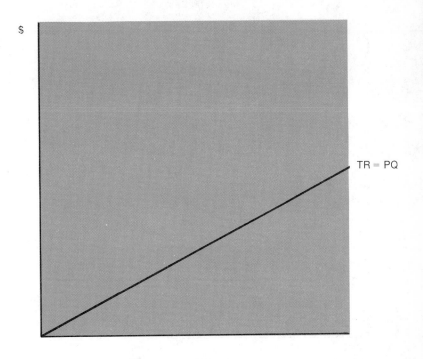

Relationship Between Output and Total Revenue

OUTPUT

Figure 16–1

severance pay. The firm may then be reluctant to lay off workers, and thus the labor cost becomes fixed and independent of the level of output. These qualifications make the actual classification of costs into fixed and variable more difficult, but they do not invalidate the concept that some costs are fixed and independent of the level of output, while other costs vary with the level of output.

Fixed costs are independent of output

Fixed costs do not vary with the level of output and hence are the same whatever the level of the operations of the firm. Fixed costs (FC) are equal to some constant (a), which may be expressed by the following simple equation:

(2) $FC = a.$

In Table 16–1 the fourth column gives the fixed costs of operation. These fixed costs are $1000 if the firm produces ten or 100 units of output. The relationship between output and fixed costs is shown in Figure 16–2 as a horizontal line (FC) that crosses the Y axis at a, the fixed dollar amount ($1000). The line FC has no slope, because fixed costs neither rise nor fall with the level of output. They are independent of the level of output.

Variable costs (VC) change with the level of output: the

Relationship Between Output and Fixed, Variable, and Total Costs

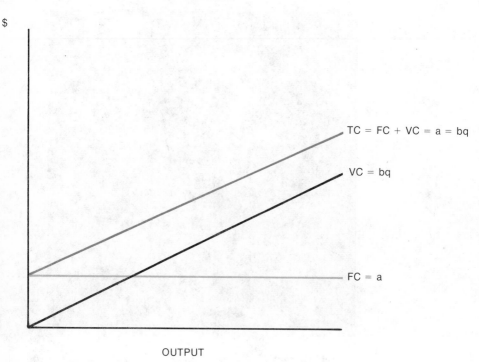

OUTPUT

Figure 16–2

more output the firm produces, the larger the total variable costs of production. This relationship may also be expressed by a simple equation: variable costs are some proportion of output. In symbolic form that is,

(3) $$VC = bQ.$$

The equation states that variable costs are some proportion (b) of output, where b is the per unit variable cost of production. As the level of output rises, then variable costs rise in proportion to the increase in output. This relationship is shown in the fifth and sixth columns in Table 16–1, which gives the per unit variable costs ($1) and total variable costs of production. At zero level of output there are no variable costs. Each additional unit of output then adds $1 to the firm's variable costs. Thus at 200 units of output these costs are $200, and at 1000 units of output these costs have risen to $1000.

The total variable costs are represented in Figure 16–2 by the line VC. The variable costs line passes through the origin, which indicates that if operations were to cease, the firm would have no variable costs of operation. This is different than fixed costs, which still exist even if the firm ceases production. For example, during a strike certain costs (i.e., interest expense) do not disappear just because the firm ceases production. While the firm may not be incurring variable costs during a strike, the fixed costs continue. A plant that is not operating because of a strike may not generate output and sales, which puts pressure on management to settle the strike before the fixed costs become an intolerable burden.

Total costs (TC) of production are the sum of fixed costs and variable costs (i.e., TC = FC + VC = a + bQ). In Table 16–1 total costs of operation are shown in the seventh column, which is the sum of columns four and six. In Figure 16–2 the total costs are illustrated by TC, which is the vertical summation of FC and VC.

When a firm breaks even, its total costs of production are equal to its total revenues. The firm is neither making profits nor experiencing losses. If the firm were to produce less, it would experience losses. Management knows that it must produce at least that level of output in order to cover all its costs. If management does not believe that the breakeven level of output can be produced and sold, then it must make some changes. For example, it may decide to produce the output but also seek to find a means to reduce the per unit costs of production.

The breakeven level of output may be found by a simple formula. At the breakeven point total costs must equal total revenue. In equation form that is,

(4) $$TR = TC.$$

By substituting equations (1), (2), and (3) into equation (4)

Variable costs depend on the level of output

Total costs: FC + VC

Method to determine the breakeven level of output

and solving for the breakeven level of output (Q_B), this level of output is as follows:

$$PQ_B = a + bQ_B$$

$$PQ_B - bQ_B = a$$

$$Q_B (P - b) = a$$

(5) $$Q_B = \frac{a}{P - b}$$

(Equation (5) employs a subscript. In this case a particular level of output is being discussed. The Q represents any level of output. By adding the subscript B, one particular level of output is being denoted.)

Since (a) is the fixed cost of production and (b) is the per unit variable cost of output, the formula for the breakeven level of output (Q_B) expressed in words is as follows:

$$Q_B = \frac{\text{Fixed costs}}{\text{Price of product} - \text{per unit variable cost}}$$

If this formula is applied to the numerical example in Table 16–1, the breakeven level of output is the following:

$$Q_B = \frac{\$1000}{\$2 - \$1}$$

$$Q_B = 1000$$

This answer is the same that is obtained in the eighth column of Table 16–1, which gives the profits of the firm. These profits are determined by subtracting column seven (total cost) from column three (total revenues). The breakeven point is also illustrated in Figure 16–3, which combines the first two figures. As may be seen in Figure 16–3 and Table 16–1, the firm's total cost exceeds its total revenue for all levels of output below 1000, and the firm makes profit at all levels of output greater than 1,000. It breaks even when it produces and sells 1,000 units of output.

USES FOR BREAKEVEN ANALYSIS

Uses

(1) Changes in price
or costs

Besides indicating the level of output that must be achieved to avoid losses, breakeven analysis is a means for management to analyze the effects of changes in prices and costs. For example, what would be the effect of a decline in the price of the product? If, as the result of increased competition, the price of the product were to fall from $2.00 to $1.50, breakeven analysis indicates the

Determination of the Breakeven Level of Output

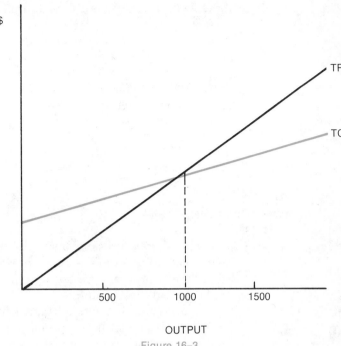

OUTPUT

Figure 16–3

firm must now produce at least 2000 units of output [$1000/($1.50 − $1.00) = 2000] in order to meet its total costs. While the decrease in price may produce an increase in sales, can management anticipate a sufficient increase to absorb 2000 units of output? An example of a change in costs may be the suggestion of the advertising department for an increased campaign to increase sales. Management may use breakeven analysis to ascertain by how much the level of output must be expanded to cover the increased advertising expense. If the advertising campaign adds $.25 per unit to the cost of the item, then the breakeven point becomes:

$$\frac{\$1000}{\$2 - \$1.25} = \$1333$$

The advertising campaign will result in the firm experiencing losses unless a level of sales of 1333 units can be anticipated.

Breakeven analysis may also be used to analyze the substitution of fixed for variable costs. This substituting of fixed costs for variable costs is an important decision often faced by a firm's management. For example, the firm may be able to purchase a piece of equipment that reduces the per unit variable cost of production but increases the fixed costs of operation. This sub-

(2) Substituting fixed for variable costs

stitution may also increase the level of output necessary to breakeven. If, in the above example, the fixed cost rises to $1500 and the per unit variable cost drops from $1.00 to $.80, then the breakeven level of output rises from 1000 to 1250 [$1,500/($2 − $.80)]. Thus, while the equipment may be cost saving if the management anticipates a larger level of output, it may also turn the firm into a losing operation should the level of sales decline.

These examples illustrate the types of situations and problems to which management may apply breakeven analysis. They do not exhaust all the possible situations, however. When a firm is considering introducing a new product, the analysis may then be used to determine the level of sales necessary to produce a profit. By determining this minimum level of sales, the analysis aids managerial planning and decision making.

An Example of Breakeven Analysis

This section presents a simple example employing breakeven analysis and the equations presented in the previous section. Simple problems for the student to work through are given at the end of the chapter.

A large firm, Corporation X, has investments in many areas of consumer goods. It is a primary manufacturer of cosmetics, nonprescription drugs, and candies. The firm sells all these items through a variety of department and drug stores. Corporation X has a strong marketing department and well-developed marketing channels. These channels, however, are not being used to capacity, and the firm is interested in developing products that can be marketed with its current line of products. One possibility is a line of paper goods (stationery, greeting cards, and other paper goods). Such products may be readily marketed through the firm's existing marketing network. However, paper products require substantial investment in fixed equipment. Management must determine the level of sales necessary to breakeven in order to help justify the investment in the new plant and equipment.

The marketing department has estimated that sales for the next four years will be as follows:

1977	1978	1979	1980
$25,000,000	38,000,000	42,000,000	44,000,000

The cost to produce a unit of output is $.75, while the packages of paper may be marketed wholesale for $1. Such a price permits retailers to maintain their profit margins and still sell the product competitively. The cost of the plant and equipment necessary to produce the paper products is estimated to be $10 million.

From the above information the equations presented in the previous section may be solved. Total revenue is

(1)
$$TR = P \times Q$$

$$TR = \$1\ Q$$

This gives the estimated total revenue for any level of output. The fixed costs necessary to acquire the plant and equipment are

(2)
$$FC = a$$

$$FC = \$10,000,000$$

And the variable costs are

(3)
$$VC = b\ Q$$

$$VC = \$.75\ Q$$

This equation gives the estimated total variable costs for all levels of output. For the firm to break even, total revenue must equal total costs.

(4)
$$TR = TC$$

$$\$1\ Q = \$10,000,000 + \$.75\ Q$$

Hence, the breakeven level of output is

(5)
$$Q_B = \frac{a}{P - b}$$

$$Q_B = \frac{\$10,000,000}{\$1 - \$.75} = 40,000,000$$

For the firm to break even it must produce 40 million units of output and sell each unit at $1. Failure to achieve this level of output and sales will result in the firm experiencing losses on its new line of paper products. The sales estimates indicate that this breakeven level will not be achieved for two years but that sales in subsequent years will be profitable.

It should be noted that while the above analysis indicates the new line of paper products will eventually be profitable, this information is insufficient evidence to justify the investment. Alternative investments should be considered, but breakeven analysis does not examine other alternatives. Selecting among competing investments is a major topic in finance and will be covered in Chapter 23, Capital Budgeting. However, for the purpose of this chapter, this example illustrates how breakeven analysis is used to determine the minimum level of sales neces-

Breakeven analysis is not a substitute for capital budgeting

sary to avoid losses. Additional weaknesses in breakeven analysis are discussed in the next section.

WEAKNESSES IN BREAKEVEN ANALYSIS

(1) Accuracy of the data

Breakeven analysis requires data, and the analysis can only be as good as the data that are used. Estimating accurately the data, such as the variable cost of production or the response of buyers to changes in price, may be difficult. While the collection of data and the computing of statistics may be done by a firm's engineers and technicians, management must be aware of the degree of accuracy of the data. The results of breakeven analysis should be interpreted in light of the accuracy of the data.

(2) Emphasis is not on profits and maximization of value

Management also needs an awareness of the limitations and assumptions of breakeven analysis. Breakeven analysis is limited to identifying the level of output at which the firm ceases to operate at a loss and begins to make profits. The analysis offers little insight as to the best level or profit maximizing level of output that management should seek to obtain. Reliance on breakeven analysis may then direct management's attention away from profits and value maximization.

(3) Linear functions

Another weakness of simple breakeven analysis is that it is built on linear functions. These functions assume (1) that the price of the product is constant, and (2) that the per unit variable costs are constant. The analysis also assumes that no matter how many units are produced the firm will be able to sell the outputs at that given price. Economics, however, teaches that in order to sell additional units of output, the firm may have to *lower its price*. The assumption of constant per unit variable costs may also be invalid, for it implies that the firm produces the first unit of output and the ten-thousandth unit at the same per unit variable cost. Economics, however, teaches that firms will experience diminishing returns and thus *per unit variable costs will rise*.

These assumptions may significantly reduce the reliability of simple breakeven analysis. Failure on the part of management to be aware of these assumptions may result in the misuse of the analysis or inaccurate interpretation of the results. Breakeven analysis only indicates the minimum level of output that must be achieved in order to avoid losses. It should be used in conjunction with other tools to determine which courses of action are in the best interests of the firm and its owners.

NONLINEAR BREAKEVEN ANALYSIS

Management may seek to overcome some of these difficulties by using different specifications of the total cost and total revenue functions. Management may adopt the approach used by economists that suggests (1) that total costs rise more rapidly as diminishing returns begin and capacity is reached and (2) that total revenue increases at a decreasing rate as the price of the product is lowered to sell more output. These costs and revenue relationships are illustrated in Figure 16–4. Fixed costs are the same as in the previous illustrations, but per unit variable costs rise as output increases, and this causes total costs to rise more rapidly as output increases. Total revenues rise more slowly as the firm lowers its price in order to induce people to purchase the additional output.

When the assumptions of a constant price of the product and constant per unit variable costs of production are removed, breakeven analysis is altered. As may be seen in Figure 16–4, there are now two breakeven points (Q_1 and Q_2). A firm may generate losses by producing too much of a product as well as too little, for this additional output is more expensive to produce and does not generate sufficient revenues to cover the costs. Management now knows that the most profitable level of operations lies between output Q_1 and Q_2. If management anticipates sales outside this range, then it must take steps to alter the scale of

Nonlinear breakeven analysis may produce two breakeven levels of output

Non-Linear Costs and Revenue Functions

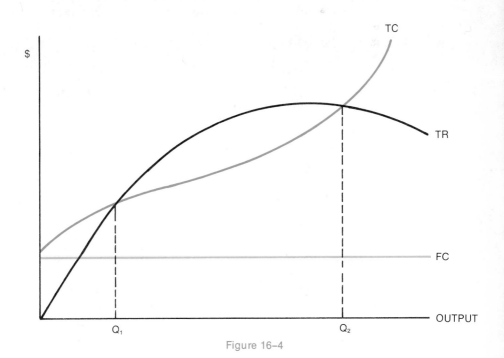

Figure 16–4

operations. The firm cannot produce a level of output above Q_2 and below Q_1 efficiently and profitably. Hence, if management anticipates such a level of sales, it should change the scale of operation in order to avoid losses.

While nonlinear breakeven analysis may give management more information, the analysis is more difficult to perform. The response of buyers to lower product prices and the rate at which per unit variable costs rises are necessary information. Small firms may lack the facilities for estimating this data. Even larger firms with computer facilities may find this analysis expensive and perhaps inaccurate. Management has to ask, "Is the more sophisticated, nonlinear analysis worth the additional cost?" For many firms the answer is "no," and for these firms the simple linear breakeven analysis is sufficient for planning managerial decisions.

DEGREE OF OPERATING LEVERAGE

Responsiveness of profits to change in output

Another tool used in planning is the degree of operating leverage which measures the responsiveness of changes in the level of profits to changes in the level of output. This measure gives management an indication of the response in profits that it can expect if the level of sales is altered. Specifically, the degree of operating leverage is defined as the percentage change in profits divided by the percentage change in the level of output. In symbolic terms this ratio may be represented as follows:

(6) $$\epsilon = \frac{\%\Delta\pi}{\%\Delta Q}$$

The symbols are defined as follows:

ϵ = the degree of operating leverage
Δ = change
π = profits
Q = output

This ratio answers the following type of question: if output is increased by 10 per cent, by what percentage will profits increase? If the degree of operating leverage is 2, then a 10 per cent increase in the level of output will increase the level of profits by 20 per cent. A large degree of operating leverage indicates that small fluctuations in the level of output will produce large fluctuations in the level of profits.

THE RELATIONSHIP BETWEEN THE
DEGREE OF OPERATING LEVERAGE AND
BREAKEVEN ANALYSIS

The simplest way to illustrate the relationship between the degree of operating leverage and breakeven analysis is to re-arrange the ratio present above and compare it with Figure 16–5. This figure is divided into two components; the top half reproduces the total costs and total revenues from Figure 16–3. The bottom half shows the relationship between output and profits. In either component at levels of output below Q_1, the firm is operating at a loss. At Q_1 level of output, the firm is making neither profits nor losses but is breaking even. At levels of output above Q_1, the firm is making a profit. The profit or loss position of the firm that is illustrated by the bottom half of the figure is essentially no different than the material on the top half. Thus at Q_2 the fact that the firm is making losses of "ab" may be read off either the top or bottom half of Figure 16–5. At Q_3 the profits of "cd" may also be read off of either half. For the purpose of showing the relationship between the degree of operating lever-age and breakeven analysis, the lower half, the relationship between profits and the level of output, will be used.

The degree of operating leverage was defined as the per-centage change in profits divided by the percentage change in output. This was expressed symbolically in equation (6). The percentage change in profits was $\%\Delta\pi$ and $\%\Delta Q$ represented the percentage change in output. These terms in equation (6) may be rearranged as follows:

(7)
$$\%\Delta\pi/\%\Delta Q = \frac{\Delta\pi}{\pi}\Big/\frac{\Delta Q}{Q} = \frac{\Delta\pi}{\Delta Q}\cdot\frac{Q}{\pi}$$

In this form the degree of operating leverage consists of two factors that are multiplied. The first component ($\Delta\pi/\Delta Q$) is the slope of the total profit line in Figure 16–5. The second compo-nent (Q/π) is the reciprocal of a point on the profit line. For example, Point A is a particular combination of output and profits such as 600 units of output and profits of $300. If the slope of the profit function is equal to 2, then the degree of operating lever-age at point A is

$$2 \times 600/300 = 4$$

This indicates that if management increases the level of output by 10 per cent, then the level of profits will rise by 40 per cent. Thus an increase in output from 600 units to 660 units (a 10 per cent increase) will produce an increase in profits from $300 to $420 (a 40 per cent increase). Thus by computing the degree of

Relationships Between Output and Profits

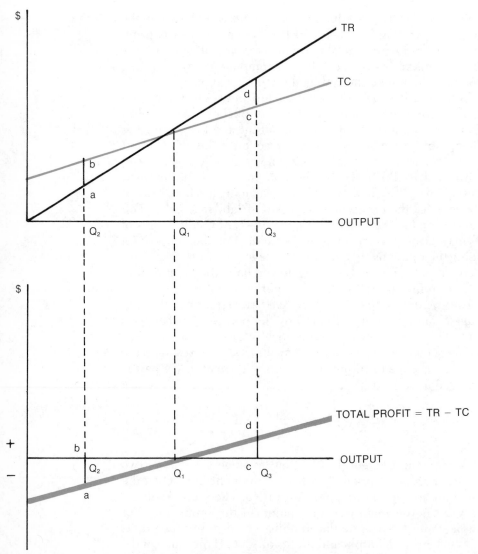

Figure 16–5

operating leverage management has an indication of the response in profits to a change in the level of output.

The decomposing of the degree of operating leverage into
two component pieces helps reveal the relationship between the
degree of operating leverage and breakeven analysis. At the
breakeven level of output (Q_1 in Figure 16–5), the level of profits
is zero. When zero profit is substituted into the ratio Q/π, the
value of the ratio becomes infinite (or undefined). Thus at zero

profits the degree of operating leverage is infinite which tells management that a small percentage change in the level of output will produce very large percentage change in the level of profits. This is exactly what management should expect. The percentage change in profits is very large because previously the firm was either operating at a loss or breaking even.

As the firm continues to increase output above Q_1. the degree of operating leverage falls. While the slope of the profit line ($\Delta\pi/\Delta Q$) is not affected as output increases, the other component of the degree of operating leverage declines. The ratio of Q/π declines as the level of output and profits rises. Thus the degree of operating leverage falls as output increases which indicates to management that a fluctuation in the level of output will have an effect on the level of profits, but this effect diminishes as the firm reaches a higher level of output.

Operating leverage falls as firm approaches maximum profits

AN ALTERNATIVE METHOD FOR DETERMINING THE DEGREE OF OPERATING LEVERAGE

The following is an alternative way to express the degree of operating leverage:

(8)
$$\epsilon = \frac{\text{Revenue minus variable costs}}{\text{Revenue minus total costs}}$$

In symbols this is

(8)
$$\epsilon = \frac{Q\ (P - V)}{Q\ (P - V) - F}$$

The symbols are as follows:

Q = the level of output
P = the price of the product
V = the per unit variable cost
F = the fixed cost

In this form the degree of operating leverage is easier to compute, but it is also easy to forget that the degree of operating leverage is the ratio of two percentage changes and that it is a measure of the responsiveness of profits to changes in the level of output. This alternative form masks the definition of the degree of operating leverage and thus may lead to incorrect interpretation.

How equation (8) may be applied is illustrated by the following example. A firm is able to sell a unit of output for $5.00. Each unit has a variable cost of $3.00, and the fixed costs of operation are $1000. What is the degree of operating leverage at 1000 units? By substituting the numbers in equation (8), the degree of operating leverage is

$$\epsilon = \frac{1000\ (\$5 - \$3)}{1000\ (\$5 - \$3) - \$1000} = 2$$

The number 2 then indicates that if the firm increases output by 10 per cent, profits will rise by 20 per cent. This increase is easily verified, for at 1000 units the level of profits is $1000.

$$
\begin{aligned}
\text{TR} &= \$5000 \\
-\ \text{TC} &= \$3000 + 1000 \\
\hline
\text{profits} &= \$1000
\end{aligned}
$$

If output is increased by 10 per cent to 1100 units, profits become $1200, which is 20 per cent higher.

$$
\begin{aligned}
\text{TR} &= \$5500 \\
-\ \text{TC} &= \$3300 + 1000 \\
\hline
\text{profits} &= \$1200
\end{aligned}
$$

Alternative method highlights the importance of fixed costs

This alternative method to determine the degree of operating leverage points out the importance of fixed costs. The greater the fixed costs, then the smaller will be the denominator in the ratio, and hence the larger will be the degree of operating leverage. Firms with small fixed costs will not have large amounts of operating leverage. For such firms the level of output necessary to generate profits is small and fluctuations in profits with changes in level of output are smaller. Firms with larger amounts of fixed costs have to produce a larger level of output in order to spread these costs, and thus such firms have higher degrees of operating leverage.

OPERATING LEVERAGE AND RISK

High degree of operating leverage implies high degree of risk

The previous discussion suggests that profits will rise and fall more rapidly for a firm with a high degree of operating leverage. This section compares the degree of operating leverage for two industries, airlines and retailing, and shows how this operating leverage affects the level of risk associated with each industry.

Airlines have large fixed costs

The airlines are an excellent example of an industry that has a large amount of operating leverage. A large proportion of their costs are relatively fixed (e.g., interest and depreciation on the planes and equipment). Equally important is that, once the plane is in the air, the cost of the flight is basically the same whether the plane carries one person or a full load. The difference between breakeven and a profitable flight is often a matter of just a few passengers. Once this breakeven number of passengers is reached, the profitability of the flight rises rapidly because the fixed costs are being spread over an ever increasing number of passengers. Thus, once a profitable level of operation is reached, the level of profits rises very rapidly with further increases in the level of output (passengers carried). Airlines then have a large degree of operating leverage, for a small percentage change in the number of passengers carried will produce a much larger percentage change in profits.

Retailing is an entirely different type of operation. The firm may have few fixed costs (e.g., rent for the building) and many variable costs. As the firm expands output, these variable costs (e.g., wages, financing to carry inventory) also expand. Such operations do not have a large degree of operating leverage, for, as sales expand, there is not a large expansion in profits.

Figure 16–6 compares an airline with a retailer and illustrates how changes in sales have more impact on profits of the firm with the high degree of operating leverage. The top half of the figure is a breakeven chart for an airline; the bottom half is a breakeven chart for a retailer. For ease of comparison both the breakeven level of output (Q_B) and the total revenue curve (TR) are identical for both firms. The differences between the two firms entirely rests upon the nature of their cost curves. The retailer has lower fixed costs (OR versus OS), but the total cost curve for the retailer rises more rapidly.

The effect of these differences in costs (i.e., the difference in operating leverage) can be seen by moving along the horizontal axis. If output increases from Q_B to Q_1, the profits are greater for the airline than for the retailer (AB versus CD). If output decreases to Q_2, the losses are greater for the airline (EF versus GH). The airline experienced greater fluctuations in profits and losses for the same change in output because it has the higher degree of operating leverage.

This fluctuation in earnings implies that the airline is the riskier firm. In periods of declining sales, it will experience greater losses than the retailer. Firms with a higher degree of operating leverage are generally riskier than firms with a lower degree of operating leverage. Firms with the small degree of operating leverage may not achieve a rapid increase in profits as sales expand. However, they will not experience rapid declines in the level of profits when sales decline, because most of their costs are variable costs which also decrease with the decrease in output and sales.

These differences in operating leverage indicate that some businesses are inherently more risky than others. Risk emanates from two sources, the nature of the business and how the business is financed. These risks are called "business risk" and "financial risk," respectively. Airlines then have a high degree of business risk while retailers, especially those selling staples

Earnings fluctuate

Fluctuations in earnings indicates risk

Business risk

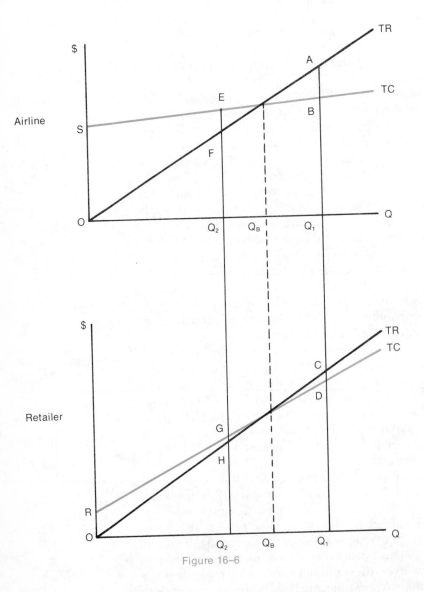

**Breakeven Analysis For An Airline
And A Retailer**

Figure 16–6

such as food and clothing, may not have this high degree of
business risk. (Financial risk is discussed below in Chapter 21.)

Management's goal is to maximize the value of the firm.
Excessive risk, however, diminishes the worth of a firm. While
risk cannot be avoided by business, management can follow
actions that reduce the impact of risk. For example if a firm has a
high degree of operating leverage (i.e., a high degree of business
risk), then management may avoid using an excessive amount of

*Excessive operating
leverage may reduce
the value of the firm*

debt financing. This would reduce financial risk so that the combined elements of business and financial risks are not excessive.

In summary, measuring operating leverage, like determining the breakeven level of output, is another tool that management may use in planning the level of operations. Operating leverage points out the importance of fixed costs and increases management's ability to perceive how fluctuations in sales will produce fluctuations in the level of profits. The degree of operating leverage shows how increasing the level of fixed costs will affect the firm's profits. Management needs to be aware that such an increase in fixed costs will increase (1) fluctuations in profits as sales fluctuate and (2) the level of output necessary for the firm to be profitable. These, in turn, increase the element of risk and may reduce the value of the firm. Hence excessive amounts of operating leverage will be detrimental to the firm's owners, for it decreases the value of their investment.

SUMMARY

This chapter has added two techniques to management's kit of tools to analyze current operations and to plan future operations. The first technique is breakeven analysis, which has a variety of uses. It may be employed to analyze the effects on profits and losses of fluctuations in sales and costs. Since the technique tells management what level of sales is necessary to avoid losses, it is particularly useful when management is anticipating introducing a new product or entering a new field.

The degree of operating leverage is a measure of the responsiveness of profits to changes in output. It brings to the foreground the importance of fixed costs relative to variable costs. Firms that have high fixed costs have a high degree of financial leverage. The firm must achieve a higher level of output and sales in order to earn profits. In effect, the firm has to spread the overhead. Firms whose costs primarily vary with output do *not* have a high degree of operating leverage. They may achieve profits at a lower level of output. However, once profitable levels of output have been achieved, the firm with the high degree of operating leverage will experience more rapid increases in profits with further increases in output.

KEY WORDS AND TERMS

fixed costs	total revenue
variable costs	breakeven level of output
total costs	degree of operating leverage

QUESTIONS FOR THOUGHT AND DISCUSSION _____

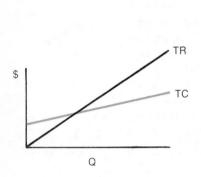

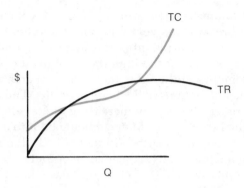

1. What happens to the breakeven level of output in the above graphs if fixed costs are increased (i.e., a parallel upward shift)?

2. If the management of a firm were considering introducing a new product, should they use breakeven analysis? If so, should the linear or nonlinear version be used? What will probably be the most difficult (and probably most important) part of constructing this analysis?

3. Why is the degree of operating leverage different for a bus company and a retailer? For a given percentage change in sales, which firm may experience the greater change in profits? Why will the use of debt financing increase the element of risk if the firm has a high degree of operating leverage?

4. A firm has the following cost and revenue functions:

$$TR = 4Q$$
$$TC = 3000 + 3Q$$

(a) What is the breakeven level of output?
(b) If the level of output is 5000 units, what is the degree of operating leverage?
(c) If the output increases to 10,000 units, what happens to the degree of operating leverage?
If the firm changes its costs so the new cost schedule is $TC = 5000 + 2.5\,Q$, what happens to (1) the breakeven level of output and (2) the degree of operating leverage at 5000 and 10,000 units of output?

5. A firm can produce a new product by either of two methods. With method A the fixed costs are $10,000 and the variable costs are $3 a unit. With method B the fixed costs are $20,000 and the variable costs are $2.50 a unit. The output sells for $4.00 a unit. What is the breakeven level of output for each method and which should the firm prefer if it anticipates rising sales?

Chapter 17

PLANNING: FORECASTING AND BUDGETING

Learning Objectives

- Differentiate between forecasting and budgeting.
- Identify the assets and liabilities that automatically vary with the level of sales.
- Illustrate the per cent of sales technique method of forecasting.
- Describe the use of estimated equations to forecast.
- Construct a cash budget.
- Explain the purpose of the cash budget.

"What we plan we build"

Phoebe Cary (Dreams and Realities)

Forecasting is an important part of a business activity. This is particularly true with forecasts of the financial needs of the firm. Since all assets must be financed, it is crucial to the financial health of the company to forecast the anticipated level of assets in order to plan for their financing. There are several techniques for such forecasting, and this chapter will briefly cover several of them. None of these techniques can forecast with complete accuracy, so the chapter will consider not only the techniques but also their potential biases.

After forecasts are made, the firm can make plans based on the forecasts. Budgets can be constructed that employ the estimates. The last part of this chapter considers one of these budgets, the cash budget. This budget uses forecasts of sales, receipts, and disbursements to plan the firm's need for short-term finance. The cash budget identifies when the firm will have excess cash and when its cash position will be deficient. This information lets the financial manager prepare a financing plan before the funds must be acquired. Such planning will give the financial manager time to find the most advantageous source of funds.

PER CENT OF SALES

The per cent of sales technique for forecasting financial requirements isolates the assets and liabilities that change with the level of sales and expresses each as a per cent of sales. These percentages are then used to forecast the level of each asset and liability. The forecasted increase in the level of assets must be financed and the increased level of liabilities will automatically finance some of the increase in assets. The difference between the increase in the assets and the liabilities must be financed by other means.

Assets and liabilities expressed as a per cent of sales

Percent of sales uses those assets and liabilities that automatically vary with sales

What assets vary with the level of sales? Consider a firm with the following balance sheet:

ASSETS		LIABILITIES AND EQUITY	
Cash	$100	Accounts payable	$200
Accounts receivable	300	Bank note	200
Inventory	300	Other current liabilities	100
Plant and equipment	500	Long-term debt	300
	$1200	Equity	400
			$1200

Several of the assets will vary with the firm's level of sales. A higher level of sales will require that the firm carry more inventory and will also increase the accounts receivable, as credit sales should expand if all sales increase. The level of cash may also rise with increased cash sales, and the firm will want to increase its level of cash holdings to meet the expanded liquidity needs, such as the payroll associated with higher sales volume.

While cash, inventory, and accounts receivable increase as sales rise, other assets do not automatically expand with increased sales. The plant and equipment may not be increased but will be used at a higher level of capacity. If the level of sales rises sufficiently, more plant and equipment must be acquired, but no automatic increase in these fixed assets must occur as sales volume increases.

All the assets that increase with the higher level of sales must be financed. The funds to finance these assets must come from somewhere, and one source is any liability that also expands with the level of sales. If liabilities increase sufficiently, they will cover the expansion in assets, but if they do not, then the firm must find additional financing in order to operate at the higher level of sales.

Assets must be financed

Accounts payable are the primary liability that increases with expanded sales. This expansion in the accounts payable occurs because the firm's suppliers increase goods sold to the firm on credit, and other expenses such as wages and salaries automatically expand. These accounts payable are the primary source of finance that automatically expands with the level of

Accounts payable are an automatic source of finance

operations of the firm. The other short-term liabilities such as notes payable and the current portion of long-term debt due this fiscal year do not automatically expand with the level of sales and thus are not automatic sources of finance.

Example of per cent of sales

How the per cent of sales technique of forecasting works may be illustrated by the previous balance sheet. After identifying the assets and liabilities that vary with the level of sales, they are expressed as a per cent of sales. Thus if the firm has inventory of $300 and sales of $2000, inventory is 15 per cent of sales ($300/$2000). The following exhibit expresses all the assets and liabilities in the previous balance sheet that vary with the level of sales as a percentage of sales (assuming a level of sales of $2000):

ASSETS		LIABILITIES	
Cash	5%	Accounts payable	10%
Accounts receivable	15%		
Inventory	15%		

The per cent of sales for the assets and liabilities that do not automatically increase with the level of sales has not been determined. Thus, as may be seen from the exhibit, the ratio of all assets that vary with sales is 35 per cent, and the ratio for liabilities is 10 per cent.

Once the percentage has been determined and the anticipated level of sales has been forecasted, the anticipated level of sales is multiplied by each percentage to determine the anticipated level of each asset and liability necessary to sustain that level of sales. For example, if management anticipates the level of sales will rise to $2400 (a 20 per cent increase), then the per cent of sales technique will forecast the following level of assets and liabilities for each asset and liability that varies with sales:

ASSETS		LIABILITIES	
Cash	$120	Accounts payable	$240
Accounts receivable	360		
Inventory	360		

In this case the per cent of sales method of forecasting states that the level of inventory will rise to $360 ($2400 × .15), the level of accounts receivable will be $360 ($2400 × .15), and the level of cash will be ($2400 × .05). The automatic expansion in assets is $140, which may be found by multiplying the increase in sales ($400) by the 35 per cent, which is the sum of the ratios of all assets that vary with the level of sales.

Simultaneously with the increase in assets, the accounts payable will rise to $240 ($2400 × .10). The total increase in assets is $140, while the increase in liabilities is $40. This $40 increase in liabilities will finance only part of the increase in assets. $100 ($140 − $40) of assets will require other sources of financing. Management may expect that the firm will operate at a profit, and these profits can be retained to finance the additional assets. But profits after taxes must be at least $100 to finance the expansion in assets. If management cannot anticipate after-tax profits of $100, then an outside source of finance (such as a bank loan) will have to be found to finance the anticipated increase in assets necessitated by the expansion in sales.

The above example illustrates the per cent of sales technique of forecasting. Obviously it is a very simple technique, for in effect it asserts that if an asset or liability is some per cent of sales and sales expand by some per cent then the assets and liabilities will also expand by the same per cent. The proportion of the assets to sales is maintained; it remains constant. This proportion is illustrated by Figure 17–1, which shows the relationship between sales and inventory. The horizontal axis is the level of sales, and the vertical axis is the level of inventory. A similar graph may be drawn for any asset or liability that varies with sales. Point A represents the current level of sales (S_1) and the level of inventory (I_1). If a line is drawn through point A and the origin, the slope of the line ($\Delta I / \Delta S$) represents the per cent of sales. This relationship is summarized by the following equation:

The assumption: the proportions are fixed

(1) $$I = bS$$

Relationship Between Inventory and Sales

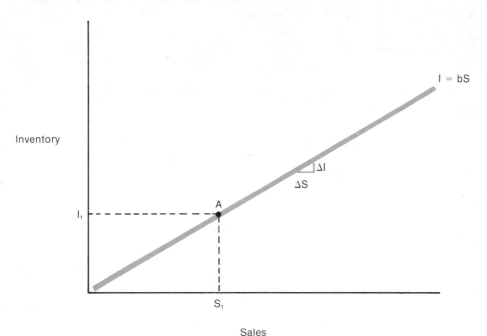

Sales

Figure 17–1

S is the level of sales; I, the inventory; and b is the per cent of sales. The ratio of current inventory to current sales determined the per cent of sales which in this case is also the slope of the line. Once this percentage has been determined, then it is easy to predict the level of inventory associated with any level of sales. In the above example, inventory was 15 per cent of sales. Thus if sales are $1000, inventory will be $150 ($1000 × .15). If sales expand to $20,000, then inventory must expand to $3000 ($20,000 × .15). By this method, all that is necessary to project the level of the asset is (1) the ratio of the current level of that asset to current sales and (2) the anticipated level of sales.

Simplicity versus accuracy

Obviously the per cent of sales method of forecasting is very simple. Unfortunately, however, it may produce biased and inaccurate estimates. If such estimates understate the financial needs, they may cause the firm to have financial difficulties, for finding additional credit rapidly may be difficult. If the technique over-predicts the financial needs, it may cause the firm to borrow more than is necessary and hence cause the firm to pay unnecessary interest expense.

One source of the potential bias is that the per cent of sales method assumes that the current percentage will hold for all levels of sales. This assumption need not be true. For example, the firm may be able to economize on inventory as the firm becomes larger. Thus inventory as a per cent of sales may decline as the level of sales rises. The converse may also be true as sales decline. The firm may continue to carry items even though sales have diminished, or there may be a lag after the decline in sales before the firm recognizes which items are moving slowly and ceases to carry them. Thus inventory as a per cent of sales may rise when the level of sales declines.

While the per cent of sales technique of forecasting may produce biased estimates, it is still employed as a tool of forecasting for two reasons. First, it is very simple and may be computed with ease. Second, if the change in sales is relatively small, then the estimate will probably not be significantly biased. The larger the increase in sales, the more the estimate will be incorrect; but if management is concerned with only a small change in the level of sales, the per cent of sales method of forecasting financial needs may be sufficient.

REGRESSION ANALYSIS

Inventory as a per cent of sales may vary

One method to overcome this bias is to consider the relationship between the asset or liability and sales over several years. For example, Table 17–1 depicts a firm's level of inventory and sales for the last five years. This information indicates there is a positive relationship between the level of inventory and sales, but inventory as a per cent of sales has declined. If this

TABLE 17–1 Five-Year Level of Inventory and Sales

YEAR	SALES	INVENTORY	INVENTORY AS A PER CENT OF SALES
1977	$2000	$600	30%
1976	1700	530	31
1975	1400	500	36
1974	1200	470	39
1973	1000	400	40

decline continues, then the use of a percentage determined from only one year's observations will overpredict the necessary level of inventory.

This relationship between sales and inventory is plotted in Figure 17–2, which also indicates the positive trend between sales and inventory, for the points are rising. Using the graph in this form, however, may be difficult. For example, it may be difficult to project the level of inventory if the level of sales rises to $2500. This problem may be overcome if the points are expressed as an equation. The technique that summarizes the points in equation form is called regression.

Relationship may be expressed as a simple equation

Linear regression analysis is relatively easy if the firm has access to computer facilities. The technique estimates the following two important elements: the intercept of the Y axis and the slope of the line. Figure 17–3 reproduces the points in Figure 17–2 but in addition passes a line through the points so that the relationship between inventory and sales is expressed by the following simple linear equation:

(2) $$I = a + bS$$

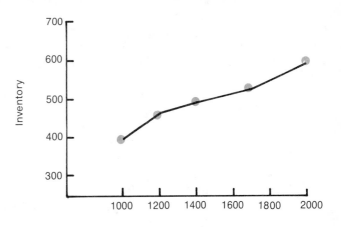

Trend in Inventory and Sales

Sales

Figure 17–2

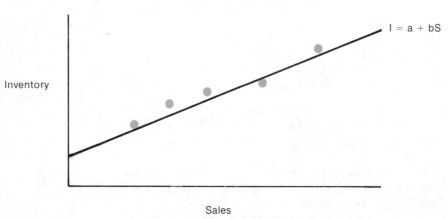

Figure 17–3

The vertical intercept (a) gives the level of inventory the firm carries even when there are no or very few sales. The rate at which the line rises is the slope ($\Delta I/\Delta S$), and this is represented by the symbol b. Regression analysis estimates *numerical* values for a and b, the intercept and the slope.

Equation may be used to forecast
For this firm, regression analysis indicates that the equation for the relationship between inventory and sales is:

$$I = 421 + .054S$$

Once the firm has the estimated equation, it can then forecast the level of inventory for any level of sales. For example, if sales are $3000, then the equation estimates that the level of inventory will be $583 which is obtained from the equation by substituting $3000 for S and solving for I:

$$I = 421 + .054 (3000); I = 583$$

Can estimate nonlinear and multivariate equations
The above example is simple linear regression analysis. Regression analysis may be nonlinear and may include more than two variables (multiple regression). For example, the level of inventory may be related not only to the level of sales but also to other variables such as the season of the year or the availability of credit. Multiple regression analysis is a means to isolate the effects of several variables on the level of inventory. However, nonlinear and multiple regression are topics of advanced courses and will not be pursued here.

While nonlinear and multiple regression analysis will not be developed, it is desirable to compare simple linear regression with the per cent of sales forecasting techniques. The per cent of sales technique is a simple case of regression analysis in which there is no intercept and the slope is determined by the origin and one observation. The per cent of sales technique then assumes that the present ratio of inventory to sales is constant and is the slope of the equation. On the basis of that assumption, the technique then projects the level of inventory. Regression analysis, however, does not make that assumption and estimates an equation using several observations that relate inventory and sales.

The differences in the predictive power in the two techniques are illustrated in Table 17–2, which is based upon the previous example. The first column gives sales, and the second and third columns give the estimated level of inventory. The second column uses the per cent of sales method that assumes that the ratio inventory to sales is constant (30 per cent of sales). The third column uses the regression equation $I = 421 + .054S$, which was estimated on the basis of data for past levels of inventory and sales.

Regression analysis may be more accurate

As may be seen in Table 17–2, the higher the anticipated level of sales, the larger the estimated level of inventory. But the estimated level of inventory is larger for the per cent of sales method than for the regression technique. Thus the per cent of sales techniques may be over-estimating the desired level of inventory. For example, if as the firm grows there are economies in inventory management, then the level of inventory need not grow as rapidly. Thus, the ratio of inventory to sales will decline. Under these circumstances the regression analysis gives a better estimate of the desired level of inventory and is the more accurate predictor.

CASH BUDGET

"Budget" is a cash term frequently encountered concerning financial matters. A budget is an estimate of receipts and disbursements for a period of time, and even individual households as well as firms may have such plans. They are important predictive tools, for they enumerate the anticipated flows of revenues and expenditures for the firm and household. In addition to

Budgets: a planning tool

TABLE 17–2 Comparison of Per Cent of Sales and Regression Techniques of Forecasting

SALES	PER CENT OF SALES FORECAST	REGRESSION ANALYSIS FORECAST
	(Inventory = .30 Sales)	(Inventory = 421 + .054 Sales)
$1500	$450	$502
2000	600	529
2500	750	556
3000	900	583

being a planning device, budgets may also be used as a tool of control. Individual departments within the firm can have budgets which constrain their ability to spend or require that excess spending decisions be made by higher management. The budgets then act as a constraint on the firm's divisions and give management more internal control of the firm's operations. The budget may also be used as a tool to judge performance. Was the budget maintained? Which divisions within the firm overextended their budgets? By comparing the actual performance with the anticipated performance, management may be able to identify sources of financial problems.

An estimate of receipts and disbursements

The period of time for a budget is variable and depends on the nature of the firm and the purpose of the budget. Some budgets may be for short periods of time, six months, for example. A firm with seasonal or fluctuating sales may develop a budget that covers the season. Other budgets may cover many years. For example, a public utility may have a budget for capital spending on plant and equipment that covers planned expenditures and revenues for many years.

Time dimension may vary

Budgets are particularly useful planning tools for short time periods. An important example of short-term budgeting is the cash budget which is used to predict the short-term needs of the firm for cash. Once the cash budget has been constructed, then the financial manager can plan for the management of the cash during periods of excess cash and for the acquisition of cash when it is so needed. The cash budget thus helps the financial manager to determine not only that cash is needed but also when it is needed. This element of time is crucial, for the financial manager can contact sources of short-term credit in advance of the need for funds. Such early contact will indicate that management is aware of its financial needs, and this should increase the confidence of the lenders in the firm's management. Such confidence may in turn result in more favorable terms which reduce the cost of the funds.

Cash budget helps financial planning

While the cash budgets of firms in different industries will vary because the flow of expenditures and revenue differs, the desirability of good cash management applies to all firms. Emphasis on the management of cash has recently increased. This may in part be explained by the recent high yields on short-term assets. Also the short-term money market is very well developed, for there are a variety of short-term assets (e.g., Treasury bills, certificates of deposits, commercial paper). Thus there are many assets in which excess funds may be put to work. Good management of cash is an important means to increase the profitability of the firm. The cash budget, which indicates when the firm will have excess cash and when it will need short-term credit, is an integral tool in planning the management of cash.

Excess cash should be invested in short-term securities

The cash budget is basically a table relating time, disbursements, and receipts. The units of time may be monthly, weekly,

A table of disbursements and receipts

or even daily. For purposes of exposition, only a monthly cash budget will be developed. The cash items are grouped into inflows (receipts) and outflows (disbursements). The difference between the inflows and the outflows is the summary that indicates to the financial manager whether to expect excess cash which needs to be invested or cash deficiencies which must be financed.

The construction of a simple cash budget for the fall season may be illustrated by the following example. The financial manager has determined the following anticipated sales for the next seven months:

Cash budget employs estimates

May	$15,000	August	50,000	November	10,000
June	20,000	September	40,000		
July	30,000	October	20,000		

Thirty per cent of the sales are for cash, and 70 per cent are on credit. Of the credit sales, 90 per cent are paid after one month, and 10 per cent are paid after two months. Thus the financial manager expects that of the anticipated sales of $15,000 in May, $4500 will be for cash ($15,000 × .3) and $10,500 will be on credit ($15,000 × .7). Of these credit sales $9450 will be collected after one month ($10,500 × .9), and $1050 will be collected after two months ($10,500 × .1).

If the firm owns any other assets that will become cash during the time period, those assets must also be included in the cash budget. For example, if the firm owns a short-term asset valued at $10,000 that will be due on June first, it must be included in the cash budget. Since the purpose of the cash budget is to determine the excess or shortage of cash that the firm will experience, all cash items must be included in the budget. Noncash expenses like depreciation are excluded.

In this case, the firm's sales are seasonal, so it will seek to build up inventory in anticipation of the seasonal business. As the inventory is produced, the labor and materials must be paid for. The estimated expenditures for wages and materials for the season are:

May	$30,000	August	30,000	November	3000
June	25,000	September	10,000		
July	38,000	October	5000		

These estimated expenditures indicate that the buildup in inventory occurs in June, July, and August. The sales, however, occur primarily in July, August, and September. The sales lag after the buildup of inventory; thus there will be a drain on the firm's cash.

Besides the expenditures that vary with the level of output, the firm has expenses that do not vary with the level of operations. These include interest and rent of $1000 a month and administrative expenses of $2000 a month. The firm also has to make an estimated quarterly income tax payment in September of $2500 and a payment of $1000 on August first to retire part of a debt issue. Management likes to maintain a minimum cash balance of $10,000 as a safety valve in case there is an emergency. The firm's cash position at the beginning of May is $12,000, which exceeds the desired minimum level of cash balances.

The financial manager now combines the above information to obtain estimates of the monthly net increase or decrease in the firm's cash position. (The budget may be constructed on a weekly, monthly, or quarterly basis depending on the time available for its construction, the need for extreme accuracy, and the volatility of the entries.) The monthly cash budget is illustrated in Table 17–3. The first part of the table presents the estimated cash that the firm receives monthly. The first line of the table gives the estimated sales, and the next four lines give the estimated cash generated by the sales. The second line enumerates the cash sales; the third line gives the collections that occur on the credit sales after a month, and the fourth line gives the credit collection that occurred two months after the sales. In the table the arrow shows when May's credit sales yield cash receipts. The fifth line gives other sources of cash payments (i.e., the short-term debt instrument that matures). The sum of lines two through five is the monthly cash receipts of the firm and is given in line six.

The second part of the table enumerates the firm's monthly cash disbursements. Line seven gives the monthly expenses that vary with the level of sales; while line eight gives the expenses that do not vary with the level of output (i.e., the interest, rent, and administrative expenses). The ninth line gives other cash disbursements (i.e., the $2500 tax payment and the $1000 debt retirement payment). The sum of all the monthly cash payments is given in the tenth line.

The third part of the table summarizes the first two parts and indicates if the firm has a net inflow or outflow of cash during the month. Thus the cash budget establishes if the firm has excess cash that it can use to purchase short-term income earning assets (like a certificate of deposit) or has insufficient cash which requires that the firm find short-term financing. The eleventh line is the difference between lines six and ten; it gives the net inflow of cash during the month. The twelfth line gives the firm's cash position at the beginning of the month. The sum of the eleventh and twelfth lines gives the firm's cash position at the end of the month, which is given in line thirteen. The minimum desired level of cash is given in the fourteenth line. The difference between cash position at the end of the month and the desired minimum level of cash is given in the fifteenth line of the table. This is the important line for it indicates that the firm will have either excess cash generated by operations during the month or a cash deficiency.

TABLE 17–3   Monthly Cash Budget (For a Firm with a Fall Season)

		MAY	JUNE	JULY	AUGUST	SEPTEMBER	OCTOBER	NOVEMBER	DECEMBER	JANUARY
Part 1										
1	Anticipated sales	$ 15000	$ 20000	$ 30000	$ 50000	$40000	$ 20000	$ 10000		
2	Cash sales	4500	6000	9000	15000	12000	6000	3000		
3	Accounts collected (one month lag)		9450	12600	18900	40500	25200	12600	6300	
4	Accounts collected (two month lag)			1050	1400	2100	4500	2800	1400	700
5	Other cash receipts		10000							
6	Total cash receipts	4500	25450	22650	35300	54600	35700	17400		
Part 2										
7	Variable cash expenses	3000	25000	38000	30000	10000	5000	3000		
8	Fixed cash expenses	3000	3000	3000	3000	3000	3000	3000		
9	Other cash expenses				1000	2500				
10	Total cash disbursements	6000	28000	41000	34000	15500	8000	6000		
11	Cash gain (or loss) during the month (line 6 minus line 10)	(1500)	(2550)	(18450)	1000	39100	27700	11400		
Part 3										
12	Cash position at beginning of month	12000	10500	7950	(10500)	(9500)	29600	57300		
13	Cash position at end of month (line 12 minus line 11)	10500	7950	(10500)	(9500)	29600	57300	69700		
14	Desired level of cash	(10000)	(10000)	(10000)	(10000)	(10000)	(10000)	(10000)		
15	Excess (or shortage) of cash (line 13 minus line 14)	500	(2050)	(20500)	(19500)	19600	47300	58700		

How is the information on the cash budget interpreted? The process of interpretation may be illustrated by considering several months. For example, during the month of May the firm has a net loss of cash of $1500 (line 11), but since the firm began the month with $12,000 in cash, it has enough cash to cover the anticipated cash loss and still maintain its desired level of cash holdings. This is indicated in line 15 which shows that there is excess cash of $500 over the desired level of cash balances. In the month of June cash disbursements once again exceeded receipts (by $2550). The extent to which the cash expenditures exceeded the receipts, however, was reduced by the receipt of the $10,000 payment on the short-term asset. Thus it appears that the financial manager was previously aware of the firm's cash needs in June and July and so purchased a short-term asset that matured in June. However, even with this extra inflow of cash, the cash position at the end of the month drops to $7950 (line 13) which is less than the desired level of cash balances by $2050 (line 15). The financial manager would then have to decide to let the cash position fall below the desired minimum or to borrow the $2050 to maintain the desired minimum level of cash.

In July the difference between the cash outflows and cash receipts grows even larger. Anticipated cash payments exceed cash receipts by $9500 before allowance is made for the desired desired level of cash are added, the firm is short $20,500 (line 15), minimum level of cash. When the actual cash outflow and the and this cash deficiency continues through August. Thus the financial manager can anticipate that the firm will need $20,500 of short-term financing to cover the firm's cash needs for July and August. After August the firm's cash position improves as the cash from its credit sales flows into the firm. In September the firm will have generated $19,600 in excess cash, and after September the firm's cash position continues to improve. Thus the financial manager can anticipate having excess cash that can be used to purchase a short-term income earning asset that matures when the cycle begins again.

Cash budget
forewarns when
short-term finance
will be needed

The cash budget helps the financial manager to establish that the firm will need short-term external finance and when the firm will need this external finance. In the above example, the financial manager can anticipate that the firm will need external short-term funds in June, July, and August. The financial manager also knows when the cash will be generated that may be used to retire the short-term debt. Thus the financial manager can approach the lender with the following information: (1) the firm's cash needs, and (2) estimates concerning when the firm will be able to repay the loan. The financial manager can plan now for this loan and may be able to shop around for terms. By preparing the cash budget, the financial manager can not only anticipate the firm's financial needs but also arrange for the necessary finance in advance. Such planning should increase the lender's confidence in the management, and this may result in more favorable credit terms.

This chapter has covered several tools that the financial manager may use to forecast the firm's cash needs. The simplest technique is the per cent of sales method of forecasting, but its accuracy is open to question. Regression analysis is a more sophisticated forecasting tool. While the computer has decreased the difficulty of performing this type of analysis, its accuracy depends upon the quality of the data and the proper specifications of the variables and the functions. Thus regression analysis may be a useful tool only to firms with sufficient resources to perform the analysis well.

Budgeting is another tool for financial planning and control. The cash budget which enumerates cash inflows and outflows is a particularly useful tool, for it enables management to plan its short-term cash needs. By constructing such a budget, management is able to better plan its financial strategy, for the cash budget indicates both the timing and the amount of the firm's short-term need for finance.

per cent of sales
slope
intercept
regression
receipts
disbursements
cash budget

1. Budgeting is a means by which management in a large firm may control operations. Is such budgeting also necessary in a small firm? What role can a cash budget play in a firm of any size?

2. A firm uses the per cent of sales method of forecasting. Its inventory is 12 per cent of sales, while accounts receivable are only 6 per cent of sales. If sales double, what happens to the level of inventory and accounts receivable? What assumption

has been made by this technique of forecasting? Is this assumption more valid for small or large changes in sales?

3. Why may accurate data be more important than the forecasting methods used?

4. A firm with sales of $1000 has the following balance sheet:

ASSETS		LIABILITIES AND EQUITY	
Accounts receivable	$200	Trade accounts payable	$200
Inventory	$400	Long-term debt	$600
Plant	$800	Equity	$600

It earns 10 per cent on sales (after taxes) and pays no dividends.
(a) Determine the balance sheet entries for sales of $1500 using the per cent of sales method of forecasting.
(b) Will the firm need external financing to grow to sales of $1500?
(c) Construct the new balance sheet and use newly issued long-term debt to cover any financial deficiency.

5. A firm has the following monthly pattern of sales.

January	$100
February	$300
March	$500
April	$1000
May	$500
June	$300
July	$100

(60 per cent of the sales are on credit and are collected after a month.)

The company pays wages each month that are 60 per cent of sales and has fixed costs of $100 a month. In March it receives $200 from a bond that matures. In April and July it makes a tax payment of $200 and seeks to have $150 in cash at all times. Construct a cash budget that indicates the firm's monthly needs for short-term financing.

Chapter 18

MANAGEMENT OF SHORT-TERM ASSETS

Learning Objectives

- Identify the costs of carrying inventory.
- Determine the economic size of an inventory order.
- Differentiate between LIFO and FIFO.
- Explain why LIFO is preferred during periods of inflation.
- Describe costs and benefits of offering credit.
- Prepare a schedule that ages accounts receivable.
- Explain the purpose of cash management.
- List several alternatives to holding excess cash.

"Yesterday is a cancelled check; tomorrow is a promissory note; today is ready cash."

Hubert Tinley

This chapter considers managing short-term assets. The following chapter is concerned with their financing. These assets are frequently referred to as the working capital that flows through the firm. The firm acquires inventory which is subsequently sold for either cash or credit. Then the credit sales are collected, the cash may be reinvested in inventories, and the cycle is repeated.

All assets must be financed; inventory, accounts receivable, and cash are all uses of funds. The financial manager must determine the best use for the firm's funds, and thus part of his role is to establish the firm's policy for managing working capital. He must anticipate the firm's needs for inventory and its ability to collect its accounts receivable. Any excess cash must be put to work by investing short-term, income earning assets or by retiring debt.

This chapter covers several aspects of working capital management. The first section deals with inventory: the inventory cycle, the optimal order quantity, and valuation. The next section of the chapter is devoted to the management of accounts receivable. The chapter ends with a discussion of cash management. A common theme throughout the chapter is the need to finance these assets and to earn a return sufficient to justify the use of the funds. This return is, of course, related to the potential benefits offered by the specific asset versus the costs associated with carrying the asset. However, maximization of the value of the firm requires that short-term assets, like long-term assets, must offer a return equal to or greater than the firm's cost of capital. Thus the financial manager needs to be aware of the benefits and costs of a particular policy that affect the management of the firm's working capital.

THE INVENTORY CYCLE

Inventory flows
through the firm

A firm produces output to sell or buys items wholesale and then retails the product. In either case the firm currently acquires inventory to sell in the future. This inventory must be paid for; it must be financed by either borrowed funds or equity. The more rapidly the firm turns over the inventory, the less finance is necessary to carry the inventory. (In Chapter 15, Ratio Analysis, one of the important ratios used to analyze the firm was the inventory turnover.) Rapid turnover indicates that the firm is able to sell the inventory quickly, and hence the firm ties up less of its funds in inventory. Rapid turnover, however, is not by itself desirable, for such turnover may result in the firm not having inventory available when there are buyers. Being out of stock may result in the loss of sales and profits. Thus, while rapid inventory turnover will decrease the firm's financial needs, it may also result in lower profits for the firm.

Graphic illustration
of the inventory cycle

The inventory cycle is illustrated by Figure 18–1. The firm initially purchases inventory (AB) and sells this inventory over time. Thus, as time passes, some inventory is sold, and the stock of inventory is drawn down. After a period of time (T_1), the inventory is sold and the stock is depleted. The firm then purchases new inventory (AB), and the cycle is repeated $(T_1$ to $T_2)$.

Safety stock

In reality a firm would not let its inventory fall to zero before it restocked its shelves. Instead it will seek to maintain a minimum level of inventory (i.e., a safety stock) to assure that the item is always available for sale. Such a safety stock is illustrated in Figure 18–2. The minimum level of inventory (i.e., the safety stock) is OA. The inventory order is next added to the safety stock, so that the firm has a maximum inventory of OB which consists of the safety stock OA and the order AB. This total inventory is drawn down as sales are made. Once the inventory has decreased to the safety stock, then the firm reorders.

The firm could avoid reordering the inventory by increasing its initial purchase. By doubling its initial purchase, this firm could double the time before it has to reorder. This is illustrated by Figure 18–3, which reproduces Figure 18–2 and adds a larger

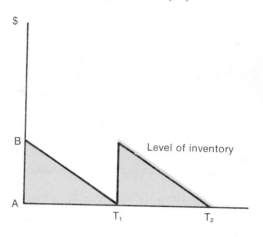

Figure 18–1

Simple Inventory Cycle
Including A Safety Stock

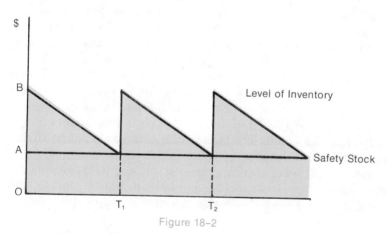

Figure 18–2

Longer Inventory Cycle

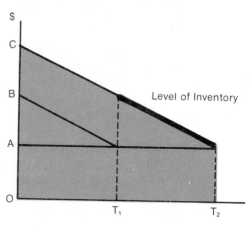

Figure 18–3

inventory purchase (AC) that is twice AB. The inventory OC is sufficient to last to T_2 before the firm must reorder and repeat the procedure. Of course, the firm could avoid all inventory cycles if it has sufficient inventory. However, all inventory must be financed. It costs money to carry the inventory, and hence management should determine the best level of inventory to purchase to reduce the cost of carrying it. '

The Economic Order Quantity

The trade off between order costs and carrying costs

The optimal size of an order of inventory is commonly called the "economic order quantity" (EOQ), which seeks to minimize the cost of carrying and processing inventory. This cost has several components, and minimizing one component may significantly increase the cost of another component. What are these costs? First, there is the cost of placing the order, which includes fees such as shipping and brokerage and the cost to the firm of processing the order. Generally, the larger the order or the less frequent the order is made, the lower these expenses are when expressed as a percentage of the inventory. For example, the cost of placing an order for 100 units every month may be $200, but the cost of placing an order for 200 units every two months is $300. While the total cost of the larger order is higher, the cost per unit is lower. The cost per unit of the smaller, more frequent order is $2 ($200/100), but the per unit cost of the larger order is only $1.50 ($300/200). The larger order permits a reduction in the per unit cost of the order.

A second set of costs are those associated with carrying the inventory. These costs include not only insurance, storage, and handling expenses but also the cost of the finance necessary to carry the inventory. Inventory, like any other asset, must be financed, and this cost must be included to determine the economic order quantity. All these carrying costs increase as the size of the inventory increases. Thus these expenses will tend to offset the lower per unit costs of larger orders. The job of management then is to balance the savings from larger orders with the increased carrying costs.

Equation (1) is a very simple method to determine the economic order quantity.

(1)
$$EOQ = \sqrt{\frac{2SO}{C}}$$

The symbols in this equation are defined as follows:

EOQ = the economic order quantity
C   = the per unit cost of carrying the inventory for a specified period of time

S   = the number of units of the item sold during a specified time period

O   = the cost of placing an order

How the formula works may be illustrated by the following simple example. A firm uses 10,000 units of an item each year, and it cost the firm $10 to carry each unit. The cost of an order is $50. When these values are substituted into Equation (1), the economic order quantity is determined as follows:

$$EOQ = \sqrt{\frac{2(10,000)(50)}{10}} = 316$$

Thus each order for inventory should be 316 units because orders of that size are most economical.

The effect of a change in the cost of carrying the inventory or the cost of processing an order may be illustrated by this equation. For example, if the costs of an order rise from $50 to $100, the economic order quantity becomes

Effect of changing ordering or carrying costs

$$EOQ = \sqrt{\frac{2(10,000)(100)}{10}} = 447$$

Thus the increase in the cost of the order raises the best reorder size from 316 to 447 units. If the carrying costs were to rise from $10 to $20, the EOQ declines from 316 to

$$EOQ = \sqrt{\frac{2(10,000)(50)}{20}} = 224$$

It is important to note that these changes in costs do not produce proportionate changes in the economic order quantity. The doubling of the order costs does not double the economic order quantity, and a doubling of the carrying costs does not result in halving the optimal order. There is more than one variable affecting the optimal order quantity. If one variable changes and the others are unaffected, there is no reason to assume there will be a proportionate change in the economic order quantity. Hence there is no simple proportionate relationship between one component of the costs and the EOQ.

The above model for the economic order quantity is, of course, an oversimplification for several reasons. First, sales do not necessarily occur as smoothly as the decline in inventory in Figures 18–1 to 18–3 suggest. Second, there may be a lag between when the firm orders the inventory and when it receives the inventory. Third, the cycles need not be of equal length. The model,

Simplifying assumptions

however, does point out that the firm purchases inventory, draws down its stock, and then reorders, and that optimal financial management requires determining the most economic quantities to order. This model can be expanded to include such considerations as the safety stock, quantity discounts, changing costs of credit, and delays in processing orders. While the model may be expanded and made more sophisticated, the basic concept is not altered. It still seeks to determine the size of the order that minimizes the total costs of carrying and processing inventory. Since management seeks to maximize the value of the firm, determining this optimal order quantity is just another facet of the many roles management must perform.

INVENTORY VALUATION

Fluctuating prices
affect cost of
inventory

The inflation of the 1970s points out the importance of valuation of inventory on a firm's earnings and income taxes. A firm purchases inventory at different times during its fiscal year. During periods of fluctuating prices, the cost of inventory will vary. The firm then subsequently sells the inventory and an important question arises: which units of the inventory were sold? Were the first units of inventory the first to be sold, or were the last units of inventory the first units to be sold? During periods of fluctuating prices, such as the recent inflation, this is an important question, because depending on the answer the firm's profits and income taxes are affected.

Two methods of
inventory valuation:
(1)FIFO; (2) LIFO

There are two prevalent means to value inventory. The first method says that the first units of inventory that are purchased are the first units sold. This system is called first in, first out (FIFO). The second method says that the last units of inventory that are purchased are the first units to be sold. Under this system the newest inventory is sold first. This system is called last in, first out (LIFO). If the firm sold all of its inventory and carried over no inventory from one year to another or if prices did not fluctuate, the difference between the two methods is not important. However, firms do carry inventory from one fiscal year to another; hence it is important to establish which items of inventory are actually sold. This determination becomes even more important during periods of fluctuating prices because the cost of the inventory fluctuates. For example, during a period of inflation the cost of the inventory will probably increase during the year. Under this condition the selection of the method of inventory valuation then affects the firm's profit and income taxes.

How this effect occurs may be illustrated by the following example. A firm purchases 100 units of inventory every two months. As a result of the inflation the cost of the inventory increases during the year. The following schedule gives the date of purchase and the cost of the inventory.

	PRICE PER UNIT	TOTAL COST OF INVENTORY
January	$1.00	$100
March	1.04	104
May	1.06	106
July	1.08	108
September	1.11	111
November	1.15	115
		$634

During the year the firm purchased 600 units of inventory for a total cost of $634. During the period in which the firm was purchasing the inventory, it was also selling it for $1.30 a unit. Total sales were 500 units for total revenues of $650. The firm thus ended the year with 100 units of inventory to sell during the next year. How much profit did the firm earn during this year? The answer will be influenced by the method of inventory valuation that is selected because the cost of the inventory rose during the year.

If FIFO is used, the first inventory is sold first. Thus the firm sold the 500 units of inventory acquired from January to September, and this inventory cost $519. If LIFO is used, the last inventory was sold first. Thus the firm sold the 500 units acquired during March through November, and this inventory cost $534. The effect on the firm's earnings of the choice of LIFO or FIFO is illustrated by the following simple income statements. The first statement is constructed using FIFO, and the second statement is constructed using LIFO.

	FIFO INCOME STATEMENT	LIFO INCOME STATEMENT
Receipts	$650	$650
Cost of Goods Sold	519	534
Income	$131	$116

The profits of the firm are higher in the FIFO income statement because the cost of the goods sold is less. The use of the lower inventory valuation thus produces higher profits, and these higher profits will result in the firm having to pay higher income taxes. In effect the cost of the inventory acquired during the year has been understated which creates the illusion of higher profits. Thus during periods of inflation some of a firm's profits may be illusionary resulting from using the FIFO method of inventory valuation. If the firm had used LIFO to evaluate the inventory, profits would be less, and thus the taxes on its income would be less. During a period of inflation the use of LIFO may give a better indication of the firm's true profitability because LIFO uses the higher cost of goods sold to determine profits.

Many firms did switch from FIFO to LIFO during 1974, a year of rapid inflation; as a result, their profits were lower. Frequently management of publicly held corporations made special

Profits and taxes are currently higher under FIFO

Many firms switched from FIFO to LIFO

efforts to inform their stockholders that the lower earnings were the result of change in inventory valuation and not a decrease in profitability. For example, Reynolds Metals reported 1974 earnings per share of $6.23 and then noted that earnings would have been $7.18 if FIFO had been used instead of LIFO to evaluate the inventory. Management wanted the stockholders to be aware of the effect on earnings of the switch from FIFO to LIFO, for the earnings were significantly lower.

While the above example illustrates that LIFO will result in lower earnings and taxes, the choice between the two methods during a period of inflation is not so clear cut. Management has to consider not only the tax consequences but also the importance that creditors and investors place on the firm's earnings. LIFO will reduce the firm's corporate income tax, but this reduction is achieved by lower profits. The firm may then appear to be less profitable to investors and creditors, who may not be aware of the inflationary bias on profits that FIFO has during a period of inflation. This reduction in profitability may reduce the value of the firm's stock or decrease the quality of its debt which in turn increases the cost of credit. Thus management must determine which is more desirable: the appearance of higher profits obtained by using FIFO versus lower corporate income taxes that result from the use of LIFO. If interest rates are high and the stock's price is low, management may conclude the cost of losing funds to the Federal Government in higher taxes is too expensive to justify the appearance of higher profits and thus adopt the LIFO method of inventory valuation.

MANAGEMENT OF ACCOUNTS RECEIVABLE

Credit sales produce accounts receivable

Accounts receivable arise through credit sales. Sales may be for cash or for credit. If the firm accepts credit, it is accepting a promise of payment in the future. The firm must determine its credit policy, and there are several factors management should consider when determining the firm's willingness to accept credit sales. As in all financial decisions, these factors involve the potential benefits versus the costs associated with the policy. The potential benefit of accepting credit is increased sales, for credit is a competitive device to encourage sales. Many consumers use credit extensively and many firms, especially retailers, also buy on credit. Thus to increase the level of sales, the firm may extend credit.

Cost of offering credit

But credit involves costs. There are the obvious processing fees, for the firm must bill its credit customers and keep records. These processing costs have encouraged many firms to accept credit cards instead of directly billing customers. Thus cards such as BankAmericard (VISA) or Master Charge have become alternative methods for firms to offer credit. The retailer accepts

the card and lets the issuing agent process and collect the accounts receivable. The retailer, however, only collects some
percentage of the credit sales, such as 98¢ on every $1.00, with
the 2¢ going to the collecting agent. While this arrangement
reduces the potential proceeds of the sale, it virtually eliminates
the processing costs.

Offering credit also involves the possibility of loss, for not all
credit sales are collected, as some purchasers will default. Of
course, many accounts are of excellent quality, as is illustrated by
the accounts receivables of utilities. These accounts are generally
of high quality because the company can force payment by
threatening to discontinue service. One method of increasing
the safety of accounts receivable is to require the buyer to pledge
the merchandise against the loan. In case of default the seller
will repossess the goods, which may then be resold. However,
the goods are now used, and the seller may be unable to sell them
for the full value of the account receivable. In such a case the
seller still has a claim on the buyer for the balance but may never
be able to collect that claim.

The possibility of
loss through default

While the ability to use merchandise as collateral to secure
an account receivable will increase the quality of the account
receivable, such use of merchandise for collateral is not practical
for many goods and services. Instead its use is primarily limited
to durable goods such as cars. When the account receivable is not
secured, then the probability of collecting the account is reduced
and the risk of loss is increased. This risk of loss is a very
important element in determining a firm's credit policy. Obviously, if the firm suffers considerable losses, it must protect itself
in some way. The firm may then grant credit sparingly or under
extreme terms, such as very high interest rates, which encourage
buyers to use cash. Also the firm can seek to protect itself by
charging more for its products in which case all buyers share in
the cost of the losses on the credit sales.

Not all acounts
receivable can be
supported by
collateral

Accounts receivable like all assets must be financed. They
are a use of funds and hence divert funds away from other uses.
As will be explained in Chapter 22, a firm must earn on all
investments a return equal to or greater than its cost of capital.
Funds tied up in accounts receivable are no different than funds
tied up in plant and equipment. Hence there must be a return on
these accounts. While some accounts do earn interest, all accounts must offer an implied return or benefit (i.e., increased
sales) to justify the use of the funds. If the accounts do not yield
this return, then they are decreasing the profitability of the firm.

Accounts
receivable are a use
of funds

As was explained in Chapter 15 (Ratio Analysis), accounts
receivable may be analyzed by the use of a turnover ratio such as
annual sales/accounts receivable or average collection period.
The faster the accounts receivable turnover, the faster they are
collected and turned into cash. A high turnover is desirable, but
it may also indicate a stringent credit policy. While such a policy

Methods to analyze
management of
accounts receivable:
(1) Turnover ratios

may result in fewer losses on credit sales, it may also imply the loss of credit sales. The firm must balance the tradeoff between a stringent credit policy and potential risk of loss on credit sales.

(2) Aging schedule
Another tool used to analyze credit sales is to age the accounts. This is basically a table that shows the length of time each account has been outstanding (i.e., unpaid). Aging the accounts thus identifies those accounts that are slowly converting into cash. How this technique works is illustrated by the following very simple example. A firm has total accounts receivable of $1000 which are composed of five customers. The amount and number of days outstanding for each account are as follows:

CUSTOMER	AMOUNT OF THE ACCOUNT	NUMBER OF DAYS OUTSTANDING
A	$300	45
B	100	70
C	100	20
D	200	35
E	300	15

From this information the following table can be constructed:

	DOLLAR VALUE	PER CENT OF TOTAL ACCOUNTS RECEIVABLE
Accounts outstanding 30 days or less	$400	40%
Accounts outstanding 30 to 60 days	$500	50%
Accounts outstanding over 60 days	$100	10%

By analyzing the length of time the accounts have gone unpaid, management is able to determine that 60 per cent of its accounts receivable take over a month to collect and that 10 per cent require more than two months.

Policy is a balancing
of costs and benefits
If its financial manager frequently ages the receivables, a pattern or norm will be established. Then if the percentage of slow accounts increases, the financial manager has identified a problem and can take action to force collection or acknowledge the accounts to be bad and discontinue carrying them at the stated value on the firm's books. However, the financial manager should remember that slow accounts are not necessarily bad and that they may eventually be collected. In many cases a firm's best or most important customers may be slow payers. This may be especially true if the buyer is larger than the seller and accounts for a major portion of the smaller firm's sales. Such a buyer has the power to ride the credit, and the small supplier may not press for payment because it fears loss of future sales.

In summary, a firm's credit policy, like all economic decisions, involves a balancing of offsetting variables. By offering credit, a firm may increase sales and profits, but with these increased sales come increased costs. There is the cost of processing collections, the cost of financing the accounts, and the risk of loss. Like any investment decision, a firm's credit policy considers the potential benefits of offering credit versus the increased expenses. If the present value of these benefits exceeds the present costs, then the firm extends credit, for such a credit policy will enhance the value of the firm.

CASH MANAGEMENT

After inventory flows through the firm into sales, and when accounts receivable have been collected, the financial manager must decide what to do with the cash. Cash management is important because, as was explained earlier, the firm must have sufficient liquidity to meet its obligations as they come due. However, liquidity reduces profitability because cash itself earns nothing. The cash must be used to purchase an income earning asset in order to increase profitability.

Excess cash is invested in short-term liquid assets

Recently, management of cash was considered unimportant. However, with the increase in short-term interest rates in the 1970s and the technological advances of the age of computers, cash management has increased in importance. The purpose of such management is to minimize the amount of cash held so that excess cash may be invested in income earning assets, especially liquid, short-term financial assets such as Treasury bills or commercial paper.

A firm holds cash for two reasons: to make transactions and as a precaution. While individuals may also hold cash for an additional reason to speculate on a decline in security prices, firms probably hold a minimal amount of cash or even no cash at all for speculative purposes. Firms are not in business to speculate on changes in security prices but to make profits through the production and sale of goods and services. The demand for money for transactions is the result of a lack of synchronization of receipts and disbursements. Money flows into the firm and the firm makes monetary payments, but there is no reason to anticipate that the cash inflows and the cash outflows will be synchronized. The firm then may have to acquire and hold cash and subsequently pay it out as the bills come due. The firm will also maintain a cash balance for precautionary purposes. These cash holdings would be used to meet an emergency. Such a safety stock of cash was considered in the previous chapter in the section on the cash budget.

*Reasons for holding cash:
(1) transactions;
(2) precautions*

There are a variety of short-term liquid assets that the financial manager may purchase with the firm's excess cash. These short-term assets are purchased in the "money market." This

Money market instruments

term differentiates short-term assets that are very liquid from long-term securities which are purchased in the "capital market."

The features of many money market instruments are discussed in various sections of this text. The safest short-term asset is the Treasury bill (which was discussed in Chapter 6). These bills are readily available and may be resold with ease should an unexpected need arise for the funds. A second possible short-term investment is commercial paper issued by large corporations with good credit ratings. (Commercial paper is discussed in more detail in the next chapter on the sources of short-term finance.) The third major money market instrument is the negotiable certificate of deposit sold by financial intermediaries, especially commercial banks.

These three short securities do not exhaust all the possibilities available to the financial manager. The firm's excess cash may be invested in short-term debt issued by state and municipal governments. Such investments not only offer the advantage of tax-free income but also are comparable in quality to other money market instruments. There are two general types, project notes and tax anticipation notes.

Project notes are issued by the United States Department of Housing and Urban Development to finance local federal programs such as urban renewal and low-rent housing. The proceeds are used for site improvements, construction, and various short-term cash needs before more permanent financing is arranged. All the short-term financing needs of various projects are lumped together and sold in the private market under the common title of "project notes." Since project notes have the full faith and credit backing of the United States Government, these tax exempt notes are as safe as Treasury bills.

Tax anticipation notes are issued by municipalities to finance current operations before tax revenues are received. As the taxes are collected, the proceeds are used to retire the debt. Similar notes are issued in anticipation of revenues from future bond issues and other sources such as revenue sharing from the Federal Government. While these anticipation notes do not offer the safety of the project notes, the interest is exempt from federal income taxation. Commercial banks and security dealers maintain secondary markets in them. So the notes may be readily liquidated should the firm need ready cash.

While there are a variety of money market instruments available, they all have common features. In particular, they are short-term debt instruments that may be readily converted into cash. Hence they may be used by the financial manager as an alternative to holding cash. The financial manager should match anticipated cash payments (such as income taxes or dividends) with the maturity dates of the debt instruments. Then, by investing the excess cash in these money market instruments, the

Treasury bills

Commercial paper

Certificates of deposit

Project notes

Tax anticipation notes

financial manager will assure not only that the firm will have the liquidity to meet its obligations but also increase its profitability.

In the previous chapter, the cash budget was used to help plan for the firm's cash need. The financial manager may also use inventory models to plan the firm's cash holding. In effect, the cash is treated like inventory and drawn down as payments are made. Once the level of the safety stock is reached, the firm's cash balances are restored, and the process is repeated. The question then becomes: What is the optimal amount of cash that the firm should acquire (i.e., what is the best or most economic level of cash holdings)?

This optimal quantity of cash is related to (1) the interest lost by holding cash instead of an income earning asset; (2) the brokerage fees and any other expenses associated with converting short-term liquid assets to cash; and (3) the total amount of money paid out during the time period. In terms of Equation (1) presented above, these variables are C, O, and S, respectively. By using the equation, it is easy to see that an increase in interest rates (i.e., an increase in C) will cause the optimal cash holdings to fall, and an increase in brokerage fees (i.e., an increase in O) will cause the desired level of cash holdings to increase.

EOQ model may be applied to cash management

How Equation (1) may be applied to cash is illustrated by the following simple example. The firm makes $100,000 in payments during the year and is able to earn 5 per cent on short-term funds that are invested. The firm pays $100 in brokerage, handling, and various fees every time it transfers funds from an income earning asset to cash. What is the optimal transfer of funds from short-term income earning assets to cash? The answer is as follows:

$$EOQ = \sqrt{\frac{2(100,000)(100)}{.05}} = 20,000$$

The firm should transfer funds from short-term assets that earn 5 per cent to cash in units of $20,000. If short-term interest rates were to rise to 10 per cent, the unit would decline to $14,142.

While the equation indicates a particular amount should be transferred from short-term liquid assets to cash, the firm may not be able to achieve such a switch. Many short-term liquid assets are not issued in denominations such as $20,000. For example, negotiable certificates of deposit are issued in units of $100,000. Thus the firm could not in reality liquidate $20,000 of negotiable certificates of deposit. Also during the year the firm may receive cash from other sources, and this, too, will alter the amount of cash that must be obtained by liquidating assets. Such inflows of cash will have to be considered in designing the best policy for cash management. But the basic principle remains the same. The financial manager must provide for the firm's needs for cash, that is, have sufficient cash on hand to meet current liabilities as they come due. Temporary excess holdings of cash should be invested in safe money market instruments to increase the firm's interest income.

SUMMARY

This chapter has covered several aspects of the management of working capital. Emphasis was placed on determining the optimal size of inventory orders, and management of accounts receivable and cash. Since all inventory and accounts receivable must be financed, it is important to determine the optimal quantity of inventory to order and the best credit policy. The firm should not tie up its sources of finance in excess inventory or unprofitable accounts receivable.

This chapter has been devoted to acquiring and managing short-term assets. Having determined what short-term assets the firm will seek to use, the next facet of the financial manager's job is to determine how these assets will be financed. Short-term assets may be financed by either short- or long-term debt or equity. The type of financing is important as the financial manager seeks to balance the benefits and costs associated with the various short-term sources. However the long-term sources are discussed in Chapters 25 and 26, after the discussion of investments in fixed assets.

KEY WORDS AND TERMS

inventory cycle	credit policy
safety stock	Treasury bills
economic order quantity (EOQ)	negotiable certificate of deposit
LIFO	commercial paper
FIFO	project note
aging accounts receivable	tax anticipation note

QUESTIONS AND PROBLEMS FOR THOUGHT AND DISCUSSION

1. How will the following affect the amount of cash a firm has?
   (a) an increase in the turnover of accounts receivable
   (b) an increase in administrative expenses
   (c) an increase in cash dividends
   (d) an increase in the rate banks charge for short-term credit

2. What is the optimal order quantity if
   (a) the per unit carrying cost is $2?
   (b) the cost of placing an order is $10?
   (c) the number of units sold a year is 1000?
   What happens to the EOQ if the number of units sold rises to
   1200 and the cost of placing an order rises to $12?

3. Why, during a period of falling prices, will the use of FIFO
   instead of LIFO result in lower profits? When will firms
   prefer to use LIFO?

4. If a firm has a slow turnover of its receivables, why may that
   decrease its profitability? Why may increasing the turnover
   result in lower sales?

Chapter 19

SOURCES OF FUNDS: SHORT-TERM DEBT

Learning Objectives

* Describe the main elements of commercial bank loans.
* Explain compensating balances and their effect on the cost of a loan.
* Determine the cost of trade credit.
* List the advantages of offering trade credit and the advantages of accepting it.
* Differentiate between the types of commercial paper.
* Explain how pledging or factoring accounts receivable are a source of short-term finance.

> "A promise made is a debt unpaid."
> *Robert William Service*

Many firms must produce goods, pay employees, and meet various other expenses before they can sell output and collect revenues. During the time it takes the firm to produce its output and collect its revenues, it has the need for short-term credit to meet running expenses as they come due. In addition, the firm may sell on credit and receive the proceeds from the sale in the future. These short-term assets must be financed. While the previous chapter considered the management of current assets, this chapter will consider how they may be financed with short-term liabilities.

Some firms may have funds that they can use to acquire current assets. Money invested by a firm's owners, funds obtained by retaining earnings, or funds obtained by issuing long-term debt may be used by the firm to cover its short-term financial needs. However, if the firm has put these funds to work elsewhere (e.g., plant and equipment), it will have to obtain short-term financing. While the primary source of such financing is the commercial banking system, there are a variety of additional sources of short-term finance.

This chapter covers the various sources of short-term finance: commercial bank loans, trade credit, commercial paper, and secured loans. These sources are not available to all firms, and there are significant differences in the terms and cost of each type of credit. The financial manager must maintain the firm's ability to meet short-term obligations as they come due. This involves analyzing the different sources of short-term finance and determining their costs. Then the financial manager selects that source which is best suited for meeting the financial needs of the firm.

COMMERCIAL BANK LOANS

Commercial banks are concerned with liquidity, and thus they want to make loans that are of a relatively short duration. Therefore commercial banks are a primary source of short-term finance. Bank loans are used by virtually all types of firms, but the primary users of this type of loan are retailers and wholesalers. Firms that have large amounts of fixed assets do not use short-term bank financing to purchase the fixed assets, for such financing is inappropriate. Such long-term assets should be financed by long-term financing such as bonds or equity. Retailers and wholesalers, however, are primarily concerned with short-term assets, and bank financing is an appropriate means to finance these assets. The primary users of bank credit are small firms. While this does not mean that large firms do not use bank financing, the proportion of a firm's financing that is obtained from commercial banks declines as the size of the firm increases. Larger firms have access to other sources of finance and thus do not have to rely so heavily on commercial banks. These firms have the ability to obtain a larger variety or wider range of financing.

The concern with liquidity

A loan from a commercial bank is a package that is individually negotiated between the borrower and the bank. Since the loans are individually negotiated, it is important for the potential borrower to maintain an excellent relationship with the banker. The negotiated package will include the size of the loan, the maturity date, the amount of the interest, any security requirements such as the pledging of specific assets of the firm or the subordination of other debt, and other limitations on the financial activity of the firm. Since the bank is lending its funds, the bank is generally in the position to demand financial constraints on the company. For example, the bank may demand that the firm maintain a minimum current ratio such as 2 to 1, or the bank may place limitations on the ability of the firm to pay dividends.

Loans are individually negotiated

Besides lending money, the bank may provide other services to the firm. For example, the bank may be a source of useful information. The bank's economists may be used for economic forecasts, or the bank may be a source of information on the financial condition of the borrower's credit customers. If the firm has foreign transactions, the bank can handle foreign exchange. These services may be advantageous to the firm and help justify borrowing from one bank instead of another if it offers superior services.

Line of credit

The firm may borrow a specific amount of money, or it may arrange for the right to borrow up to a specific amount of funds. This latter is called a line of credit. The bank grants the firm the option to borrow whenever the firm needs the money. As the firm's need for short-term funds arises, the firm draws on the line of credit. The credit line thus offers the borrower the flexibility to use the credit only when it is needed. Under this type of arrangement, the firm has a source of short term finance but does not have to use the funds. Interest is paid only on the funds actually used plus a small fee on the unused balance of the credit line. Even with this fee the credit line may be inexpensive compared with the cost of other sources of short-term credit which require that the debt be outstanding for a specified period of time.

The prime rate

The cost of any type of bank loan varies with the quality of the borrower and the conditions of the loan. The bank's best customers (i.e., the best credit risks) are charged the "prime rate" while other customers may be charged the prime plus a percentage such as 2 per cent. Thus, if the prime rate is 7.5, then the rate is 9.5 per cent. The prime rate fluctuates, and thus any interest rate that is tied to the prime rate may be very volatile. For example, the prime rate was 5¼ per cent in July, 1972, 7¾ per cent in July, 1973, and 12 per cent in July, 1974. The increase from 5¼ to 12 per cent in two years illustrates the potential volatility of the prime rate. These fluctuations in the prime rate are related to the demand for short-term money and the supply of credit available. During periods of tight money, the rate can rise drastically to ration the scarce credit. How rapidly the prime rate can rise is illustrated by the fact that it rose from 8¾ per cent in March, 1974, to 11½ per cent in May, 1974, a period of just three months. While this period is unique, it does illustrate that short-term interest rates can significantly fluctuate during a short period of time.

How to determine the simple interest rate

The effective cost of a bank loan may not be the stated rate of interest. The effective cost is related to the interest charge, the amount of money that the borrower can use, and the length of the loan. There are subtle means that the commercial bank has to increase the effective cost of the loan by altering the amount of proceeds of the loan that the firm can use or the length of time the loan is outstanding. Equation (1) may be used to determine the true or effective cost of a loan. This cost is also referred to as the "simple" interest rate.

$$(1) \quad \frac{\text{Interest paid}}{\substack{\text{Proceeds of the loan} \\ \text{that the borrower} \\ \text{may use}}} \times \frac{12}{\substack{\text{Number of months} \\ \text{that the firm has} \\ \text{use of the proceeds}}} = \substack{\text{Effective} \\ \text{annual cost} \\ \text{of the loan}}$$

How commercial banks increase the effective interest cost of a loan may be illustrated by several examples that use this equation. All the subsequent examples will be based on the following simple loan: $1000 at 6 per cent for one year. The borrower has $1000, and if the loan is retired at the end of the year and the borrower pays the $60 interest at that time, the cost of the loan is

$$\frac{\$60}{\$1000} \times \frac{12}{12} = 6\%$$

The borrower has the use of the $1000 for the entire year and pays $60 for the use of the proceeds; thus the effective rate of interest is 6 per cent.

The bank may require that the borrower pay the interest in advance, that is, the bank requires that the loan be discounted. The borrower does not receive $1000 but gets $940 ($1000 − $60). In effect the borrower is paying $60 for the use of $940, which increases the cost of the loan. Instead of an interest rate of 6 per cent, the interest rate is

Discounting in advance increases the interest cost

$$\frac{\$60}{\$940} \times \frac{12}{12} = 6.38\%$$

By discounting the loan in advance the bank has caused the true cost of interest to rise from 6 per cent to 6.38 per cent.

A second method for affecting the cost of the loan is for the bank to require that the borrower maintain compensating balances. A compensating balance is some proportion of the outstanding loan (such as 20 per cent) that the bank requires the borrower to keep in an account in the bank. The amount of compensating balances and the account in which they are kept may be subject to negotiation. Of course, the net effect of these balances depends on the terms. If the borrower must maintain a compensating balance of 20 per cent, then the cost of the loan is significantly increased because the borrower has use of only 80 per cent of the borrowed funds. The cost of the loan now becomes:

Compensating balances also may increase interest costs

$$\frac{\$60}{\$800} \times \frac{12}{12} = 7.5\%$$

The borrower is in effect paying $60 for the use of $800, and the effective cost of that loan is 7.5 per cent, which is considerably higher than the stated 6 per cent interest cost.

If the compensating balances are placed in a savings account (and this is possible, for each loan is individually negotiated), then the effective cost of the loan will not be 7.5%, because the borrower will earn interest on the funds in the savings account. For example, if the borrower is permitted to place the funds in a savings account that pays 5 per cent, then the $200 will earn $10 in interest. The net interest that the borrower now pays for the loan is $50; so the effective interest rate for the loan is

$$\frac{\$50}{\$800} \times \frac{12}{12} = 6.25\%$$

This effective cost is still greater than the stated 6 per cent.

Another factor that affects the true interest cost of a loan subject to compensating balances is the extent to which the borrower maintains funds in accounts at the bank. In Chapter 17 it was suggested that a firm will seek to maintain some amount of cash on hand to serve as a safety stock. This money may simultaneously serve as a compensating balance. Thus, if this borrower maintains a checking account of $100, then only an additional $100 must be kept in the account to meet the 20 per cent required compensating balances. In this case the borrower has the use of $900 of the $1000 loan, and the effective interest rate becomes:

$$\frac{\$60}{\$900} \times \frac{12}{12} = 6.67\%$$

As these examples illustrate, the effect of compensating balances on the cost of the loan is influenced by a variety of factors. These include the amount of funds that must be diverted from the loan to an account in the bank, the type of account, and the borrower's policy of maintaining funds in the account independently of the required compensating balance. However, the important question is always the same: does the compensating balance increase the true cost of the loan? It is this effective cost that is important, and the financial manager should determine this cost in order to be able to compare it with the other sources of short-term credit.

Installment loans

Another way that the bank may increase the interest cost of a loan is to require that the loan be paid off in installments. Instead of paying the loan in one lump sum at the end of the loan's duration, the loan is retired in equal installments. The monthly payments may be determined by adding the principal and the amount of interest and dividing by the number of pay periods. If the above loan is paid off in equal monthly installments, then the monthly installment is $88.33[($1000 + $60)/12]. The repayment schedule for this installment loan is given in Table 19–1. Each month the borrower pays $88.33, which is $5 in interest and

$83.33 in principal. After six months the loan is reduced to $500, but the monthly interest is still $5.00.

With this installment loan the borrower has the use of only one half of the proceeds for the duration of the loan. At the end of six months the borrower will have retired $500 of the loan and has only the use of $500. The average amount of proceeds that the borrower may use for the duration of the loan is $500. Thus the effective interest cost becomes:

$$\frac{\$60}{\$500} \times \frac{12}{12} = 12\%$$

which is significantly higher than the stated 6 per cent interest cost of the loan. By reducing the time that the borrower has, the use of the proceeds causes the effective interest cost of the loan to rise. The amount of this increase depends upon how rapidly the principal is being retired (i.e., how long the borrower has the use of the proceeds).

Installment loans are frequently employed by consumers to finance purchases of durable goods (e.g., a car). Before truth-in-lending legislation, the lender would not necessarily inform the borrower of the effective interest rate of the loan. Instead, the interest would be stated as some percentage such as 6 per cent, but, since the principal was being retired in installments, the effective cost was considerably higher. Truth-in-lending legislation has altered this practice, for now the lender is required to inform the borrower not only the amount of interest that must be paid (which is called the finance charge) but also of the effective rate of interest. Thus the legislation requires that borrowers be informed by the lenders of the true cost of the debt.

Installment loans should not be confused with mortgage loans, which also involve equal monthly payments. In the case of

Frequently used to finance consumer purchases

TABLE 19-1 Repayment Schedule for $1000 Installment Loan

NUMBER OF PAYMENT	PAYMENT ON INTEREST	PAYMENT ON PRINCIPAL	BALANCE OF LOAN
1	$5	$83.33	$916.67
2	5	83.33	833.33
3	5	83.33	750.00
.	.	.	.
.	.	.	.
.	.	.	.
6	5	83.33	500.00
.	.	.	.
.	.	.	.
.	.	.	.
10	5	83.33	166.67
11	5	83.33	83.33
12	5	83.33	.00

Are different than
mortgage loans

mortgages the amount of interest paid each month depends on the amount of principal that is still outstanding. Since the interest rate is charged only on the outstanding principal, the effective cost of the loan is equal to the stated interest cost. As the borrower makes payments and reduces the principal, the amount of interest paid is also reduced.

An example of part of a mortgage repayment schedule is presented in Table 19–2. The first column gives the number of the payment, and second and third columns break the monthly payment into the payments for interest and principal. The last column gives the balance due on the loan. As may be seen from the table, as payments are made, (1) the amount of the principal declines; (2) the amount of interest paid each month declines; and (3) the rate at which the principal is repaid increases. In the early years of the mortgage, most of the payment covers the interest charges, but during the latter life of the mortgage most of the payment retires the principal.

Repayment schedule
for installment loan
and mortgage
compared

The difference between the installment loan and a mortgage can be seen by comparing Table 19–1, the repayment schedule for the installment loan, and Table 19–2, the repayment schedule for the mortgage. The monthly payments are equal in both cases. The dollar amount of interest paid declines and the amount of principal retired monthly increases in the mortgage repayment schedule. The interest rate, which is paid on the balance of the mortgage, is a fixed percentage. Hence the interest payment declines each month because the amount of principal declines. For the installment loan the interest paid and the principal retired each month are constant. The interest is not figured on the remaining balance of the loan but on the initial

TABLE 19–2   Repayment Schedule for a $25,000 Mortgage Loan

INTEREST RATE: 7¼%	MONTHLY PAYMENT: $180.71		TERM: 25 YEARS
Number of the Payment	Payment on Interest	Payment on Principal	Balance of Loan
1	$151.04	$ 29.67	$24,970.33
2	150.86	29.85	24,940.48
3	150.68	30.03	24,910.45
4	150.50	30.21	24,880.24
.	.	.	.
.	.	.	.
.	.	.	.
150	107.92	72.79	17,789.78
151	107.48	73.23	17,716.55
152	107.40	73.67	17,642.88
.	.	.	.
.	.	.	.
.	.	.	.
297	4.26	176.45	528.70
298	3.19	177.52	351.18
299	2.12	178.59	172.59
300	1.04	172.59	.00

amount borrowed. Thus the effective interest rate rises each month because the borrower has a smaller loan but is paying the same dollar amount of interest.

In summary, commercial bank credit is the primary source of short term finance. It is usually much cheaper than alternative sources such as trade credit. The prime disadvantage of borrowing from commercial banks is the extent to which the bank imposes restrictions on the firm. The bank is concerned with its liquidity and seeks to protect its investment. Therefore it will demand those restrictions that it believes are necessary to insure repayment. These restrictions may be viewed by the borrower as excessive and thus encourage the use of other sources of short-term finance.

TRADE CREDIT

Trade credit is the most important source of short-term finance for small firms, especially retail establishments. It is, however, a very expensive source, and the financial manager should be aware of the cost of this type of credit. Trade credit arises when a supplier sells goods but does not demand immediate payment. Instead, the purchaser is permitted to choose between immediate payment or payment in the future. For immediate payment, or for payment within a short time period such as ten days, the buyer is given a discount such as 2 per cent off the purchase price. If the buyer does not remit during the first ten days, then payment in full must be made within a specified time period, such as 30 days. These terms are written 2/10, net 30, which means a 2 per cent discount for payment within the first ten days or the net (i.e., full) price within 30 days. These terms of trade have no mention of credit or interest payments and thus may not appear to be a source of short-term credit. But inventory must be financed, and goods acquired by trade agreements are no exception. When trade credit is used, the source of the finance is the supplier who lets the buyer have the use of the goods before having to pay for them.

Source of trade credit is the supplier

Used to finance inventory

That these trade agreements are a source of finance may be illustrated by T accounts. A supplier sells goods to a retailer but does not receive immediate payment for the goods. Instead the supplier accepts the retailer's promise to pay in the future. Excluding any profit or loss for the supplier, the effect on each firm's balance sheet is as follows:

SUPPLIER		RETAILER	
Assets	Liabilities	Assets	Liabilities
Goods ↓ Accounts receivable ↑		Inventory ↑	Accounts payable ↑

The supplier has accepted an account receivable for the output, and the retailer has received the goods which are now part of inventory. The retailer does not immediately pay for the inventory but accepts a new liability, the account payable. This increase in liabilities is the source of funds that is financing the increase in inventory.

Trade credit may expand as inventory expands

This type of arrangement may be very beneficial to a firm that must carry a large amount of inventory. As the firm expands its inventory, then its suppliers expand their credit. The expansion of trade credit then is in response to the expansion in inventory and comes automatically without the need for the firm to seek funds elsewhere. If the firm is able to turn over the inventory rapidly, it may obtain cash quickly enough to pay the suppliers without having to use other sources of credit. For example, if the terms of trade credit are 2/10, net 30, then the firm has the use of the goods for a month before payment is due. If the inventory turns over once a month, then trade credit may be sufficient to cover the entire inventory. Of course, the firm is still paying the high cost of trade credit. If the firm is able to turn over the inventory only six times a year (i.e., every two months), then trade credit will carry only one half of the firm's inventory. Since the terms of trade are for one month and the inventory turns over every two months, the firm must find other sources of finance to cover the cost of maintaining the inventory for the second month.

The important question that the financial manager must consider is whether trade credit is the best source of finance for carrying the inventory. This is the question of the cost of trade credit versus the cost and availability of other sources of finance.

May appear to be free

It may appear that trade credit is free, for the supplier is permitting the buyer to use the goods for no explicit interest charge. That, however, is a misconception of what constitutes the *price* of the goods and the *interest charge*. In finance, the price of the product

The discount should be viewed as interest

is considered to be the discounted price. The discounted price is the price that the buyer pays if cash is available and the buyer promptly pays for the goods. The net price then includes the purchase price plus a penalty for not paying the bill promptly. This penalty should be treated as the interest charge for the use of the goods. Thus, if an item costs $100 and is supplied under the following terms 2/10, net 30, then the price of goods is $98, and the firm has ten days in which to pay it. If the firm does not or cannot meet that price within ten days, then it pays a finance charge (i.e., interest) of $2 for the use of that good for the next twenty days. When expressed in those terms, the interest charge is clearly seen.

The effective cost of trade credit

How expensive trade credit really is may be seen when the interest cost is expressed in annual terms. This calculation may be done with relative ease by Equation (2).

$$(2) \qquad \frac{\text{Percentage discount}}{\text{Pay period minus the discount period}} = \frac{X}{360}$$

The component parts of the equation are the percentage discount, the number of days the credit is extended (i.e., the pay period minus the discount period), and X/360, which is the term that converts the cost (X) to an annualized basis. When the terms are substituted into this equation, the cost of trade credit is determined. For 2/10, net 30 the cost of credit is:

$$\frac{.02}{30-10} = \frac{X}{360}$$
$$36\% = X$$

On an annual basis 2/10, net 30 costs 36 per cent simple interest, which is quite expensive compared with other sources of credit.

Equation (2) may be used to illustrate the factors that affect the cost of trade credit. Since the X/360 is constant, it is the terms on the left hand side of the equation that ultimately affect the cost of trade credit. The cost of trade credit is thus related to (1) the amount of the discount, and (2) the length of time that the buyer has the use of the goods. An increase in the amount of the discount increases the cost of trade credit. An increase in the payment period reduces the cost of trade credit. Both of these statements may be explained with the aid of the above equation.

The variables that affect the cost of trade credit

An increase in the discount in effect reduces the price of the goods and increases the cost of carrying the goods on credit. If the discount were 3 per cent instead of 2 per cent (i.e., 3/10, net 30), then the firm pays $97 for the goods during the first ten days and a $3 penalty for the use of the goods after the discount period. By the equation the cost of credit becomes:

An increase in the discount increases the effective cost

$$\frac{.03}{30-10} = \frac{X}{360}$$
$$54\% = X$$

The cost of trade credit now is 54 per cent, which is higher than the 36 per cent cost of trade credit when the terms are 2/10, net 30. The increase in the discount then increases the cost of trade credit, for the penalty is larger (i.e., the interest charge is greater). Thus, if a supplier wants to induce prompt payment, one method is to increase the discount. This tells the buyer that credit is more expensive and should encourage the buyer to find credit elsewhere and pay the supplier promptly.

An increase in the payment period means that the buyer has the use of the goods longer, and thus the cost of trade credit is less. If the payment period is increased from 30 days to 60 days (i.e., 2/10, net 60), then the cost of the trade credit becomes:

An increase in the pay period reduces the cost

$$\frac{.02}{60-10} = \frac{X}{360}$$
$$14.4\% = X$$

By lengthening the payment period from 30 to 60 days, the effective cost of the trade credit is reduced from 36 to 14.4 per cent. The cause of the reduction in cost is, of course, the fact that the buyer has the use of the goods for 30 additional days but does not have to pay a higher penalty for the longer time period. If a supplier wishes buyers to use trade credit, then increasing the length of the payment period reduces the cost of trade credit and encourages increased use of this source of credit.

The above equation may be used to compare that cost of different terms of trade credit. Such comparisons will permit management to select among the most advantageous terms of trade credit. Such selection is important if the firm has sufficient funds to pay promptly some but not all of its suppliers. If, for example, a firm faces the following terms of credit:

(a) 2/10, net 30

(b) 3/10, net 30

(c) 2/15, net 30

it can determine that the cost of each is as follows:

$$\text{(a)} \quad \frac{.02}{30-10} = \frac{X}{360}$$
$$36\% = X$$

$$\text{(b)} \quad \frac{.03}{30-10} = \frac{X}{360}$$
$$54\% = 4$$

$$\text{(c)} \quad \frac{.02}{30-15} = \frac{X}{360}$$
$$48\% = X$$

Thus, by determining the cost of each of the terms of trade credit, management knows that its scarce funds should be used to pay (b) first because it is the most expensive of the three terms of credit.

When to time
payments

If a firm uses trade credit, when should it make payments? If a firm intends to pay the discount price and thereby not accept trade credit, the payment should be made as late as possible. If possible, the payment should be made on the last day of the discount period. The price that the seller is charging includes the cost of supplying the goods during the discount period. Thus the purchaser should seek to take advantage of this "free" use of the goods during the entire discount period, for the price paid includes this use of the goods. If the buyer is unable to make the payment by the end of the discount period, payment should be made at the end of the pay period. Once the discount period has passed, the buyer has to pay the cost of the trade credit. There is nothing to be gained by paying early. If early payment is made, the cost of trade credit is increased, for the buyer does not have the use of the credit for the entire period.

While the terms of trade credit set the cost of the credit, what affects these terms? Trade credit is very competitive, and suppliers are aware that the terms they offer may affect the sale of their output. By offering more generous terms, the supplier may be able to execute a sale. The terms of credit then become a means to differentiate one supplier from another. As each supplier tries to encourage sales by offering trade credit, the terms of the various offers should tend to be similar, for competition will force the suppliers to offer comparable terms.

If trade credit is so expensive, why is it used? There are several explanations for the use of trade credit. First, it is very convenient. By deferring payment until the end of the pay period, the buyer automatically receives the trade credit. Second, the buyer may use trade credit without being aware of the cost of the credit. Trade credit may be considered (incorrectly) to be free, for the buyer may believe that the true cost of the good is the net price instead of the discounted price. Such thinking leads buyers to conclude that they are receiving the free use of the goods for the entire time period. Third, trade credit avoids several sources of financial interrogation. A public offering of securities is subject to the security laws, and banks scrutinize the financial condition of the borrower before a bank loan is granted. Trade credit, however, may automatically come from suppliers who do not require the buyer to be subjected to this financial analysis. Fourth, the buyer may lack an alternative source of credit. While bank credit is cheaper, it may not be available to risky small firms. Suppliers, however, need outlets for their goods and offering trade credit may be a way to assure themselves of buyers for their goods. These suppliers are usually larger firms with established sources of credit. They are able to borrow at cheaper rates from their sources and in turn pass on the credit to the small retail firms. The sellers cannot exist without their markets. Trade credit may assure the existence of these markets by offering a source of finance to small firms that may lack alternative sources of finance.

Advantages of trade credit

This section has covered the mechanics and cost of trade credit, but in reality trade credit may work differently. Buyers may stretch the terms of credit by either (1) remitting the discounted price after the payment period instead of the net price, or (2) "riding the credit" and paying after the payment period. This latter situation may occur if the buyer has not sold the inventory and does not have the funds to pay off the suppliers. Such practices, of course, reduce the cost of credit. When such practices occur, the suppliers then must decide if they want to

Riding the credit

enforce the terms of the credit or be lenient and let the credit ride. In many cases the suppliers may not enforce the terms, for they need the retailers to purchase their goods. If the supplier's cost of credit is significantly lower than the cost of trade credit, then the supplier may be able to afford to let the retailers ride the terms of credit. Such extensions of the credit, however, cannot be indefinite. Eventually the supplier must decide how rapidly it wants to collect its accounts receivable. While suppliers may be lenient and not enforce the terms of trade, the cost of funds will force them eventually to seek to collect payment.

COMMERCIAL PAPER

Commercial paper is an unsecured short-term liability of a corporation. The debt usually matures in two to six months. It may have a maturity date of only one day, but it never has a maturity date beyond nine months (270 days). It is issued in denominations as small as $5000, but the larger denominations are more common. Since there are no specific assets backing commercial paper, only companies with exceptionally good credit are able to issue this type of promissory note. These firms issue commercial paper to meet temporary needs for cash, and they frequently refinance the commercial paper by issuing long-term debt or equity. The commercial paper then serves as a temporary source of funds prior to more permanent financing.

A substitute for short-term bank financing

Commercial paper is a substitute for other types of short-term debt financing, especially bank loans. It is usually cheaper than bank credit, for the interest cost is generally about .5 per cent less than the prime rate. Commercial paper does not require compensating balances, but the investment community frequently insists on unused credit lines to support commercial paper. This means that compensating balances may be indirectly required to issue commercial paper. However, other restrictions are not placed on the company. Thus the effective cost differential between the prime rate and the rate on commercial paper is probably greater than the .5 per cent difference between the interest rate on bank loans and the interest paid on commercial paper.

Commercial paper does not pay a stated amount of interest. Instead the paper is sold at a discount. Thus a $1,000,000, sixty day note may be sold for $980,000. When the note matures, the buyer receives $1,000,000 and thus earns $20,000 on the investment of $980,000. To figure the effective interest cost, Equation (1), which illustrates the cost of bank's credit, may be used. In this example the effective cost is

$$(1) \qquad \frac{20,000}{980,000} \times \frac{12}{6} = 4.08\%$$

Commercial paper may be issued by firms and sold directly to buyers. This is called *direct paper*. Direct sales of commercial paper require a sales staff or an investment banker who is willing to place the paper. Thus such sales require sufficient volume of commercial paper to justify the sales expense. Direct paper constitutes the bulk of the commercial paper issued. The remaining sales of commercial paper are made through dealers (dealer paper). Commercial paper is purchased by banks, insurance companies, financial institutions, pension funds, and companies that have excess liquidity and need a short-term investment. Individual investors rarely have a sufficient amount of cash to participate in the market for commercial paper, especially when it is issued in large denominations like $100,000.

Since commercial paper is unsecured, it is not issued by financially weak firms, for no one would purchase it. Thus the vast majority of firms are unable to issue commercial paper. While commercial paper is issued by corporations with excellent credit, occasionally a firm defaults on its commercial paper. Perhaps the most celebrated case is the Penn Central Railroad. Penn Central had issued commercial paper and was thrown into bankruptcy when it was unable to retire the commercial paper when it came due. This failure to retire or refinance the commercial paper caused large losses for the firms that had purchased it. This loss then made it more difficult for other firms to sell their commercial paper. For a period of time after the Penn Central bankruptcy, only the best quality paper could be sold.

SECURED LOANS

Inventory, accounts receivable, or any other sound short-term asset (e.g., government security) may be used to secure a short-term loan. This collateral then serves to protect the loan because the lender has a lien against the asset. This security should increase the availability of credit and reduce the interest cost of the loan to the borrower.

Secured loans are made by commercial banks and other financial institutions. These lenders make their profits through the lending process; they do not want to take title to the pledged assets. If they are forced to take the pledged asset, they can choose either to hold the asset or to liquidate it. Liquidation will rarely bring the face value of the asset; thus the lender will not grant a loan for the entire value of the pledged asset. Instead the bank or finance company may lend some proportion, such as 70 per cent of the asset's stated value. The borrower must have some equity in the asset that will be lost in case of default and seizure of the asset. This equity then is a margin of safety for the creditor. The amount that the creditor will lend against the

---

Marginal notes:

Types of paper: (1) Direct; (2) Dealer

Unsecured but generally safe

Assets may be used for collateral

Lenders do not want title to the collateral

pledged asset depends on the quality of the pledged asset, the ease with which the creditor believes that the asset can be liquidated should the debtor default, the anticipated liquidation value, and the transaction costs of liquidation. A firm's short-term assets are not equally desirable for pledging against short-term loans. Inventory is less liquid than accounts receivable, and hence lenders are less willing to accept inventory as collateral. Lenders instead prefer the accounts receivable or marketable securities.

Factoring: selling accounts receivable

There are two methods for using accounts receivable as a means to obtain short-term financing. The firm may pledge the accounts receivable and thus retain them, or the firm may sell them. The process of selling the accounts receivable is called factoring. The sale price is less than the face value of the accounts receivable (i.e., they are sold at a discount). The bigger the discount, the larger the cost of using this source of short-term finance. However, if the firm needs cash, selling the accounts receivable is a means to obtain immediate cash. This type of financing offers a major advantage for the seller, because the seller is no longer concerned with collecting the accounts receivable. The risk of collecting accounts receivable is transferred to the buyer (i.e., the factor). However, there are two means by which the factor may control this transfer of risk. First, the factor will usually demand approval of credit sales by the firm. When the firm receives an order on credit, it may be required to have the sale approved by the factor. If the factor believes that the credit sale is a bad risk, then approval may be denied (i.e., the factor refuses to accept the account receivable). Thus the firm will have to choose between refusing the credit sale or carrying the account itself. Second, the factor may accept the account receivable but only at a substantial discount. The larger the discount, then the greater the incentive not to factor the account receivable. The firm must then decide if its cash needs are sufficient to accept the larger discount. Either of these two techniques reduces the risk to the factor of buying the account receivable.

Short-term finance should not be used to finance long-term assets

While selling the firm's accounts receivable or pledging them (or any other short-term asset) is a means for the firm to finance short-term cash needs, such finance should never be used to finance the long-term financial needs such as the purchase of plant and equipment. Short-term finance should only be used to finance short-term cash needs, for if the firm uses short-term finance to carry long-term assets, the firm must continually refinance the assets. The firm would be in an extremely precarious position if it were unable to refinance the short-term debt when it used the funds to finance long-term assets.

Advantages of borrowing from finance companies

Pledging short-term assets offers the firm a cost advantage over other sources of finance. The security for the loan reduces the cost of obtaining short-term finance from credit companies, and secured loans are much cheaper than trade credit. Secured credit from finance companies is, however, generally more expensive than credit from commercial banks. The advantage of using finance companies instead of commercial banks rests on (1) the ability to use banks in addition to this secured credit (if the need should arise); and (2) avoidance of the restrictions placed on the firm by the commercial bank. While these restrictions may not have stated costs, the management of the firm may feel that there are implicit costs in the restrictions and thus avoid bank credit when other sources of short-term financing exist.

SUMMARY

This chapter has considered the various sources of short-term finance. While commercial banks are the most important general source of short-term finance, trade credit, commercial paper, factoring, and other secured loans may be significant sources of funds for some firms. Each of these sources has specific features that argue for its use under certain conditions. Since short-term assets are frequently financed by short-term sources, the financial manager must know the various sources of short-term finance and their advantages and costs.

Short-term sources should not be used to finance long-term assets. Such sources must be continually refinanced or retired. Long-term investment may not produce funds sufficiently rapidly to retire the short-term debt, and the terms of refinancing may be unfavorable. Using short-term debt to finance long-term assets will certainly increase the element of risk and reduce the value of the firm.

KEY WORDS AND TERMS

line of credit	trade discount
prime rate	ride the credit
effective interest rate	direct paper
compensating balance	dealer paper
installment loan	lien
mortgage	factoring

QUESTIONS AND PROBLEMS FOR THOUGHT AND DISCUSSION

1. If a firm needs credit to finance its inventory, where can it get the funds? How will the firm select between alternative sources of credit? Is the cost of the funds the only relevant consideration?

2. If you were a supplier and your customers had a high rate of failure, would you increase or decrease the cash discount when stating the terms of trade credit? Would you lengthen or shorten the discount period?

3. If a firm needs funds to finance purchases of plant and equipment, should it use trade credit or a credit line with a commercial bank as the source of these funds?

4. Why do discounted loans and installment loans yield a true rate of interest that is greater than the rate of interest stated on the principal (i.e., the coupon rate)? To determine the true interest rate, what factors should be considered? What role does truth-in-lending legislation play in informing borrowers of the cost of a loan?

5. Firm A borrows $1,000,000 from a commercial bank. The bank charges an annual rate of 7 per cent and requires a compensating balance of 10 per cent of the value of the loan. If the firm averages deposits of $75,000, what is the approximate effective interest cost of the loan?

6. Which of the following terms of trade credit is the more expensive?
   (a) A 3 per cent cash discount if paid on the fifteenth day with the bill due on the forty-fifth day (i.e., 3/15, net 45).
   (b) A 2 per cent cash discount if paid on the tenth day with the bill due on the thirtieth day (i.e., 2/10, net 30).

Chapter 20

TIME VALUE OF MONEY

Learning Objectives

- State why a dollar received today is more valuable than a dollar received tomorrow.
- Differentiate between a lump sum payment and an annuity.
- Differentiate between compounding and discounting.
- Know how to read an interest table.
- Apply the interest tables to solve problems.

"Money makes money. And the money that money makes makes more money."

Benjamin Franklin

If $100 is deposited in a savings account today in a commercial bank, how much will the savings account be worth a year later? If $100 is deposited every year for ten years in the savings account, how much will the account be worth after ten years? If $100 is in a savings account today, how much was deposited in the account a year ago? These questions are illustrative of a major concept in finance: the time value of money. A dollar today is not equivalent to a dollar in the future. That is the time value of money.

The time value of money is one of the most crucial concepts in finance. A financial decision is made at a point in time. For example, an investor buys stock now, or a firm decides to invest in a new plant or replace old equipment in the present. The potential returns from these investments occur in the future; the returns occur over a period of time. There has to be a means to compare these future returns with the present cost of these investments. Such comparisons are the domain of capital budgeting, which is covered in Chapter 23. To understand capital budgeting, it is necessary to understand the time value of money.

This chapter will consider the following four cases: (1) the compound value of a dollar; (2) the compound sum of an annuity; (3) the present value of a dollar; and (4) the present value of an annuity. After each has been explained, several examples of how these concepts are used are given in the last section of the chapter.

THE COMPOUND VALUE OF A DOLLAR

Funds (1) earn interest and

If $100 is invested in a savings account that pays 5 per cent annually, how much money will be in the account at the end of the year? The answer is easy: $100 plus $5 interest for a total of $105. This answer is derived by multiplying 5 per cent and $100, which gives the interest earned during the year, and then adding this interest to the initial principal. This simple calculation may be expressed in algebraic form. These equations employ subscripts which represent time. The subscript o means the present, 1 means the first year, and n means any year. If P_0 is the initial principal ($100) and i is the interest rate (5 per cent), then the principal after one year (P_1) will be $100 + .05 \times \$100 = \$105$, or

$$(1) \qquad\qquad P_0 + iP_0 = P_1$$

(2) Accumulate over time

How much will be in the account after two years? This answer is obtained in the same manner as above, by adding the interest earned during the second year to the principal at the beginning of the second year. That is, $105 + .05 \times \$105 = \$110.25$, which may be expressed in the following algebraic terms:

$$(2) \qquad\qquad P_1 + iP_1 = P_2$$

After two years the initial $100 will have grown to $110.25; the savings account has earned $10.25 interest. This interest is composed of $10 interest on the initial principal and $.25 interest that is earned during the second year on the $5 interest earned during the first year. This earning of interest on interest is called *compounding*. Money deposited in savings accounts is frequently referred to as compounding, for interest is earned on both the principal and on previously earned interest.

The words "interest" and "compounded" are frequently used together. For example, advertisements for savings accounts may say that interest is compounded daily, or the cost of a loan may be stated as being 12 per cent compounded annually. In the above example, interest was compounded annually since it was earned only once during the year. In many cases interest is not compounded annually but quarterly, semiannually, or even daily. The more frequently the compounding (i.e., the more frequently the interest is added to the principal) the more rapidly the money is put to work to earn even more interest.

How much will be in the account at the end of three years? This could be answered by the same general method used above by taking the amount in the account at the end of the second year ($110.25) and adding to it the interest earned during the third year (5 per cent times $110.25). That is, $110.25 + $5.5125 = $115.76. It would be expressed algebraically as:

(3) $$P_2 + iP_2 = P_3$$

By continuing this method one could figure out how much will be in this account at the end of 20 or more years, but that obviously is a lot of work. Fortunately there is a much easier way to determine how much the $100 will grow to in a given number of years. This is done by the use of an interest table called the "compound value of a dollar."

Table 20–1 is an example of an interest table that gives the compound value of a dollar. The interest rate at which the dollar is compounded annually is read horizontally across the top of the table. The number of years is read vertically along the left hand margin. If one wants to know the amount the $100 will grow to in three years at 5 per cent, first find the interest factor (1.158) and multiply it by $100. That yields $115.80, which is the answer that was derived above by working out the calculations (except for rounding off). If one wanted to know the amount the $100 would grow to after 25 years at 5 per cent compounded annually, then multiply the $100 by the interest factor 3.386 and derive the answer, $338.60. Thus if $100 were placed in a savings account that annually paid 5 per cent interest, there would be $338.60 in the account after 25 years.

Interest tables ease calculations

Interest tables for the compound value of a dollar are based on a general formulation of the simple equations used above. To obtain the amount in the savings account at the end of year one, the equation was

Compound value of a dollar may be determined for any interest and any time period

(1) $$P_0 + iP_0 = P_1$$

which may be written as

$$P_0 (1 + i) = P_1$$

To obtain the amount after two years, the equation was

(2) $$P_1 + iP_1 = P_2$$

which may be written as

$$P_1 (1 + i) = P_2$$

Since P_1 equals $P_0 (1 + i)$, then the amount in year two may be expressed as

(3) $$[P_0 (1 + i)] (1 + i) = P_2$$

TABLE 20–1   The Compound Value of a Dollar

YEAR	1%	2%	3%	4%	5%	6%	7%
1	1.010	1.020	1.030	1.040	1.050	1.060	1.070
2	1.020	1.040	1.061	1.082	1.102	1.124	1.145
3	1.030	1.061	1.093	1.125	1.158	1.191	1.225
4	1.041	1.082	1.126	1.170	1.216	1.262	1.311
5	1.051	1.104	1.159	1.217	1.276	1.338	1.403
6	1.062	1.126	1.194	1.265	1.340	1.419	1.501
7	1.072	1.149	1.230	1.316	1.407	1.504	1.606
8	1.083	1.172	1.267	1.369	1.477	1.594	1.718
9	1.094	1.195	1.305	1.423	1.551	1.689	1.838
10	1.105	1.219	1.344	1.480	1.629	1.791	1.967
11	1.116	1.243	1.384	1.539	1.710	1.898	2.105
12	1.127	1.268	1.426	1.601	1.796	2.012	2.252
13	1.138	1.294	1.469	1.665	1.886	2.133	2.410
14	1.149	1.319	1.513	1.732	1.980	2.261	2.579
15	1.161	1.346	1.558	1.801	2.079	2.397	2.759
16	1.173	1.373	1.605	1.873	2.183	2.540	2.952
17	1.184	1.400	1.653	1.948	2.292	2.693	3.159
18	1.196	1.428	1.702	2.026	2.407	2.854	3.380
19	1.208	1.457	1.754	2.107	2.527	3.026	3.617
20	1.220	1.486	1.806	2.191	2.653	3.207	3.870
25	1.282	1.641	2.094	2.666	3.386	4.292	5.427
30	1.348	1.811	2.427	3.243	4.322	5.743	7.612

YEAR	8%	9%	10%	12%	14%	15%	16%
1	1.080	1.090	1.100	1.120	1.140	1.150	1.160
2	1.166	1.188	1.210	1.254	1.300	1.322	1.346
3	1.260	1.295	1.331	1.405	1.482	1.521	1.561
4	1.360	1.412	1.464	1.574	1.689	1.749	1.811
5	1.469	1.539	1.611	1.762	1.925	2.011	2.100
6	1.587	1.677	1.772	1.974	2.195	2.313	2.436
7	1.714	1.828	1.949	2.211	2.502	2.660	2.826
8	1.851	1.993	2.144	2.476	2.853	3.059	3.278
9	1.999	2.172	2.358	2.773	3.252	3.518	3.803
10	2.159	2.367	2.594	3.106	3.707	4.046	4.411
11	2.332	2.580	2.853	3.479	4.226	4.652	5.117
12	2.518	2.813	3.138	3.896	4.818	5.350	5.936
13	2.720	3.066	3.452	4.363	5.492	6.153	6.886
14	2.937	3.342	3.797	4.887	6.261	7.076	7.988
15	3.172	3.642	4.177	5.474	7.138	8.137	9.266
16	3.426	3.970	4.595	6.130	8.137	9.358	10.748
17	3.700	4.328	5.054	6.866	9.276	10.761	12.468
18	3.996	4.717	5.560	7.690	10.575	12.375	14.463
19	4.316	5.142	6.116	8.613	12.056	14.232	16.777
20	4.661	5.604	6.728	9.646	13.743	16.367	19.461
25	6.848	8.623	10.835	17.000	26.462	32.919	40.874
30	10.063	13.268	17.449	29.960	50.950	66.212	85.850

This equation uses the term $1 + i$ twice, for P_0 is being multiplied by $1 + i$ twice. Thus it is possible to write equation (3) as

(3) $$P_0 (1 + i)^2 = P_2$$

The amount to which a dollar will grow may always be expressed in terms of the initial dollar (i.e., P_0). The general formula for finding the amount to which a dollar will grow in "n" number of years (compounded annually) is

(4) $$P_0 (1 + i)^n = P_n$$

Thus the general formula for finding the compound value of a dollar for any number of years consists of (1) the initial dollar (P_0), (2) the interest factor $(1 + i)$, and (3) the number of years (n). Since the interest factor is raised to the nth power, construction and use of interest tables are obviously necessary to answer all but the simplest problems.

The student should note two things concerning the interest tables used in this book. First, they are expressed in annual terms. For example, Table 20–1 is the compound value of $1 compounded *annually*. Tables may be constructed for other time periods, such as a month or a day. Second, some pocket calculators (e.g., models sold by Texas Instrument or Hewlett-Packard) can be used to solve problems that require interest tables. Students who have access to these calculators may find them to be an excellent substitute for interest tables. It is quite possible that in the near future electronic calculators will have made interest tables obsolete.

Pocket calculators may also be used

THE COMPOUND SUM OF AN ANNUITY

How much will be in a savings account after three years if $100 were deposited annually in the account? Conceptually this question is no different than the compound value of a dollar except that the payment is not one lump sum at the beginning but an annual payment of equal installments. This is an example of an annuity which is the periodic payments of equal amounts. In this example an annual deposit of $100 is made into a savings account, and the question is how much will be in the account at some future date. Of course, the money placed in the account will earn interest and the interest will be compounded. One means to ascertain how much will be in the account would be to compound $100 at 5 per cent for three years, then compound $100 at 5 per cent for two years, and then compound $100 at 5 per cent for one year. At the beginning of the fourth year (when the last payment is made) all the deposits and the interest would be summed to obtain the amount in the account. This process is

Annuity: series of equal payments

summarized in Table 20–2. The left hand column gives the date of each $100 deposit. Each row then gives the interest earned on the deposit. For example, the $100 deposit made on January 1, 1976, earned $5 on January 1, 1977, and $5.25 on January 1, 1978. The last row gives the total deposits, interest, and the amount in the account ($431.01) on January 1, 1978.

Annuity tables

While it is possible to derive the sum of the annuity in this manner, it is very cumbersome. Interest tables have been developed that facilitate these calculations. Table 20–3 is an example of such a table that gives the sum of an annuity of $1.00 for selected years and selected interest rates. The number of years is read vertically at the left, and the interest rate is read horizontally across the top. The table is used as follows. If one wants to know the compound value of an annuity of $100 at 5 per cent for four years (four annual $100 payments with interest being earned for three years), then multiply $100 by the interest factor found in the table (four years at 5 per cent). The interest factor is 4.310, and thus the value of an annuity is $100 times 4.310 = $431.00, which was the same answer that was derived by obtaining the compound value of each $100 and adding them.

THE PRESENT VALUE OF A DOLLAR

The opposite of compounding: discounting

In the preceding sections the amount to which a dollar grows was considered. In the following sections the reverse situation is discussed. How much is a dollar received ten years from now worth today? How much would an annual payment of $1000 for 20 years after a person retires cost him today? These questions incorporate the time value of money, but instead of asking to how much the dollar will grow at some future day, they ask how much that dollar in the future is worth now. These are questions of *present value*, while the preceding questions concerned *future value*.

Determining the present value

If $100 is deposited in a savings account and earns 4 per cent annually, $104 is in the account at the beginning of the second year. When compounding, the question is, if $100 is deposited in a savings account that earns interest, how much will be in the

TABLE 20–2

DATE OF DEPOSIT	AMOUNT OF DEPOSIT	INTEREST EARNED			TOTALS
		1/1/76	1/1/77	1/1/78	
1/1/75	$100	$5	$ 5.25	$ 5.51	$115.76
1/1/76	100	—	5.00	5.25	110.25
1/1/77	100	—	—	5.00	105.00
1/1/78	100	—	—	—	100.00
	$400	$5	$10.25	$15.76	$431.01

account at some future date? Present value asks if, at the beginning of the second year, $104 is in a savings account that pays 4 per cent annually, how much was deposited in the account at the beginning of the first year? The process by which this question is answered is called discounting. The future amount is *discounted* back to the present in order to determine its *present* value.

The compound value of a dollar is found by the following general equation:

$$(4) \qquad\qquad P_0 (1 + i)^n = P_n$$

The present value (P_0) is found by dividing the future value (P_n) by the discount factor $(1 + i)^n$. This is expressed in Equation 5.

$$(5) \qquad\qquad P_0 = \frac{P_n}{(1 + i)^n}$$

The equation states that, if the future amount is discounted by some interest factor, the present value of that amount is determined. Working with discount factors that are raised to some large power (n) is, of course, difficult, but interest tables have been developed that permit the calculation of present values. An example of a present value table is Table 20–4, which gives the present value of a dollar for selected interest rates and years. The interest factors are read horizontally across the top, and the number of years is read vertically along the left. To determine the present value of a dollar that will be received in five years when the current interest rate is 5 per cent, multiply the dollar by the interest factor .784, which is found from the table under the 5 per cent column and row for 5 years. The present value of the dollar then is $1.00 × .784 = $.78. The dollar to be received in five years is worth $.78 today. In other words, if $.78 is deposited in a savings account and earns 5 per cent interest annually, then the account will have $1.00 after 5 years. Thus a dollar received after five years is presently worth only $.78 today if interest rates are 5 per cent.

Present value tables

The present value of a dollar today thus depends upon (1) the length of time and (2) the interest factor. The further into the future the dollar will be received and the higher the interest rate, then the lower the present value of the dollar. This is illustrated by Figure 20–1, which gives the relationship between the present value of a dollar and the length of time at various interest rates. As may be seen from the graph, a dollar to be received after 20 years is worth considerably less than the dollar to be received after five years when both are discounted at 7 per cent, and both are perceptibly worth less than when they are discounted at 2 per cent. The higher the rate at which the future is discounted, the less a dollar in the future is worth now.

Present value depends on time and the interest factor

TABLE 20–3   Sum of an Annuity of $1 for N Years

YEAR	1%	2%	3%	4%	5%	6%
1	1.000	1.000	1.000	1.000	1.000	1.000
2	2.010	2.020	2.030	2.040	2.050	2.060
3	3.030	3.060	3.091	3.122	3.152	3.184
4	4.060	4.122	4.184	4.246	4.310	4.375
5	5.101	5.204	5.309	5.416	5.526	5.637
6	6.152	6.308	6.468	6.633	6.802	6.975
7	7.214	7.434	7.662	7.898	8.142	8.394
8	8.286	8.583	8.892	9.214	9.549	9.897
9	9.369	9.755	10.159	10.583	11.027	11.491
10	10.462	10.950	11.464	12.006	12.578	13.181
11	11.567	12.169	12.808	13.486	14.207	14.972
12	12.683	13.412	14.192	15.026	15.917	16.870
13	13.809	14.680	15.618	16.627	17.713	18.882
14	14.947	15.974	17.086	18.292	19.599	21.051
15	16.097	17.293	18.599	20.024	21.579	23.276
16	17.258	18.639	20.157	21.825	23.657	25.673
17	18.430	20.012	21.762	23.698	25.840	28.213
18	19.615	21.412	23.414	25.645	28.132	30.906
19	20.811	22.841	25.117	27.671	30.539	33.760
20	22.019	24.297	26.870	29.778	33.066	36.786
25	28.243	32.030	36.459	41.646	47.727	54.865
30	34.785	40.568	47.575	56.085	66.439	79.058

YEAR	7%	8%	9%	10%	12%	14%
1	1.000	1.000	1.000	1.000	1.000	1.000
2	2.070	2.080	2.090	2.100	2.120	2.140
3	3.215	3.246	3.278	3.310	3.374	3.440
4	4.440	4.506	4.573	4.641	4.770	4.921
5	5.751	5.867	5.985	6.105	6.353	6.610
6	7.153	7.336	7.523	7.716	8.115	8.536
7	8.654	8.923	9.200	9.487	10.089	10.730
8	10.260	10.637	11.028	11.436	12.300	13.233
9	11.978	12.488	13.021	13.579	14.776	16.085
10	13.816	14.487	15.193	15.937	17.549	19.337
11	15.784	16.645	17.560	18.531	20.655	23.044
12	17.888	18.977	20.141	21.384	24.133	27.271
13	20.141	21.495	22.953	24.523	28.029	32.089
14	22.550	24.215	26.019	27.975	32.393	37.581
15	25.129	27.152	29.361	31.772	37.280	43.842
16	27.888	30.324	33.003	35.950	42.753	50.980
17	30.840	33.750	36.974	40.545	48.884	59.118
18	33.999	37.450	41.301	45.599	55.750	68.394
19	37.379	41.446	46.018	51.159	63.440	78.969
20	40.995	45.762	51.160	57.275	72.052	91.025
25	63.249	73.106	84.701	98.347	133.334	181.871
30	94.461	113.283	136.308	164.494	241.333	356.787

TABLE 20–3   Sum of an Annuity of $1 for *N* Years *(Continued)*

YEAR	16%	18%	20%	24%	28%	32%
1	1.000	1.000	1.000	1.000	1.000	1.000
2	2.160	2.180	2.200	2.240	2.280	2.320
3	3.506	3.572	3.640	3.778	3.918	4.062
4	5.066	5.215	5.368	5.684	6.016	6.362
5	6.877	7.154	7.442	8.048	8.700	9.398
6	8.977	9.442	9.930	10.980	12.136	13.406
7	11.414	12.142	12.916	14.615	16.534	18.696
8	14.240	15.327	16.499	19.123	22.163	25.678
9	17.518	19.086	20.799	24.712	29.369	34.895
10	21.321	23.521	25.959	31.643	38.592	47.062
11	25.733	28.755	32.150	40.238	50.399	63.122
12	30.850	34.931	39.580	50.985	65.510	84.320
13	36.786	42.219	48.497	64.110	84.853	112.303
14	43.672	50.818	59.196	80.496	109.612	149.240
15	51.660	60.965	72.035	100.815	141.303	197.997
16	60.925	72.939	87.442	126.011	181.87	262.36
17	71.673	87.068	105.931	157.253	233.79	347.31
18	84.141	103.740	128.117	195.994	300.25	459.45
19	98.603	123.414	154.740	244.033	385.32	607.47
20	115.380	146.628	186.688	303.601	494.21	802.86
25	249.214	342.603	471.981	898.092	1706.8	3226.8
30	530.312	790.948	1181.882	2640.916	5873.2	12941.0

YEAR	36%	40%	50%	60%	70%	80%
1	1.000	1.000	1.000	1.000	1.000	1.000
2	2.360	2.400	2.500	2.600	2.700	2.800
3	4.210	4.360	4.750	5.160	5.590	6.040
4	6.725	7.104	8.125	9.256	10.503	11.872
5	10.146	10.846	13.188	15.810	18.855	22.370
6	14.799	16.324	20.781	26.295	33.054	41.265
7	21.126	23.853	32.172	43.073	57.191	75.278
8	29.732	34.395	49.258	69.916	98.225	136.500
9	41.435	49.153	74.887	112.866	167.983	246.699
10	57.352	69.814	113.330	181.585	286.570	445.058
11	78.998	98.739	170.995	291.536	488.170	802.105
12	108.437	139.235	257.493	467.458	830.888	1444.788
13	148.475	195.929	387.239	748.933	1413.510	2601.619
14	202.926	275.300	581.859	1199.293	2403.968	4683.914
15	276.979	386.420	873.788	1919.869	4087.745	8432.045
16	377.69	541.99	1311.7	3072.8	6950.2	15179.0
17	514.66	759.78	1968.5	4917.5	11816.0	27323.0
18	700.94	1064.7	2953.8	7868.9	20089.0	49182.0
19	954.28	1491.6	4431.7	12591.0	34152.0	88528.0
20	1298.8	2089.2	6648.5	20147.0	58059.0	159350.0
25	6053.0	11247.0	50500.0	211270.0	824370.0	3011100.0
30	28172.0	60501.0	383500.0	2215400.0	11705000.0	56896000.0

TABLE 20–4 Present Value of a Dollar

YEAR	1%	2%	3%	4%	5%	6%	7%	8%	9%	10%	12%	14%	15%
1	.990	.980	.971	.962	.952	.943	.935	.926	.917	.909	.893	.877	.870
2	.980	.961	.943	.925	.907	.890	.873	.857	.842	.826	.797	.769	.756
3	.971	.942	.915	.889	.864	.840	.816	.794	.772	.751	.712	.675	.658
4	.961	.924	.889	.855	.823	.792	.763	.735	.708	.683	.636	.592	.572
5	.951	.906	.863	.822	.784	.747	.713	.681	.650	.621	.567	.519	.497
6	.942	.888	.838	.790	.746	.705	.666	.630	.596	.564	.507	.456	.432
7	.933	.871	.813	.760	.711	.665	.623	.583	.547	.513	.452	.400	.376
8	.923	.853	.789	.731	.677	.627	.582	.540	.502	.467	.404	.351	.327
9	.914	.837	.766	.703	.645	.592	.544	.500	.460	.424	.361	.308	.284
10	.905	.820	.744	.676	.614	.558	.508	.463	.422	.386	.322	.270	.247
11	.896	.804	.722	.650	.585	.527	.475	.429	.388	.350	.287	.237	.215
12	.887	.788	.701	.625	.557	.497	.444	.397	.356	.319	.257	.208	.187
13	.879	.773	.681	.601	.530	.469	.415	.368	.326	.290	.229	.182	.163
14	.870	.758	.661	.577	.505	.442	.388	.340	.299	.263	.205	.160	.141
15	.861	.743	.642	.555	.481	.417	.362	.315	.275	.239	.183	.140	.123
16	.853	.728	.623	.534	.458	.394	.339	.292	.252	.218	.163	.123	.107
17	.844	.714	.605	.513	.436	.371	.317	.270	.231	.198	.146	.108	.093
18	.836	.700	.587	.494	.416	.350	.296	.250	.212	.180	.130	.095	.081
19	.828	.686	.570	.475	.396	.331	.276	.232	.194	.164	.116	.083	.070
20	.820	.673	.554	.456	.377	.312	.258	.215	.178	.149	.104	.073	.061
25	.780	.610	.478	.375	.295	.233	.184	.146	.116	.092	.059	.038	.030
30	.742	.552	.412	.308	.231	.174	.131	.099	.075	.057	.033	.020	.015

YEAR	16%	18%	20%	24%	28%	32%	36%	40%	50%	60%	70%	80%	90%
1	.862	.847	.833	.806	.781	.758	.735	.714	.667	.625	.588	.556	.526
2	.743	.718	.694	.650	.610	.574	.541	.510	.444	.391	.346	.309	.277
3	.641	.609	.579	.524	.477	.435	.398	.364	.296	.244	.204	.171	.146
4	.552	.516	.482	.423	.373	.329	.292	.260	.198	.153	.120	.095	.077
5	.476	.437	.402	.341	.291	.250	.215	.186	.132	.095	.070	.053	.040
6	.410	.370	.335	.275	.227	.189	.158	.133	.088	.060	.041	.029	.021
7	.354	.314	.279	.222	.178	.143	.116	.095	.059	.037	.024	.016	.011
8	.305	.266	.233	.179	.139	.108	.085	.068	.039	.023	.014	.009	.006
9	.263	.226	.194	.144	.108	.082	.063	.048	.026	.015	.008	.005	.003
10	.227	.191	.162	.116	.085	.062	.046	.035	.017	.009	.005	.003	.002
11	.195	.162	.135	.094	.066	.047	.034	.025	.012	.006	.003	.002	.001
12	.168	.137	.112	.076	.052	.036	.025	.018	.008	.004	.002	.001	.001
13	.145	.116	.093	.061	.040	.027	.018	.013	.005	.002	.001	.001	.000
14	.125	.099	.078	.049	.032	.021	.014	.009	.003	.001	.001	.000	.000
15	.108	.084	.065	.040	.025	.016	.010	.006	.002	.001	.000	.000	.000
16	.093	.071	.054	.032	.019	.012	.007	.005	.002	.001	.000	.000	
17	.080	.060	.045	.026	.015	.009	.005	.003	.001	.000	.000		
18	.069	.051	.038	.021	.012	.007	.004	.002	.001	.000	.000		
19	.060	.043	.031	.017	.009	.005	.003	.002	.000	.000			
20	.051	.037	.026	.014	.007	.004	.002	.001	.000	.000			
25	.024	.016	.010	.005	.002	.001	.000	.000					
30	.012	.007	.004	.002	.001	.000	.000						

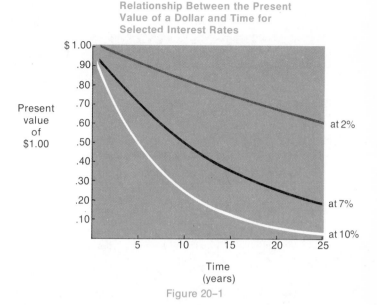

Relationship Between the Present
Value of a Dollar and Time for
Selected Interest Rates

Figure 20–1

THE PRESENT VALUE OF AN ANNUITY

Frequently future sums are not isolated, one-shot payments. For example, the return on an investment may occur for many years. As periodic payments may be made and the amount accumulates (the compound value of an annuity), so may a set of periodic payments be received over time. When equal payments are made annually, this flow of receipts is called an annuity. The present value of these future payments may be determined by obtaining the present value of each payment and summing these present values. This approach is illustrated by the following example of an annuity.

A future annuity's current value

PAYMENT	YEAR	INTEREST FACTOR	PRESENT VALUE
$100	1	.943	$ 94.30
100	2	.890	89.00
100	3	.840	84.00
			$267.30

The recipient expects to receive $100 at the end of each year for three years and wants to know how much this set of annual payments is currently worth if 6 per cent can be earned in alternative investments. The recipient may find the present value of each of the $100 payments and sum these individual present values and derive a present value of $267.30.

To simplify this calculation, interest tables have been developed for the present value of an annuity. An example of such a table is Table 20–5. The interest factors are selected interest rates that are read horizontally across the top and the number of

Present value tables for annuities

TABLE 20-5 Present Value of an Annuity of One Dollar

YEAR	1%	2%	3%	4%	5%	6%	7%	8%	9%	10%
1	0.990	0.980	0.971	0.962	0.952	0.943	0.935	0.926	0.917	0.909
2	1.970	1.942	1.913	1.886	1.859	1.833	1.808	1.783	1.759	1.736
3	2.941	2.884	2.829	2.775	2.723	2.673	2.624	2.577	2.531	2.487
4	3.902	3.808	3.717	3.630	3.546	3.465	3.387	3.312	3.240	3.170
5	4.853	4.713	4.580	4.452	4.329	4.212	4.100	3.993	3.890	3.791
6	5.795	5.601	5.417	5.242	5.076	4.917	4.766	4.623	4.486	4.355
7	6.728	6.472	6.230	6.002	5.786	5.582	5.389	5.206	5.033	4.868
8	7.652	7.325	7.020	6.733	6.463	6.210	5.971	5.747	5.535	5.335
9	8.566	8.162	7.786	7.435	7.108	6.802	6.515	6.247	5.985	5.759
10	9.471	8.983	8.530	8.111	7.722	7.360	7.024	6.710	6.418	6.145
11	10.368	9.787	9.253	8.760	8.306	7.887	7.499	7.139	6.805	6.495
12	11.255	10.575	9.954	9.385	8.863	8.384	7.943	7.536	7.161	6.814
13	12.134	11.348	10.635	9.986	9.394	8.853	8.358	7.904	7.487	7.103
14	13.004	12.106	11.296	10.563	9.899	9.295	8.745	8.244	7.786	7.367
15	13.865	12.849	11.938	11.118	10.380	9.712	9.108	8.559	8.060	7.606
16	14.718	13.578	12.561	11.652	10.838	10.106	9.447	8.851	8.312	7.824
17	15.562	14.292	13.166	12.166	11.274	10.477	9.763	9.122	8.544	8.022
18	16.398	14.992	13.754	12.659	11.690	10.828	10.059	9.372	8.756	8.201
19	17.226	15.678	14.324	13.134	12.085	11.158	10.336	9.604	8.950	8.365
20	18.046	16.351	14.877	13.590	12.462	11.470	10.594	9.818	9.128	8.514
25	22.023	19.523	17.413	15.622	14.094	12.783	11.654	10.675	9.823	9.077
30	25.808	22.397	19.600	17.292	15.373	13.765	12.409	11.258	10.274	9.427

YEAR	12%	14%	16%	18%	20%	24%	28%	32%	36%
1	0.893	0.877	0.862	0.847	0.833	0.806	0.781	0.758	0.735
2	1.690	1.647	1.605	1.566	1.528	1.457	1.392	1.332	1.276
3	2.402	2.322	2.246	2.174	2.106	1.981	1.868	1.766	1.674
4	3.037	2.914	2.798	2.690	2.589	2.404	2.241	2.096	1.966
5	3.605	3.433	3.274	3.127	2.991	2.745	2.532	2.345	2.181
6	4.111	3.889	3.685	3.498	3.326	3.020	2.759	2.534	2.339
7	4.564	4.288	4.039	3.812	3.605	3.242	2.937	2.678	2.455
8	4.968	4.639	4.344	4.078	3.837	3.421	3.076	2.786	2.540
9	5.328	4.946	4.607	4.303	4.031	3.566	3.184	2.868	2.603
10	5.650	5.216	4.833	4.494	4.193	3.682	3.269	2.930	2.650
11	5.988	5.453	5.029	4.656	4.327	3.776	3.335	2.978	2.683
12	6.194	5.660	5.197	4.793	4.439	3.851	3.387	3.013	2.708
13	6.424	5.842	5.342	4.910	4.533	3.912	3.427	3.040	2.727
14	6.628	6.002	5.468	5.008	4.611	3.962	3.459	3.061	2.740
15	6.811	6.142	5.575	5.092	4.675	4.001	3.483	3.076	2.750
16	6.974	6.265	5.669	5.162	4.730	4.033	3.503	3.088	2.758
17	7.120	6.373	5.749	5.222	4.775	4.059	3.518	3.097	2.763
18	7.250	6.467	5.818	5.273	4.812	4.080	3.529	3.104	2.767
19	7.366	6.550	5.877	5.316	4.844	4.097	3.539	3.109	2.770
20	7.469	6.623	5.929	5.353	4.870	4.110	3.546	3.113	2.772
25	7.843	6.873	6.097	5.467	4.948	4.147	3.564	3.122	2.776
30	8.055	7.003	6.177	5.517	4.979	4.160	3.569	3.124	2.778

years is read vertically at the left. To determine the present value of an annuity of $100 received for three years when interest rates are 6%, obtain the interest factor for three years at 6%. This interest factor is 2.673; then multiply the $100 by the interest factor. Thus the present value of the annuity is $267.30, which is the same value that was derived by obtaining each of the individual present values and summing them. $267.30 is the price that one would be willing to pay at the present for three annual payments of $100 when the return on alternative investments is 6 per cent.

As with the present value of a dollar, the present value of an annuity is related to the interest rate and the length of time. The lower is the interest rate and the longer is the duration of the annuity, then the greater is the current value of the annuity. These relationships are illustrated in Figure 20–2, which gives the relationship between the length of time of the annuity, the interest rate, and the present value of the annuity. As may be seen from the graph, the lower the interest rate and the longer the annuity, the greater its present value.

USES OF PRESENT VALUE AND COMPOUND INTEREST TABLES

The concept of the time value of money is crucial to financial decision making. Decisions are made at a point in time but the

Examples of the time value of money

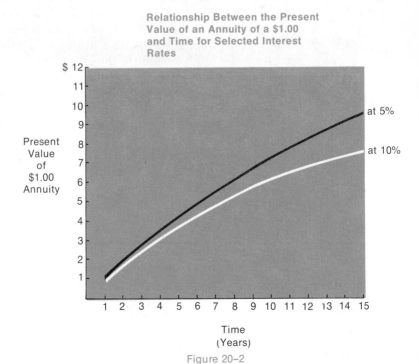

Relationship Between the Present Value of an Annuity of a $1.00 and Time for Selected Interest Rates

Time
(Years)

Figure 20–2

returns generated by the decisions occur over time. This is true not only for financial decisions made by firms but also for decisions made by creditors and investors. This section is devoted to several problems that employ the concept and the interest tables. These examples are illustrative of the variety of questions that involve the time value of money, and should also give the reader some practice in the use of the tables. Additional problems are given at the end of the chapter. You should attempt to solve these problems, for such practice is desirable, as interest tables will be used in subsequent chapters.

A means to help select the correct interest table

You may find the following grid helpful in determining which of the interest tables to use in solving a particular problem.

	ONE PAYMENT	SET OF PAYMENTS (ANNUITY)
COMPOUND VALUE	Table 20–1	Table 20–3
PRESENT VALUE	Table 20–4	Table 20–5

There are four interest tables. Two involve a set of payments (an annuity), and two involve a single payment. The top of the grid shows the single payment and the annuity. If a problem involves one of these two cases, it *excludes* the others. The interest tables also involve time. Two tables involve the future (the compound value tables), and two involve the present (the present value tables). The left hand side of the grid gives the compound value and the present value. If a problem is concerned with one of these, it excludes the other. This grid permits you to determine which table to use. For example, you are given the problem: "The gross national product rose from $284 billion in 1950 to $977 billion in 1970. What is the annual rate of growth?" You realize this is not a set of equal payments, and hence the grid tells you to exclude Tables 20–3 and 20–5. The problem involves one amount ($284) growing to another amount ($977). This is an example of compound value, and hence the grid tells you to exclude Tables 20–4 and 20–5. Thus the grid has indicated that Tables 20–3, 20–4, and 20–5 should be excluded. Then you should use Table 20–1 to solve this problem.

PROBLEM 1

A person accepts a job that pays $8000 a year and anticipates annual raises of 7 per cent. How much will this individual earn after ten years? This problem involves the compounding of a dollar and may be restated as: How much will $8000 grow in ten years at 7 per cent? The interest factor for 7 per cent for ten years found in Table 20–1 is 1.967. Thus, $8000 × 1.967 = $15,736. After ten years the person can anticipate earning $15,736, on the basis of a 7 per cent raise each year.

PROBLEM 2

If a company earned $1 a share in 1965 and $3.11 in 1974, what has been the rate of growth in earnings? This problem also concerns the compound value of a dollar, but in this case the final value is given and the interest factor is the unknown. The question asks what interest factor must $1 be multiplied by to obtain $3.11. The problem may be set up as follows:

$$\$1 \ (1 + i)^{10} = \$3.11$$

By dividing both sides by $1, the equation becomes:

$$(1 + i)^{10} = 3.11$$

Look in Table 20–1 in the row for ten years for an interest factor of 3.11. An interest factor of 3.11 is found under 12 per cent; one dollar will compound to $3.11 in ten years at 12 per cent. The earnings growth rate then is 12 per cent.

This problem is an example of an important use of an interest table, for the beginning and ending values (such as earnings per share or an investment in a security) are frequently known, but the annual growth rate is unknown. The growth rate is determined by dividing the beginning value into the end value and locating that resultant quotient in a compound value of a dollar table for the number of years that have elapsed. The growth rate in earnings per share or in the value of one's portfolio or even the rate at which goods are inflating may be estimated by this simple technique.

PROBLEM 3

If inflation continues (i.e., if prices continue to increase) at 8 per cent annually for the next five years, how much will today's dollar be worth? This is a present value question, although it may not appear to be one. Reworded, this question is: $1 received five years from today is currently worth how much if the interest factor is 8 per cent? In Table 20–4 (the present value of a dollar) the interest factor for five years at 8 per cent is .681. Thus today's dollar will be worth only $.681 five years from now if the rate of inflation is 8 per cent annually.

PROBLEM 4

If a person wants to accumulate $15,000 to make the down payment on a home at the end of five years, how much will have to be saved each year if the savings earn 6 per cent? This problem involves the compound sum of an annuity, but in this case the final sum and the interest rate are known, but the annual payments are unknown. Table 20–3 (the compound sum of an annuity) is used to answer this problem, and the table indicates an interest factor of 5.637 for five years at 6 per cent. The equation then is set up as follows: 5.637X = $15,000. Divide the $15,000 by the interest factor and the quotient indicates that the individual must save $2661 annually. If this amount is saved annually and invested to earn 6 per cent annually, then after five years the individual will have accumulated $15,000 in interest and principal.

This problem is illustrative of a question often asked by prospective homeowners who desire to purchase a home. The use of the interest table permits the prospective homeowner to plan the amount of savings that must be realized annually to achieve the downpayment. While Table 20–3 assumes one lump payment each year and thus cannot tell how much must be saved each month, it does give an indication of how much the prospective homeowner must annually save to raise the money.

SUMMARY

This chapter has considered the time value of money. A dollar received today and a dollar received in the future are not equal. The current dollar may be used to purchase goods and services now or may be invested to earn interest. The dollar received in the future cannot be used to purchase goods and services currently, nor will it earn interest. Future dollars then are worth less than current dollars, and that is the essential point of the time value of money.

Future and present dollars are brought together by interest factors. A dollar in the present will grow to more dollars in the future as the present dollar earns interest, and future dollars may be discounted back to the present by interest factors. By the use of interest factors it is possible to compare present and future dollars.

The ability to compare future dollars with present dollars is crucial to financial decision making. Many financial decisions involve the current outlay of money, for investments are made in the present. The returns on these investments, however, occur in the future. How interest factors are used to aid financial decision making by bringing together these future returns with the present investment expenditures is the subject of Chapter 23. The next chapter, however, is concerned with a firm's cost of capital and the interest factors employed by a specific firm.

KEY WORDS AND TERMS

compounding
annuity
future value
present value
compound value of one dollar
compound value of one dollar annuity
present value of one dollar
present value of one dollar annuity

QUESTIONS AND PROBLEMS FOR THOUGHT
AND DISCUSSION

1. (a) If a person currently earns $10,000 and inflation continues at 8 per cent for ten years, how much must the person make to maintain his purchasing power?

   (b) College graduates in 1965 could expect a starting salary of about $5000. In 1975 they could achieve starting salaries of $10,000. If the rate of inflation were 8 per cent during that time period, which group of students had the higher standard of living?

   (c) If a person bought a $50,000 home in 1970 and sold it in 2000, what would be the value of the house if the annual rate of inflation were 8 per cent during the 30 years?

   (These questions show the potential impact of inflation. Annual price increases may not be substantial. However, when they are compounded over a period of years, the effect can be astounding. It is probably only a matter of time before nickels, dimes, and quarters become obsolete.)

2. If a father wants to have $20,000 to send a child to college, how much must he invest annually for 18 years if he earns 5 per cent on his funds? (Any current student who subsequently becomes a parent and wants to send the child to college should make this calculation early in the child's life.)

3. An investor buys a share of Continental Telephone for $14½. The company pays $1.16 a year cash dividend and permits the investor to reinvest dividends in the company at the stock's market price. If the price of the stock and the dividend remain constant, how many shares will the investor have accumulated after ten years?

(This problem illustrates one means to accumulate savings. Many companies have instituted dividend reinvestment plans. Since the stockholders never receive the money, they cannot spend it. Thus such plans offer the investor an easy and sometimes even cheaper method to accumulate shares. However, such plans currently do not permit the deferral of income taxes permitted by the retirement plans covered in Question 6.)

4. Series E bonds are purchased at a discount (e.g., $18.75) and after a period of time (e.g., six years) may be redeemed (e.g., $25).
   (a) What is the annual rate of interest earned on these bonds?
   (b) What is the annual rate of interest if the discounted price were $15 instead of $18.75?
   (c) What is the annual rate of interest if the time period is reduced from six to five years?
   (Virtually everyone is aware of Series E Bonds. When they were first issued, the length of time that the bonds had to be held to earn the full amount of interest was ten years. Currently they must be held 5 years and 10 months to earn 5½ per cent. By reducing that time period, the Federal Government has increased the rate of interest. The same effect could have been achieved by lowering the price of the bonds and maintaining the maturity date. Bonds that were issued many years ago (e.g., 1942) and that are still outstanding currently earn the higher interest rates. Such bonds may be redeemed at the owner's option. Under present law all Series E Bonds must be redeemed in 1982, after which time additional interest will not be accrued.)

5. A company has two investment possibilities and each offers the following flows of cash:

	YEAR 1	YEAR 2	YEAR 3
A	$1400	$1700	$1800
B	1500	1500	1500

If the firm can earn 10 per cent in other investments, what is the present value of investments A and B? If each investment costs $4000, is the present value of each investment greater than the cost of the investment? (This question is a very simple example of one method of capital budgeting [Chapter 23]). This technique permits the firm to rank alternative investments and help select the potentially most profitable investment.)

6. A 40-year-old man decides to put funds into a retirement plan. He can save $2000 a year and earn 7 per cent on this savings.

How much will he have accumulated when he retires at the age of sixty-five? At retirement how much can he withdraw each year for twenty years from his accumulated savings if his savings continue to earn 7 per cent?

(This question illustrates the basic elements of pension plans. A sum of money is systematically set aside. It earns interest so that by retirement a considerable amount has been accumulated. Then the retired person draws on the fund until it is exhausted or death occurs in which case the remainder of the fund becomes part of the estate. Of course, while the retired person draws on the fund, the remaining principal continues to earn interest. Recent changes in the federal income tax laws now permit workers who are not covered by pension plans to set up their own plans through a financial institution such as a commercial bank. These plans not only permit the building of retirement funds but also defer federal income taxes.)

Chapter 21   FINANCIAL LEVERAGE

Learning Objectives

* Define financial leverage.
* Explain the potential effect of financial leverage on earnings.
* Explain the potential effect of financial leverage on risk.
* Identify the importance of taxes to debt financing.
* Show how preferred stock is a source of financial leverage.
* Illustrate how individuals may employ financial leverage.

"The human species is composed of two distinct races, the men who borrow, and the men who lend."

Charles Lamb

There are many concepts in finance, but no concept is more important than that of financial leverage. In the minds of some businessmen the successful use of financial leverage to increase profits is the "name of the game." Since it is such an important concept, this entire chapter will be devoted to financial leverage, how it is obtained, the risk involved in using it, and how the individual as well as the businessman may use financial leverage.

Financial leverage is the use of another person's money in return for a fixed payment and a promise to return the money. If a firm borrows funds, it issues debt and must make a fixed payment for the use of the money. This fixed payment is called interest. The debt must be retired (i.e., paid off). The firm may also obtain financial leverage by an equity claim on its earnings but giving the purchaser preference or prior claim on the earnings. Since the purchaser has a preferred claim, his stock is called preferred stock. Preferred stock has a fixed dividend and thus is similar to debt, for the interest payments on debt are fixed. However, preferred stock does not mature, and hence there is no need to pay back the money.

The firm agrees to make fixed interest or dividend payments because the firm *anticipates* being able to earn more with the money than it has agreed to pay. This will increase the return on the common stockholder's investment. The creditors are willing to lend the firm the money because the firm offers a fixed return. The creditors receive a relatively assured flow of income from the loans but do not bear the risk of owning and operating the business. If the creditors have the skills, they might enter the business themselves. There are, however, many people who lack either the skills or the desire to enter a particular business and are satisfied to let the firm use the money for the promised fixed return. They are, of course, aware that the firm anticipates earning more money with their money than the firm has agreed to pay.

Management wants to maximize the value of the firm's equity and should follow policies that increase the wealth of the firm's stockholders. Since the use of financial leverage may increase the return to the common stockholders, management may seek to use financial leverage. If financial leverage is used, it may also increase the firm's level of risk. Thus management must seek to find the best or optimal amount of financial leverage, for insufficient use of leverage will decrease the stockholder's return, while excessive use will subject the stockholder to excessive risk.

HOW FINANCIAL LEVERAGE INCREASES INVESTORS' RATE OF RETURN

How financial leverage works may be shown by a very simple example. Firm A needs $100 capital to operate and may acquire the money from the owners of the firm. Alternatively, it may acquire part of the money from stockholders and part from creditors. If the management acquires the $100 from stockholders, the firm uses no debt financing and is not financially leveraged. The firm would have the following simple balance sheet:

Return on equity without using financial leverage

ASSETS	LIABILITIES & EQUITY
Cash $100	
	Equity $100

Once in business the firm generates the following simplified income statement:

Sales	$100
Expenses	80
Gross profit	20
Taxes (50%)	10
Net profit	$ 10

What is the return that the firm has earned on the owners' investment? The answer is 10 per cent, for the investors contributed $100 and the firm earned $10 after taxes. The firm may pay the $10 to the investors in cash dividends or may retain the $10 to help finance future growth. Either way, however, the owners' rate of return on their investment is 10 per cent.

Return on equity using financial leverage

By using financial leverage, management may be able to increase the owners' rate of return on their investment. What happens to their rate of return if management is able to borrow part of the capital needed to operate the firm? The answer to this question depends upon (1) what proportion of the total capital is borrowed and (2) the interest rate that must be paid to the creditors. If management is able to borrow 50 per cent ($50) of the firm's capital needs at an interest cost of 5 per cent, the balance becomes:

ASSETS	LIABILITIES AND EQUITY
Cash $100	Debt $50
	Equity $50

Since the firm borrowed $50, it is now obligated to pay interest. Thus the firm has a new expense that must be paid before it has any earnings for the common stockholder. The simple income statement now becomes:

Sales	$100.00
Expenses	80.00
Gross profit	20.00
Interest expense	2.50
Taxable income	17.50
Taxes	8.75
Net profit	$ 8.75

The use of debt causes the total net profit to decline from $10 to $8.75. What effect does this have on the owners' rate of return? It increases from 10 per cent to 17.5 per cent. Why did this reduction in the net profit produce an increase in the owners' rate of return? The answer is that the owners invested only $50, and that $50 earned them $8.75. They made 17.5 per cent on their money, whereas previously they earned only 10 per cent.

The importance of the fixed interest payment

There are two sources of this return. First, the firm borrowed money and agreed to pay a fixed return of 5 per cent. The firm, however, was able to earn more than 5 per cent with the money, and this additional earning accrued to the owners of the firm. Second, the entire burden of the interest cost was not borne by the firm. The federal tax laws permit the deduction of interest as an expense before determining taxable income, and thus this interest expense is shared with the government. The greater the corporate income tax rate, then the greater the portion of this interest expense borne by the government. In this case 50 per cent or $1.25 of the interest expense was borne by the government in lost tax revenues. If the corporate income tax rate were 60 per cent, the government would lose $1.50 in taxable income by permitting the deduction of the interest expense. These then are the two sources of the additional return to the owners; the additional money earned on the borrowed capital and the tax dollars lost by the federal government.

As was seen in the above example, a firm's management may increase the owners' rate of return by the use of debt, i.e., the use of financial leverage. By increasing the proportion of the firm's assets that are financed by debt (by increasing the debt ratio), management is able to increase the rate of return on the owners' equity. Table 21-1 shows various combinations of debt financing as measured by the debt ratio and (1) the resulting earnings for the firm and (2) the rate of return on the investors' equity. The table was constructed on the assumption that the interest rate is 5 per cent no matter what proportion of the firm's assets were financed by debt. This unrealistic assumption will be dropped later in the chapter. Figure 21-1 plots the material presented in Table 21-1. From both the table and the figure it may be seen that as the debt ratio rises, the rate of return on the owner's equity not only rises but rises at an increasing rate. This dramatically indicates how the use of financial leverage may significantly increase the rate of return on a firm's equity.

Larger use of debt financing can further increase return on equity

FINANCIAL LEVERAGE AND RISK

Since the use of financial leverage increases the owners' rate of return, the question becomes, Why not use ever-increasing

TABLE 21-1 Relationship Between Debt Ratio and the Rate of Return on Equity

DEBT RATIO	0%	20	50	70	90
AMOUNT OF DEBT OUTSTANDING	$ 0	20	50	70	90
EQUITY	$100	80	50	30	10
SALES	$100	100	100	100	100
EXPENSES	$ 80	80	80	80	80
GROSS PROFIT	$ 20	20	20	20	20
INTEREST EXPENSE (5% INTEREST RATE)	$ 0	1	2.50	3.50	5
TAXABLE INCOME	$ 20	19	17.50	16.50	15
INCOME TAXES (50% TAX RATE)	$ 10	9.50	8.75	8.25	7.50
NET PROFIT	$ 10	9.50	8.75	8.25	7.50
RATE OF RETURN ON EQUITY	10%	11.87	17.5	27.5	75.0

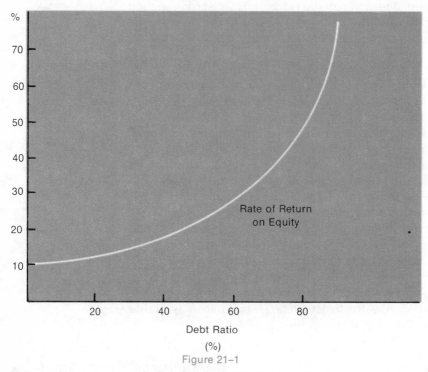

Figure 21–1

Use of Financial Leverage and the Return on Equity

Increased use of debt financing increases financial risk

Fluctuations in sales then produce larger fluctuations in earnings for the leveraged firm

amounts of debt financing? The answer is that, as the firm becomes more financially leveraged (i.e., as the debt ratio rises), the firm becomes more risky. This increase in risk increases (1) the potential for fluctuations in the owners' returns and (2) the interest rate that the creditors charge for the use of their money.

That the use of financial leverage increases the potential risk to the owners may be seen by employing the simple example presented in the previous section. What happens to the rate of return on the equity if sales were to decline by 10 per cent (from $100 to $90) and expenses were to remain the same? The income statements for the financially unleveraged and leveraged firms becomes as follows:

	UNLEVERAGED FIRM (0% DEBT RATIO)	LEVERAGED FIRM (50% DEBT RATIO)
Sales	$90.00	$90.00
Expenses	80.00	80.00
Gross profit	$10.00	$10.00
Interest	—	2.50
Taxable income	$10.00	$ 7.50
Taxes	5.00	3.75
Net profit	$ 5.00	$ 3.75

The 10 per cent decline in sales produces substantial declines in the earnings and the rates of return on the owners' investment in both cases. For the unleveraged firm the rate of return is now 5 per cent ($5/$100); for the financially leveraged firm the rate of return plummets from 17.5 per cent to 7.5 per cent. The decline is greater for the financially leveraged firm than for the unleveraged firm. Why does the return decline more for the leveraged firm than for the unleveraged firm? The answer rests with the *fixed* interest payment. When the firm borrowed the capital, it agreed to make the fixed interest payment. This agreement is a legal obligation that the firm must pay or default on the loan. The fixed interest payment, which was a source of the increase in the owners' rate of return when sales were $100, becomes the cause of the larger decline in the owners' rate of return when the firm's sales decline. If the firm had been even more leveraged (i.e., if the debt ratio had been greater), the decline in the rate of return on the owners' investment would have been even larger. This suggests a general conclusion: the greater the proportion of a firm's assets that are financed by fixed obligations, then the greater the potential fluctuation in the owners' rate of return. Small changes in revenue or costs will produce larger fluctuations in the firm's earnings.

> The earnings' fluctuations are caused by the fixed interest payment

Firms that use large amounts of financial leverage are viewed by creditors as being risky. Creditors may refuse to lend to a highly leveraged firm or do so only at higher rates of interest or more stringent loan conditions. As the interest rate increases, the owners' rate of return on their equity in the firm diminishes. This may be seen in the example presented in Table 21–2, which illustrates what happens to the investors' rate of return as the interest rate rises. Table 21–2 is based on the example in Table 21–1. The first case (A) is taken directly from Table 21–1 and illustrates the rate of return if the interest is held constant as more debt is employed. The second case (B) assumes that interest rates rise as the debt ratio increases to compensate creditors for the increased risk. The last row in each case gives the rate of

> Increase in risk will lead to higher interest rates

TABLE 21–2   Relationship Between Increased Interest Rates and the Rate of Return on the Investors' Equity

DEBT RATIO	0%	20	50	70
(A) Gross Profit	$20	20	20	20
Interest at 5%	$ 0	1	2.50	3.50
Taxable income	$20	19	17.50	16.50
Rate of return on investors' equity	10%	11.87	17.50	27.50
(B) Gross Profit	$20	20	20	20
Interest rate	5%	5%	7%	10%
Interest expense	$ 0	1	3.50	7
Taxable income	$20	19	16.50	13
Rate of return on investors' equity	10%	11.87	16.50	20.8

return on the owners' equity, and, as would be expected, the increased interest expense causes the owners' rate of return to diminish. However, even though the rate of return diminishes, it may still exceed the rate of return obtained when no debt was used, and thus financial leverage is still favorable.

Financial leverage
may still be favorable
even though interest
rates rise

As long as the rate of return on all the assets exceeds the after tax cost of debt (i.e., the interest rate adjusted for the tax savings), financial leverage is favorable and will increase the return on the owners' investment. In the first example presented in this chapter, the firm earned 20 per cent before taxes on its assets. Financial leverage then is favorable if interest rates are 12 per cent, 15 per cent, or even 18 per cent. It is only at 20 per cent that financial leverage becomes unfavorable, for then the interest charges have risen sufficiently to absorb every dollar earned on the borrowed money. If the firm financed operations by $50 equity and $50 debt at 20 per cent, it would have the following income statement:

Sales	$100
Expenses	80
Gross profit	20
Interest	10
Taxable income	10
Taxes	5
Net profit	$ 5

The rate of return on the equity is 5 per cent, which is exactly the rate of return earned on the equity by the unleveraged firm.

Federal income tax
laws encourage the
use of debt financing

Why can interest rates be so high and financial leverage still be favorable? A major reason for this result is the ability of the firm to deduct the interest expense before determining taxable income. If a firm's income tax rate is 50 per cent and the interest rates are 12 per cent, 15 per cent, or 18 per cent, the after-tax cost to the firm is only 6 per cent, 7.5 per cent, and 9 per cent, respectively. Only when the after-tax cost of debt exceeds the rate earned on the firm's assets is financial leverage unfavorable. The ability to share the interest expense with the government significantly encourages the use of debt to obtain financial leverage. Corporations, whose federal income tax rate is 48 per cent, share almost half of the interest expense with the federal government. From the firm's viewpoint, a dollar paid in interest to creditors reduces the firm's taxes by $.48. The true interest cost of the dollar is only $.52, and thus the tax laws become a major incentive to use financial leverage.

FINANCIAL LEVERAGE THROUGH PREFERRED STOCK FINANCING

In the preceding sections we saw how financial leverage was achieved through the use of debt. Financial leverage may also be acquired through the use of preferred stock, for preferred stock has a fixed dividend which is similar to the fixed interest payment on borrowed money. The significant differences between debt and preferred stock financing are that the dividend on the preferred stock is not a contractual obligation and is not a tax-deductible expense and that the company does not have to retire the preferred stock. The fact that the dividend is not a contractual obligation is the major advantage for preferred stock financing. Preferred stock is less risky than debt financing because, if the firm falls on bad times and is unable to meet the dividend payment, the owners of the preferred stock cannot force the firm to make the payment. In the case of debt, however, if the firm fails to pay the interest, the creditors can take the firm to court to force payment or force bankruptcy.

Preferred stock is a less risky means to obtain financial leverage

Lacks tax advantage

Although preferred stock financing is a less risky means to acquire financial leverage, the other significant difference between it and debt financing argues strongly against the use of preferred stock. Since interest is a tax-deductible expense and the preferred dividends are not, the effective cost of debt financing is cheaper. If a firm borrows money at 8 per cent, the true cost of the money is reduced as a result of the tax laws. If a firm issues preferred stock and pays an 8 per cent dividend, the true cost to the firm is 8 per cent. Since the cost of debt financing is shared with the government, firms tend to use debt instead of preferred stock as a means to obtain financial leverage.

The tax law also reduces the amount of financial leverage that a firm may obtain with preferred stock. The difference in the rates of return to the common stockholder that result from the use of debt and preferred stock financing is illustrated in the following example. The firm issues $50 worth of common stock and needs an additional $50. It may issue either $50 of debt with a 5 per cent interest rate, or $50 of preferred stock with a 5 per cent dividend. In either case the firm acquires $50 and pays out $2.50 in either interest or dividends. However, the earnings available to the common stockholder are larger when debt is used instead of preferred stock. This is shown in the following income statements:

	DEBT FINANCING	PREFERRED STOCK FINANCING
Sales	$100.00	$100.00
Expenses	80.00	80.00
Gross profit	$ 20.00	$ 20.00
Interest	2.50	—
Taxable income	$ 17.50	$ 20.00
Taxes	8.75	10.00
Net profit	$ 8.75	$ 10.00
Preferred dividends	—	2.50
Earnings available to common stock	$ 8.75	$ 7.50

When debt financing is used, the earnings are $8.75, while the earnings are only $7.50 when the preferred stock is used. Thus the rate of return on the common stockholders' investment is larger (17.5 per cent versus 15 per cent) when debt financing is used. The ability of the firm to share the interest expense of obtaining financial leverage with the federal government encourages the use of debt financing instead of preferred stock financing. The use of preferred stock financing has declined over time, and this decline is partially explained by the unfavorable tax treatment afforded preferred stock.

Differences in the Amount of Financial Leverage Used by Firms

While virtually every firm uses some financial leverage, there are differences in the degree to which it is used. This was illustrated in Tables 15–1 and 15–2. Table 15–1 presented the debt ratio for several industrial firms, and Table 15–2 presented the debt ratios for selected telephone companies. As these tables indicated, there are differences among firms in the use of financial leverage as measured by the debt ratio.

Some firms have a high degree of financial risk

Some firms are more financially leveraged by the nature of the business enterprise, and this financial leverage will influence the behavior of the firms in the industry. Commercial banks are an excellent example. Banks have high debt ratios because most assets acquired by commercial banks are financed by their deposit liabilities. Small changes in the revenues of commercial banks will produce larger fluctuations in the earnings after interest and taxes. Bankers are well aware of this financial leverage and are less willing to take inordinate risks. The nature of their operations and banks' high degree of financial leverage require that bankers be inherently conservative.

Airlines have both financial and operating leverage

Other firms need large amounts of fixed equipment to operate, and they may also be highly leveraged if they have financed this equipment through the issuance of debt. The airlines are an excellent example of an industry that has a large investment in equipment that has been frequently financed by debt. This high degree of financial leverage in part explains the large fluctuations in earnings of airline companies. Table 21–3 presents the debt ratio and earnings per share for selected airlines over a period of years. The information in the table indicates that there have been large and sudden fluctuations in the earnings per share of airlines. These fluctuations have resulted from changes in the demand for the service and the cost to produce the service. But these fluctuations are magnified by the use of debt financing. For example, TWA finances three fourths of its assets with debt and has experienced fluctuations in earnings from a deficit of

TABLE 21–3   Earnings Per Share and Debt Ratios of Selected Airlines
(Source: Standard and Poor's Corporate Records and Annual Reports.)

| | AMERICAN AIRLINES | | EASTERN AIRLINES | | NATIONAL AIRLINES | | TWA | |
	EPS	Debt Ratio	EPS	Debt Ratio	EPS	Debt Ratio	EPS	Debt Ratio
1975	$(.72)	73.3%	$(2.65)	79.5%	$1.33	65.3%	$(6.68)	81.8%
1974	.72	61.3	.37	70.0	3.58	70.2	(2.01)	77.9
1973	(1.69)	62.4	(2.73)	68.5	2.36	66.3	3.25	75.6
1972	.20	64.1	1.02	76.3	2.34	65.4	3.01	75.6
1971	.13	61.7	.32	75.2	(.46)	57.7	.11	74.4
1970	(1.30)	64.5	.39	77.2	.44	56.5	(6.39)	77.7

$6.39 per share in 1970 to earnings of $3.25 per share in 1973, then back to a deficit of $6.68 per share in 1975.

DEGREE OF FINANCIAL LEVERAGE

In the previous section financial leverage was measured by the debt ratio. Another measure of financial leverage is the degree of financial leverage, which is the percentage change in earnings available to the firm's owners divided by the percentage change in earnings before interest and taxes (EBIT). The earnings available to the owners are net earnings after interest and taxes have been paid. The degree of financial leverage then is expressed by the following ratio:

Responsiveness of net earnings to changes in earnings before interest and taxes

$$(1) \qquad \frac{\text{percentage change in earnings}}{\text{percentage change in EBIT}}$$

This ratio measures the *responsiveness* of earnings available to the common stockholders relative to earnings available to pay creditors, the government, and the owners. If a firm's earnings rise by 60 per cent when earnings before taxes and interest increase by 20 per cent, then the degree of financial leverage is 3. This is shown by the following equation:

$$(2) \qquad \frac{\text{percentage change in earnings}}{\text{percentage change in EBIT}} = \frac{60\%}{20\%} = 3$$

This indicates that when earnings before interest and taxes increase by $1, then earnings after taxes and interest increases by $3. The financial leverage magnifies the earnings available to the firm's owners.

The larger the numerical value of this ratio, the greater the degree of financial leverage. Fluctuations in earnings before interest and taxes will produce greater fluctuations in earnings after interest and taxes if the firm uses a large amount of financial leverage. The degree of financial leverage then is a means to measure the responsiveness of earnings available to the firm's owners to changes in the earnings before interest and taxes are paid.

INDIVIDUALS' USES OF FINANCIAL LEVERAGE

Financial leverage is used by individuals as well as firms

While the discussion up to now has centered on the use of financial leverage by firms, individuals may also use financial leverage. This usage primarily occurs in the following three cases: (1) financing homes through mortgages; (2) purchasing securities on margin; and (3) using consumer credit. In each case the individual makes a down payment (equity) and agrees to pay interest and retire the principal. This is essentially no different than a firm borrowing money to finance purchases of plant, equipment, or inventory. The individual receives the same potential benefits as a firm and is subject to the same risks.

(1) Home mortgages

When an individual purchases a home, a down payment is made and the balance of the money is borrowed. If the home costs $50,000 and the down payment is $15,000, then the remaining $35,000 must be borrowed. The home owner makes interest payments on the loan and periodically repays the principal. If the interest rate is 8 per cent, then the homeowner makes initial interest payments of approximately $2800 annually. These payments may be deducted from the homeowner's income before determining the income that is subject to federal tax. Like the firm, the homeowner shares the borrowing cost with the government. If the homeowner's tax bracket is 25 per cent, the savings is $700 in taxes (.25 × $2800). Thus the interest cost is really only $2100. If the house is sold after a year for $60,000, what is the return on the investment? The profit on the sale is $10,000, but the interest expense was $2100 (after the tax saving). Thus the homeowner receives $7900 (before any commissions or taxes on this gain) on an investment of $15,000. That is a rate of return in excess of 50 per cent on the funds invested. If the homeowner had paid the full purchase price of the home, the return would have been only 20 per cent ($10,000/$50,000). By borrowing part of the purchase price and thereby using financial leverage, the homeowner was able to increase the return on the capital. Of course, the homeowner is subject to risks, for if the price of the home were to decline, the use of financial leverage magnifies the loss. For example, if the price of the house had declined from $50,000 to $40,000, the individual receives only $5000 after paying off the $35,000 mortgage and would have sustained a loss on the investment. However, the recent trend of rising prices of homes argues strongly in favor of purchasing a home and financing the purchase through a mortgage. As long as this trend continues, such purchases may prove to be a sound method for obtaining living space, and the use of mortgages may increase the return on the homeowners' investment.

The purchase of securities on margin is similar to purchasing a home with a mortgage. The investor makes a down payment (called margin) and borrows the difference. If the price of a stock is $50 and the margin requirement is 60 per cent, then the investor must invest $30 and may borrow the remaining $20. Interest is paid on the amount that the investor borrows. This interest expense may be shared with the federal government, for the interest is deductible from income before determining the investor's taxable income. If the price of the security rises, then the investor will reap a larger return on the investment than would be possible had the entire cost of the investment been paid.

(2) Securities on margin

For example, if the price of the stock rose from $50 to $70, an investor earns 40 per cent ($20/$50). If margin is used and 40 per cent of the purchase price is borrowed, the investor would have committed only $30 and thus earned 67 per cent ($20/$30) on the money. If, however, the price of the security had declined, then the use of margin would have magnified the loss. Thus the potential for greater profits and losses in the security markets is available to the investor who uses financial leverage to purchase securities.

The use of consumer credit is essentially no different than purchasing a home or securities with borrowed funds. The consumer in this case takes the return in the form of current services from the goods. Instead of saving sufficient income to purchase the goods, the consumer purchases the goods with borrowed funds and repays the loan as income is generated. The consumer pays interest on the money borrowed to finance the purchase, and presumably the value that the consumer places on the current flow of services from the goods exceeds the cost of financing the purchase. This cost can be substantial, however, for consumer loans may carry interest rates of 12 per cent or greater. The consumer is also subject to increased risk. If the individual should fail to make the finance payments, the goods will be repossessed, and the consumer will lose any equity in them. Thus financial leverage also applies to consumer credit. It increases the users' potential return, for they can have the goods at once instead of having to wait to purchase them. But it also subjects consumers to increased financial risks. This increased potential return and increased financial risk thus applies to all users of financial leverage.

(3) Consumer credit

SUMMARY

This chapter has contained a discussion of financial leverage. All assets must be financed. There are two sources of this finance—debt and equity. If the firm uses debt financing or preferred stock, it is financially leveraged. If the firm is able to earn more with the funds (acquired by issuing debt) than it must pay in interest, the residual accrues to the equity. Thus, by successfully using debt financing, the firm increases the earnings available to the owners, and the return on their investment is increased.

While the successful use of debt financing increases earnings, it also increases the element of risk. The terms of the debt must be met. If the firm experiences a decline in sales or profit margins, it must still pay the interest and retire the debt. Failure to do so may result in bankruptcy. Thus, while the use of debt financing may increase earnings during periods of success, the opposite is true during periods of difficulty. Then the use of debt financing reduces earnings, as the firm must meet the fixed obligations of its debt financing.

While most firms do use some debt financing, there can be significant differences in its use among firms. Management must decide to what extent it is willing to employ financial leverage. Some managements are more willing to take risk, and their firms are more financially leveraged. Thus it is possible to find differences in the use of debt financing among firms in the same industry. However, the ultimate judge of these financing decisions is their effect on the value of the firm. Excessive use of debt financing will reduce the value of a firm. Hence management should seek to find that combination of debt and equity financing which offers the advantage of financial leverage without exposing the firm to excessive risk.

KEY WORDS AND TERMS _____

> financial leverage
> debt
> interest
> federal taxes
> preferred stock
> degree of financial leverage
> consumer credit
> margin
> financial risk

QUESTIONS AND PROBLEMS FOR THOUGHT
AND DISCUSSION _____

1. In many managers' minds, financial leverage is the name of the game. What is meant by this? What are the possible risks and rewards associated with financial leverage? Do you think

there may be considerable differences in the use of financial leverage by firms in the same industry?

2. What feature of preferred stock makes it a source of financial leverage? Since both debt and preferred stock are means to obtain leverage, why will a debt issue with a 5 per cent yield achieve more leverage than an equal amount of preferred stock with a 5 per cent dividend? If tax laws were changed to equalize the differences, would a firm prefer to use debt or preferred stock?

3. Financial leverage is associated with financial risk. As a firm becomes more financially leveraged, why does it become more risky? How will creditors seek to protect the funds they have lent? Why may the value of the firm's stock decline as the firm becomes more financially leveraged? Go to your library and compare the debt ratios, sales, and earnings of General Motors, Ford, and Chrysler. What conclusions may you draw from your analysis?

4. Given: funds needed to start the business: $100.

> sales: $200
> expenses: $150
> tax rate: 50% of profits

(a) What is the profit the owners will receive if they put up the $100?

(b) If the firm borrowed $50 of the initial $100 at 10 per cent interest, what is the profit the owners will receive?

(c) What is the rate of return of the investment in each case? Why is the rate of return to the owners in (b) larger than the rate of return in (a)?

(d) If expenses rise to $175, what will be the rate of return on the owners' investment in (a) and (b)?

(e) In which case will the rate of return fall more? Why?

(f) What generalization can you draw from the above?

Chapter 22 THE COST OF CAPITAL

Learning Objectives

- Explain why the cost of capital depends on the alternative uses for the funds.
- Identify the components of a firm's capital structure.
- Differentiate between the impact of taxes on the cost of debt and preferred stock.
- Compute the cost of capital.
- Isolate the effect of increased use of debt on the cost of capital.
- Determine the optimal capital structure.

"A measure of the unwillingness of those who possess money to part with liquid control over it."

John Maynard Keynes

A firm's sources of finance are not free, because both debt and equity investors anticipate a return on their funds. This return is a cost to the firm that the financial manager must cover in order to maintain the value of the firm. Creditors and equity investors have many possible uses for their money. If a firm does not earn for them a sufficient return for the use of their money, they will certainly take their funds elsewhere. Such a withdrawal of funds will decrease the value of the firm.

The financial manager must know the costs of the firm's sources of finance (i.e., its cost of capital) in order to judge investment opportunities. To increase the value of the firm, an investment must earn more than the cost of funds necessary to finance the investment. The determination of the firm's cost of capital then is necessary for the correct application of the capital budgeting techniques discussed in the next chapter.

This chapter is devoted to the cost of capital and how it is determined. The cost of capital is not just the interest cost of a loan. Instead, it is an average of the cost of the various components (i.e., debt and equity) of a firm's finances. In the sections below, each of the component costs is discussed. Then a simple example of the process by which the financial manager determines the cost of capital is presented. In the last section, the optimal capital structure of AT&T and how its management is seeking to maintain that structure are discussed.

COST OF DEBT

The cost of debt is related to (1) the interest rate, (2) the corporate income tax rate, and (3) risk. If a firm borrows money and pays 8 per cent for the use of that money, then the before-tax interest rate is 8 per cent. The tax laws, however, permit the deduction of interest before computing taxable income. The interest expense is shared with the federal government, and the amount of this sharing depends on the firm's marginal income tax rate. For many incorporated businesses, the tax rate on additional income is 48 per cent, which reduces the cost of debt by nearly one-half. For example, if a firm has a marginal tax rate of 48 per cent and issues bonds that pay 8 per cent interest, then the cost of debt is 4.16 per cent. This percentage is easily found because the cost of debt (k_d) is the interest rate times one minus the firm's marginal tax rate (t). Thus, for this firm

Factors affecting the cost of debt

cost of debt = before-tax interest rate (1 − marginal tax rate)

$$.0416 = .08 (1 - .48)$$

This cost of debt is expressed in equation form in Equation (1):

(1) $$k_d = i(1 - t)$$

Once again you will note the use of subscripts. Since this chapter is concerned with the various components of a firm's cost of capital, the subscripts will denote the specific source being discussed, such as debt (d) or preferred stock (p) or common stock and retained earnings (e).

The cost of debt is the cost at which new debt may be issued; it is not the cost at which debt was issued in the past. If a firm has debt that was issued ten years ago with a fixed interest rate below the current interest rate, it is the current interest rate that is used to determine the firm's cost of capital. When the older debt was issued, the rate was used to determine the firm's cost of capital at that time. The firm's cost of debt today is the current cost of obtaining debt, not its historic cost. Current cost is the interest rate that the firm must presently pay to borrow the money adjusted for the tax deduction.

Current and not historical cost

The cost of debt is also dependent upon the riskiness of the firm. As the firm becomes more risky, creditors will want higher interest payments to compensate them for the increased risk. The risk is related to the nature of the business (i.e., business risk) and the degree of financial leverage (i.e., financial risk). The more the

Increase in risk will increase interest rate

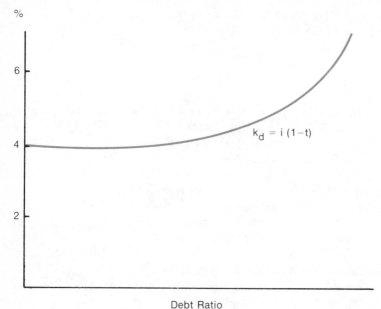

Figure 22–1
Cost of Debt

firm uses debt financing, the greater the potential for it to fail to meet its debt obligations. As the firm's debt ratio increases, then the interest rate on borrowed money will increase. This is illustrated by the line k_d in Figure 22–1. As the debt ratio increases, the cost of debt may be stable as the firm initially uses more financial leverage without significantly increasing risk for the creditor. Eventually the cost of debt starts to rise as the debt ratio increases, because creditors demand more interest to compensate them for the increased risk of loss.

COST OF PREFERRED STOCK

No tax advantage for preferred stock

The cost of preferred stock is dependent upon the cash dividend and the market price of the preferred stock. Since the dividends are paid after taxes, there is *no tax adjustment* as there is with interest payments. The cost is the yield necessary to induce investors to purchase the preferred stock. This yield or cost (k_p) is the dividend (D_p) divided by the price (P_p). This is expressed simply in Equation (2):

$$(2) \qquad k_p = \frac{D_p}{P_p}$$

Cost of preferred is the dividend yield

If a preferred stock pays a dollar dividend and has a market price of \$12, then the cost of the preferred stock is

$$(2) \qquad k_p = \frac{\$1.00}{\$12.00} = .08333$$

The 8.33 per cent is the cost of the funds if the firm currently uses preferred stock financing.

For a new issue of preferred stock, the company should use the net price after selling the stock, which deducts the expense of selling the shares. For example, if this firm issued new preferred shares and had to pay an underwriting fee of 7 per cent, it would net only $11.16 [$12.00(1 − .07)] per share. Thus the cost of preferred stock financing would be

$$k_p = \frac{\$1.00}{\$11.16} = 8.96\%$$

The cost of selling new shares to the public raises the cost of preferred stock. In this case the cost increased by over half a percentage point.

From the viewpoint of the firm, the cost of preferred stock is significantly higher than the cost of debt. This cost differential results from federal income tax laws and is not the result of the public's willingness to pay more for debt securities. Even though preferred stock is a means to obtain financial leverage, the increased cost of this financial leverage argues for the use of debt securities to obtain financial leverage. In recent years there has been relatively little preferred stock financing (unless the preferred stock was issued as part of a merger or is convertible into the common stock of the company). While the preferred stock does not legally bind the firm to pay dividends and meet other indenture agreements, its additional cost overshadows these advantages of the preferred stock.

Cost of preferred exceeds cost of debt

COST OF EQUITY (COMMON STOCK AND RETAINED EARNINGS)

The cost of equity is the return required by investors in common stock. The cost of equity is an opportunity cost concept; it is the return that these investors require of the firm in order to meet their alternative uses of the money. This cost applies to both new shares of common stock and to retained earnings, for investors could use the funds generated by the profits but retained by the firm. The firm must be able to meet the investors' alternative uses for the money in order to justify retaining the earnings.

Alternative uses of funds

Investors purchase stock with the anticipation of a total return consisting of dividend yield and capital gains. The dividend yield is the dividend (D) divided by the price of the stock (P_e). The capital gains is the increase of the price of the stock, which is related to the growth rate (g) of the firm's earnings. If the firm is consistently able to achieve growth in earnings, then dividends can be increased, and the price of the shares will rise.

Total return: (1) dividends; (2) capital gains

This increase in the value of the shares produces capital gains for the stockholders.

Equity investors' required return (i.e., the cost of equity, k_e) is the sum of the dividend yield plus the capital gains, which is expressed algebraically in Equation (3):

(3)
$$k_e = \frac{D}{P_e} + g$$

Flotation costs
If the firm is issuing new shares, then a modification in Equation (3) is necessary. Since there are flotation costs (i.e., selling costs), the company cannot issue new shares at the current market price of the stock. Thus the price of the common stock in Equation (3) must be reduced by the flotation costs of the new stock. Obviously, the greater the flotation costs, the smaller the amount obtained by the firm for each share sold and the greater the cost of new equity financing. For the purpose of this chapter these flotation costs are ignored, but you should be aware of these selling costs and their effect on the cost of equity.

How this cost of equity may be applied is shown in the following example. A firm's earnings are growing annually at the rate of 7 per cent, and the common stock is expected to pay $1.00 a share dividend. If the common stock is currently selling for $25, then the cost of equity for the firm is

$$k_e = \frac{\$1.00}{\$25} + .07$$

$$k_e = .11$$

This 11 per cent cost tells the management of the firm that investors require 11 per cent return on their investment in the stock. Currently that return is being achieved by a 4 per cent dividend yield and the 7 per cent growth in earnings. Failure on the part of management to continue to achieve this 11 per cent return for the common stockholders will result in a decline in the price of the common stock.

A method to value a company
This equation is also useful in another form. By mathematical manipulation, this equation may be expressed as follows:

(4)
$$P_e = \frac{D}{k_e - g}$$

In this form the equation is a method to find the value of a firm.*

---

*To be mathematically precise, the dividend component of the equation should be the dividend paid during the first year. That is the current dividend (D_0) plus the growth in the dividend during the year (gD_0). Thus the dividend paid during the first year (D_1) is $D_1 = D_0 + gD_0 = D_0(1 + g)$.

Equation (4) indicates what stock price is necessary to justify the purchase of the stock by an investor who knows his required rate of return and the anticipated growth rate and dividend yield of the company. If the investor's required rate of return is 11 per cent and the firm is expected to pay $1.00 dividend and grow annually at a rate of 7 per cent, then the price of the common stock will be

$$P_e = \frac{\$1.00}{.11 - .07}$$

$$P_e = \$25$$

If the price of the common stock exceeds $25, then the investor will view the stock as overpriced and not purchase it. If, however, the price is below $25, then the investor will view the stock as being underpriced and thus will purchase it.

Equation (4) suggests several reasons why security prices fluctuate. According to the equation, a stock's price is related to (1) the growth rate of earnings (g); (2) the cash dividend (D); and (3) investor's required rate of return (k_e). If any of these factors were to change, the stock's price would also change. If the company is unable to maintain its growth rate, then the earnings and dividends will increase more slowly, and the price of the stock will fall. If the firm unexpectedly reduces its cash dividend, then the price of the stock will fall (unless the firm is able to reinvest its earnings and increase the growth rate sufficiently to overcome the decrease in dividends). If investors' alternative uses for money increase, then their required rate of return on common stock will rise and cause security prices to fall. Thus, as interest rates rise, the required return on common stocks must increase, for investors can earn higher yields on debt instruments. Stock prices must fall in order to be competitive with these debt instruments. The same may be true if the rate of inflation increases, for investors may put money into physical goods such as real estate, art, and gold, for their prices are inflating. To be competitive (i.e., to offer similar yields), stock prices will have to decline (unless the inflation also produces sufficient increases in the firm's growth rates and dividends).

> Reasons why security prices fluctuate

As the above discussion indicates, the cost of equity may be viewed from the standpoint of either the firm or the investors. In either case the same variables are being considered: the dividend of the firm, the growth rate in earnings, the price of the common stock, and the required rate of return that investors demand. Implicit in this formulation of the cost of equity is the risk class of the firm. If the risk class of the firm is altered by the financing decision, then the investors' required rate of return will be altered. As the firm becomes more risky, the required rate of return will rise as investors require more return to compensate them for the additional risk.

This risk is related to the nature of the business and the financial leverage employed by the firm. As additional debt is used to finance the assets of the firm, the risk to the common stockholder is increased and the required rate of return will rise. The relationship between financial leverage and the required rate of return is illustrated in Figure 22–2, which relates the cost of equity (k_e) and the firm's debt ratio. The relationship between the cost of debt and the firm's debt ratio was illustrated in Figure 22–1. In both cases the cost of equity and the cost of debt may be constant over a range of debt ratios, but ultimately these costs start to rise as the firm becomes more financially leveraged and hence more risky. Thus the additional use of debt financing increases not only the cost of debt but also the cost of equity.

COST OF CAPITAL

The cost of capital to the firm is an average of the costs of debt, preferred stock, and equity. The cost of capital is, however, not just a simple average but a weighted average with the weights dependent upon the proportion of the firm's assets financed by each component. How this average is determined is

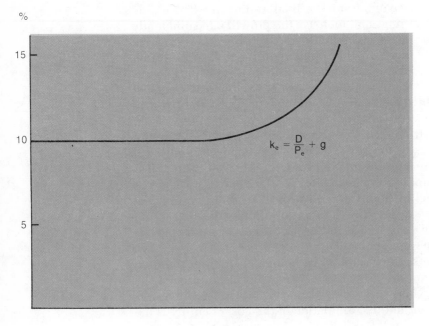

Debt Ratio

Figure 22–2

Cost of Equity

illustrated by the example below. A firm has the following balance sheet:

ASSETS	LIABILITIES AND EQUITY	
Total assets $1000	Total debt	$400
	Preferred stock	100
	Common stock and retained earnings	500

The firm has determined that the current cost of each type of
financing is as follows:

Cost of debt	4.16%
Cost of preferred stock	8.33%
Cost of equity	11.00%

The proportion of the firm's asset financed by each type of
financing is

Debt	40%
Preferred stock	10%
Common stock	50%

These proportions are found by dividing the amount of each type
of financing by the firm's total assets. For debt the proportion is
400/1000 = 40 per cent. For preferred stock, it is 100/1000 = 10
per cent; and for common stock plus the retained earnings the
proportion is 500/1000 = 50 per cent. If this combination of
financing is the firm's optimal capital structure, these proportions are used to determine the firm's minimum cost of capital.
However, if the firm is using too much of one source and too little
of another, the use of book proportions will give an inaccurate
cost of capital. (The determination of this optimal capital structure is developed in the next section.)

To find the cost of capital, multiply the proportion of each
component of the optimal capital structure by their respective
costs and add the results. For this firm that yields:

The cost of capital is a weighted average

	COST	×	WEIGHT	=	WEIGHTED COST
Debt	4.16	×	.40	=	1.664
Preferred stock	8.33	×	.10	=	.833
Common stock	11.00	×	.50	=	5.500
		Cost of capital		=	7.997

For this firm the average weighted cost of capital is 7.997 per
cent. The firm must earn at least 7.997 per cent on its investments
in order to maintain its present value. This 7.997 per cent cost of
capital is the discount factor that will be used in the following
chapter to determine the net present value of an investment.

If a firm does earn 7.997 cents after taxes on the investment
of a dollar, then the firm has 1.664 cents to pay the interest, .833

cent to pay the dividends on the preferred stock, and 5.5 cents to pay dividends to the common stock or reinvest in the company so that it may grow. The 7.997 cents cover the cost of each individual component of the firm's cost of capital.

Firm must cover its cost of capital

If the company earns more than 7.997 per cent, then it is able to pay its debt expense and the preferred stock dividends, and it will have more than is necessary to meet the expected return of the common stockholders. Their return will exceed the required 11 per cent on the equity. For example, if the firm earns 10 per cent (i.e., 10 cents), then 1.664 cents is paid to creditors and .833 cent goes to the preferred stockholders. That leaves 7.503 cents for the common stockholders, and the firm may increase its dividends or increase its growth rate by reinvesting the earnings. Either way, investors will bid up the price of the stock. Since the return on an investment in the stock exceeded investors' required rate of return, the value of this firm is increased.

OPTIMAL CAPITAL STRUCTURE

Use of debt initially reduces cost of capital

The cost of debt is cheaper than the cost of equity. Debt is cheaper because it is less risky than ownership (i.e., the obligations to the creditors must be met before the stockholders are rewarded), and the government permits the deduction of interest expense before determining taxable income. Management may decrease the firms' cost of capital by substituting cheaper debt for equity. However, as the proportion of assets financed by debt rises, the firm becomes riskier, and the cost of both debt and equity rises. What management needs to determine is the optimal combination of debt and equity financing that minimizes the firm's cost of capital. Once that optimal capital structure has been determined, then management must seek to maintain that combination of debt and equity financing, for it is the firm's optimal capital structure.

Determining the optimal combination of debt and equity financing

The process of determining the optimal capital structure is illustrated in Table 22–1. The first column in the table presents the firm's debt ratio. The second and third columns give the cost of debt and the cost of equity, respectively. (To ease the calculation, it is assumed this firm has no preferred stock.) The cost of debt is less than the cost of equity, and both are constant over a considerable range of debt ratios. The cost of both debt and equity starts to rise as the firm becomes more financially leveraged. The fourth column presents the weighted average cost of capital, which incorporates the cost of debt and the cost of equity, each weighted by the proportion of the assets they finance.

If the firm is entirely financed by equity, then the average weighted cost of capital is the cost of equity. As the firm uses debt and substitutes the cheaper debt financing for equity financing, the average weighted cost of capital is reduced. As the debt ratio rises, the average weighted cost of capital still declines. This

TABLE 22-1   Determination of the Optimal Capital Structure

DEBT RATIO (DEBT/TOTAL ASSETS)	COST OF DEBT (k_d)	COST OF EQUITY (k_e)	WEIGHTED COST (k)
0	4	10	.10
10	4	10	.094
20	4	10	.088
30	4	10	.082
40	4	10.5	.079
50	5	11	.080
60	6	12	.084
70	8	13.5	.097
80	10	16	.112
90	15	20	.155

decline in the average weighted cost of capital does not continue indefinitely, as the firm substitutes the cheaper debt. Both the cost of debt and the cost of equity begin to increase, because creditors and investors believe that more financial leverage increases the riskiness of the firm. The initial increases in the cost of debt and the cost of equity may be insufficient to stop the decline in the weighted cost of capital. But as the costs of debt and equity continue to increase, the average weighted cost of capital reaches a minimum and also starts to increase. In the table this minimum occurs at a debt ratio of 40 per cent (i.e., 40 per cent debt financing to 60 per cent equity financing). As additional debt is used, the costs of both debt and equity rise sufficiently to cause the weighted cost of capital to increase. The firm's optimal capital structure then is with a debt ratio of 40 per cent.

This determination of the optimal capital structure is also illustrated by Figure 22-3, which plots the cost of debt, the cost of equity, and the average weighted cost of capital given in Table 22-1. As is readily seen in the graph, when the debt ratio increases, the average weighted cost of capital (k) initially declines, reaches a minimum at a debt ratio of 40 per cent, and then starts to increase. The optimal capital structure is reached at the minimum point on the average weighted cost of capital schedule. The financial manager should acquire this combination of financing because it is the minimum cost of funds.

Optimal capital structure illustrated graphically

This minimum cost of capital should be used to judge potential investments; it will be employed by the capital budgeting techniques discussed in the next chapter. As the firm expands and makes additional investments in plant and equipment, it must also expand its sources of finance. These additional sources should maintain the firm's optimal capital structure. Additional (or marginal) investments are financed by additional (or marginal) funds. As long as the optimal capital structure is maintained, then additional funds should cost the same as the

Cost of capital is used in capital budgeting

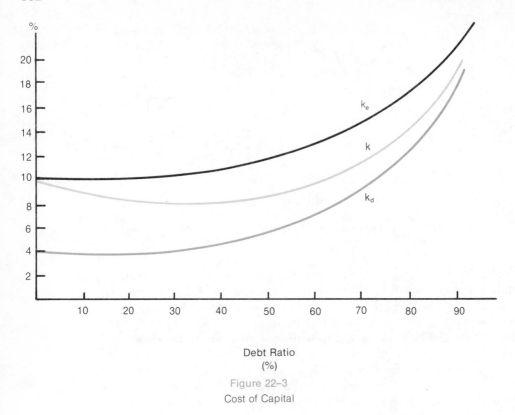

Debt Ratio
(%)
Figure 22–3
Cost of Capital

cost of all of funds (unless the investments increase the element of risk).

For many firms, the optimal capital structure is a range of debt ratios. In the example presented in Table 22–1 and Figure 22–3, the average weighted cost of capital does not vary significantly between a debt ratio of 30 to 50 per cent. This indicates that the effect of substituting cheaper debt financing on the firm's cost of capital is achieved when 30 per cent of the firm's assets are debt financed. Additional use of debt, however, does not start to increase the cost of capital until over 50 per cent of the assets are debt financed. Thus the optimal capital structure is a range of debt to equity financing and not just a specific combination of debt to equity.

That the optimal capital structure is a range and not a specific combination is important from a practical viewpoint. New issues of debt or common stock are made infrequently, and when they are issued, the dollar amount of the issue may be substantial. A firm will not bother to issue new securities for a trivial amount of money because of the cost of issuing the securities. Thus, when new securities are issued, the debt ratio may be significantly altered. Unless the optimal capital structure were a range of debt ratios, every new issue of securities would alter the firm's cost of capital. Since the optimal debt structure is a range,

Optimal capital structure may be a range of debt ratios

A range increases flexibility

then a firm has flexibility in the issuing of new securities and may tailor the security issues for market conditions. For example, if the price of the firm's stock is high, management may issue new stock instead of debt. Or, if management anticipates that interest rates will increase in the future, then it may choose to issue debt now and use equity financing at some future date. This flexibility in the type of securities issued is in part the result of the optimal capital structure being a range of debt to equity financing. But even the existence of a range does not mean (1) that the firm can always use the same type of financing, and (2) that a firm should avoid seeking to find the optimal capital structure. Finding the optimal capital structure, like finding the most profitable level of output, is required if the management of the firm wants to maximize the value of the firm.

AT&T'S OPTIMAL CAPITAL STRUCTURE

AT&T is an excellent example of a firm seeking its optimal capital structure. AT&T is the nation's largest telephone company, and telephone operations require a large investment in plant and equipment. In 1975 alone the company needed $9.4 billion to meet its capital requirements.

An example of optimal capital structure

To meet its capital needs, AT&T has sold to the public many issues of bonds as well as new shares of common stock. The company has a triple A rating for its bonds and has always been able to market issues of new securities. However, AT&T cannot issue bonds and exclude issuing new stock, because this would increase the degree of financial leverage and risk. Issuing only debt would result in a higher cost of capital.

Even though excessive debt financing will increase a firm's cost of capital, AT&T during the last decade has issued a substantial amount of debt to meet its needs for long term capital. During the decade 1965–1975 AT&T's debt rose from $9.1 billion to over $29 billion. The debt ratio was 31 per cent in 1965, 43 per cent in 1970, and reached a high of 50.4 per cent in 1975. Reasons for this increased use of debt include (1) increased cost of plant and equipment as a result of inflation, and (2) a decrease in the price of its stock, which means that fewer dollars are raised by issuing new shares.

AT&T's management has become very concerned by this increased use of debt financing. While the management certainly understands the concept that successful use of financial leverage increases a firm's per share earnings, it also understands that increased use of debt financing increases the element of risk. In particular the management of AT&T does not want to lose the firm's triple A credit rating. If the debt's rating were lowered, future debt issues would require higher interest rates, which could reduce profitability and lead to higher telephone rates.

To reduce the need for debt financing, AT&T now places more emphasis on internally generated funds and new equity financing as a means to raise capital. In its 1975 annual report, the firm stated that, of its $9.4 billion capital requirement, $6.6 billion was met by internally generated funds, and only $2.8 billion was obtained through external financing. Of the $2.8 billion, over $1 billion was raised through issuing new stock. As a result of the retention of earnings and new issues of stock, AT&T was able to reduce its debt ratio for the first time in over a decade. Furthermore, management stated its intention to continue to reduce the debt ratio, and a target debt ratio of 45 per cent has been established. Management thus views the firm's optimal capital structure as consisting of 45 per cent debt and 55 per cent equity. Such a capital structure provides the advantages of financial leverage without unduly increasing the element of risk to creditors and stockholders.

SUMMARY

This chapter has considered the cost of capital of a firm. This cost is an average of the firm's cost of debt, preferred stock, and common stock weighted by the proportion of the firm's assets that each finances. The cost of capital thus is not just the cost of borrowing money, nor is it the rate of return that the firm is earning on its assets or equity. The cost of capital is a weighted average of the cost of the firm's sources of finance.

The cost of capital differs for firms in different industries. Some industries are inherently riskier than others, and thus the cost of capital must be higher. Furthermore, the cost of capital may differ for firms within the same industry if they are employing different combinations of financial leverage. However, all firms should seek to find that combination of debt and equity financing that minimizes the cost of capital. That combination of debt and equity is the firm's optimal capital structure and will maximize the value of the firm. It is this cost of capital that will be used in the next chapter on capital budgeting.

KEY WORDS AND TERMS

cost of debt
cost of preferred stock
cost of equity
opportunity cost
total return
flotation costs
optimal capital structure

1. What is the cost of debt? What is the cost of common stock? Why is the cost of debt less than the cost of common stock? Why should a firm not use all equity financing? Why does the cost of debt start to rise as the debt ratio increases?

2. Given the following information about a firm:

dividend per share	$1.00
price of the stock per share	$20.00
growth rate in earnings and dividends	5%
debt ratio	30%
marginal tax rate	40%
interest rate	8%

What is the firm's cost of debt? What is the firm's cost of capital? If the firm uses more debt and less equity financing, what will happen to the firm's cost of capital? Why?

3. Using the following equation:

$$P_e = \frac{D}{k_e - g}$$

how will each of the following affect a stock's price?
(a) An increase in risk.
(b) A decrease in corporate income taxes.
(c) A reduction in the firm's growth rate.

Chapter 23   CAPITAL BUDGETING

Learning Objectives

* Determine the payback period for an investment.
* Identify the weaknesses in payback method.
* Determine the net present value and the internal rate of return.
* Differentiate between the net present value and the internal rate of return.
* Adjust capital budgeting techniques for risk.
* Apply discounted cash flow techniques to select investments.

"Goodness is the only investment that never fails."

Henry David Thoreau

Capital budgeting is one important application of the interest factor. Capital budgeting is a technique for selecting among alternative investments in assets whose lives exceed one year. It seeks to answer such questions as (1) to buy a new machine and replace an old machine (the replacement decision); (2) to expand the level of operation of the firm by purchasing new plant and equipment; or (3) to purchase one of two competing new machines that perform the same task. These decisions are crucial to the life and profitability of the firm. Failure to make profitable investments will certainly reduce the value of the firm. Since capital budgeting techniques aid in this decision-making process, they are crucial to increasing the wealth of the firm and its stockholders.

This chapter is concerned with these techniques. It is an involved topic, one to which an entire text could be devoted. The treatment in this chapter will only indicate the essence of the subject; at best, it lays the groundwork for you to pursue the subject in more advanced courses. Even if you do not intend to pursue the study of finance, the chapter will give you a basis for understanding the concept. Since many firms use capital budgeting, all students of business need an understanding of its purposes and techniques.

Three methods for selecting among competing uses of long-term capital are covered in this chapter: (1) payback period, (2) internal rate of return, and (3) net present value. All three methods aid in the decision to purchase a fixed asset *now*, but the benefits from the investments occur to the firm *in the future*. Understanding this time element is very important, for an investment is made in the present, but the cash flow generated by the investment occurs in the future. Thus all capital budgeting techniques require a forecast of the anticipated cash flow (i.e., profits plus depreciation). The need for good forecasts and reliable data is as crucial for capital budgeting as the correct application of the techniques. This chapter, however, is concerned with capital budgeting techniques.

Investments are made in the present. The returns occur in the future

All three techniques rank different investment proposals and thereby facilitate the selection process. The payback period is by far the easiest of the three and by far the poorest, for it ignores several important considerations, especially the cost of capital and time value of money. The other two techniques do not have these weaknesses. They do require more mathematical calculations, but the use of computers has significantly reduced the tediousness of these calculations. Management may now devote its energies to the collection of the relevant data and the applications of the data under differing sets of assumptions. With continued use of computers and more knowledge by management of capital budgeting techniques, it is safe to assume that the use of capital budgeting techniques will continue to increase.

THE PAYBACK PERIOD

The payback method ranks alternative investment opportunities by how rapidly the initial amount invested is recouped. The more rapidly the money is returned, the more desirable the investment. If a firm has the following three alternative investments (each of which cost $1000) to select among, B is preferred because it recoups the cost of the investment in three years, while A and C take four years.

Payback stresses the return of the cost of the investment

	A	B	C
Year 1	$250	$333	$400
2	250	333	100
3	250	333	400
4	250	333	100
5	250	333	400

The cash flow (profits plus depreciation) from B is the fastest and therefore it is to be preferred.

The method is
simple but has
serious weaknesses

Obviously the payback method is a very simple means to rank alternative investment projects. If a firm has $1,000,000 to. allocate among alternative investments and the following schedule of projects with their respective payback periods, then the firm will select projects E, B, and D and reject projects A, C, F, and G because E, B, and D return their initial investments quicker and use the firm's available resources (i.e., the $1,000,000).

PROJECT	COST	PAYBACK PERIOD (IN YEARS)
A	$500,000	4.3
B	300,000	3.2
C	600,000	5.1
D	200,000	4.1
E	500,000	2.0
F	400,000	6.0
G	100,000	7.0

The payback method is obviously a very simple way of making capital budgeting decisions. There are many flaws in the technique, but it is better to use the payback method than to use nothing. It does put the emphasis on rapid return of the intitial cost. The inability to predict the future accurately implies that placing emphasis on the near future may be a desirable means to select among alternative investments. Thus, while the payback method is criticized on theoretical grounds, its potential use on pragmatic grounds cannot be discarded.

The criticisms of the payback method do illustrate why the other capital budgeting techniques are superior. Users of the payback method should at least be aware of its weaknesses even if they choose not to adopt the superior methods of capital budgeting.

The weaknesses of the payback method are as follows: (1) the interest factor is omitted; (2) cash flows after the payback period are ignored; (3) the timing of the cash flows is ignored; and (4) no attempt is made to adjust for the degree of risk. Each of these weaknesses will be briefly discussed. How these weaknesses may be overcome will be examined in the section on the internal rate of return and the net present value methods of capital budgeting.

Payback (1) omits
the interest
factor

The omission of the interest factor means that the payback method does not differentiate between a dollar earned today and a dollar earned tomorrow. This raises two problems. First, if the payback period is four years, the payback method has nothing to say about what may be earned on the money earned in the first year during the remaining three years. Second, the omission of the interest factor ignores alternative uses of the money, for nothing is said about what the money invested in the asset could earn if it were invested elsewhere. Basically the payback method analyzes the following schedule of anticipated cash flows for an investment that costs $1000:

TIME PERIOD	CASH FLOW
Year 1	$300
2	400
3	100
4	200
5	200

and says that the payback period is four years. It says nothing about any alternative uses (such as Federal Government securities) or what may be earned on the $300 cash flow received during the first year. Certainly this money may be put to work in subsequent years.

This problem is compounded when the second weakness, the timing of the cash flow, is also considered. If the payback method is strictly applied, it cannot differentiate between the following two investments that cost $1000 each:

(2) Ignores the timing of the cash flows

TIME PERIOD	CASH FLOW A	CASH FLOW B
Year 1	$400	$100
2	300	200
3	200	300
4	100	400

Both investments take four years to return the initial investment and therefore are equal according to the payback method. Of course, A is superior to B (by common sense), since the cash flow is greater in the early years and hence that money may be reinvested profitably elsewhere. But the payback method does not explicitly consider the timing of the cash flows. The failure of the payback method to take into consideration (1) the timing of the cash flows and (2) the time value of money are two very serious defects in this technique.

The payback method does not consider cash flows received after the payback period. The failure to consider subsequent cash flow after the payback period means that this technique will select investment A over B (if both investments cost $1000), even though B will yield cash flow significantly longer than A.

(3) Ignores cash flow after the payback period

TIME PERIOD	CASH FLOW A	CASH FLOW B
Year 1	$250	$200
2	250	200
3	250	200
4	250	200
5	0	200
6	0	200

Common sense indicates that B is better than A because A recoups only the cost of the investment. It offers no profit at all, because the sum of the yearly cash flows just covers the cost of the investment. Thus an investment must yield cash flow after the payback period in order to be profitable, and even then the investment may not be profitable when the interest earned by an alternative investment is considered. The payback method, however, is only concerned with recouping the dollar cost of the investment and ignores any other costs and cash flow generated after the payback period.

(4) Fails to
consider risk

The payback method also fails to consider risk. This question of risk may be illustrated by the following example of an investment that a person may consider. In 1974 an investor could have purchased the following $1000 bond: Pan Am 4.5 per cent for a price of $140. The payback period is 3.1 years ($140/$45). Why is the payback so rapid? Stated another way, why is the price so low? The answer is that the bond is very risky; the interest may not be paid or the principal is not safe. The quick payback is the result of the bond market's discounting the bond because of the high degree of risk. Certainly one should not invest in securities solely on the basis of quick payback, because the element of risk is being ignored. And the same generalization applies to investing in fixed assets by the firm.

In summary, the payback method places the emphasis on the quick return of the cost of an investment. It is not concerned with the profitability of the investment or the time value of the money. Many investments, however, have very long payback periods. For example, pharmaceuticals may require years of research and testing. While this payback period is long, the product may be very profitable once marketed. Power plants operate for years, and the payback on a college education is also very long. Investments in research, plants, or education are discouraged by the payback method of capital budgeting. It biases the investment decision in favor of short-term investments.

Payback is
frequently used

While the payback method is consistently criticized, it is frequently used. The reasons for this use are (1) it is readily understood, (2) it is extremely easy to apply, and (3) it avoids making projections into the more distant future. The more uncertain the future, then the stronger may be the case for use of the payback. In the minds of many businessmen, dollars received in the distant future are worth very little today, for the future is very uncertain. Thus, while the payback method has little support on theoretical grounds, it has support on pragmatic grounds. It is easy to perform and places the emphasis on the immediate return of the cost of the investment. The small businessman may simply lack the time, knowledge, or equipment to do more sophisticated types of capital budgeting. The payback method provides a means to rank investment alternatives and make selections among alternatives.

NET PRESENT VALUE AND INTERNAL RATE OF RETURN INTRODUCED

The net present value and internal rate of return methods of capital budgeting are very similar. They both overcome the disadvantages of the payback method, for both techniques explicitly use the time value of money and all the cash flow generated by an investment. Both recognize that an investment is made and then the cash flow generated by the investment occurs over a period of time. This flow over time must be compared with the present cost of the investment and the cost of the funds necessary to finance the investment in order to determine if the investment should be made.

The comparison of an investment with alternative uses of the funds is necessary to determine if the investment will increase the value of the firm. If the return on an investment is less than the firm's cost of capital, then that investment should not be made. Such an investment will reduce the value of the firm because there are better, alternative uses of the funds. Discounted cash flow methods of capital budgeting use the cost of capital to judge an investment against alternative uses of the funds necessary to finance the investment. Hence they indicate the investment's true profitability. Selecting among alternative investments by using discounted cash flow techniques (i.e., the net present value and the internal rate of return) will increase the value of the firm, for these techniques exclude investments that do not cover the firm's cost of capital.

Net present value and internal rate of return use the same variables

The difference between the net present value and the internal rate of return methods of capital budgeting lies in the interest factor that each employs. While this difference is important and is the subject of advanced work in capital budgeting, the treatment here will stress how the two techniques work and how they overcome the disadvantages of the payback method of capital budgeting.

In the following discussion of the two techniques, the following terms and symbols will be used:

C: the cost of making an investment.

$R_1, R_2, \ldots R_n$: the cash flow generated by the investment in years one, two, and on through the last year (n) that the investment generates cash flow.

S_n: the salvage value (if any) of the investment at the end of its useful life.

PV: the present value of the investment.

k: the cost of capital to the firm.

r: the internal rate of return on an investment.

n: the number of years that it is anticipated that the investment will generate a cash flow.

THE NET PRESENT VALUE

Net present value
discounts future
cash flows

The net present value technique of capital budgeting determines the present value of the cash flows from an investment and subtracts them from the cost of the investment. This technique is illustrated by the following example. A firm may make an investment that costs $1000 and has the following estimated cash flows:

YEAR	CASH FLOW
1	$300
2	400
3	500
4	300

At the firm's
cost of capital

It is estimated that after the four years have elapsed the equipment may be sold for $100 (i.e., that the equipment has a salvage value of $100). The firm is now faced with the question of whether it should make this investment. In order to answer this question the firm needs to know the present value of the cash flow and the salvage value. In order to determine the present the firm must have (1) the interest factor (i.e., the cost of capital) and (2) a present value table. If the cost of capital is 8 per cent then the present value of the investment is the sum of the present value of each of the cash flows and the salvage value. The following is illustrative of the process of determining the present value of this investment:

YEAR	CASH FLOW	×	INTEREST FACTOR	=	PRESENT VALUE
1	$300		.926		$ 277.80
2	400		.857		342.80
3	500		.794		397.00
4	300		.735		220.50
Salvage value	100		.735		73.50
					$1311.60

The individual present values are summed to obtain the present value of the investment. In this case the present value is $1311.60. The present cost of making this investment is $1000. The net present value of this investment then is $311.60 ($1311.60 − $1000). Therefore the investment should be made, for the net present value is positive which indicates that the investment is profitable.

And determines the
net present value

The net present value method may be stated in more formal terms. First, determine the present value of an investment (PV) by discounting the cash flow (R) generated each year (R_1, R_2 ... R_n) and the salvage value (S_n) by the firm's cost of capital (k). Thus the present value of the investment is as follows:

Stated algebraically

$$(1) \quad PV = \frac{R_1}{(1 + k)^1} + \frac{R_2}{(1 + k)^2} + \cdots + \frac{R_n}{(1 + k)^n} + \frac{S_n}{(1 + k^n)}$$

Second, determine the net present value (NPV) of the investment by subtracting the cost (C) of the investment from the present value of the investment. That is:

(2) $$NPV = PV - C$$

If the net present value is positive, the investment is profitable and should be undertaken by the firm. If the net present value is negative, then the investment is unprofitable, and the firm should not make the investment. The acceptance and rejection criteria for the net present value method of capital budgeting are summarized as follows:

The acceptance criterion

Accept the investment if
$$PV - C = NPV \geqslant 0$$
Reject the investment if
$$PV - C = NPV < 0$$

This approach to capital budgeting requires that a firm determine the net present value of all possible investments and undertake those investments that have a positive net present value. Accepting all investments with a positive net present value requires a crucial assumption that the firm has or can obtain sufficient financing for all the investments. If the additional investments make the firm riskier, the firm may be able to raise sufficient capital only if it agrees to pay higher returns. This higher return will increase the cost of capital and make some of the investment projects unacceptable.

INTERNAL RATE OF RETURN

The internal rate of return method of capital budgeting finds that rate of return which equates the present value of the cash flows and the present cost of the investment. This particular rate of return is called the "internal rate of return." In effect the internal rate of return method sets up the following equation:

Internal rate of return equates the present value and cost

(3) $$\text{Present cost} = \frac{\text{Present value of the cash flow + the}}{\text{present value of the salvage}}$$

The method may be illustrated by the same example used to illustrate the net present value approach. The information is substituted into the equation as follows:

$$\$1000 = \frac{300}{(1+r)^1} + \frac{400}{(1+r)^2} + \frac{500}{(1+r)^3} + \frac{300}{(1+r)^4} + \frac{100}{(1+r)^4}$$

Then the equation is solved for the unknown r, the internal rate of return. While the equation may appear to be formidable, it may be solved with ease by computers.

The equation may also be solved by trial and error. This is done by selecting a rate of return and solving for r. If the r does not equate the two sides of the equation, another r is selected until one is found that equates both sides of the equation. Obviously such a procedure is tedious to perform manually.

How the trial and error method works may be illustrated by using the above example. If a rate of return of 10 per cent is selected and used in the equation to determine the present value of the cash flow, the present value of the investment is found to be:

$$\$1251.80 = (300)(.909) + (400)(.826) + (500)(.751) \\ + (300)(.683) + (100)(.683)$$

This present value is larger than the cost of the investment; thus the internal rate of return must be greater. The cash flow must be discounted at a higher rate to equate the present value and the present cost of the investment. If a rate of return of 24 per cent is selected, then the present value becomes:

$$\$962.50 = (300)(.806) + (400)(.650) + (500)(.524) + (300)(.423) \\ + (100)(.423)$$

This present value is less than the cost of the investment; thus the internal rate of return must be lower. By continuing this process, the internal rate of return (which equates the present value of the cash flows and the cost of the investment) may be found. In this case that internal rate of return is approximately 20 per cent, since at that rate of return the present value of this investment is $1009.80, which is approximately equal to the cost of the investment ($1000).

Internal rate of return ranks investment proposals

The internal rate of return method is used to select investments in the following manner. This rate of return is computed for each investment opportunity. Then the internal rates of return are ranked from the highest to the lowest; the investment with the highest rate of return is made first. All investments with an internal rate of return greater than the firm's cost of capital are profitable and should be undertaken. For example, a firm has the following investment opportunities and has computed the internal rate of return on each investment:

INVESTMENT	COST OF INVESTMENT	INTERNAL RATE OF RETURN
A	$1000	11%
B	500	8
C	1500	9
D	300	12
E	800	7

If the firm's cost of capital is 10 per cent, then only investments A and D should be made for a total outlay of $1300. If the cost of capital were to decline to 6 per cent, the firm should make all the investments for a total expenditure of $4100.

This approach to capital budgeting is summarized by Figure 23–1, which plots the cost of capital and internal rate of return on the vertical axis and the total investment (I) on the horizontal axis. The graph is downward sloping, indicating that as the internal rate of return declines, there are more investments available. This is exactly what one would anticipate; a larger number of investments offers smaller returns. The firm then accepts all investment whose internal rate of return is equal to or greater than the firm's cost of capital. In the graph the cost of capital is k_1. Therefore the firm makes all investments to I_1 for at that level of investment the internal rate of return is equal to the firm's cost of capital.

The internal rate of return method of capital budgeting may be summarized in symbolic terms. The internal rate of return is that r, which equates:

Internal rate of return stated algebraically

(3) $$C = \frac{R_1}{(1 + r)^1} + \cdots + \frac{R_n}{(1 + r)^n} + \frac{S_n}{(1 + r)^n}$$

and the criteria for accepting an investment is if

$r \geqslant k$, accept the investment
$r < k$, reject the investment

While the above are the acceptance criteria, many firms that use the internal rate of return approach do not take all investments with an internal rate of return greater than the cost of capital. Instead they establish a higher rate of return (or "hurdle rate") that is used as the acceptance criterion for selecting in-

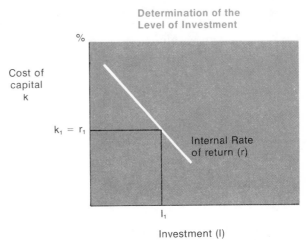

Determination of the Level of Investment

Figure 23–1

vestments. For example, if the cost of capital is 10 per cent, the firm may make all investments with an internal rate of return in excess of 15 per cent. Such a hurdle rate helps the firm provide for risk because it excludes the investments with the lowest anticipated internal rates of return.

INTERNAL RATE OF RETURN AND NET PRESENT VALUE COMPARED

The internal rate of return and net present value methods of capital budgeting are very similar. Both methods use all the cash flows generated by an investment, and both consider the timing of those cash flows. Both methods also explicitly incorporate the time value of money into the analysis. If the two methods are placed next to each other,

Net present value

$$(2) \qquad NPV = \frac{R_1}{(1 + k)^1} + \ldots + \frac{R_n}{(1 + k)^n} + \frac{S_n}{(1 + k)^n} - C$$

Internal rate of return

$$(3) \qquad 0 = \frac{R_1}{(1 + r)^1} + \ldots + \frac{R_n}{(1 + r)^n} + \frac{S_n}{(1 + r)^n} - C$$

Difference revolves around the discount factor

The only difference is the discount factor. The net present value approach uses the firm's cost of capital to discount the cash flow. The internal rate of return method determines that rate of return which equates the present value of the cash flows and the present cost of the investment (i.e., makes the net present value zero). The use of different discount factors does result in different statements of the acceptance criterion. For the net present value approach, an investment must yield a positive net present value to be accepted. For the internal rate of return method, the investment's internal rate of return must exceed the firms' cost of capital to be accepted. Under some circumstances the methods yield conflicting results (which is one reason why advanced study of capital budgeting is an involved area of study). However, for the purposes of this text, the two methods are complimentary means to select among alternative investments.

RISK

Investment decisions involve uncertainty. Costs of operations may prove to be higher than expected or sales may be lower. Changes in laws and regulations may occur or more competitors may enter the field. All these future events are uncertain, and some may reduce the future cash flows generated by the investment. If management had perceived these uncertainties, then they may not have made the investment.

Either technique may incorporate risk by (1) adjusting for probability of occurrence or

Capital budgeting techniques need to consider these uncertainties. The element of risk may be incorporated into discounted cash flow analysis by either of two methods. First, all the cash flows may be adjusted for their probability of occurrence. How this is applied is illustrated by the following example. The estimated cash flow from an investment is $100, $300, and $400. The probability of each cash flow occurring is 90 per cent, 70 per cent, and 50 per cent, respectively. These cash flows are next multiplied by the probability of occurrence to obtain the adjusted cash flows: $90, $210, and $200. It is these adjusted cash flows that are discounted by the firm's cost of capital in order to determine the present value of the investment. If the firm's cost of capital is 10 per cent, then the present value of this investment is:

$$\$405.47 = \frac{90}{(1 + .10)^1} + \frac{210}{(1 + .10)^2} + \frac{200}{(1 + .10)^3}$$

This present value is considerably lower than the present value of $639.10 which is obtained if the adjustment for probability of occurrence is not made.

(2) Adding a risk premium

The second method adjusts the discount factor by adding a risk premium. Some investments are known by management to be riskier than others. To adjust for these differences in risk, an adjustment factor is added to the firm's cost of capital. The greater the risk, the greater the adjustment factor that is added. This technique may also be illustrated by the above example. Instead of adjusting the cash flows by the probability of occurrence, a risk premium is added to the firm's cost of capital. If this risk premium is 4 per cent, then the present value of the investment is:

$$\$588.40 = \frac{100}{1 + .10 + .04} + \frac{300}{(1 + .10 + .04)^2} + \frac{400}{(1 + .10 + .04)^3}$$

This is lower than the present value of $639.10, which is determined when the risk premium is omitted. Thus the present value of the cash flow is reduced by the addition of the risk factor, and the investment is less attractive.

Measurement of risk is difficult

Discounted cash flow methods of capital budgeting may be altered to incorporate risk. The actual measurement of this risk, however, may be very difficult. For example, how can a drug firm estimate the probability that a particular research project will lead to a marketable product? While the inclusion of adjustments for risk may increase the accuracy of capital budgeting, it can do so only if the estimates of risk are accurate. The problem area then is not the inclusion of risk into the analysis but accurately measuring it. In many cases this measurement may prove to be highly subjective or inaccurate. In these cases capital budgeting will also be inaccurate, for it can select investments only on the basis of the data being used. Accurate data then is crucial to accurate capital budgeting decisions.

CAPITAL BUDGETING AND UTILITIES

The previous discussion has been very theoretical, and you may have wondered if this theory is applied by firms. Surveys of larger firms indicate that the answer is yes, and the trend in use is increasing as more firms analyze investment alternatives and make investment decisions through the use of discounted cash flow techniques. These managers realize that theoretical models permit simplification and generality. Discounted cash flow techniques emphasize the important considerations: (1) the revenues generated by the investments, (2) the cost of the investment, and (3) alternative uses of the funds.

The willingness on the part of management to use capital budgeting techniques is influenced in part by the nature of the business. The reliability of the analysis is related to the quality of the data and estimates used. Accumulating accurate data can be expensive. In industries where estimates may be relatively inexpensive to obtain, firms tend to use discounted cash flow techniques. For example, a survey of electric utilities indicated that over 90 per cent of them use discounted cash flow methods for choosing among competing alternative investments.

Utilities (1) have large investment in plant and equipment

There are several reasons why electric utilities are willing to use these techniques. First, most of their investments are long term (plant and equipment). Electric utilities do not have large investments in inventory. Their accounts receivable are of high quality; few resources are diverted to the collecting of these accounts. Instead, the emphasis is on having sufficient capacity (i.e., plant and equipment) to meet the public's demand for electricity. Hence utilities are always planning for the future and estimating the demand for electricity.

(2) Can make accurate estimates

Second, electric utilities are able to make reasonably accurate estimates of costs, including labor, fuel, depreciation, and taxes. However, even if their estimates are not accurate, they are able to recoup losses. Utilities are regulated and are permitted to earn only a fair return. Hence if revenue estimates are incorrect and the firm does not earn its allowable profit, the regulatory commissions permit it to increase rates until the firm does earn the allowed rate of return. If an industrial firm underestimated costs and experienced losses, it might be unable to raise its prices to restore profitability.

(3) Know their cost of capital

Third, since utilities are regulated and permitted a fair return on their capital, these firms know their cost of capital. While estimating the cost of capital may be difficult for other firms and can be a stumbling block in the application of sophisticated capital budgeting techniques, utilities are virtually given a cost of capital. They are not permitted to earn more than the allowed rates of return. This target rate of return may be employed as the firm's cost of capital to evaluate investment alternatives.

How a utility may use the net present value method of capital budgeting can be illustrated by the following example. The company has two alternative methods for generating electricity. Plant A uses oil for the production of electricity; Plant B uses nuclear fuel. The nuclear plant is more expensive to build but cheaper to operate. To choose between the two, the utility first estimates the cash flows. Then it discounts the cash flows by the cost of capital to determine the present value of the cash flows. Lastly, it determines the net present value by subtracting this present value from the present cost.

For Plant A the annual cash flows are $100; for Plant B they are $175. Plant A costs $1000, but Plant B costs $1700. Both plants will last 20 years and the firm's cost of capital is 7 per cent. The net present value of each investment is as follows:

Plant A:

$$NPV = \frac{\$100}{(1 + .07)^1} + \cdots + \frac{\$100}{(1 + .07)^{20}} - \$1000 = \$114.70$$

Plant B:

$$NPV = \frac{\$175}{(1 + .07)^1} + \cdots + \frac{\$175}{(1 + .07)^{20}} - \$1700 = \$307.25$$

(Since the cash flow is $100 in each year for A and $175 each year for B, annuity tables may be used. These cash flows are obviously simplifying assumptions.) In this example Plant B, the nuclear plant, is the more profitable alternative because it has the higher net present value. If the regulatory authority permits the utility to install Plant B, the utility will earn more than the 7 per cent it is permitted. To earn only 7 per cent, the net present value would have to be zero. This excess profit may result in the utility being required to lower its rates in the future to bring down its profits to the allowed rate of return.

Political and social issues also affect investment decisions

This example is typical of the problem currently facing many electric utility companies. Nuclear plants are more expensive to build than alternative means to generate electricity, but nuclear plants may produce cheaper electricity in the future. Capital budgeting techniques then favor the selection of nuclear power plants over plants employing other fuels. The problem for utility companies, however, is not estimating revenues and expenses, nor is it the application of discounted cash flow methods of capital budgeting. The problems lie in getting permission to build nuclear plants from regulatory agencies and the Atomic Energy Commission. Hence investment decisions are not just the result of financial analysis. Political and social issues may also affect investment decisions. Thus, while discounted cash flow analysis may indicate that an investment is profitable, such an investment may not be possible when political or social factors are considered.

THE REPLACEMENT DECISION

Equipment has a finite life and must be replaced. This need for replacement is obvious once the equipment is worn out. New equipment, however, may be developed that offers the firm savings before the old equipment needs to be replaced. This raises the question of whether the firm should retain the old, less productive equipment or replace it with the new, cost-saving equipment. This replacement decision, like the decision to invest in new plant and equipment, should be approached by capital budgeting techniques. The new equipment must have a positive net present value to justify replacing the old equipment.

Many factors influence the decision to replace

The following factors influence this net present value: (1) the potential savings from the new equipment; (2) the cost of the new equipment; (3) the firm's income tax rate; (4) the salvage value or price for which the old equipment may be sold; (5) the depreciation on the new and old equipment; and (6) the firm's cost of capital. To make the replacement decision, the firm must determine the net present value of the new equipment in light of these factors. Some of the factors produce cash inflows for the firm, while others result in cash expenditures. For example, purchasing the new equipment will result in a cash outflow, but the savings from the new equipment will increase the firm's cash flow. The question basically reduces to: "Does the present value of these cash inflows exceed the present value of the cash outflows?" If the present value of the cash inflows exceeds the present value of the cash outflows, then the replacement should be made. If the present value of the cash inflows is less than the present value of the cash outflows, the replacement should not be made.

Isolate cash inflows and outflows

First, the firm must determine all the cash inflows. The potential savings from the new equipment is a cash inflow, for the new equipment will increase the profits for the firm. The depreciation on the new equipment is treated as if it were a cash inflow because this non-cash expense will produce cash flow in the future. The salvage value, or price at which the old equipment may be sold, is a cash inflow, for when the old equipment is sold, the firm will receive payment. Thus the primary cash inflows are (1) the potential savings, (2) depreciation charges on

the new equipment, and (3) any salvage value on the old equipment. Next the firm must determine the cash outflows, such as
the purchase price of the new equipment, for purchasing the
new equipment will require payment. The depreciation on the
old equipment which will be lost when the old equipment is
replaced is also a cash outflow. Finally, the firm must consider its
corporate income tax rate, which will affect the cash flows by
reducing the firm's profits.

How the replacement decision should be made may be
illustrated by a simple example. A firm has an opportunity to
replace an old machine with a new machine that costs $1000 and
will save the firm $100 a year. The old machine still operates and
may be sold for its book value of $500. Both the old and new
machines have anticipated lives of five years and are depreciated
on a straight line basis with no salvage value. Thus the depreciation on the new equipment will be $200 a year ($1000/5), while
the depreciation on the old equipment is $100 a year ($500/5).
The firm's income tax rate is 40 per cent, and its cost of capital is 9
per cent.

The information may be arranged as in Table 23–1 to isolate
the cash inflows from the cash outflows. The top half of the table
gives the cash inflows, while the bottom half gives the cash
outflows. The entries in the table may be explained as follows.
The cost savings from the new equipment is $100 and increases
the profits by $100. Taxes, however, reduce the profits to $60.
This $60 is anticipated for five years. The present value of this

TABLE 23–1

	GROSS	TAXES (40% TAX RATE)	NET (AFTER TAX)	TIME PERIOD	INTEREST FACTOR	PRESENT VALUE
Cash Inflows:						
Cost savings from the new equip- ment	$ 100	$40	$ 60	5 years	3.890*	$ 233.40
Depreciation on the new equip- ment	200	80	120	5 years	3.890*	466.80
Proceeds from the sale of old equipment	500	—	500	the present	1	500.00
						$1199.20
Cash Outflows:						
Cost of the new equipment	1000	—	—	the present	1	1000.00
Depreciation on the old equip- ment that is lost	100	40	60	5 years	3.890*	233.40
						$1233.40

Net present value: $1199.20 − $1233.40 = $−34.20

*The interest factor is the present value of an annuity for five years at 9%.

$60 discounted at the firm's cost of capital (9 per cent) for five years is $233.40 ($60 × 3.890). The depreciation on the new equipment is $200 a year, which reduces the firm's profits but increases its cash flow. The net effect after tax of this cash flow (depreciation expense) is $120, which will occur for five years. The present value of this $120 cash flow for five years is $466.80. The sale of the old equipment raises $500 now and thus has a present value of $500. The sum of the individual present values are $1199.20.

The bottom half of the table gives the cash outflows that result from making the replacement. The new equipment costs $1000, and that must be paid now. The old equipment, which will be sold, is not fully depreciated. The firm will lose this cash flow that would have been generated if the replacement had not occurred. Thus replacing this equipment produces a loss in depreciation which is treated as a cash outflow. In this example, $100 depreciation expense is lost each year, and the present value of this lost cash flow is $233.40. The sum of the present value of the cash outflows is $1233.40. The present values of these cash outflows are then subtracted from the present value of the cash inflows in order to determine the net present value of replacement.

Determine the net present value

In this example the net present value is $−34.20, which indicates that the replacement of the old equipment by the new equipment should not occur. The cash inflows from the new equipment are insufficient to justify the replacement. While this example is very simple, it does give the basic mechanics of the replacement decision. The mechanics become more complex as other factors are considered, such as a tax loss or gain on the old equipment or differences in the expected lives of the new and old equipment. However, the basic concept and approach are not altered by adding additional factors. The basic approach still remains to determine the net present value of the cash inflows and cash outflows. As long as the present value of the cash inflows exceeds the present value of the cash outflows, then the firm should replace the old equipment with the new equipment, for this replacement is profitable and will increase the value of the firm.

SUMMARY

This chapter has considered alternative means to choose among investment opportunities. Firms are faced with many investment decisions, such as whether to expand the size of the plant, to replace old equipment, or to refund a debt issue with new debt. Management thus needs methods to aid in this decision making.

Three methods were considered in this chapter. The

payback period is the easiest technique but suffers from several weaknesses. The other two methods, net present value and the internal rate of return, involve discounting cash flows and are superior and more accurate than the payback method. Firms with the resources to perform this type of analysis should use discounted cash flow techniques to facilitate choosing among alternative investment opportunities. These methods will identify investments whose return will exceed the firm's cost of capital. By selecting those investments management will increase the value of the firm, since they are superior to the alternative uses of the funds.

_____ KEY WORDS AND TERMS

payback period
present cost
discounted cash flow
net present value
internal rate of return
cash flow
salvage value
acceptance criterion
hurdle rate
probability of occurrence
replacement

QUESTIONS AND PROBLEMS FOR THOUGHT
_____ AND DISCUSSION

1. What is the difference between investment in plant and equipment and investment in securities? Why does investment value rise when interest rates fall? Does this decline apply to securities as well as to plant and equipment?

2. Explain the effect that each of the following has on the present value of an investment:
   (a) An increase in interest rates.
   (b) An increase in investors' required rate of return on equity.
   (c) An increase in the estimated cash flow from the investment.
   (d) An increase in the element of risk.

3. If you were the financial manager of a city and the legislative body asked you for an opinion on whether to build a school or a freeway, how would you respond? Would your method of analysis be different if you were the financial manager of a college and the trustees asked for an opinion on whether to build a gymnasium or a library?

4. Why may it be advantageous for a firm to replace equipment before it wears out? What factors will influence that decision, and what techniques should the firm use?

5. The cost of capital for a firm is 10 per cent. The firm has two possible investments with the following cash flows:

	YEAR 1	YEAR 2	YEAR 3
Investment A	$300	200	100
Investment B	$200	200	200

(a) Each investment costs $400. Which investment should the firm make?

(b) What is the internal rate of return for the two investments? Which investment should the firm make? Is this the same answer you obtained in (a)?

(c) If the cost of capital rises to 12 per cent, which investment should the firm make?

(d) If the cost of capital declines to 8 per cent, which investment should the firm make?

6. A $1000 asset has an expected life of five years. It generates $400 in earnings before depreciation and taxes. If the firm's cost of capital is 6 per cent and the tax rate is 50 per cent, what is the net present value if the firm uses straight line depreciation? If the firm uses the double declining balance method of depreciation what is the net present value? What is the source of the difference in the net present values? (Use a 40 per cent rate of depreciation in the double declining balance method.)

Chapter 24

SOURCES OF FUNDS: ISSUING SECURITIES

Learning Objectives

- State the role of the investment banker.
- Illustrate the mechanics of marketing a new security issue to the general public.
- Isolate the effect that risk has on the offer price of new securities.
- Define preemptive rights, dilution, and rights offering.
- List the determinants of the value of a right.
- Describe the costs and advantages of private placements.

"If you need a tax loss, buy new issues."

George Stigler

Most of the financing of growth by a firm is through internally generated funds: retained earnings. But firms may not generate sufficient earnings to finance all the desired levels of growth, and so the firm is forced to seek outside financing. Sources of outside financing, besides commercial banks, include private placements with financial institutions such as insurance companies or pension funds and the sale of securities to the general public. This chapter is devoted primarily to issuing securities to the general public through investment bankers and rights offerings. The private placement is discussed briefly at the end of the chapter.

INVESTMENT BANKING

The Role of the Middleman

A firm could sell securities directly to the public, but that would be an expensive and time-consuming process. The firm may contact its current stockholders and creditors and ask them

Direct sale to the general public is inefficient

to purchase the new securities. Then it may have to advertise the securities or even peddle them from door to door. While this scenario is in part hyperbole, it points out that there is a cost to selling new securities, and this cost may be very high if the firm seeks to sell the securities itself. Thus the firm employs help in marketing the securities; it uses the services of an investment banker, who sells new securities to the general public. In effect the investment banker is a middleman who channels money from investors to the firm that needs the capital.

Term "investment banker" is misleading

Investment banking is an important financial institution, but confusion exists concerning it. Part of the confusion may be the result of the misnomer: investment banker. An investment banker is often not a banker, and an investment banker does not invest. Instead the investment banker is frequently a brokerage firm such as Merrill Lynch, Pierce, Fenner and Smith, or First Boston Corporation. While these brokerage firms may own securities, they do not buy and hold the newly issued securities for investment purposes.

Investment bankers are middlemen

What they do perform is a middleman function that brings together individuals with money to invest and firms that need financing. Since brokerage firms have many customers, they are able to sell new securities without the costly search that the individual firm may have to make in order to sell its securities. Thus, while the firm must pay for the services of the investment banker, it is able to raise external finance cheaper through the investment banker than by selling the securities itself.

The Mechanics of Underwriting

If a firm needs external funds, then it will approach a brokerage firm to discuss an underwriting. The term "underwriting" refers to the process of selling new securities. It also implies that the firm selling the securities and not the firm issuing the shares bears the risk associated with a decline in security prices. This is developed subsequently in the section on types of agreements.

Each underwriting is individually negotiated

The firm needing finance and the brokerage house discuss the amount of funds needed, the type of security to be issued, the price and any special features of the security, and the cost to the firm of issuing the securities. All these factors are negotiated between the firm seeking capital and the investment banker. If mutually acceptable terms are agreed upon, then the investment banker will be the underwriter of the securities, for the investment banker will be responsible for selling the securities and raising the capital. Since the underwriting started with a particular brokerage firm, that firm is called the originating house, and it manages the underwriting. The originating house need not be just a single firm if the negotiation involved several firms. In this case several firms join together to manage the underwriting of the securities and sell them to the general public.

Frequently the originating house does not seek to sell all the securities by itself but forms a syndicate to market the securities. The syndicate is a group of brokerage houses that have joined together to underwrite the securities. Each member of the syndicate is responsible for his portion of the securities. After the underwriting has been completed, the syndicate is dissolved.

Underwriter forms a selling group

The use of a syndicate has several advantages. The syndicate has access to more potential buyers for the securities, and by using a syndicate the number of securities that each brokerage firm must sell is reduced. This increase in potential customers and decreased amount that each broker has to sell should increase the probability that the issue of securities will be sold. As is explained below, the underwriters want to be successful; they want to sell the securities. Since members of the syndicate are likely to be geographically dispersed, the new securities will be sold to a geographically dispersed public. This is an additional advantage of using a syndicate if the firm is anticipating applying for listing the securities on the New York Stock Exchange, for one of the exchange requirements is a geographical dispersion of the securities.

Types of Agreements

The agreement between the investment banker and the firm may be of two types. The investment banker may agree to purchase (i.e., to underwrite) the entire issue of securities and sell them to the general public. This guarantees a specified amount of money to the firm issuing the securities. Or the investment banker may make a "best efforts" agreement, in which the best efforts to sell the securities will be made, but there is no guarantee that a specified amount of money will be raised. The former agreement places the risk of selling the securities on the investment banker, and most sales of new securities are of this type. The underwriters purchase all the securities, pay the expense of the underwriting, and bear the risk of the underwriting. Of course, the underwriters anticipate recouping the expenses through the sale, but they bear the risk of failing to sell the entire issue of securities. Since they have agreed to purchase the entire issue, the underwriters must pay the firm for all the securities even if the syndicate is unable to sell them.

Difference between underwriting and best efforts

It is for this reason that the pricing of the securities is crucial. If the initial offer price is too high, then the syndicate will be unable to sell the securities. If this occurs, the investment bankers have the following two choices: (1) purchase the securities with their own money, or (2) let the market find a lower price level that will induce investors to purchase the securities. Both choices are painful. If the underwriters purchase the securities, they either tie up their own funds that may earn a

Importance of not overpricing the issue

higher return elsewhere, or they will have to borrow the funds to pay for the securities. Like any other firm, the investment banker does not have unlimited access to borrowed funds, and these borrowed funds cost money. Thus the decision to support the price of the securities will cost the investment bankers in foregone opportunities for their own capital or (and this case is the more likely) require that they borrow substantial amounts of capital. In either case the profit margins on the underwriting are substantially decreased, and they may even experience a loss on the underwriting.

Letting the price find its own level

Instead of supporting the price, the underwriters may choose to let the price of the securities fall. Then the inventory of unsold securities can be sold and the underwriters do not tie up capital or have to borrow money from their credit sources. If the underwriters make this choice, they force losses on themselves when the securities are sold at less than cost. But they also force losses on customers who bought the securities at the initial offer price. The underwriters certainly do not want to inflict losses on these customers. If they continually experience losses, these buyers will not participate in the future, and the underwriters' market for future security issues will vanish. Thus the investment bankers do not seek to overprice a securities issue, for overpricing will ultimately result in experiencing losses.

Important not to underprice

There is also an incentive not to underprice the issue. If the issue is underpriced, all the securities will be readily sold and their price will rise. The buyers of the securities will be satisfied, for the price of the securities increased as a result of the underpricing. The initial purchasers of the securities reap windfall profits, but these profits are really at the expense of the company whose securities were underpriced. If the underwriters had priced the securities at a higher price, the company would have raised more capital. If underwriters consistently underprice the securities, firms will use other investment bankers to underwrite their securities. Underwriting is a very competitive business, and each security issue is individually negotiated. Hence, if one investment banker consistently underprices, firms will use competitors to underwrite their securities.

Marketing the Securities

The prospectus: a source of factual information concerning the securities being sold

Once the terms of the negotiations have been agreed upon, the managing house may issue a preliminary prospectus, often referred to as a red herring because of the red lettering on the title page. This lettering points out that the information is subject to amendment and that the securities cannot be sold until they are approved by the SEC. The cost of printing is borne by the underwriters, who recoup this cost through the underwriting fees. This preliminary prospectus describes the company and the securities to be issued. It includes the firm's income and balance sheets, its current activities (such as a pending merger or labor negotiation), the regulatory bodies to which it is subject, and the nature of its competition. The preliminary prospectus is thus a detailed document concerning the company and is, unfortunately, usually tedious reading.

The preliminary prospectus does omit the price of the securities, for that will be determined on the day the securities are issued. If the market should weaken or strengthen, then the price of the securities may be adjusted for the change in market conditions. In fact, if the market weakens sufficiently, the firm has the option to postpone or even cancel the underwriting.

When the shares are approved for issue by the SEC, a final prospectus is published. It is virtually identical to the preliminary prospectus except that the price of the security, the underwriting discount, the proceeds to the company, and more recent financial data are added. The red lettering is also deleted. Figure 24–1 illustrates the cover sheet for a final prospectus for James

450,000 Shares

JAMES RIVER CORPORATION

OF VIRGINIA

Common Stock
($.10 par value)

Of the 450,000 shares offered hereby, 340,000 are being sold by James River Corporation of Virginia and 110,000 are being sold by certain Selling Shareholders (see "Principal and Selling Shareholders"). The Company will not receive any of the proceeds from the sale of shares by the Selling Shareholders.

The Common Stock of James River is traded in the over-the-counter market. On June 29, 1976, the closing representative bid and asked prices as reported by NASDAQ were $17¼ and $18¼, respectively.

THESE SECURITIES HAVE NOT BEEN APPROVED OR DISAPPROVED BY THE SECURITIES AND EXCHANGE COMMISSION NOR HAS THE COMMISSION PASSED UPON THE ACCURACY OR ADEQUACY OF THIS PROSPECTUS. ANY REPRESENTATION TO THE CONTRARY IS A CRIMINAL OFFENSE.

	Price to Public	Underwriting Discount (1)	Proceeds to Company (2)	Proceeds to Selling Shareholders
Per Share	$17.75	$1.20	$16.55	$16.55
Total	$7,987,500	$540,000	$5,627,000	$1,820,500

(1) See "Underwriting."
(2) Before deducting expenses estimated at $115,000 payable by James River.

The shares are offered by the several Underwriters when, as and if delivered to and accepted by them, and subject to prior sale, withdrawal of such offer without notice and certain other conditions.

Kidder, Peabody & Co.
Incorporated

Scott & Stringfellow, Inc.

Wheat, First Securities, Inc.

The date of this Prospectus is June 30, 1976

Figure 24–1
The title page from the James River Corporation prospectus.

River Corporation. The names of the managing underwriters are in large print at the bottom. These managing underwriters formed the syndicate that sold the shares to the general public.

Firm's Cost of Underwriting

Fees paid by the firm

The firm's cost of the underwriting is the difference between the price of the securities to the general public and the proceeds to the firm. In the above example, this cost is $1.20 a share, or 7.25 per cent ($1.20/$16.55) of the firm's proceeds. The underwriting fee varies with each underwriting, but there are several identifiable factors that influence it. First, the fee (as a percentage of the offer price) declines as the dollar amount of the underwriting increases. Certain costs of the underwriting are fixed, such as the printing expense of the prospectus. The larger the issue, the more securities there are for this expense to spread over, and thus the cost per security is less. Second, the securities of large, well-known companies have smaller fees, for the public is more aware of the company and is more willing to buy the shares. Third, the small company pays a much larger fee, because the underwriters must be compensated for (1) the additional risk in the underwriting and (2) the cost of the additional search necessary to find buyers. Fourth, the underwriting fees also depend on the type of security, for the cost of issuing bonds is less than stock. Financial institutions such as banks and insurance companies may buy large blocks of debt securities more readily than large blocks of stock. Thus the cost of finding buyers for bonds is less than for stock, and this cost saving results in lower fees for underwriting bonds than stock.

In addition to the fees the underwriter may receive indirect compensation. This may take the form of the right (or option) to buy additional securities (usually at a substantial discount) or membership on the board of directors. Such indirect compensation may be as important as the fees because it unites the underwriter and the firm. After the initial sale the underwriter often becomes a market maker for the securities. Thus a continuing relationship between the firm and the investment banker may be beneficial to both.

Volatility of the New Issue Market

New issue market is volatile

The new issue market is extremely volatile. There have been periods when the market seemed willing to purchase virtually any security that was for sale. And there have been periods during which new companies were simply unable to raise money, and large companies did so only under onerous terms. Figure 24–2 illustrates this volatility. The column on the top is the anticipated calendar of new securities for the week of Oc-

Coming Financing

WEEK'S PROBABLE CORPORATE OFFERINGS (a)

Issue	Amount	Description	Probable Offering Date	Principal Underwriter
New Jersey Power & Light Co.	$8,000,000	Bonds—Monday—Competitive		
Seeman Brothers, Inc.	421,600 shs	Common—Monday—Courts & Co.		
Gibraltar Financial Corp.	400,000 shs	Common—Monday—White, Weld		
Consumers Power Co	$55,000,000	Bonds—Tuesday—Competitive		
Transcontinental Gas Pipe Line Co.	$40,000,000	Bonds—Tuesday—White, Weld		
Southern Pacific Co.	$9,900,000	Certificates—Tuesday—Competitive		
Western Gear Corp.	1,050,000 shs	Common—Tuesday—Blyth		
Cleve Pak Corp.	1,050,000 shs	Common—Tuesday—Dean Witter		
Specialty Restaurants Corp.	315,101 shs	Common—Tuesday—Dean Witter		
Page Airways, Inc.	300,000 shs	Common—Tuesday—Allen		
Lightolier, Inc.	290,000 shs	Common—Tuesday—Paine, Webber, Jackson & Curtis		
Elder-Beerman Stores Corp.	250,000 shs	Common—Tuesday—Walston		
International Aluminum Corp.	250,000 shs	Common—Tuesday—Dean Witter		
Crawford & Co.	225,000 shs	Common—Tuesday—Courts		
General Education Services Corp.	215,000 shs	Common—Tuesday—C. E. Unterberg, Towbin		
Sam Goody, Inc.	160,000 shs	Common—Tuesday—Walston		
Aero-Tech, Inc.	120,000 shs	Common—Tuesday—Mitchum, Jones & Templeton		
Felsway Shoe Corp.	100,000 shs	Common—Tuesday—Blair		
Connecticut Light & Power Co.	$40,000,000	Bonds—Thursday—Competitive		
Wilson Sporting Goods Co.	$35,000,000	Debentures—Thursday—Lehman Brothers		
New Jersey Bank & Trust Co.	$7,192,500	Conv. Notes—Thursday—Drexel Harriman Ripley		
Bandag, Inc.	$2,500,000	Conv. Debs.—Thursday—Bacon, Whipple		
Tower Fund, Inc.	1,250,000 shs	Common—Thursday—Weis, Voison, Cannon		
Sargent Industries, Inc.	500,000 shs	Common—Thursday—W. E. Hutton		
Sea Containers, Inc.	457,142 shs	Common—Thursday—Burnham		
American Building Maintenance Industries	242,000 shs	Common—Thursday—Lehman Brothers		
Flower Industries, Inc.	200,000 shs	Common—Thursday—Courts		

a-Tentative schedule, depending on SEC clearance, market conditions or other factors.

NEW OFFERINGS FILED

Pacific Gas & Electric Co.	$60,000,000	Bonds—Competitive
Quebec Hydro-Electric Commission	$50,000,000	Debentures—First Boston
Province of Nova Scotia	$35,000,000	Debentures—Halsey, Stuart
San Francisco & Oakland Helicopter Airlines, Inc.	$2,500,000	Conv. Debs.—J. Barth
Schott Industries, Inc.	450,000 shs	Common—Van Alstyne, Noel
Tropical Gas, Inc.	230,000 shs	Common—Glore Forgan, Wm. R. Staats
Kane-Miller Corp.	212,500 shs	Common—None
Hamburger Hamlets, Inc.	170,000 shs	Common—Dempsey-Tegeler

COMING FINANCING

WEEK'S PROBABLE CORPORATE OFFERINGS

Company	Amount	Type	Due Date	Moody's Rating	S&P Underwriters
MONDAY					
Michigan Wisconsin Pipe Line	$50,000,800	Bonds—1994—A—Competitive—A			
TUESDAY					
Gen'l Motors Acceptance	$250,000,000	Debentures—1999—Aaa—Morgan Stanley & Co. AA			
Bucyrus-Erie Co.	$50,000,000	Debentures—1999—A—Paine, Webber—A-			
Central Illinois Light	$25,000,000	Bonds—2004—Aa—Competitive—A			
	750,000 shs	Common—Blyth Eastman Dillon			
Southern Railway	$15,000,000	Certificates—1975-89—Aa—Competitive			
Florida Power Corp.	450,000 shs	Preferred—Aa—Kidder, Peabody—A			
Northwestern Pub. Serv. ....160,000 shs		Common—Stone & Webster Securities			
WEDNESDAY					
Commonwealth Edison Co.	$125,000,080	Bonds—1979—Aaa—Competitive—AA			
THURSDAY					
International Harvester	$150,000,000	Debentures—2004—A—Morgan Stanley—A			
NEW OFFERINGS FILED					
Baltimore Gas & Electric	$75,000,000	Bonds—Competitive			
	2,500,000 shs	Common—First Boston Corp.			
Iowa Elec. Light & Power	$30,000,000	Bonds—Competitive			
Columbia Gas System	1,000,000 shs	Preferred—Competitive			
Northern States Power	300,000 shs	Preferred—Competitive			

Reprinted with permission of Dow Jones.

Figure 24–2

New financing for selected weeks.

tober 21, 1968, as published by *Barron's*. The column on the bottom is the new issue calendar for the week of June 3, 1974. The difference is obvious. In the former case there are many new issues of stock and issues of bonds; many of these companies are small and they are issuing only 200,000 to 300,000 shares, which will raise one or two million dollars. In the second case only a few well-known firms (in particular, utilities) were issuing securities, for the market conditions would not permit the sale of new securities by unproven firms.

Buying new
issues can be
risky

The new issue market is volatile not only as regards the number of securities being offered but also regarding the price changes of the new issues. When the new issue market is "hot," it is not unusual for the prices to rise dramatically. Several examples of this spectacular performance are presented in Table 24–1, which presents the offering prices of the new issues and the prices during the first month after the shares were issued. The table also gives the stock's prices several years later. Some of the prices dramatically rose after the securities were initially issued, but they then quite as dramatically fell. CP Products is illustrative of the volatility of new issues. The shares initially sold for $13 in 1972, then rose to $28 but were worth less than $1.00 only two years later in 1974.

Participation by an investor in the new issue market when firms are "going public" (i.e., selling shares to the general public for the first time) subjects the investor to much risk. But IBM and Xerox Corporation went public once, and the hope of finding another IBM causes the buyers to forget sometimes their common sense and to omit fundamental financial analysis. When this occurs, many financially weak firms are able to raise capital by issuing shares. These stocks may command prices far in excess of the intrinsic value of the earning capacity of the firm. And, as is frequently the case, these prices subsequently decline to prices that are indicative of the earning power of the firm.

TABLE 24–1   Price Performance of Selected New Issues

COMPANY	ISSUE PRICE	PRICE DURING FIRST MONTH AFTER ISSUE DATE	MARKET PRICE (8–16–74) OR (8–30–74)
Arrow Automotive Ind.	$17	$22½	$ 3½
CP Products	13	28	½
Graves Truck Line	16	20¼	8¼
Midland Glass	10¾	10⅞	3¾
Mobile America	15	32½	1⅜
Naum Bros.	8¾	11	1¼
Onan	19	23⅞	11½
Rucker Pharmacal	10.30	16¼	7¼
Telco Marketing	21	31½	1½
Tidewell Industries	15	33	1½
Unity Buying Service	16½	27⅝	7

Sources: *Barrons*, March 20, 1972, p. 57, and April 8, 1972, p. 57; *Pink Sheets*, August 16, 1974; and *Standard and Poor's Stock Guide*, September, 1974.

RIGHTS OFFERINGS

Some companies have granted their stockholders preemptive rights. This privilege gives the stockholders the right to maintain their proportionate share of ownership in the company. Thus, if the company wants to raise additional funds by issuing more shares of common stock, the company must first offer these shares to its current stockholders. The stockholders are not required to buy the shares; they have the privilege of purchasing or refusing them. If the current stockholders do purchase the shares, they maintain their proportional ownership of the company.

Firms that have granted these preemptive rights will use rights offerings when they issue new stock. This offering gives the stockholder the option to purchase additional stock at a predetermined price. This predetermined price must be below the market price of the stock to induce purchases of the new shares. Evidence of this option is called a right, which is issued to all stockholders of the company as of a specified day. Since the option is a privilege to purchase the stock at a discount, the option has value. The following example explains (1) the mechanics of a rights issue and (2) the determination of the value of a right.

A company whose stockholders have preemptive rights needs $1,000,000. The firm's stock is selling for $60 a share, and it currently has 1,000,000 shares outstanding. Management believes the firm can raise the money by issuing 200,000 new shares of common stock at a price of $50. This is a 20 per cent increase in the number of shares outstanding. Since the current stockholders have preemptive rights, the firm offers them the right to purchase the new shares in proportion to their current ownership. A person with 5 shares is given the option to buy one new share. The stockholder will be sent five rights (one for each share), and each right will be the option to purchase .2 shares. The stockholders may exercise these rights or sell them to someone who would like to purchase the new shares.

What will be the market price of these rights if the stockholder decides not to exercise the rights but to sell them? The intrinsic value of the rights (i.e., their true value as an option) is found in the following way. The stockholder has 5 shares worth $300 (5 × $60). If the new share is purchased, the stockholder obtains it for $50 and now has 6 shares worth $350. The average cost of a share is $58.33 ($350/6). The difference between the average cost of the six shares of stock and the exercise price of the rights is the intrinsic value of the rights. In this case the intrinsic value is $58.33 − $50 = $8.33 for five rights, or $1.67 for one right. In this case such a sale would raise approximately $8.33.

The stockholder may determine this "rights-on" value of a

Preemptive rights protect stockholders from dilution

Rights: the option to buy new shares

Rights have intrinsic value

How to determine the value of a right

right (i.e., the value of the rights before they are detached from the stock) by the use of a simple formula:

(1)
$$V = \frac{P_m - P_e}{n + 1}$$

The symbols are defined as follows:

V: the value of a right
P_m: the current market price of the stock
P_e: the exercise price of the right (which is also referred to as the subscription price)
n: the number of rights necessary to purchase one share

If the stockholder applies this formula to the above example, the value of a right is $1.66.

$$V = \frac{\$60 - \$50}{5 + 1}$$

$$V = \frac{10}{6} = \$1.66$$

The value of a right is easy to calculate, and the formula is easy to remember for the subscripts tell the user which prices (market price and exercise price) to use. The formula also points out the fact that the issuing of the new shares will increase the number of shares outstanding. That is why the denominator is $n + 1$ and not just n. There will be one new share for every n shares outstanding; the old shares will be diluted by the issuing of the new shares.

What affects the value of a right

The intrinsic value of a right is related to the market price of the common stock, the exercise (or subscription) price of the right, and the number of rights necessary to purchase a new share. When the firm offers the stockholders the rights, the firm must fix (1) the number of rights necessary to purchase a new share, and (2) the exercise price of the rights. The market price of the stock, however, may continue to fluctuate and hence cause the intrinsic value of the right to fluctuate. The market price of the right may, however, be greater than its intrinsic value. If speculators anticipate that the price of stock will rise, they will bid up the price of the right. It will sell for a premium over its intrinsic value. If the stock's price does rise, then these speculators may realize profits as the value of the rights also rise. Such a price increase does not affect the exercising of the rights. It may, however, indicate that the exercise price was too low and that management could have raised the same amount of money with fewer shares priced more dearly.

If the price of the common stock were to decline, the whole rights issue could fail if the price of the stock falls below the exercise price of the right. In the above example, if the price of the common stock were to decline to $48 a share, then the rights are worthless. No one will exercise the rights to buy the stock at $50 a share when the shares can be purchased on the open market at $48. In order to make certain that the rights offering does not fail but does raise the money desired by the company, management must price the new shares at a sufficient discount. Thus a rights offering presents management with something of a dilemma. If the exercise price of rights is too high, management risks the possibility of having the rights offering fail. However, the lower the exercise price of the rights, the larger the number of shares that must be issued in order to raise a given sum of money. Establishing the exercise price of a rights issue is obviously a major consideration in a rights offering.

The time dimension of a rights offering

The issuing of rights occurs over time. Figure 24–3 illustrates the time frame of a rights offering. On January 1, there is nothing known by stockholders about a rights offering. Then, on January 10, the announcement of the rights offering is made to the general public that stockholders owning the shares at the close of business on January 31 will receive the rights to purchase the new shares. From January 10 through January 31 the stock continues to trade in the open market, and anyone who purchases the stock during that time period and holds the stock until February gets the rights to purchase the new shares. During this time period the price of the stock includes the value of the rights, and the stock trades with the *rights on* (i.e., the rights are still embodied in the stock). In effect, the $60 price for the stock is the sum of the value of the rights and the value of the stock. The $60 then represents the $1.66 value of the rights and the $58.34 value of the stock.

On February 1, purchasers of the stock no longer received the rights; the stock is trading exclusive of the rights, or *ex rights*. Purchasing the stock after January 31 means the purchaser may

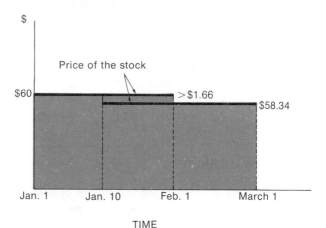

Figure 24–3
Time dimension of a rights offering.

not participate in the rights offering, and the purchaser's shares have been diluted because the new shares are being issued. The price of the stock must decline on February 1 by the value of the right ($1.66) to account for the dilution of the existing shares. The stockholders, who purchased the shares prior to February 1, now receive their rights from the company. They may exercise them or sell them in the open market, for the rights now exist independently of the common stock. The only constraint on these stockholders is that they act by the expiration date of the right, March 1.

The investor who purchased the stock for $60 in January does not suffer any loss when the rights are distributed and the price of the stock declines. This investor owns the stock worth $58.34 and the right worth $1.66. The total value is still $60. All that happened is that the rights have been separated from the common stock, and investors may hold or sell either or both of them. The issuing of rights does not decrease the stockholder's wealth. Any loss in wealth will occur only if the stockholder fails to exercise or sell the rights, for the right to purchase the new shares ultimately expires and the option ceases.

While a rights issue may appear to decrease the wealth of existing stockholders because the price of the stock declines, this is not so. The stockholder receives an option with a value equal to the decline in the price of the stock. This maintaining of the *current stockholders'* wealth is an essential difference between a rights offering and a stock offering to *new* investors. If the new stock is sold to the general public, and if the stock is sold at a discount to induce new investors to purchase the stock, then existing stockholders do suffer losses. Their proportion of ownership is reduced, and the price of their shares declines because of the dilution of ownership. It is precisely these losses that preemptive rights are seeking to stop.

A rights offering then is a means for a company to raise money from its current stockholders. By offering the current stockholders new shares in proportion to their present ownership, it gives the current stockholders an opportunity to maintain their proportionate ownership. If they do not want to purchase the new shares, the current stockholders may sell the rights. In either case, their wealth is not reduced as it may be if the new shares are sold to new stockholders at a discount, which causes the price of all existing shares to decline.

PRIVATE PLACEMENT

With the recent growth in large financial institutions, there has developed an important source of capital for firms other than retained earnings and new issues of securities to the general public. This source is the directly negotiated private placement of securities with pension funds, insurance companies, and other financial institutions that have large amounts of cash to invest. Such private placements of securities offer advantages to both sides.

The advantages to the firm are primarily the saving in underwriting fees and the availability of large amounts of cash quickly. Even if an investment banker acts as a broker between the financial institution and the firm, the investment banking fee is smaller for a private placement than an issue of new securities sold to the general public. This reduced fee is the direct result of lower costs to the underwriter who does not have the expenses associated with a public underwriting. This cost saving may be substantial for a small firm seeking to raise a modest sum of money.

Advantages of private placement: (1) lower fees, (2) speed

Another advantage to the firm is that it does not have to meet the SEC's disclosure requirements. These disclosure requirements are for the protection of the investing public, and presumably the financial institution does not need this protection. From the firm's viewpoint, the disclosure statement is a cost when securities are issued to the public and perhaps a source of information to its competitors that the firm would like to avoid divulging.

(3) Avoids disclosure

An advantage to both the firm and the financial institution is that the terms of securities may be tailored to the needs of both parties. For example, the firm may be able to sell a bond of intermediate length to a financial institution when the general public may not be willing to accept intermediate length debt.

(4) Tailor-made offering

There are, however, several important disadvantages of using private placements that involve the restrictive covenants that may be part of the agreement. Since the financial institution is giving up the money, it may seek to decrease its risk of loss by building into the agreement restrictive covenants that may prove to decrease significantly the flexibility of the borrower. The purpose of these covenants is not to hinder the firm's operation but to protect the lender's investment.

The disadvantage: restrictive covenants

The firm may be restricted in its ability to incur additional debt. This covenant may (1) limit the type of debt that the firm may issue or (2) require the firm to maintain a certain current ratio or debt ratio. The lender may also require that the debt issue have a sinking fund feature, a non-refundability clause, or a call premium (these features are explained in the next chapter on debt). The sinking fund eases the retirement of the debt, but the other two restrictive covenants may be particularly painful. Non-refundability means that the firm cannot pay off the loan before it is due. If interest rates subsequently decline, the firm cannot refinance this issue. A call premium means the firm must pay more than the principal if it retires the debt before maturity. A call premium does not make early retirement impossible, but it does make it more costly.

Covenants may also require the maintaining of a minimum amount of working capital to protect the lender against the deterioration of the borrower's ability to pay its current liabilities. This covenant may be stated as a minimum dollar amount or as a percentage of the loan. Covenants may also restrict the ability of the firm to pay dividends, salaries, types of investments made by the firm, and mergers. All these restrictive covenants may be part of a private placement, and since each placement is separately negotiated, the individual terms will vary with the bargaining powers of the parties and the conditions of the money and capital markets at the time of the agreement.

SUMMARY

This chapter has covered a variety of ways that firms may obtain sources of outside capital. New securities may be issued through investment bankers or sold directly to current stockholders through a rights offering. Securities may also be sold to financial institutions through a private placement.

Many firms primarily rely on internally generated funds to finance operations and expansion and rarely use these sources of outside financing. Some industries, such as utilities, frequently issue new securities and do use investment bankers, rights offerings, and private placements. These sources of capital may be employed by firms in various industries as a means to acquire the funds necessary to finance and expand operations.

KEY WORDS AND TERMS

investment banker   offer price
underwriting   underwriting fee
best efforts   preemptive rights
red herring   rights offering
prospectus   rights on
originating house   ex rights
syndicate   private placement

QUESTIONS AND PROBLEMS FOR THOUGHT AND DISCUSSION

1. What role in the underwriting process does each of the following play?
   (a) the managing house
   (b) the syndicate
   (c) the prospectus

    (d) the underwriting discount
    (e) the SEC (refer to Chapter 9)

    Could any of these be omitted from the process?
    What may be the effect of omitting any particular part of the
    underwriting process?

2. Go to your library and find information in Standard and Poor's
   or Moody's on the following firms that recently went public.
   (a) Daniel International
   (b) Four Seasons Nursing Centers of America
   What subsequently happened to the earnings and the price of
   the shares of each company? Were the firms good investments? Why do investors buy new issues? Why in periods of
   tight money and low security prices are firms unable to go
   public?

3. If a company went public at $30 a share and the price of the
   stock immediately rose to 35–36, who receives the windfall
   gain? Did the supply of this stock exceed the demand? From
   the viewpoint of the underwriter, was this a successful underwriting? Why would the underwriter not want to overprice
   a new issue?

4. Risk is associated with the selling of new securities. Who
   bears the risk in a "best efforts" sale of securities? Why do
   firms prefer an underwriting to a "best efforts" sale? What risk
   is there to the investor who purchases the securities?

5. What is the difference between an underwriting and a private
   placement? Which tends to cost more with regard to (a) fees
   and (b) implicit costs? Under what conditions would a firm
   prefer each of these methods of raising funds?

6. A company decides on a rights offering to sell new shares. It
   needs $2,000,000 and currently has 1,000,000 shares out-
   standing. The current price of the stock is $13, and the firm
   believes that it can sell the new shares at $10.
   (a) If each share receives a right, how many shares will be
      required to buy a new share?
   (b) If the rights offering is successful, how many shares will
      the firm have outstanding?
   (c) What is the value of a right before it is detached and
      exercised?
   (d) By how much must the price of the stock decline when the
      rights are detached and exercised?
   (e) Why does the price of the stock decline?
   (f) What would happen if the price of the stock were to de-
      cline to $9 before the rights were exercised?

Chapter 25

SOURCES OF FUNDS: LONG-TERM DEBT

Learning Objectives

- Identify the general characteristics of all long-term debt instruments.
- Isolate the feature(s) that distinguish each type of bond.
- State the role of bond ratings.
- Calculate the pricing of a bond.
- Explain the inverse relationship between interest rates and bond prices.
- Explain the methods for retiring debt.

"Pay every debt as if God wrote the bill."

Ralph Waldo Emerson

Many corporations have issued long-term debt to finance expansion of plant and equipment. When the firm's internally generated funds (profits and depreciation) are insufficient to finance the expansion, the firm may issue long-term debt. Financing fixed assets by long-term debt offers the firm the advantages of financial leverage, and the debt may be retired by the cash flow generated by the plant and equipment.

This chapter is concerned with the long-term debt of corporations and covers (1) the characteristics common to all long-term debt and (2) the different types of debt. Long term debt initially may be purchased by institutions in a private placement or by individuals through a public offering. Once the debt has been issued, it may be bought and sold on the organized security exchanges or in the over-the-counter market. Thus the debt must have a market price, and this chapter considers how that price is determined. The debt must also be paid off; the last section of this chapter is devoted to the retirement of long-term debt.

CHARACTERISTICS OF ALL DEBT INSTRUMENTS

Debt instruments: (1) pay interest, (2) mature

All debt instruments have similar characteristics. They are liabilities of their issuers for a specified amount, called the principal. Virtually all debt has a maturity date; it must be paid off by a specified date. If maturity occurs after a year, it is long-term debt. When this debt is issued, the length of time to maturity can range from a few years to 20 or 30 years. The owners of debt instruments receive payments (interest). Interest should not be confused with other forms of income, such as cash dividends paid by common and preferred stock. Dividends come from the firm's earnings, while interest is an expense. Sometimes interest is called *yield* and may be expressed in two ways: *current yield* and *yield to maturity*. The difference between the two is discussed subsequently in the section on pricing of bonds.

Each debt agreement has terms that the debtor must meet, and these are stated in a legal document called the *indenture*. One of the most frequent requirements is the pledging of collateral that the borrower must put up to secure the loan. For example, the collateral for a mortgage is the building. Other assets, such as securities or inventory owned by the borrower, may also be pledged to secure the loan. If the borrower defaults on the loan (i.e., if the borrower fails to pay the interest or fails to meet other terms of the indenture), then the creditor may seize the collateral and sell it to recoup the principal.

(3) Have an indenture

Other examples of common loan restrictions are (1) limits on dividend payments, (2) limits on the issue of additional debt, and (3) the requirement to maintain a current ratio of at least 2 to 1. These examples do not exhaust all the possible conditions of a given loan. Since each loan is separately negotiated, there is ample opportunity for subtle differences among loan agreements. The important point, however, is that if any part of the loan agreement is violated, the creditor may declare that the debt is in default and that the entire loan is due. Default is not just the failure to pay the interest. Failure to meet any of the indenture provisions places the loan in default, even though the interest is still being paid.

(4) Possible restrictions

Many debt instruments are purchased by investors who may be unaware of the terms of the indenture. Even if they are aware of the terms, the investors may be too geographically dispersed to take concerted action in case of default. To protect their interests, a *trustee* is appointed for each bond issue. It is the trustee's job to see that the terms of the indenture are upheld and to take remedial action if the company should default on the terms of the indenture. If the firm should default on the interest payments or other terms of the indenture, the trustee may take the firm to court on behalf of all the bondholders in order to protect their principal.

The role of the trustee: protect the bond holders

Another characteristic of all debt is risk—risk that the interest will not be paid, risk that the principal will not be repaid, risk that the price of the debt instrument may decline, and risk that inflation will continue. Risk of default on interest and principal payments varies significantly with different types of debt. The

Sources of risk: (1) default

debt of the Federal Government has no risk of default on its interest payments and principal repayments. The reason for this absolute safety is that the government has the power to print money. The government can always issue the money necessary to pay the interest and repay the principal.

The debt of firms and individuals is not so riskless, for both may default on their obligations. To aid potential buyers of debt instruments, there have developed credit rating services (Moody's, Dun and Bradstreet, and Standard and Poor's). These services rate the degree of risk of a debt instrument. The following exhibit illustrates the risk classification offered by Moody's. High quality debt receives a rating of Aaa, while poorer quality debt receives progressively lower ratings. While not all debt instruments are rated, the service does cover a significant number of debt obligations.

Moody's Bond Ratings

Aaa	Bonds of highest quality
Aa	Bonds of high quality
A	Bonds whose security of principal and interest is considered adequate but may be impaired in the future
Baa	Bonds of medium grade that are neither highly protected nor poorly secured
Ba	Bonds of speculative quality whose future cannot be considered well assured
B	Bonds that lack characteristics of a desirable investment
Caa	Bonds in poor standing that may default
Ca	Bonds of a high degree of speculation and often in default
C	Lowest rating for bonds having little probability of any investment value

Source: *Moody's Bond Record*, December, 1976.

These ratings play an important role in the marketing of debt obligations. Since the risk of default may be substantial for poor quality debt, some financial institutions and investors will not purchase debt with a low credit rating. If a firm's or municipality's debt rating falls, it may have difficulty selling its debt. Corporations and municipal governments thus seek to maintain good credit, for good credit ratings reduce the cost of borrowing and increase the marketability of the debt.

(2) Price fluctuations

Debt is also subject to the risk of price fluctuations. Once it has been issued, the market price of the debt will rise or fall depending on market conditions. If interest rates rise, then the price of debt must fall so that its fixed interest payment is competitive. The opposite is true if interest rates decline. The price of debt must rise, for the fixed interest payment makes it more attractive, and buyers bid up the debt's price. Why these fluctuations in the price of debt instruments occur is explained in more detail in the subsequent section on the pricing of debt instruments.

There is, however, one feature of debt that partially compensates for the risk of price fluctuations. The holder knows that the debt ultimately matures; the principal must be repaid. Thus, if the price falls and the debt instrument sells for a discount (i.e., less than the face value), the value of the debt must appreciate as it approaches maturity. For on the day it matures, the full amount of the principal must be repaid.

The final risk that all creditors must endure is inflation, which reduces the value of money. During inflation the debtor repays the loan in money that purchases less. If the lenders anticipate inflation, they will demand a higher rate of interest to help protect their purchasing power. For example, if the rate of inflation is 8 per cent, the creditors may demand 10 per cent, which nets them 2 per cent in real terms. While the inflation causes the real value of the capital to deteriorate, the high interest rate partially offsets the effects of inflation. Thus creditors must demand a rate of interest at least equal to the rate of inflation to maintain their purchasing power.

(3) Inflation

TYPES OF DEBT INSTRUMENTS

Corporate Bonds

Corporations issue many types of bonds, as the following list indicates:

Variety of corporate debt

> mortgage bonds
> equipment trust certificates
> debentures
> subordinate debentures
> income bonds

Other types of bonds include the convertible debentures and variable interest rate bonds. These are discussed in more detail later in this chapter. Each type of bond has characteristics that differentiate it from the others. Purchasers should be aware of the differences, for some types of bonds are decidedly more risky.

MORTGAGE BONDS

Mortgage bonds are issued to purchase specified fixed assets, and the assets are pledged to secure the debt. If the firm should default on the interest or principal repayment, the cred-

Mortgage bonds have collateral

itors may take title to the pledged property. They may then choose to operate the fixed asset or to sell it. While the pledging of property may decrease the lender's risk of loss, the lender is not interested in taking possession and operating the property. Lenders earn their income through interest payments, not by the operation of the fixed assets. Such lenders are rarely qualified to operate the assets if they were to take possession of them. If they are forced to sell the assets, they may find few buyers and have to sell at distress prices. For example, if a school defaults on interest on the mortgage payments on its dormitories, what can the creditors do with the buildings if they take possession of them? While the pledging of the assets increases the safety of the principal, the lenders prefer the prompt payment of interest and principal.

EQUIPMENT TRUST CERTIFICATE

Equipment trust certificates finance equipment

Equipment trust certificates are issued to finance specified equipment, and the assets are pledged as collateral. These certificates are primarily issued by railroads and airlines to finance rolling stock and airplanes, and this equipment is the collateral. This collateral is considered to be of excellent quality, for unlike other fixed assets this equipment may be readily *moved* and sold to other railroads and airlines should the firm default on the certificates.

DEBENTURES

Debentures are unsecured

Debentures are unsecured promissory notes of a company supported by the general credit of the firm. This type of debt is more risky, for in case of default or bankruptcy, the secured debt is redeemed before the debentures. Some debentures are *subordinate debentures*, and these are even riskier because they are subordinate to all other debts of the firm. Even unsecured debt has a superior position to the subordinate debenture. These are among the riskiest of debt issued and usually have significantly higher interest rates or other features, such as convertibility in the stock of the company, to compensate the lenders for the increased risk.

Financial institutions often prefer a firm to sell debentures to the general public. Since the debentures are general obligations of the company, they do not tie up assets of the company. If the firm needs additional money, it can use these assets as collateral. The financial institutions will be more willing to lend the firm the additional funds because of the collateral. If the assets had been previously pledged, the firm would lack this flexibility in its financing.

While the use of debentures may not decrease the ability of the firm to issue additional debt, default on the debentures usually means that all superior debt is in default. A frequent indenture clause stipulates that, if any of the firm's debt is in default, all debt issues are in default, in which case the creditor may declare the entire debt to be due. Thus a firm should not overextend itself through excessive use of unsecured debt any more than it should use excessive amounts of secured debt.

INCOME BONDS AND REVENUE BONDS

Income bonds require that the interest be paid only if the firm earns it. If the firm is unable to cover its other expenses, then it is not legally obligated to pay the interest on these bonds. These are the riskiest of all types of bonds and are rarely issued today by corporations. There is, however, a type of bond frequently issued by state and local governments that is similar to income bonds. These are *revenue bonds*, which pay the interest only if the revenue is earned. Examples of this type are the bonds issued to finance toll roads. The interest on the debt is paid if the tolls generate sufficient revenue (after the operating expenses) to cover the interest payments.

Income bonds pay interest only if earned

Forms of Bonds

Bonds may be issued in the following two forms: (1) registered as to principal and interest, and (2) registered only as to principal with coupons attached. Registered bonds are similar to stocks, and the interest payments are sent to the registered owner. Coupon bonds are entirely different. The owner of the bond has to detach the coupon and send it to the paying agent to collect the interest. In the past most bonds were of the coupon variety, and people who were on a fixed income were frequently called "coupon clippers." Today bonds are issued in both types. Any investor who is concerned with the form can learn from a bond guide such as Moody's or Standard and Poor's which bonds are coupon bonds and which are registered bonds. If the bond issue has both types, then the investor may specify to the broker the type desired when the bond is purchased.

Registered bonds, coupon bonds

An example of a coupon bond is given in Figure 25–1. Portions of the bond are reproduced. The coupons are numbered from 1 to 50, and each represents a six-month interest payment. This Georgia and Florida Railroad 6 per cent Income Non-Mortgage Debenture certainly was not a good investment. It still has all the coupons attached. This means that not one interest payment was made. While bonds are debt obligations, this particular bond is a debenture (i.e., not secured) and an income bond. Thus the debtor is obligated to pay the interest only if earned. This railroad did not earn sufficient revenues to meet the first interest payment. Writing the word "Gold" across the face of the bond certainly did not turn this piece of paper into metal!

Figure 25–1
Coupon bond.

Figure continued on the opposite page

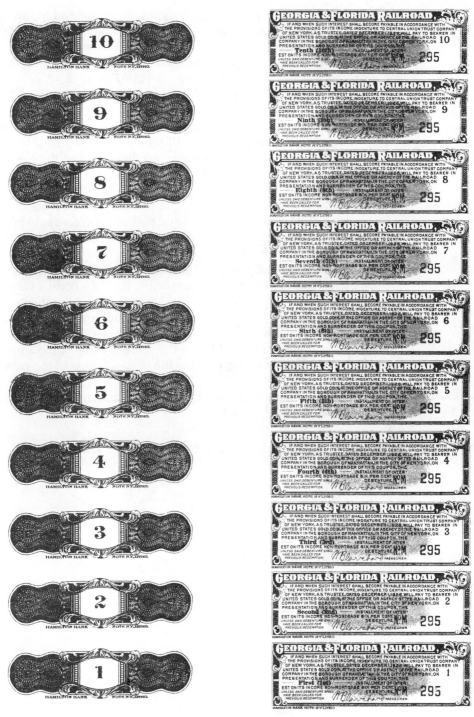

Figure 25–1 *Continued*

The Price of a Bond

Bonds may be sold

Many bonds are sold to the general public and are traded daily like stocks, and some of them are listed on the New York Bond Exchange. Trades on the exchange are reported by financial newspapers. For example, on January 28, 1977, the *Wall Street Journal* listed the transactions in Figure 25–2 in AT&T bonds. How these entries are read is illustrated by the AT&T 2¾s82. This listing is for a $1000 AT&T bond that has a 2¾ per cent coupon and matures in 1982. The current yield on this bond is 3.2 per cent, and 12 of these $1000 bonds traded during the day on the exchange. The high price was $851.25, and the low and closing prices were $851.25; there was *no net change* from the previous day.

Bond prices fluctuate

While bond prices fluctuate daily, the price of a bond (in a given risk class) is primarily related to (1) the interest paid by the bond, (2) the interest investors may earn on competitive bonds, and (3) the maturity date of the bond. A bond is a debt instrument that makes periodic interest payments (usually semiannually), which are similar to annuity payments. Part of a bond's value is the present value of all the interest payments. At maturity the principal is repaid, which is similar to a lump sum payment in the future. Part of a bond's value is the present value of this principal. The price of a bond today is the present value of the annuity (i.e., the interest payments) plus the present value of the principal.

Determination of a bond's price

The price of a bond may be expressed in terms of the present values formulas from Chapter 20:

$$(1) \qquad P_B = \frac{I_1}{(1+i)^1} + \frac{I_2}{(1+i)^2} + \cdots + \frac{I_n}{(1+i)^n} + \frac{P}{(1+i)^n}$$

New York Exchange Bonds

Friday, January 28, 1977

CORPORATION BONDS

Volume, $19,520,000

Bonds	Cur Yld	Vol	High	Low	Close	Net Chg
ATT 2¾s82	3.2	12	85⅛	85⅛	85⅛	.....
ATT 3¼s84	4.2	29	78⅞	78⅛	78⅛	− ¼
ATT 4⅜s85	5.3	16	83⅜	82⅝	83	+ ⅜
ATT 2⅝s86	3.7	2	70	70	70	.....
ATT 3⅞s90	5.5	36	70⅝	70⅛	70⅝	− ¼
ATT 8¾2000	8.2	443	107⅛	106¾	107	+ ¼
ATT 7s01	7.7	105	91	90½	91	+ ½
ATT 7⅛s03	7.7	210	92¼	91½	92¼	+ ⅜
ATT 8.80s05	8.2	224	107	106⅝	107	.....
ATT 7¾s82	7.6	63	102⅞	102½	102½	− ⅜
ATT 8⅝s07	8.2	227	105⅝	105¼	105⅝	+ ⅛

Figure 25–2

Transaction in AT&T bonds. (Reprinted with permission of Dow Jones.)

The terms are:

P$_B$: the current price of the bond
  I: the annual interest payment (with the subscripts indicating the year)
  n: the number of years to maturity
  P: the principal
  i: the current interest rate

Interest is usually paid semiannually. Thus Equation (1) could be modified to include semiannual compounding. Such modification does not change the general form of the equation but has been omitted to reduce its complexity.

The calculation of the bond's price is illustrated by the following example. A firm has a $1000 bond that pays 6 per cent ($60) annually and matures in three years. When these values are substituted into equation (1), it becomes:

$$P_B = \frac{60}{(1 + i)} + \frac{60}{(1 + i)^2} + \frac{60}{(1 + i)^3} + \frac{1000}{(1 + i)^3}$$

All that is needed to solve for the price of the bond is the current interest rate, which is the interest rate being paid by competitive bonds of the same length of time to maturity and risk. If the competitive bonds yield 6 per cent, then the price of this bond will be par ($1000), for

$$\$1000 = \frac{\$60}{(1 + .06)} + \frac{\$60}{(1 + .06)^2} + \frac{\$60}{(1 + .06)^3} + \frac{\$1000}{(1 + .06)^3}$$

$$\$1000 = \$56.60 + \$53.40 + \$50.38 + \$839.62$$

If competitive bonds are selling to yield 10 per cent, this bond will be unattractive to investors. They will not be willing to pay $1000 for a bond yielding 6 per cent when they could buy competing bonds that yield 10 per cent. In order for this bond to compete with the other bonds, its price must decline sufficiently to yield 10 per cent. In terms of Equation (1):

Higher interest rates drive bond prices down

$$P_B = \frac{\$60}{(1 + .1)} + \frac{\$60}{(1 + .1)^2} + \frac{\$60}{(1 + .1)^3} + \frac{\$1000}{(1 + .1)^3}$$

$$\$900.53 = \$54.55 + \$49.59 + \$45.08 + \$751.31$$

the price of the bond must decline approximately to $900 and sell for a *discount* (i.e., a price less than the stated principal) to be competitive with the other bonds. At that price investors will earn $60 a year in interest and $100 in capital gains, for a total annual return of 10 per cent on their investment. The capital gain occurs because the bond was purchased for $900, but, when the bond matures, the holder receives $1000.

Lower interest rates drive bond prices up

If interest rates were to fall, the price of the bond would have to rise. If interest rates decline to 4 per cent, then the price of the bond is:

$$\$1055.50 = \frac{\$60}{(1 + .04)} + \frac{\$60}{(1 + .04)^2} + \frac{\$60}{(1 + .04)^3} + \frac{\$1000}{(1 + .04)^3}$$

The bond is selling for a premium (i.e., a price greater than the stated principal). While it may seem impossible for the price of a bond to sell for a premium, it must do so if interest rates fall below the rate of interest stated on the bond.

This example leads to a general conclusion concerning bond prices and changes in interest rates: they are *inversely* related. When interest rates rise, bond prices decline. When interest rates fall, bond prices rise.

This example also illustrates the difference between the current yield and the yield to maturity. The *current yield* on a bond is the annual interest payment divided by the price of the bond. If a $1000 bond pays $60 a year and is purchased at a discount for $900, then the current yield is 6.7 per cent ($60/$900). The *yield to maturity* considers not only the current yield but also any increase or decrease in the price of the bond at maturity. In the above example the bond sold for a discount; so the yield to maturity on an investment in this bond is the current yield plus the appreciation in the price of the bond. In this case the yield to maturity is 10 per cent, a current yield of 6.7 per cent, and price appreciation of $100.

The current yield and the yield to maturity will be equal only if the bond sells for par. If the bond sells for a discount, then the current yield is less than the yield to maturity. These differences in yields are illustrated by the following AT&T bond. The issue pays $32.50 annually and matures in 1984. In November, 1976, it sold at a discount for 76½ (i.e., $765 for $1000 face value). That bond has a current yield of 4.2 per cent. The yield to maturity is approximately 7.2 per cent. This yield to maturity is found by using the equation presented above.

$$\$765 = \frac{\$32.50}{(1 + r)} + \cdots + \frac{\$32.50}{(1 + r)^8} + \frac{\$1000}{(1 + r)^8}$$

$$r = 7.2\%$$

If an investor purchased this bond, the yield to maturity exceeds the current yield.

If a bond sells for a premium, then the current yield is greater than the yield to maturity. This is illustrated by the 8¾ per cent AT&T bond that matures in 2000. It sold for $1060 (i.e., at a premium). The current yield is 8.25 per cent, and the yield to maturity is 8.17 per cent. An investor who seeks current income will prefer to purchase bonds selling near or above par.

Many investors may prefer purchasing bonds at a discount. They will collect some current income and receive a capital gain (which is taxed at the lower long-term capital gains tax rate) when the bond matures.

The relationship between the price of a bond and interest rates suggests a means to make profits in the bond market. All that the investor needs to know is the direction of future changes in the interest rate. If investors anticipate that interest rates will decline, then they expect bond prices of a given maturity to rise. This price increase must occur, for previously issued bonds must have the same yield as currently issued bonds. The reverse is also true, for if investors anticipate that interest rates will rise, then they are also anticipating that bond prices will decline. This decline must occur for previously issued bonds to have the same yield as currently issued bonds. Thus if investors can anticipate the direction of change in interest rates, they can also anticipate the direction of change in the price of bonds.

Investors, however, may anticipate incorrectly and suffer losses in the bond market if they are incorrect as to the direction of change in the interest rate. If they buy bonds and interest rates rise, then the market value of the bonds must decline, and the investors will have suffered capital losses. These investors, however, have something in their favor—the bonds must ultimately be retired. Since the principal must be redeemed, an investment error in the bond market will be corrected as the bond's price rises when the bond approaches maturity. The capital losses will eventually be erased. The correction of the error, however, may take years, during which time the investors have lost the higher yields on bonds issued after their initial investments.

Anticipation of changes in interest rates can lead to profits

CONVERTIBLE BONDS

Convertible bonds are a hybrid type of security. Technically they are debt: the bonds pay interest that is a fixed obligation of the firm, and the bonds have a maturity date. But these bonds have a special feature—they may be converted into a specified number of shares of common stock. Thus the value or market price of these bonds depends on both the value of the stock and the interest that the bonds pay.

This type of bond offers the investor the advantages of debt and equity. If the price of the common stock rises, then the value of the bond must rise. The investor thus has the opportunity for capital gain should the price of the common stock rise. If, however, the price of the common stock does not appreciate, the investor still owns a debt obligation of the company on which the

Convertible bonds combine debt and equity

company must pay the interest and retire at maturity. Thus the investor has the safety of an investment in a debt instrument.

Advantages of
convertible bonds
The convertible bond also offers the firm several advantages. First, if the firm gives investors the conversion feature, it is able to issue the bond with a lower rate of interest. Second, the conversion price is set above the market price of the stock when the bond is issued. Thus when the bond is converted, the firm issued fewer shares than would have been issued if the firm had sold common stock. Therefore the current stockholders' position is less diluted by the issuing of new shares. Third, when the convertible bond is issued, the management of the firm does not anticipate having to retire the bond. Instead, management anticipates that the bond will be converted into stock, and this conversion ends the necessity to retire the debt. Fourth, when the bond is converted, the transfer of debt to common stock increases the equity base of the firm and decreases its debt ratio. Since the firm is less financially leveraged, it may be able to issue additional debt.

Were a popular
source of finance
Convertible bonds appear to offer advantages to both investors and firms, and they were a popular financing vehicle in the 1960s. Firms would issue these bonds, and, after the price of the stock rose, the bonds would be converted into the common stock of the company. The burden of debt (the interest payments and retirement) painlessly disappeared. Unfortunately the sharp decline in security prices in the 1970s means that many convertible bonds have not been converted. They still exist on the firm's balance sheet as debt and require interest payments, and they must ultimately be retired like any other type of bond. These convertible bonds obviously have not been painlessly converted into common stock, and only time will tell if retiring them will be a burden that some firms will be unable to bear.

VARIABLE INTEREST RATE BONDS

Variable instead of
fixed interest
payments
Prior to the mid-1970s, once bonds were issued the amount of interest was fixed. With the advent of increased inflation in the 1970s, corporations started issuing bonds with variable interest rates. Citicorp was the first major American firm to offer variable interest rate bonds to the general public. These bonds were not the first examples of variable interest rate bonds, however, for there had been prior issues in the United States, and variable interest rate mortgages have existed in other countries for years.

The unusual
Citicorp bond
Two features of the Citicorp bond were unique when it was issued. These are as follows: (1) a variable interest rate tied to the interest rate on Treasury bills, and (2) the right of the holder of the bond to redeem it at its face value. The interest rate of the Citicorp bond is one per cent above the average Treasury bill rate during a specified time period. When the bonds were issued, the initial interest rate paid by the bonds was 9.7 per cent. This

variability of the interest rate means that if short-term interest rates rise, then the interest rate paid by this bond will increase. The bond's owner participates in any increase in short-term interest rates. Of course, if the short term interest rates decline, then the holder of the bond will earn a lower rate of interest.

The second unique feature of the Citicorp bond is that the holder of the bond has the option to redeem the bond for its face value two years after it was issued. This option will subsequently recur every six months. Thus the holder knows that the principal can be obtained twice a year. If the holder needs the money quicker, the bond may be sold, for it is traded on the New York Bond Exchange. Thus the Citicorp bonds are very liquid debt instruments that also offer the holder an opportunity to participate in higher short-term interest rates (if they occur).

These bonds were issued in small denominations, initially in units of $5000, but they are traded in units as small as $1000. Many short-term debt instruments are issued in large denominations, such as $100,000, and that excludes the small investor. The Citicorp bonds were especially designed to attract the money of the small investor by offering an opportunity to participate through the variable interest in the high yields experienced in the short-term money market when the bonds were issued.

Designed to attract small investors

The Citicorp bond was very competitive with other short-term investments available to small investors. If an investor owns a two year certificate of deposit that earns 6 per cent, then the Citicorp bond is an attractive, alternative investment. The certificate of deposit earns more than a savings account, but, if the investor needs the money before two years elapse, a penalty is paid if the certificate of deposit is cashed. If this investor purchases the Citicorp bond, then 9.7 per cent is earned during the first year and an undetermined amount in the second year. After two years the investor may redeem the bond (just as the certificate of deposit matures). If the investor needs the money earlier, the bond may be sold on the exchange at the current market price. In this case the investor may lose some of the principal through the sale (just as interest would be lost if the certificate of deposit were to be cashed prematurely). Thus the Citicorp bond compared favorably with the certificate of deposit except that the interest in the second year was not known. However, it was very doubtful when the bonds were issued that this interest would be less than the amount paid by the certificate of deposit.

Was competitive with savings accounts

These bonds were severely criticized by savings and loan associations and other savings institutions, for the bonds initially offered investors higher yields than the savings institutions are allowed (by law) to pay. These institutions feared that deposits would be withdrawn and the money used to purchase the new bonds. Why would savers continue to place money in savings accounts if they could earn more interest and have virtually the same liquidity as the savings account? While it may not be possible to prove or disprove the fears of the savings institutions, the initial demand for the Citicorp bond was sufficient, since the company was able to sell $600,000,000 of the bonds. The success of the Citicorp issue led to imitators such as the Chase Manhattan, and there now exist several issues of similar variable interest rate bonds.

After these variable interest rate bonds were issued, short-term interest rates did decline. The Citicorp bond paid only 6.6 per cent during the second year, but that still exceeded the 6 per cent paid by the two year certificate of deposit. The decline in short-term interest rates also resulted in a decline in investor fascination with variable interest rate bonds. However, these variable interest rate debt instruments demonstrate an essential point in finance: money will flow from one investment to a more attractive alternative. This flow of funds among alternative investments may alter the money available to finance certain types of purchases. Since savings institutions primarily finance mortgages, any flow of deposits from these savings institutions reduces the credit available to finance homes. While the innovative variable interest rate bonds could not increase the total credit available, they did divert credit from the mortgage market.

RETIRING DEBT

Debt issues must ultimately be retired, and this retirement may occur on or before the maturity date of the debt. When the bond is issued, a method for periodic retirement is usually specified, for very few debt issues are retired in one lump payment at the final maturity date. Instead, part of the issue is systematically retired each year. This systematic retirement may be achieved by issuing the bond in series or by having a sinking fund.

SERIAL BONDS

Serial bonds periodically mature

In an issue of serial bonds some bonds mature each year. This type of bond is usually issued by a corporation to finance specified equipment, such as railroad cars, and the equipment is pledged as collateral. As the equipment depreciates, the cash flow generated by profits and depreciation expense is used to retire the bonds in the series as they mature.

Figure 25–3 presents an advertisement (called a tombstone) for an issue of Baltimore and Ohio Railroad equipment trust certificates. These certificates are illustrative of a serial bond. The entire issue of debt is for $7,950,000 but one-fifteenth of the certificates mature each year. The company retires $530,000 of the certificates each year as each series within the issue matures. Thus, at the end of the fifteenth year, the entire issue of certificates will have been retired.

While the Baltimore and Ohio Railroad equipment trust

NEW ISSUE   February 2, 1977

$7,950,000

Baltimore and Ohio Railroad

Equipment Trust of 1977

8% Serial Equipment Trust Certificates
(Non-callable)

These Certificates are to be dated February 1, 1977, and will mature serially in 15 annual installments of $530,000 each from February 1, 1978 to February 1, 1992, both inclusive.

Issued under the Philadelphia Plan with 20% original cash equity.

MATURITIES AND YIELDS

1978	6.00%	1983	7.65%	1988	8.00%
1979	6.55	1984	7.75	1989	8.10
1980	7.10	1985	7.85	1990	8.20
1981	7.40	1986	7.90	1991	8.20
1982	7.50	1987	8.00	1992	8.20

These Certificates are offered subject to prior sale, when, as and if issued and received by us, subject to approval of the Interstate Commerce Commission.

Merrill Lynch, Pierce, Fenner & Smith
Incorporated

The First Boston Corporation

Bache Halsey Stuart Inc.

L. F. Rothschild & Co.

Bacon, Whipple & Co.   Dain, Kalman & Quail
                                         Incorporated

J. J. B. Hilliard, W. L. Lyons, Inc.

Manley, Bennett, McDonald & Co.

Almstedt Brothers, Inc.   Burton J. Vincent, Chesley & Co.

Figure 25–3
Tombstone for a Serial Bond.

certificate is an example of a serial bond, few corporations issue serial bonds. They are primarily issued by state and local governments for capital improvements such as new school buildings. The series are then retired over a period of years by the tax revenues of the governmental unit.

SINKING FUNDS

Sinking funds are generally employed to ease the retirement of long-term corporate debt. A sinking fund is a periodic payment

A sinking fund requires a periodic payment to retire debt

for the purpose of retiring the debt issue. The payment may be made to a trustee, who invests the money to earn interest. The periodic payments plus the accumulated interest retire the debt when it matures.

Another type of sinking fund is for the firm to set aside a specified sum of money and randomly select bonds to be retired. The selected bonds are called and redeemed, and the holder

Atlantic Coast Line Railroad Company

General Mortgage 3⅝% Bonds, Series D
Due March 1, 1980

(Seaboard Coast Line Railroad Company
Successor by Merger to
Atlantic Coast Line Railroad Company)

NOTICE IS HEREBY GIVEN that, pursuant to the provisions of Section 2.01 of the Fifth Supplemental Indenture, as modified, United States Trust Company of New York, as Corporate Trustee, has drawn by lot for redemption on March 1, 1977 at 100% of their principal amount, out of moneys in the Series D Sinking Fund, $224,000 principal amount of said General Mortgage 3⅝% Bonds, Series D due March 1, 1980 bearing the following distinctive numbers:

COUPON BONDS OF $1,000 BEARING DISTINGUISHING LETTERS DM

154	1-421	1-612	2-149	3-402	3-680
184	1-443	1-644	2-189	3-426	3-711
219	1-458	1-672	2-462	3-469	3-725
224	1-476	1-697	2-503	3-478	3-755
604	1-489	1-718	2-543	3-514	3-784
914	1-513	1-730	2-575	3-532	3-824
950	1-522	1-755	2-612	3-581	3-843
1-154	1-556	1-831	2-671	3-614	3-856
1-169	1-583	1-950	2-695	3-620	3-892

FULLY REGISTERED BONDS BEARING DISTINGUISHING LETTERS RDB

Holders of the following fully registered Bonds are notified that portions thereof have been similarly called:

Bond Number	Amount Called	Bond Number	Amount Called	Bond Number	Amount Called
88	$ 2,000	229	$ 1,000	238	$ 5,000
128	1,000	230	13,000	239	6,000
174	1,000	231	9,000	240	16,000
178	1,000	232	10,000	242	2,000
206	3,000	233	15,000	244	2,000
222	2,000	235	8,000	247	3,000
223	10,000	236	38,000	251	1,000
224	18,000	237	3,000		

Holders of coupon bonds called for redemption are required to present same at the office of United States Trust Company of New York, 130 John Street, New York, New York 10038, for payment of the redemption price. Coupons due March 1, 1977 should be detached and collected in the usual manner.

Holders of fully registered bonds, of which portions have been called for redemption, are required to present and surrender same at the aforesaid office of the Corporate Trustee for payment of the redemption price on the principal amount called for redemption, and there will be issued new General Mortgage 3⅝% Bonds, Series D, of an aggregate principal amount equal to the unredeemed portions of such registered bonds surrendered. Interest payable March 1, 1977, on said fully registered bonds will be paid in the usual manner.

From and after March 1, 1977 interest on the bonds or portions thereof so called for redemption will cease to accrue.

UNITED STATES TRUST COMPANY
OF NEW YORK, *Corporate Trustee*

Dated: January 28, 1977

NOTE: Coupon Bonds Nos. 202, 2-774, 2-784, 2-785, 3-382 and 4-051, previously called for payment, have not yet been presented.

Figure 25-4

Advertisement for individual bonds being retired through a sinking fund.

must surrender the bond because it ceases to earn interest once it has been called. This type of sinking fund is illustrated by Figure 25-4, which is an advertisement taken from the *Wall Street Journal*. As can be seen, $224,000 worth of Atlantic Coast Line Railroad mortgage bonds were being retired through a sinking fund. The specific bonds being retired were selected by a lottery. Now that these bonds have been called, the owners will surrender the bonds and obtain their principal. There is no reason for the bondholders to continue to hold the bonds, for interest payments will cease. It is interesting to note at the bottom of the advertisement that some previously called bonds have not been presented for redemption. These bonds are still outstanding and are obligations of the company, but they are no longer earning interest.

REPURCHASING DEBT

If interest rates have risen and bond prices have therefore declined, a firm may seek to retire debt by purchasing it on the open market. The purchases may be made from time to time, and sellers of the bonds need not know that the company is purchasing and retiring the bonds. The company may also announce the intention to purchase and retire the bonds at a specified price. The bondholders then may tender their bonds at the specified price.

Bonds may be repurchased

The advantage of retiring debt by selling at a discount is the savings to the firm. If the firm issued $1000 bonds that are currently selling for $600, then the firm may reduce its debt by $1000 with only a $600 outlay in cash. There is a $400 saving (i.e., extraordinary gain) from purchasing and retiring the debt at a discount. For example, Trans-Lux reported to its stockholders in 1973 that it had purchased $1,000,000 worth of its convertible debentures for a price of $600,000. This generated a savings of $400,000 for the firm, which was reported as an extraordinary item on its income statement.

If bonds are purchased at a discount, an extraordinary gain will result

On the surface, this method may appear to be a desirable means to retire debt, but such appearances may be deceiving. Using money to repurchase debt is an investment decision just like buying plant and equipment. If the firm repurchases the debt, it cannot use the money for other purposes. The question is, which is the better use of the money: purchasing other income earning assets or retiring the debt? Unlike a sinking fund requirement (which management must meet), purchasing and retiring debt is a voluntary act by the firm's management. The lower the price of the debt, then the greater the potential benefit from the purchase, but the firm's management must determine if it is the best use of the firm's scarce resource—cash. For most firms the discount is not sufficient to justify purchasing the bonds. They have better alternative uses for the funds.

CALLING THE DEBT

Bonds may be
retired early
through a call

Some bonds may be called for redemption prior to maturity. If interest rates fall after a bond has been issued, then it may be advantageous for the company to issue new bonds at the lower interest rates. The proceeds then can be used to retire the older bonds with the higher interest rates. The company "calls" the older bond and retires it.

Call penalty
protects the
investor

Of course, such a refunding hurts the bondholders, who lose the higher yielding instruments. To protect these creditors, a call feature usually has a call penalty, such as a year's interest. If the initial issue had a 9 per cent interest rate, then the company would have to pay $1090 to retire $1000 worth of debt. While such a call penalty does protect bondholders, a company can still refinance if interest rates fall sufficiently to justify paying the call penalty.

Such refinancing frequently occurred during 1976, when interest yields fell significantly below the levels of the early 1970s. Utilities in particular, such as AT&T, which had issued debt with high interest rates, issued new bonds with lower interest rates, called the old debt and paid the penalty. Such refinancing sufficiently reduced the interest cost of the debt to justify paying the call penalty.

LEASING

Alternative to
owning: leasing

One important alternative source of long-term finance is leasing. Leasing is essentially renting, but while the term "renting" implies a year-to-year contract, the term "leasing" implies a contract for longer than one year. Since the contract is for more than a year, lease financing is considered to be an alternative to long-term debt as a source of finance.

A lease is a contract for the use of an asset such as plant or equipment. The firm that owns the asset (the lessee) permits the lessor to use the goods. In return the lessor enters into a contract (the lease) to make specified payments for the use of the asset. The lease is usually for a specified time period and may be renewable. In some cases the lease may be cancelled prior to its expiration date.

Leasing increases
financial leverage

The prime advantage to the lessor is the use of goods without actual ownership. Ownership remains with the lessee, who in turn must finance the asset. Thus the lessor avoids having to find finance to carry the asset. This important distinction is illustrated by the following balance sheets. Both firms initially have the same assets, liabilities, and equity.

FIRM A		FIRM B	
Assets $100	Debt $50	Assets $100	Debt $50
	Equity $50		Equity $50

Both firms decide to acquire a $50 piece of equipment. Firm A purchases the equipment and sells new debt to acquire the funds to pay for it. Firm B leases the equipment. After these transactions their respective balance sheets become as follows:

FIRM A			FIRM B	
Assets $150	Debt $100 Equity $50		Assets $100	Debt $50 Equity $50

Both firms now have the use of the equipment, but Firm A has more debt outstanding. Firm A appears to be more financially leveraged because its debt ratio is now higher. In reality, however, it is not more financially leveraged than Firm B, for Firm B also has a new contractual obligation, the lease. However, since the lease does not appear on the balance sheet, Firm B appears to be less financially leveraged.

As the above example illustrates, leasing is an alternative means to obtain the use of long-term assets. Instead of the firm using its own funds or committing itself to the terms of long-term debt, the firm commits itself to the terms of the lease. Since the lease is a fixed obligation, lease financing is comparable to debt financing.

Is an alternative to debt financing

Since leasing avoids ownership, it is frequently asserted that leasing reduces risk, especially risk associated with obsolescence through technological change. For example, if a company purchases equipment that is quickly made obsolete, then the company will still have the old equipment and hence be at a competitive disadvantage. If the company had leased the equipment instead of purchasing it, it could choose not to renew the lease and acquire new equipment. Acquiring the use of the equipment through the lease instead of purchasing made replacing the equipment easier. This reasoning has led some people to assert that leasing shifts the risk of obsolescence from the lessor to the owner, the lessee. This argument is, however, incorrect, because the lessee will seek to protect itself against the risk of loss through obsolescence by charging a higher price. If the lessee anticipates that the equipment will become obsolete, it will seek to recoup the cost of the equipment more rapidly. Hence the rental charges will be greater, which shifts the risk of loss to the user, the lessor. Thus leasing should not be justified on the grounds that it reduces risk.

But does not reduce risk

The justification for leasing rests upon whether it is the best source of finance. Acquiring the use of assets requires a source of finance. If a firm leases, it does not have to use its own funds nor does it have to borrow the funds elsewhere. Its own funds and credit sources remain available for other uses. If the firm lacks sources of finance or anticipates using its sources for other purposes, then leasing becomes an attractive alternative means to obtain the use of long-term assets.

SUMMARY

There are a variety of debt instruments that a firm may issue to obtain funds in the capital market. These debt instruments do, however, have common characteristics. The variety of types of debt and their common characteristics have been the subject of this chapter. This variety of debt instruments makes it possible for firms to issue bonds that are attractive to different types of investors. But all debt instruments are subject to risk. Even bonds that have collateral are risky because the collateral may deteriorate in value and the market price may decline if interest rates rise.

While debt instruments do subject investors to risk, they are less risky than equity instruments. Debt is an obligation of the firm. The firm must meet the terms of the indenture or be in default. Once in default, the entire debt of the company may be declared due. This threat is sufficient to force firms to attempt to meet the terms of the debt issue, thus making debt considerably safer than stock.

KEY WORDS AND TERMS

principal
maturity date
indenture
default
trustee
credit ratings
mortgage bonds
equipment trust certificate
debentures
income bonds
revenue bonds

convertible bonds
variable interest rate bonds
registered bonds
coupon bonds
coupon clippers
current yield
yield to maturity
serial bonds
sinking funds
call feature
leasing

QUESTIONS AND PROBLEMS FOR THOUGHT AND DISCUSSION

1. Given:

ISSUER OF BOND	DATE DUE	CURRENT YIELD	YIELD TO MATURITY
G. M.	1980	6.00%	8.0%
G. M.	1990	6.05%	9.0%
U. S. Government	1990	5.00%	6.5%
Lerner Stores	1980	8.10%	10.5%

How would you explain the differences in the rates of interest? What do these interest rates imply about (1) the effect of time on yields and (2) the effect of risk on yields? Rank the bonds according to risk and explain your ranking.

2. From the viewpoint of the holder of securities, what is the difference among
   (a) current yield
   (b) yield to maturity
   (c) rate of return on the investment
   When would current yield and yield to maturity be equal? When would the yield to maturity exceed the current yield? If it is generally believed that the money and credit market will be less tight, does this imply that the price of debt instruments will fall?

3. Debt must eventually be repaid. What is the difference between a serial bond issue and a bond issue with a sinking fund? If a bond issue lacks a sinking fund, how may a company retire a debt issue prior to maturity?

4. If you own a bond that pays 8 per cent (coupon rate) and matures in ten years, what is the approximate price if interest rates on comparable debt are
   (a) 6 per cent
   (b) 10 per cent
   What would be the prices if the bond matured in two years or 20 years instead of ten years? Why are these prices different?

5. Firm X has a bond outstanding with the following terms:

interest rate	10 per cent
maturity	10 years
call premium	one year's interest

   Currently the firm can issue a new bond with a ten year maturity with an 8 per cent interest rate. Should the firm call the old bond and refinance it?

Chapter 26

SOURCES OF FUNDS: EQUITY

Learning Objectives

- Isolate the features of preferred stock.
- Differentiate between preferred stock and debt financing.
- Illustrate the effect that income taxes have on cash dividends and the retention of earnings.
- Enumerate cash dividend policies.
- Explain recapitalizations: stock splits and stock dividends.
- Determine the effect of recapitalization on the wealth of stockholders.
- Describe how dividend reinvestment plans are a convenient means to accumulate shares.

"By no means run in debt: take thine own measure."

George Herbert

Equity is a major source of funds for any business. The single proprietor invests money and other assets in the business and thus has equity in the firm. Partners invest their own funds into the partnership and thus have an equity claim in the firm. Stockholders also invest their funds in corporations and have a claim on the earnings and equity of the corporation. Corporations obtain equity financing by selling stock and retaining earnings. This chapter is concerned with two aspects of corporate equity financing: preferred stock and retained earnings.

Corporations may issue and sell preferred stock to the general public to raise funds. The process of selling preferred stock is not different from the general discussion of issuing securities in Chapter 24. The discussion in the chapter covers the nature, advantages, and disadvantages of preferred stock financing.

Once corporations generate earnings, management must decide whether to retain the earnings or distribute them to stockholders. If the firm decides to retain the earnings, then it increases the stockholders' investment in the firm, which increases the ability of the firm to expand and grow. Thus the dividend policy (i.e., the policy to retain or distribute earnings) is an important aspect of equity financing. The second part of the chapter is devoted to the dividend policy of corporations and includes cash dividends, stock dividends, and stock splits.

PREFERRED STOCK

Preferred stock financing, like debt financing, is a source of financial leverage because the preferred stock pays a fixed dividend. Preferred stock, however, does not involve the legal obligations of debt, because it represents ownership. For example, the firm is not obligated to pay the fixed dividend. Thus preferred stock is a hybrid type of security that combines elements of debt and equity. Accountants treat it as equity, but, since it is a means to obtain financial leverage, preferred stock is similar to debt.

Preferred stock is similar to debt

Preferred stock is in a sense superior to common stock. Preferred stockholders are paid dividends before common stockholders, and in the case of liquidation, preferred stock is redeemed before the common stockholders receive any proceeds from the liquidation. While there is no obligation on the part of the firm to pay the preferred dividend, it is generally understood that if the firm earns sufficient profit, it will pay the dividend. However, there have been cases where the firm did earn profits and failed to pay the preferred dividends.

Preferred stock has prior claim before common stock

This section is about preferred stock; its advantages and disadvantages to the firm. The section is primarily concerned with the terms used in connection with preferred stock. While the use of preferred stock has declined because it lacks the tax advantage of debt, it is still used by utilities to raise capital.

Preferred Stock and Debt Compared

Preferred stock and debt are similar in several ways. Both instruments involve a fixed income payment to the holders. For bond holders this fixed payment is called interest; to the holders of preferred stock it is called dividends. Both bonds and preferred stock are means for the firm to obtain financial leverage, for the firm anticipates earning more on the funds obtained by issuing the securities than it is required to pay out in interest and dividends.

Bond holders and usually preferred stockholders do not have the right to vote at stockholders' meetings. Occasionally preferred stockholders have voting power. Lacking voting power, however, does not mean that bond holders and preferred stockholders lack representation. Major creditors may demand representation on the board of directors of the firm as a condition for granting the credit, and, if the preferred stock is held by a financial institution (such as an insurance company), the preferred stock may also have representation on the board of directors. Such representation may be considerably more substantive than the ability of the common stockholders to vote their shares at stockholder meetings. Thus, while bondholders and preferred stockholders may not have the power to vote, it cannot be concluded that they lack any substantive voice in the operation of the company.

While preferred stock and long term bonds are similar, their differences are significant. If the firm fails to pay the interest, the bond holders may take the firm to court to force payment of the interest or to seek liquidation of the firm (in order to protect the bondholders' principal). Preferred stockholders do not have that power, for the firm has not obligated itself to pay the dividend. If the firm should omit the preferred stock's dividend, the dividend is said to be in *arrears*. The firm does not have to remove this arrearage. In most cases, however, any omitted dividends have to be paid in the future before any dividends may be paid to the holders of the common stock. In this case the preferred stock's dividends accumulate; it is a *cumulative preferred*. Most preferred stock is cumulative, but there are examples of preferred stocks that are not. These are called *non cumulative*. For firms in financial difficulty, the difference between cumulative and non cumulative may be immaterial. Forcing the firm to pay dividends to erase the arrearage may further weaken the firm and hurt the owner of the preferred stock more than foregoing the dividend would. Once the firm has regained its profitability, erasing the arrearage may become important not only to holders of the stock but also to the company that wants to demonstrate its improved financial condition.

An example of a firm clearing the arrearage on its preferred stock is Ling Temco Vought (LTV). Dividends were suspended on the Series A Preferred Stock in 1970. The dividends accumulated for several years. Then LTV offered to exchange the preferred stock for common stock. If the preferred stockholders had accepted the offer, they would have received newly issued common stock, the preferred stock would have been cancelled, and the arrearage would cease. These stockholders, however, rejected the offer. After this rejection, LTV paid $22.50 per share in 1975 to erase the arrearage. Obviously any speculator who

Preferred stock rarely has voting rights

Differences between preferred stock and debt

(1) Arrears is not default

purchased the shares when they were selling for about $20 was well rewarded for taking that risk.

The most important difference between debt and preferred stock is that interest on debt is a tax-deductible expense while the dividend on the preferred stock is not. Preferred dividends are paid out of profit. If the corporate income tax rate is 48 per cent, then the firm must earn $1.92 before taxes in order to pay a $1.00 preferred dividend. The before tax earnings necessary to pay the preferred dividends may be found by dividing the cash dividend by 1 and then subtracting the firm's marginal tax rate. In this case, to pay the dollar dividend, the firm must earn before taxes:

$$\$1/(1- .48) = \$1.92$$

Financing with preferred stock is much more expensive than financing with debt because of the tax laws. The ability to treat the interest on debt as a tax deductible expense strongly argues in favor of debt financing instead of preferred stock to obtain financial leverage.

A third difference between debt and preferred stock is the retirement of the issue. Debt eventually must be retired, while preferred stock may be perpetual. Once the preferred stock is issued, the firm may never have to concern itself with the retirement of the preferred stock. This may be both an advantage and a disadvantage. Since the firm may never have to retire the preferred stock, it does not have to generate the money to retire it. The firm may instead use its funds elsewhere (e.g., to purchase plant and equipment). However, should the firm ever want to change its capital structure and substitute cheaper debt financing for the preferred stock, the firm may have difficulty in retiring the preferred stock. The firm may have to purchase the preferred stock on the open market, and in order to induce the holders to sell the preferred shares, the firm will probably have to bid up the price of the preferred stock. If the firm does not want to pay cash for the preferred stock, it may offer these stockholders the option of trading the preferred stock for some other security, such as common stock or debt (as LTV did in the above example). This will also probably require generous terms to induce the preferred stockholders to trade their preferred shares.

To give the firm some control over the preferred stock, it may seek to add to the preferred issue a call feature. This gives the firm the option to call and redeem the issue. While the actual terms of this call feature will vary with each preferred stock issue, the general features are similar. First, the call is at the option of the firm. Second, the call price is specified. Third, the firm may pay a call penalty (e.g., a year's dividends). Fourth, after the issue is called, future dividend payments will cease; this, of course, forces any recalcitrant holders to surrender their

(2) Dividends are not a deductible expense

(3) Perpetuity

Call feature may force retirement

stock. Such a feature gives the firm the option to retire the preferred stock in the future should financial conditions warrant the retiring of the issue.

PREFERRED STOCK: SUMMARY

Preferred stock is an inferior means to obtain financial leverage. While preferred stock is less risky than debt, corporations prefer debt financing because of the tax advantage. Thus the use of preferred stock financing declined. It now accounts for less than 5 per cent of the total corporate securities issued. However, there has been a notable increase recently as some firms have issued preferred stock to improve their debt ratios. Since preferred stock is equity, issuing preferred stock reduces the debt ratio.

The primary users of preferred stock are utilities and smaller companies who sell the preferred stock to financial institutions. Corporations such as insurance companies are willing to purchase preferred stock, primarily because of the tax laws. Only 15 per cent of these dividends are subject to federal corporate income tax. For other investors, preferred stock offers neither the safety of debt nor the growth potential of common stock. There has developed recently a different type of preferred stock that is convertible into the common stock of the company. This security, however, is really a variation of the convertible bond. It offers the investor a fixed income (the dividend) and possible capital gains if the price of stock (into which the preferred stock may be converted) rises in value.

DIVIDEND POLICY

Earnings are distributed or retained

After a corporation has earned profits, it must decide what to do with these profits: to retain them or distribute them in cash dividends. If the firm retains its earnings, it will put the funds to work by purchasing income-earning assets. This will permit the firm to grow and pay larger dividends in the future. Such retention of earnings increases the equity of the stockholders in the firm and causes the degree of financial leverage to fall (unless the firm simultaneously increases its borrowings). Such a decrease in the degree of financial leverage may be desirable, for it may reduce the riskiness of the firm and increase its future borrowing capacity. Retaining earnings thus increases the ability of the firm to finance additional growth by increasing the equity base of the firm and its borrowing capacity.

Which is the better use of funds?

If management seeks to minimize the wealth of the stockholders, then the dividend decision basically depends upon who has the better use for the money, the stockholders or the firm. Management, however, may not know the stockholders' alternative uses for the money or may choose to ignore the stockholders' alleged uses. Stockholders who do not like the dividend policy of the firm may then seek to sell their shares. The act of selling the shares will depress the price of the stock (if the sellers exceed the buyers), and thus management will be made aware of investors' attitudes toward the dividend policy. Certainly the investors in Consolidated Edison indicated dissatisfaction in 1974 when the management discontinued the cash dividends. Not only did angry stockholders voice their opinions at the annual stockholders' meeting, but they also sought to sell the stock. This selling caused its price to decline drastically within three weeks, from $18 to $7⅝ per share.

Dividends and Income Taxes

An institutional factor, federal income taxes, strongly argues for the retention of earnings at the expense of cash dividends. Dividend income is treated as ordinary income and is taxed at income tax rates. Long-term capital gains are given special tax treatment, for they generally are taxed at one-half the tax rate on ordinary income. If a company is able to reinvest its earnings and grow, then, when the investor sells the shares at a higher price (that reflects the growth), the profits from the sale are taxed at the lower long-term capital gains tax rates.

Tax laws favor retention

The following example illustrates how federal income taxes favor the retention of earnings. The example assumes that the stockholder's income tax bracket is 30 per cent and that the firm earns $100 each year. Case A illustrates the retention of earnings and the growth of the investor's investment in the firm.

Case A   Initial Capital $1000

	EARNINGS	EARNINGS RETAINED	STOCKHOLDER'S INVESTMENT
Year 1	$100	$100	$1100
Year 2	100	100	1200
Year 3	100	100	1300
Year 4	100	100	1400

After four years, the capital of the investor has grown to $1400. If the shares are sold for $1400, the investor has a long term capital gain of $400 ($1400 − $400), which is taxed at the long-term capital gains tax rate. Since, for most investors, this tax rate is one-half the individual's income tax rate, the appropriate capital gains tax rate is 15 per cent. The investor thus pays $60 ($400 × .15) in taxes and nets $340 after tax. The total value of the assets (the initial capital and the net capital gains) is $1340.

In Case B the firm distributes the annual earnings of $100 in cash dividends. The investor then pays the personal income tax of $30 ($100 × .30) and thus nets $70 after tax. After four years the stockholder will have received $400 in cash dividends, paid $120 in income taxes, and netted $280. The value of the total investment is $1280 ($1000 + $280), which is less than the $1340 the investor had after the long term capital gain was taxed at the lower capital gains tax rate.

Case B   Initial Capital $1000

	EARNINGS	EARNINGS RETAINED	STOCKHOLDER'S INVESTMENT
Year 1	$100	0	$1000
Year 2	100	0	1000
Year 3	100	0	1000
Year 4	100	0	1000

	DIVIDENDS	INCOME TAX	AFTER TAX DIVIDEND INCOME
Year 1	$100	$30	$70
Year 2	100	30	70
Year 3	100	30	70
Year 4	100	30	70
		Total:	$280

As may be seen from the above two cases, the long-term capital gains tax laws argue for the retention of earnings at the expense of the distribution of earnings in the form of cash dividends. In the above examples the difference in taxation amounted to $60. This difference would have been larger had the investor been in a higher income tax bracket and had thus lost a larger percentage of the dividend income to taxes. The differences, however, would have been smaller if the investor could have invested the dividends elsewhere and earned more than the firm earned on the retained earnings. Thus an investor could be better off by receiving the earnings if the stockholder has excellent use for the money that overcomes the difference in the tax rates.

Many investors do not have such excellent uses for the money. Thus the retention of earnings is frequently considered to be consistent with the goal of management to maximize the wealth of the stockholders. After the firm retains earnings and achieves growth, investors may be able to sell their shares and realize capital gains which will be taxed at the more favorable long-term capital gains tax rates.

Earnings Retention and Growth

Growth in earnings may lead to growth in stock price

During the 1960s dividend policy was not a major concern of management. This was a period of emphasis on growth and retention of earnings by the firm to finance that growth. Man-

TABLE 26–1   Earnings Per Share and Hi-Low Stock Prices for 1964–1972 for IBM, Johnson and Johnson, and Xerox. (Source: *Moody's Handbook of Common Stocks,* Fourth Quarter, 1976.)

YEAR	IBM		JOHNSON AND JOHNSON		XEROX	
	Earnings Per Share	Hi-Low Stock Price	Earnings Per Share	Hi-Low Stock Price	Earnings Per Share	Hi-Low Stock Price
1964	$3.20	$128–105	$.48	$13–10	$.63	$44–23
1965	3.52	142–105	.57	19–12	.93	71–31
1966	3.77	150–112	.67	22–15	1.24	89–41
1967	4.64	259–141	.76	32–18	1.48	104–65
1968	6.17	300–224	.91	36–24	1.73	109–76
1969	6.57	295–233	1.06	60–33	2.07	115–80
1970	7.10	309–175	1.50	60–37	2.39	115–65
1971	7.50	292–226	1.82	99–56	2.71	126–84
1972	8.82	341–265	2.15	133–94	3.16	171–120
Approximate annual rate of growth of earnings per share	14%		20%		20%	
Approximate annual rate of growth of stock price	12%		32%		19%	

agement retained as much of the earnings as it believed necessary to finance growth, and any residual was paid to stockholders. As may be seen in Table 26–1, it was a period of spectacular growth by major firms such as IBM, Xerox, and Johnson and Johnson. From 1964 to 1972 their earnings per share annually grew approximately 14 per cent, 20 per cent, and 20 per cent, respectively. Investors in these growth-oriented companies were rewarded as the price of the stocks rose at approximate compounded growth rates of 14 per cent, 19 per cent, and 32 per cent, respectively, in response to growing earnings. Obviously the best use of the corporate funds was to finance growth, for few investors had better alternative uses for the money. These stockholders were well rewarded for foregoing current dividend income.

With the onset of inflation in the 1970s and the increase in interest rates, dividend policy became more important. Investors had several potential uses for funds such as physical goods, whose prices investors anticipated would continue to rise or bonds that were yielding historically high interest rates. Investors had obvious alternative uses for the money earned by companies. Failure on the part of corporations to pay cash dividends or increase the dividends in response to increased earnings played a role in the decline of security prices experienced during 1973 and 1974. The dividend policy of the firm became more important to investors as they viewed the return on their investments to include not only the growth in the value of the shares but also the dividend return.

CASH DIVIDENDS

Various dividend
policies

Companies that pay cash dividends usually have a stated policy that is known by the investment community. Most American companies that pay cash dividends pay a regular cash dividend on a quarterly basis. A few companies make monthly distributions (e.g., Winn Dixie and Wrigley), and some make the distribution semiannually or annually. Frequently, in the case of semiannual and annual payments, the dollar amount is small. Instead of paying 2½ cents a share quarterly, the company pays 10 cents, which reduces the expense of distributing the dividend.

Regular quarterly
dividends

While most companies with cash dividend policies pay regular quarterly dividends, there are other types of dividend policies. Some companies pay quarterly dividends plus extras. GM pays a quarterly dividend but distributes extras twice a year if the company has a good year. Such a policy is appropriate for a firm in a cyclical industry because earnings fluctuate over time, and the firm may be hard pressed to maintain a higher level of regular quarterly dividends. By having a set cash payment, supplemented with extras in good years, the firm is able not only to maintain a fixed payment that is relatively assured but also to supplement the dividend in good years.

Payout ratio:
dividends to
earnings

Management may view the dividend policy as a distribution of a certain proportion of the earnings. The ratio of dividends to earnings is the payout ratio, which gives the proportion of the earnings the firm is distributing. For some firms this ratio has remained rather stable, which seems to indicate that management views the best dividend policy in terms of a particular payout ratio.

Irregular dividends

Some firms pay cash dividends that are irregular; there is no set dividend payment. For example, to maintain favorable tax treatment real estate investment trusts are required by law to distribute their earnings. These earnings fluctuate, thus causing the cash dividends to fluctuate. The special tax laws pertaining to these trusts then causes the trusts to have irregular dividend payments.

As earnings grow,
so may dividends

As the earnings of the company grow, the firm is able to increase its cash dividend. There is, however, a reluctance to increase the cash dividend immediately with an increase in earnings. Thus increases in dividends tend to lag after increases in earnings. The cause for this lag is management's reluctance to reduce cash dividends if earnings decline. Management apparently fears that the reduction will be interpreted as a sign of financial weakness. The reluctance to cut dividends has resulted in a tendency for management to raise dividends only when it is certain that the higher level of earnings will be maintained. If the higher level of earnings is maintained, then an increase in the dividend may be justified.

Most companies announce their dividend policy. There are many areas of a firms's operation about which investors know little and perhaps would not understand even if they did know. The dividend policy of the firm is readily understood and may have an important effect on the investors' attitude toward the firm. Some stockholders seek a flow of income from their investments and prefer stocks that pay generous cash dividends. These investors will purchase stock in companies that pay out a large proportion of the firm's earnings. Other investors prefer capital gains and purchase stocks of companies that retain earnings to finance growth. Investors need to know the firm's dividend policy. Thus it is advisable that the firm announce its dividend policy, and most firms do.

Dividend policy is usually stated

The process by which dividends are distributed takes time. The first step is the dividend meeting by the firm's directors. If they decide to distribute a cash dividend, two important dates are established. The first date determines who is to receive the dividend. On a particular day the ownership books of the corporation are closed, and everyone owning stock in the company at the end of that day receives the dividend. This is called the day of record. If the stock is purchased after the date of record, the purchaser does not receive the dividend. The stock is purchased excluding the dividend; this is referred to as *ex dividend*, for the price of the stock does not include the dividend payment. The ex dividend day is five working days before the date of record because the settlement date is five days after the transaction. In the financial papers purchases of the stock on the ex dividend day are indicated by an X. The following entry taken from the *Wall Street Journal* indicates that the stock of Sun Company traded on that day exclusive of the dividend.

The mechanics of dividend distribution

The \$.50 (i.e., \$2.00/4) quarterly dividend will be paid to the owners of record of the previous day and not to the investors who purchased the stock on the ex dividend day. In this example there was a net change of ¼ in the price of the stock for the ex dividend day. This indicates that the closing price on the previous day was \$47⅝ and not \$47⅛ as may be expected from the increase of ¼ for the day. Since the current buyers will not receive the \$.50 dividend, the net change in the price of the stock is reduced for the dividend. The net change is figured from the adjusted price (i.e., \$47⅝ minus the \$.50 dividend).

–1976-77– High	Low	Stocks	Div.	P-E Ratio	Sales 100s	High	Low	Close	Net Chg.
		– A–A–A –							
50½	30½	StW pfA	1.40	..	58	49⅞	49¼	49¼	......
6½	3⅜	SuavSho	.08e	5	50	5	4¾	4⅞	......
24⅞	14⅝	SubPrG	1.08	8	131	24⅛	23⅝	24	......
34¾	11¼	SunChm	.40	9	85	34⅜	33⅜	34	+ ½
49	26⅞	SunCo	2	6	x135	47⅜	47	47⅜	+ ¼
51	31¼	SunCo	pf2.25	..	x102	49⅝	49	49⅜	+ ⅜
28¼	20⅝	Sunbm	1.08	10	19	23¼	23	23⅛	+ ⅛
37⅛	17	Sundstr	1	8	50	34¼	33¾	34⅛	– ⅜
13⅛	9½	SunsMg	.18r	31	38	11½	11⅛	11¼	......

Selected quotations from the New York Stock Composite of security transactions. (Reprinted with permission of Dow-Jones, Inc.)

The second important date is the day that the dividend is distributed, or the distribution date. The distribution day may be several weeks after the record date, as the company must determine the owners on the record date and process the checks. The company may not perform this task itself; instead it uses its commercial bank, for which service the bank charges a fee. The final day that the dividend is received by the stockholder is thus likely to be many weeks after the board of directors announced the dividend payment.

STOCK DIVIDENDS

Stock dividends do not increase earning potential of the firm

Some firms make a practice of paying stock dividends in addition to or in lieu of cash dividends. Unfortunately the recipients frequently misunderstand what they are receiving. Stock dividends are a form of *recapitalization* and do *not* increase the assets of the firm. Since the assets and how they are managed produce income for the firm, a stock dividend does not by itself increase the potential earning power of the firm. Investors, however, may believe that stock dividends will enhance the earning capacity of the firm and the value of the stock. They mistakenly believe that the stock dividend increases the firm's assets.

In order to facilitate the demonstration of the stock dividend, the following simple balance sheet will be used:

ASSETS		LIABILITIES AND EQUITY	
Total Assets	$10,000,000	Total Liabilities	$2,500,000
		Equity: $2 par	2,000,000
		common stock	
		(2,000,000 shares	
		authorized; 1,000,000	
		outstanding)	
		Additional	500,000
		Paid in Capital	
		Retained Earnings	5,000,000

Assets, liabilities, and total equity are unaffected

Since a stock dividend is only a recapitalization, the assets and liabilities are not affected by the declaring and paying of the stock dividend. What are affected are the entries in the equity section of the balance sheet. The stock dividend transfers amounts from retained earnings to common stock and additional paid in capital. The amount transferred depends on (1) the number of new shares issued through the stock dividend and (2) the market price of the stock. If the above company issued a 10 per cent stock dividend when the price of the common stock was $20 a share, this would cause the issuing of 100,000 shares with a value of $2,000,000. This amount is subtracted from the retained earnings and transferred to the common stock and additional paid in capital. The amount transferred to common stock will be 100,000 times the par value of the stock

($2 × 100,000 = $200,000). The remaining amount ($1,800,000) is transferred to additional paid in capital. The balance sheet then becomes:

ASSETS		LIABILITIES AND EQUITY	
Total Assets	$10,000,000	Total Liabilities	$2,500,000
		Equity: $2 par common stock (2,000,000 shares authorized; 1,100,000 outstanding)	2,200,000
		Additional Paid in Capital	2,300,000
		Retained Earnings	3,000,000

The stock dividend is said to have transferred funds from retained earnings to the "permanent capital" of the firm. This statement is misleading, for no funds (or money) have been transferred. There has been an increase in the number of shares outstanding, but there has been no increase in cash and no increase in assets that may be used to earn profits. All that has happened is a recapitalization: the equity entries have been altered.

The stock dividend does not increase the wealth of the stockholder but does increase the number of shares owned. In the above example, a stockholder who owned 100 shares before the stock dividend has stock worth $2000. After the stock dividend this stockholder owns 110 shares, and the 110 shares are also worth $2000, for the price per share falls from $20 to $18.18. Why does the price of the stock fall? The answer is that there are 10 per cent more shares outstanding, but there has been no increase in the firm's assets and earning power. The old shares have been *diluted* and hence the price of the stock must decline to indicate this dilution. If the price of the stock did not fall, all companies could make their stockholders wealthier by declaring stock dividends. While it may be possible to fool some of the people some of the time, they cannot be fooled all of the time. Investors would soon realize that the stock dividend does not increase the assets and earning power of the firm, and hence investors would not be willing to pay the old price for a larger number of shares. The market price would fall to adjust to the dilution of the old shares, and that is exactly what happens.

The major misconception concerning the stock dividend is that it increases the ability of the firm to grow. If the stock dividend is a substitute for a cash dividend, then the statement is partially true because the firm still has the asset cash that would be paid to stockholders if a cash dividend had been declared. The firm, however, will still have the cash if it does not pay the stock dividend, for a firm may retain its cash and not pay a stock dividend. Hence the decision to pay the stock dividend does not increase the firm's cash; it is the decision not to pay the cash

Stockholders' wealth is unaltered

dividend that conserves the cash. When a stock dividend is paid in lieu of cash, it may even be interpreted as a screen; the stock dividend is hiding the failure to pay cash dividends.

Perhaps the primary advantage of the stock dividend is to bring to the current stockholders' attention the fact that the firm is retaining its cash in order to grow and that the stockholders will be rewarded through the retention of assets and increased earning capacity of the firm. By retaining the assets, the firm may be able to earn more than the stockholders are able to earn, which will increase the price of the stock in the future. However this same result may be achieved without the expense of the stock dividend.

THE STOCK SPLIT

Stock splits are similar to stock dividends

After the price of a stock has risen substantially, management may choose to split the stock. This split will lower the price of the stock and make it more accessible to investors. Implicit in this statement is the belief that investors prefer lower priced shares and that reducing the price of the stock will benefit the current stockholders by widening the market for their stock.

Like the stock dividend, the stock split is a recapitalization. It does not affect the assets or liabilities of the firm. It does not increase the earning power of the firm, and the wealth of the stockholder is not increased unless other investors prefer lower priced stocks and hence increase the demand for this stock.

The balance sheet used above for illustrating the stock dividend will now be employed to demonstrate a two for one stock split. In a two for one stock split one old share becomes two new shares, and the par value of the stock is halved. There are no changes in the additional paid in capital or retained earnings. All that has happened is there are now twice as many shares outstanding and each share is worth half as much as an old share.

ASSETS		LIABILITIES AND EQUITY	
Total Assets	$10,000,000	Total Liabilities	$2,500,000
		Equity: $1 par common stock (2,000,000 shares authorized; 2,000,000 shares outstanding)	2,000,000
		Additional Paid in Capital	500,000
		Retained Earnings	5,000,000

The reverse split

Stock splits may be any combination of terms, as can be seen in Table 26–2, which gives the terms of several recent stock splits. Two for one splits are the most common, and occasionally there is a reverse split (e.g., the Atlas Corporation one for five split),

TABLE 26–2   Selected Stock Splits Declared or Distributed in 1976

COMPANY	TERMS OF THE SPLIT
Ralston Purina	3 for 1
Norfolk and Western	3 for 1
Hilton Hotels	2 for 1
Automatic Data Processing	2 for 1
Diamond Shamrock	2 for 1
Eckerd Drugs	3 for 2
Allegheny Ludlum	3 for 2
American Family Corporation	5 for 4
Gulf and Western	5 for 4
Atlas Corporation	1 for 5

which reduces the number of shares and raises the price of the stock. An easy method for finding the price of the stock after the split is to multiply the stock price before the split by the reciprocal of the terms of the split. For example, if a stock is selling for $54 a share and is split 3 for 2, then the price of the stock after the split will be $54 \times \frac{2}{3} = $36.

Stock splits, like stock dividends, do not by themselves increase the wealth of the stockholder, for the stock split does not increase the assets and earning power of the firm. The split does decrease the price of the stock and thereby may increase the marketability of the stock. Thus the split stock may cause a wider distribution of ownership and increase investor interest in the company. This wider distribution may increase the wealth of the current stockholders over time. For example, it may have been rumored that a car manufacturer would split its shares to increase the distribution of the shares. This increase in the distribution may then increase interest in the product and lead to larger sales. These larger sales may result in higher profits and future increases in the price of the stock. If such a scenario were to occur, then the current stockholders may be benefited from the split, but the source of price increase in the stock is still the increase in earnings and not the stock split.

Stock splits do not increase the wealth of stockholders

DIVIDEND REINVESTMENT PLANS

Many corporations that pay cash dividends also have dividend reinvestment programs. These permit stockholders to have cash dividends used to purchase additional shares of stock. Dividend reinvestment programs started in the 1960s, but the growth in the programs occurred in the early 1970s.

There are two types of dividend reinvestment programs. In most plans a bank acts on behalf of the corporation and its stockholders. The bank collects the cash dividends for the stockholders and in some plans offers the stockholders the option of making additional cash contributions. The bank pools all the

Dividend reinvestment plans are a convenient means to accumulate shares

funds and purchases the stock on the open market. Since the
bank is able to purchase a larger block of shares, the bank receives a substantial reduction in the per share commission cost of
the purchase. This reduced brokerage fee is spread over all the
shares purchased by the bank. Thus the smallest investor to the
largest investor receives the advantage of the reduced brokerage
fees. The bank does charge a fee for its service, but this fee is
usually modest and does not offset the potential savings in
brokerage fees.

In the second type of reinvestment plan, the company issues
new shares of stock, and the money is directly rechanneled to the
company. The investor may also have the option of making
additional cash contributions. This type of plan offers the investor an additional advantage in that the brokerage fees are entirely
circumvented. The entire amount of the cash dividend is used to
purchase shares with the cost of issuing the shares being paid by
the company. There are fewer examples of this type of dividend
reinvestment plan, but since AT&T recently instituted such a
program, there may be increased use of this type of dividend
reinvestment program by other companies.

Stockholders are
"forced" to save

Besides the potential savings in brokerage fees, the major
advantage to investors of dividend reinvestment programs is the
"forced savings." Since the investor never receives the cash, he
is forced to save. Such forced saving may be desirable for investors who wish to save but have a tendency to spend money once it
is received. The programs also offer advantages to the firm. They
create goodwill and may result in some cost savings (e.g., lower
costs of preparing and mailing dividend checks). The shares
accumulated by stockholders are more likely to be retained by
these stockholders and may produce support for the price of the
company's stock. The reinvestment plans that result in the new
issue of stock increase the company's equity base and are a
source of working capital.

REPURCHASE OF STOCK

A firm with excess cash may choose to repurchase some of its
outstanding shares of stock. The effect of such an act is to decrease the number of shares outstanding. This will increase the
earnings per share and increase the degree of financial leverage
employed by the firm.

Repurchasing stock
is an alternative use
of funds

The repurchasing of shares is another example of the question of selecting among alternatives. The company may repurchase the shares because the management may believe that it is
the best use of the money. The shares may then be used in the
future in merger agreements or for the exercising of stock op-
tions. Repurchases also occur because firms believe that the
price of their shares is too low, and hence the shares are under-

valued. Repurchasing the shares then is viewed as the best investment currently available to the firm.

The repurchasing of shares may be viewed as an alternative to the paying of cash dividends. Instead of distributing the money as cash dividends, the firm offers to purchase the shares from the stockholders. This offers the stockholders several advantages. First, they have the option to sell or retain their shares. If the stockholders believe that the firm's potential is sufficient to warrant retention of the shares, they do not have to sell their shares. The option to sell the shares rests with the stockholder. Second, if the shares are sold to the company, any resulting gains may be taxed as capital gains (providing the stockholder has owned the shares for a sufficient length of time). If the company had distributed the earnings as cash dividends, then the dividends would have been taxed as ordinary income to the recipient. Since the tax rates on income exceed the tax rates on long-term capital gains, the repurchasing of shares instead of distributing cash dividends will produce tax savings for stockholders who do sell their shares.

An excellent example of the repurchasing shares is Zapata Corporation. The company sold part of its operations for a large, nonrecurring profit. The company received cash in partial payment and had to decide what to do with it. Part of the money was used for investment purposes, but the company also offered to repurchase some of its outstanding shares. When the announcement was made, the price of the stock was $19⅛. The company offered a price of $25, which was significantly above the market price of the stock. The higher price was, of course, an inducement to holders to sell their shares. Many stockholders did sell their shares back to the company to take advantage of the company's offer.

The Zapata Corporation repurchase occurred after the firm received the proceeds from the nonrecurring sale of part of its operations. Other firms, however, have considerable amount of cash and other liquid assets from their operations. This excess cash may be used to repurchase the firm's stock. The largest such repurchase occurred during February and March of 1977 when IBM offered to buy four million shares at $280 each. The total cost of repurchasing four million shares would exceed a billion dollars. However, even though the bid price of $280 exceeded the current market price, only 2.5 million shares (less than 2 per cent of IBM's outstanding stock) were offered for sale. Many IBM stockholders obviously preferred their shares to the cash.

SUMMARY

This chapter has covered preferred stock and dividend policy. Preferred stock is similar to debt, for it is a source of financial leverage. However, since preferred stock is equity, it does represent ownership in the corporation. While preferred stock financing is less risky than debt financing (because the dividends are not a legal obligation of the company), the use of preferred stock financing has declined. The prime cause of this decline is that preferred stock financing is more expensive than debt financing. The interest on debt is a tax deductible expense, but the dividends on the preferred stock are paid from earnings after taxes.

Cash dividends are a distribution of the corporation's earnings. If the firm does not distribute its earnings through cash dividends, then the firm's retained earnings are increased. This increases the investors' equity in the firm and permits an expansion of the firm's assets. Such retention of earnings may increase future earnings and enhance the value of the stockholders' investment.

Some firms pay stock dividends, thus increasing the number of shares the firm has outstanding. Such dividends are perceptibly different than cash dividends. Cash dividends require the payment of money to the stockholders, while stock dividends (and stock splits) are recapitalizations. Stock dividends and stock splits do not change the firm's assets and liabilities and hence do not alter its earning power.

KEY WORDS AND TERMS

cumulative preferred   distribution date
arrears   recapitalization
convertible preferred   stock dividend
cash dividends   stock split
payout ratio   dilution
day of record   dividend reinvestment plans
ex dividend

QUESTIONS AND PROBLEMS FOR THOUGHT AND DISCUSSION

1. Which dividend policy, a constant payout or stable dollar amount, would you prefer a firm to follow? Which policy would a retired person prefer? Would you prefer stock dividends to cash? Would the retired person prefer stock or cash dividends?

2. Go to your library and determine the growth in earnings per share of Dow Chemical for 1966–1975. What happened to the stock's price during this time period? What happened to the cash dividend during this time period? What proportion of

the firm's earnings were distributed each year? Is there a pattern in the dividend payout?

3. Why does the price of a stock decline after a 10 per cent stock dividend? What happens to the earnings per share? Why is there no effect on the firm's capacity to earn?

4. Preferred stock is equity, but from a financial viewpoint it is a source of financial leverage. Why? If you were an investor, why may you prefer the preferred stock to the common stock? Do bonds offer you the same advantages?

5. Firm A had the following items on its balance sheet:

Cash $18,000,000   Retained earnings $42,000,000
                     Common stock (2,000,000
                       shares, $50 par) $100,000,000

How would each of these accounts appear after
(a) a cash dividend of $1 per share?
(b) a 5 per cent stock dividend (fair market value is $60 per share)?
(c) a 1 for 2 reverse split?

6. The equation for the valuation of equity presented on page 326 was $P_e = D/(k_e - g)$. Using this equation, explain how the following may affect the price of the stock:
(a) A stock dividend
(b) An increase in the cash dividend
(c) An increase in interest rates
(d) An increase in the number of shares outstanding.

Chapter 27   SPECIAL TOPICS

Learning Objectives

- Isolate the types and causes of mergers.
- Enumerate the terms of a merger agreement.
- Differentiate between pooling and purchase methods of accounting.
- List the advantages offered by foreign investments.
- Identify the sources of risk associated with foreign investment.
- Illustrate how hedging may reduce risk of loss from fluctuating currency values.
- Isolate the causes of bankruptcy.
- Determine the order of payment in a bankruptcy liquidation.
- Explain why creditors may accept reorganization instead of liquidation of a bankrupt firm.

"We have forty million reasons for failure, but not a single excuse."

Rudyard Kipling

This chapter is primarily devoted to a firm's growth through mergers and foreign operations. However, many firms do not achieve growth and some even contract. Business failure is common among small firms; thus the last section is devoted to bankruptcy.

Mergers, multinational operations, and bankruptcy are all involved topics, and many schools of business devote entire courses to each. This chapter can only touch on some of the financial topics in each area. The section on mergers stresses types of mergers, their causes, and the different methods used by accountants to combine the firm's assets and liabilities. The segment on multinational firms is primarily devoted to the risks associated with foreign investments. The final part of the chapter considers bankruptcy and the reorganization of a firm and explains why creditors may be willing to accept such reorganization.

CAUSES AND TYPES OF MERGERS

Firms may expand by external as well as by internal growth.   External growth
Firms grow internally by retaining earnings and using their cash
flow to replace and expand plant and equipment. Firms expand through external growth by purchasing or merging with
an existing firm. This section is devoted to such external growth
and will briefly consider the causes of external growth and different types of mergers. The subsequent sections will discuss
how the combination of two firms may be accomplished and how
the balance sheets of the two firms are combined.

There are several reasons for external growth. First, if a firm   Reasons for
seeks to enter an industry, there are the start-up costs. The firm   mergers
must plan for the entry and contract for the plant and equipment.
This process may be not only expensive but also time consuming. The span of time from the decision to enter a new field to the
actual production and sales of the output may be many years.
Purchasing an existing firm will significantly reduce the time
necessary to enter the industry and may reduce the cost of entry.
Second, entry into a new industry has risk and is uncertain of
success. While management will not enter a new line of business
unless it anticipates earning profits, success is not assured. For
example, RCA entered the computer industry to compete with
IBM and Sperry Rand (the maker of Univac). Even though RCA
had previously been a leader in electronics, it failed to compete
successfully with the established computer firms and suffered
one of the largest losses ever incurred by a corporation. By
purchasing or merging with an existing, profitable firm, this
uncertainty and risk of loss is reduced. Third, when a firm enters
a new industry, it increases the number of firms within the
industry. This increases the element of competition and may
reduce the level of profits for all firms in the industry. Such an
increase in competition may not occur if the entering firm purchases or merges with an existing firm. Fourth, by external
growth, the firm may immediately increase its earnings per
share, and the increase in the per share earnings may in turn
increase the price of the firm's stock.

Mergers may also be justified on the grounds that the com-   Synergism
bined firm is stronger than the two individual firms. This is
called synergism. Synergism may occur when two firms with
different but complementary strengths are merged so that the
resulting firm is stronger than the sum of its parts. For example, if
one firm has a strong marketing department while another firm
has excellent product facilities but lacks marketing skills, then a
merger of the two firms may produce a firm that is stronger than
the individual firms were previous to the merger. Combining the
marketing proficiency and the production capabilities may result
in synergism. Such synergism was frequently used to justify

mergers during the merger movement of the 1960s. Firms with low profitability would be taken over on the grounds that the management of the company doing the take over could "turn around" the unprofitable firm. While it may be impossible to verify that such synergism did exist, it is an intuitively appealing explanation (or perhaps rationalization) for a firm to take over and absorb another firm.

Classification of mergers: (1) horizontal; (2) vertical

Mergers may be classified into three types: horizontal, vertical, and conglomerate. Mergers of two firms within the same industry (i.e., that produce the same products) are horizontal mergers. Thus the merger of the New York Central and the Pennsylvania Railroads was an example of a horizontal merger. Vertical mergers involve the merging of two firms in different aspects of the same industry, especially when one of the firms is a supplier for the other firm. If an automobile manufacturer merged with a producer of automobile parts, that is a vertical merger. Another example is the merger of a steel mill with an ore producer. Since steel mills buy iron ore to produce steel, the producer of the ore is one of the steel mill's suppliers. If a steel mill merged with a metal fabricator, that also is a vertical merger because the steel mill sells its product to the fabricator. Many mergers are vertical mergers, since firms seek to assure themselves of supplies of raw materials and merge with firms that are suppliers of these materials. Thus, during the energy crisis, firms that were dependent on sources of fuel would purchase suppliers. Hence coal producers became likely candidates for mergers as coal users bought coal companies to assure a supply of coal.

(3) Conglomerate

In the 1960s there developed a different type of merger between firms with diverse product lines. These conglomerations were named "conglomerate mergers," and in many cases there was no apparent relationship between the two firms. For example, Greyhound, the leader in cross-country bus transportation, took over Armour (a meat packing firm) and Dial (soaps). Public transportation and consumer products are entirely different industries, but such mergers are typical of the conglomerate merger movement. Many firms that currently have diverse product lines grew through such mergers. For example, Gulf and Western has operations in leisure time activities (Paramount Pictures), natural resources (New Jersey Zinc), consumer products, food and agricultural products, financial services, and manufacturing. Such a firm cannot be classified into any type of industry and is now referred to as a conglomerate.

Synergism was an important rationale for conglomerate mergers, for the surviving firm was presumed to be stronger and able to achieve greater growth than the individual firms could achieve by themselves. Conglomerate firms would frequently seek as merger candidates a firm whose earnings growth had been inferior or whose stock price was low relative to the firm's earnings. The conglomerate's management would assert that the merger would significantly benefit both firms, making them stronger through synergistic effects. For example, the conglomerate's managerial talent and financial skill could be applied to the merger candidate's problems, turn the firm around, and thereby achieve greater profitability. This greater profitability should then lead to higher stock prices. The lure of higher stock prices induced many stockholders and management to agree to these mergers.

Some conglomerate mergers produced (at least in the short run) phenomenal results. Through such mergers some companies were able to increase in size from small corporations to large industrial giants whose earnings growth and increase in stock prices were spectacular. Perhaps the most famous example is Ling Temco Vought (currently named LTV) that grew from a modest manufacturing firm of electronic products with sales of $154 million in 1961 to one of the country's largest industrial firms with sales in 1968 of $2.7 billion in such varied fields as food, electronics, aerospace, steel, and computer software. Such an increase in sales is an annual growth rate in excess of 100 per cent, or, in other words, sales more than doubled each year! During the same period its earnings grew from a loss of over $7 million to profits of over $24 million. The price of the stock also rose rapidly from $20 a share to a high of $169.50 in 1967.

The initial success of the conglomerates

Unfortunately for investors, LTV's amazing growth was not maintained. The growth in sales and earnings could not be maintained, and the price of the stock fell precipitously to below $10 a share in 1970. Currently the stock's price remains a mere fraction of its former high. This price performance is typical of the stock of many conglomerates, and obviously many investors suffered significant losses of their investments in these firms. Unfortunately many investors did not realize that these companies could not possibly maintain their rapid growth rates for any extended period of time. Thus the end of the period of super growth had to occur. Perhaps what surprised investors was the severity of the decline in earnings and stock prices once the rapid growth eased.

This decline in earnings of the conglomerates can be explained in part by the method used to finance their growth. The conglomerates are an excellent example of the risk associated with financial leverage, for the growth was primarily financed by debt. For example, LTV's debt expanded from $69.6 million in 1961 to $1.28 billion in 1968. This debt had the effect of increasing the growth in earning as long as financial leverage was favorable. However, when sales lagged and profit margins fell, this debt required the continued payment of fixed interest charges. Thus the earnings per share of LTV and all the conglomerates declined more rapidly than less financially leveraged firms when the economy experienced increased inflation and increased costs of production during the Viet Nam War.

Financial leverage caused earnings to fall rapidly

EXECUTING THE MERGER

External growth through a merger is an investment and should be treated in the same way as other investment decisions. The capital budgeting techniques discussed in Chapter 23 should be applied to prospective mergers. These techniques will help identify possible merger candidates and establish the terms of a merger that are acceptable to the acquiring firm.

The terms of a merger

The terms of a merger are extremely important. They include the following aspects: (1) the price paid for the acquired firm; (2) the relationship between the acquired firm's previous management and the acquiring firm's management; (3) relationships among divisions of the two firms; and (4) the relationship between the new management and labor unions affected by the merger. In some cases, the managements of the acquiring firm and the acquired firm are compatible and able to establish mutually acceptable terms. However, not every merger is between friendly partners, in which case the acquiring firm may seek to gain control from the hostile management. This may be done through a cash offer for the firm's stock at a price sufficiently high to induce the current stockholders to sell their shares. Once the acquiring firm gains control, then it may replace the old managment and merge the two companies.

Means of payment

After the price has been established, then the means of payment must be determined. The acquiring firm has basically the following three choices: (1) pay in cash; (2) issue a specified amount of debt in trade for the acquired firm's stock; or (3) issue a specified amount of stock in trade for the acquired firm's stock. These three choices are significantly different from each other from the viewpoints of both the buyer and the seller.

(1) Cash

If the firm pays cash, it is trading one asset for the acquired firm's stock. It receives the firm's assets and liabilities, but no new shares are issued, and thus their current stockholders' ownership is not diluted. Payment with cash does mean that the firm must either have the cash or a ready source of funds. From the viewpoint of the sellers the prime advantage is the receipt of money, which the sellers may use as they desire. However, since this is a cash sale of their stock, the sale is subject to capital gain tax if the stockholders sell their shares for a profit.

(2) Debt

If the firm issues debt to pay for the acquisition, it conserves its cash but increases its degree of financial leverage. This obliges the firm to meet the terms of the indenture, to pay the interest, and to retire the debt. There is, however, no dilution of their current stockholders' position, for no new shares are issued (unless the debt is convertible into the firm's stock). From the viewpoint of the sellers, the flow of interest income and the obligation of the acquiring firm to meet the terms of the indenture may be important advantages. Since the sellers have agreed to accept debt instead of cash, they may be able to negotiate a higher price to compensate them for accepting payment that is spread over several years. There is, however, a major disadvantage in accepting debt instead of cash. The Internal Revenue Service treats the acceptance of debt as no different from a cash sale. Thus for tax purposes capital gains are realized, and the sellers must pay capital gains taxes if they have made a profit on the transaction. This tax payment may be a real burden if the sellers have insufficient cash to meet their required tax obligation.

If the acquiring firm issues stock as payment, then its current stockholders' position may be diluted. This dilution depends on the earnings of the acquired company and the number of shares issued. However, no additional debt is issued that requires interest payments and eventual retirement. The sellers receive equity (i.e., stock) in the acquiring firm and can sell these shares or retain them. The shares may appreciate in value if the firm flourishes and grows, but there is no assurance that the firm will prosper, and the firm is not obligated to pay dividends. Should the value of the stock decline, the sellers may not realize the purchase price of the shares. There is, however, a major tax advantage in accepting stock as payment instead of cash or debt. The Internal Revenue Service does not treat the swapping of stock in a merger as a realized sale. The seller, who receives the new shares, has the cost basis of the old shares transferred to the new shares and does not recognize any gains or losses for the purpose of capital gains taxes. Such a transaction thus avoids the capital gains tax unless the individual investor chooses to sell the newly acquired stock. Those investors who want cash or who do not want to invest in the combined firm may sell their stock and pay any applicable capital gains taxes. Other investors, however, may continue to hold the new stock and not pay any capital gains taxes until the stock is sold in the future. This tax advantage strongly argues for accomplishing mergers through stock swaps, for stockholders may more readily accept the terms of the merger since any profits are not subject to capital gains taxes.

(3) Stock

The tax advantage of the stock swap—no realized capital gain

POOLING AND PURCHASING

There are two ways of accounting for mergers. In one case the surviving firm is considered to have "purchased" the other firm. In the other case, the two firms are consolidated and their assets and liabilities are "pooled," even though the resulting firm may retain the name of only one of the firms. While the difference between the two is an involved topic in accounting and hence beyond the scope of this text, the following discussion will give an indication of the differences between the two accounting methods.

Accounting for the merger

Two firms (A and B) have the following simple balance sheets:

FIRM A

Assets	$2000	Current liabilities	$1000
Fixed assets	3000	Long-term debt	3000
		Equity	1000
	$5000		$5000

FIRM B

Assets	$3000	Current liabilities	$1000
Fixed assets	7000	Long-term debt	3000
		Equity	6000
	$10,000		$10,000

"Pooling" is a horizontal summation

Firm B offers its stock to the owners of Firm A in trade for their stock in Firm A, and this offer is accepted. If this merger is treated as a consolidation and the assets and liabilities are pooled, the two balance sheets are combined. The balance sheets are added horizontally. Thus the new firm (Firm C) has the following balance sheet:

FIRM C

Current assets	$ 5000	Current liabilities	$2000
Fixed assets	10,000	Long-term debt	6000
		Equity	7000
	$15,000		$15,000

This new balance sheet is created by adding both firm's current assets, fixed assets, current liabilities, long-term debt, and equity. All the similar items on the two balance sheets have been combined on the new consolidated balance sheet.

"Purchase" requires establishing a value

In the case of a purchase one firm actually buys the other firm. Payment may be made for cash or the firm may issue stock or debt in trade for the stock of the acquired firm. The important issue is not, however, the means of payment but the price relative to the book value of the assets of the acquired firm. For example, if Firm B offers $5000 worth of its stock in trade for the stock in Firm A and the stockholders accept the offer, the new balance sheet of Firm B becomes:

FIRM B

Current assets	$ 5000	Current liabilities	$2000
Fixed assets	10,000	Long-term debt	6000
		Equity	7000
	$15,000		$15,000

Firm B has paid $5000 worth of its stock for $5000 worth of assets. This balance sheet is no different than the balance sheet obtained through the use of pooling. The difference between the two techniques arises when the purchase price is different than the book value of the assets of the acquired firm.

If Firm B had issued stock worth $8000 in exchange for the stock of Firm A, then Firm B is paying $8000 for assets worth (on the books) only $5000. There is a discrepancy of $3000 and the discrepancy must be accounted for. The difference between the purchase price and the book value of the assets is called goodwill. Goodwill is then added to the assets of the acquiring firm so that the new balance sheet for Firm B becomes:

FIRM B

Current assets	$ 5000	Current liabilities	$ 2000
Fixed assets	10,000	Long-term debt	6000
Goodwill	3000	Equity	10,000
	$18,000		$18,000

The effect of the purchase has been to create on the balance sheet of Firm C a new asset, goodwill.

The creation of goodwill leads to serious tax consequences. Generally accepted accounting principles now require that goodwill be depreciated, and the Internal Revenue Service requires that goodwill be depreciated *after* taxes. Thus goodwill creates a depreciation expense that reduces corporate income but does not reduce the firm's taxes. This tax law and the accounting principle thus discourage the use of the purchase method and encourage the use of pooling as the means to account for mergers. Pooling, however, can only be used when several specific conditions are met. Thus the tax laws and accounting principles encourage mergers that either meet the conditions that permit pooling or do not result in the creation of goodwill. Since many conglomerate mergers of the 1960s did result in the creation of goodwill, these changes in the tax laws and accounting principles in part discouraged the continuance of the conglomerate merger movement.

The importance of goodwill

MULTINATIONAL FIRMS

While many firms have grown through mergers, a large number of corporations have expanded operations by investing abroad. This has resulted in large multinational firms with operations in many countries. Exxon typifies this type of multinational corporate giant. Its 1975 annual report discusses operations in many geographical areas, such as the North Sea (with the cooperation of Great Britain and Norway) and in many countries (e.g., Venezuela, Surinam, French Guiana, the Netherlands, West Germany, Japan, Saudi Arabia, and Egypt). Its products, which include chemicals, coal, and nuclear fuel as well as petroleum products, are sold throughout the world, and its fleet of tankers plow the world's major bodies of water. Since Exxon

Foreign investments is another capital budgeting decision

is such a good case of the multinational firm, it will be frequently used for examples in this section.

This increase in foreign investments has primarily occurred since World War II. The initial pattern was for American firms to invest abroad; however, with the increase in foreign income and currency values, many foreign firms now invest in the United States. Thus firms from many countries (e.g., Great Britain, Germany, Japan, Iran) have invested in both plant and equipment in the United States and in American securities. Examples of firms with large exports or investments in the U.S. are given in Table 27-1.

Growth through international investments has special risks and rewards. In principle, capital budgeting techniques apply to these investments just as they apply to all other potential investments. Conceptually the decision to invest in a foreign country is no different than the decision to expand domestic production, to replace equipment, or to merge. In each case management is seeking those investments which maximize the value of the firm. Management must identify and quantify the factors that affect the cash flow from the foreign investment and then determine the investment's net present value or the internal rate of return. But management also needs to be aware that while foreign investments may offer the firm excellent opportunities for growth, they may also subject the firm to special risks. These risk factors must be considered when the decision is made to invest abroad.

The potential returns are very obvious. Foreign countries offer the firm new markets for existing products (e.g., Exxon's petroleum products). The firm already knows the technology and usually can readily transfer that technology from one country to

TABLE 27-1   Foreign Firms with Substantial Exports to or
Investments in the United States

FIRM	COUNTRY	INDUSTRY
ICI Chemical	Great Britain	chemicals
Matsushita Electric	Japan	electronics (Panasonic and Quasar)
Plessy	Great Britain	telecommunications equipment
Seagrams	Canada	distillery
SONY	Japan	electronics
Hoffman-La Roche	Switzerland	drugs
BASF	Germany	electronics
Unilever	Netherlands	consumer products (Lever Brothers, Lipton)
Royal Dutch/Shell	Netherlands/ Great Britain	petroleum
Alcan	Canada	aluminum
Saint-Gobain-Pont-a-Mousson	France	building supplies (Certain-Teed)

another. Also, operating a plant abroad may be considerably less expensive than expanding a domestic plant, for foreign labor costs may be (and frequently are) cheaper. Hence a new foreign plant that combines a new market with the most recent equipment, technology, and less expensive labor can result in considerable profit. Even if a new plant is not built, the exporting of domestically produced goods to the new market may substantially increase profits if the old plant can operate at a higher level of efficiency.

While offering potentially larger returns, foreign investments may significantly alter the firm's risk position. The firm may become more or less risky as the result of foreign investments. For example, if a firm is in a cyclical industry, it may reduce the impact of the cycle on its earnings. While economic conditions may be similar in many countries, foreign investment may reduce the impact of a domestic recession or economic stagnation. If the domestic market is weak, foreign markets may continue to be strong, and the effects of the weak domestic market on the firm's earnings are reduced. Besides reducing the impact of the economic cycle, foreign investments may reduce risk by assuring the firm a supply of raw materials. Thus many American firms invest in raw material production in foreign countries, and such investments are designed to insure the existence of the firm's source of raw materials. For example, a smelter and fabricator of metal must have a supply of ore and hence invests in foreign mining operations. By assuring itself of a source of supply, the firm reduces the riskiness of its operations.

International investment, however, may subject the firm to substantial increases in risk. Such risks are the result of local politics, lack of special knowledge, and exchange rate fluctuations. While the political climate in the United States does change, it is quite stable. Such stability may not exist in other foreign countries, or even if it does exist, the political climate can change. For example, Great Britain's attitude toward business seems to change as the government changes. When the Labour Party is in power, the chance of nationalization is considerably greater than when the Conservatives have control of Parliament.

Even when the Labour Party is in power, Great Britain is still politically very stable when compared with other countries. Many American firms with investments abroad have experienced the nationalization and expropriation of these investments. These firms may or may not receive compensation for the seized assets. For example, Cuba did not offer compensation when Fidel Castro came to power and nationalized the facilities of American firms. Venezuela, however, recently nationalized Exxon's oil investments in that country and agreed to compensate Exxon by paying $72 million in cash and $435 million in interest bearing bonds. The amount of compensation and the means of payment are frequently political questions that are

The political risk: nationalization

negotiated between governments as well as between a government and the firm whose facilities are being expropriated. Such power plays and political maneuverings are beyond the world of finance, but if a firm makes foreign investments that subject it to these problems, the element of risk can be significantly increased for the firm.

Joint projects may reduce risk

One method to reduce the political risk is for the firm to join with the foreign government in a joint project. For example, Exxon and other oil companies have had working relationships with the Arab countries which produce oil. Only in the 1970s have these countries sought complete control and ownership of the production facilities in their countries. The exact relationship between the firm and the host country varies with each agreement, but the effect is to give the foreign government remuneration from the profits of the investment. This may reduce friction and increase cooperation between the firm and the foreign government. It may also result in lower taxes and reduced chances of nationalization. Such agreements, however, usually have time durations, after which they must be renegotiated. And if there is a change in the government, the new politicians may repudiate old agreements. Hence, while joint ventures may reduce political risks, they cannot erase them.

Local legal constraints

Besides political risks foreign governments can burden the investing firm with a variety of legal constraints. For example, the country can require the firm to hire domestic labor. This will limit the ability of the firm to import specialized labor to operate the foreign plants. The foreign government may also have special laws limiting the ability of the firm to convert currencies. In this case if a firm invests capital in the country, it may be unable to take the funds out of the country. Thus any profits earned are effectively locked into the country and cannot be returned to the parent company. Certainly one of the most important constraints is the local government's tax laws. Foreign governments may tax income, the property, or the value added by the production process. The latter tax, the so-called value added tax, is particularly popular with European countries. The foreign government, however, may use tax laws to encourage investment by granting special tax concessions, such as no income or property tax for a specified time period. Such concessions are, of course, specifically designed to encourage foreign investment and are used primarily by underdeveloped nations to attract capital.

Risk from fluctuating exchange rates

There is also risk from fluctuations in exchange rates. As was explained in Part I, Chapter 7, the prices of foreign moneys change daily in relation to the demand and supply of each currency. Such exchange rate fluctuations can have a severe impact on a firm that invests abroad. Some of the largest firms in the nation (e.g., Dow Chemical, Xerox) have lost millions of dollars through currency fluctuations.

How such fluctuations may produce losses can be demonstrated by the following examples. If a firm accepts a bid for
plant and equipment in Germany and the German mark subsequently rises by 10 per cent, then the cost of the facility will
increase by 10 per cent. Such an increase in cost may convert a
profitable investment into a losing operation. Another example
of the potential source of loss from an increase in exchange rates
occurs when a firm borrows in another country and must repay in
that currency. If the value of that currency appreciates, it will
take more American dollars to retire the loan.

Exchange rate variations may also benefit the firm. For
example, if a country's currency rises in price, then previously
made investments are worth more. If the firm in the above example already had a plant in Germany, any cash flow generated by
the operation would covert into 10 per cent more dollars. Such a
10 per cent increase in the price of the mark would increase the
firm's profitability when it converted the marks to dollars. Thus
exchange rate fluctuations may help as well as hurt the firm's
financial position. For example, Reynolds Metals reported its
fourth quarter 1976 earnings were reduced by $.21 a share by
foreign currency fluctuations. In the fourth quarter of the preceding year these fluctuations increased earnings by $.83 a share.

Since exchange rates vary daily, the firm continuously runs
the risk of loss through a decline in a currency's value. The
financial manager needs to be very skilled at reducing this risk.
Such a reduction may be achieved by constantly trading currencies. The financial manager seeks to sell currencies whose price
may decline and to purchase currencies appreciating in value.
Thus if the financial manager anticipates a deterioration in the
value of French francs and an increase in the value of the German mark, francs should be sold for marks. If the price of the
franc does decline, then the marks will buy more francs in the
future. Of course, if the financial manager is wrong and the franc
rises in value, this transaction will produce a loss because the
German marks will purchase fewer French francs.

The best means for the financial manager to reduce the risk
of loss from exchange rate fluctuations is by hedging. Hedging is
achieved by the simultaneous purchase and sale of a currency.
For example, a firm contracts to buy a plant in Germany for $2
million. This payment will be made in the future and the cost of
the German marks necessary to make the payment may rise or
fall depending on fluctuations in the demand and supply of
marks. To avoid possible loss through an increase in the price of
the marks, the firm enters into a futures contract to purchase
marks (i.e., to sell dollars) for a specified price such as
$2,020,000. In effect, the firm has agreed to purchase marks and
simultaneously deliver them in payment for the plant. Thus, for
an expenditure of $20,000 (1 per cent of the total cost of the
plant), the firm has protected itself against rate fluctuations. The

*Hedging reduces
risk of loss from
fluctuations in
exchange rates*

price of the German marks and thus the price of the plant cannot exceed $2,020,000. It does not matter if the marks were to rise or fall in value, because a firm takes delivery of the marks for a specified price. If the price of the marks were to rise, the firm would be protected against loss, but conversely, if the price of the marks were to decline, the firm would not gain from the cheaper mark.

If the firm expects payment in the future, the procedure would be reversed. For example, if a firm anticipates a payment after three months in British pounds, it sells a futures contract to deliver pounds. If the pound is selling for $1.70 (i.e., called the "spot price"), the firm may agree to deliver pounds three months later for $1.69 (called the "futures price"). The firm is assured of receiving $1.69 for a pound. Thus for the cost of 1 cent a pound, the firm has protected itself from exchange rate fluctuations. The firm is protected from exchange rate deterioration, for if the pound were to decline to $1.50, the firm would still receive $1.69. Conversely, the possibility of gain is lost. If the pound were to rise to $2.00, the firm would receive only $1.69. Of course, the purpose of entering the contract is to reduce the risk of loss, and to achieve this the firm also gives up the potential for profit through currency fluctuation.

Hedging cannot erase risk

While hedging may reduce the risk of loss from fluctuations in currency values, it cannot erase it. Furthermore, if a price change is anticipated, the cost of hedging will be high. In the above example, the current price a pound was $1.70. The seller sold pounds for future delivery at $1.69. That 1 cent differential is the potential source of profit to the buyer. If the pound is still $1.70 (or above) after three months, the buyer pays $1.69 for pounds worth more than $1.69. The buyer would not be willing to make this contract if it were anticipated that the pound's price would be below $1.69 when delivery is made. Instead the buyer would be willing to purchase pounds for future delivery only at a lower price, such as $1.65 or $1.60. If a substantial price decline were anticipated, there may be no buyers for future delivery, or the price offered may be so low that sellers prefer to hold the currency and bear the risk.

Thus, sometimes, a firm cannot insure itself against loss by hedging. In addition, price changes can be sudden or larger than anticipated. These price fluctuations can have a substantial impact on a firm's profitability. For example, in 1976, Mexico devalued the peso. Even though Mexico had experienced problems in its balance of payments, the devaluation was a surprise to many people. Mexico had not changed the price of pesos in terms of dollars for 22 years (i.e., since 1954). Then the peso was suddenly devalued by 40 per cent, from 12.5 pesos equal to $1.00 to over 20 pesos equal to $1.00. It is hard to believe that a firm with operations in Mexico could have completely protected itself from such a large devaluation. Many firms reported their earnings were reduced by the devaluation. For example, Lenox, the manufacturer of fine china, reported that its third quarter 1976 earnings were reduced by $391,000. For Lenox, its Mexican operations, which account for only 8 per cent of its total sales, caused a 13 per cent reduction in its third quarter earnings as a result of the devaluation of the peso.

Once the firm has decided to make a foreign investment, it may be financed by a variety of means. The firm may use its own funds generated through cash flow or may borrow from its own domestic sources. These funds will, of course, have to be converted into the foreign country's money. The firm may also borrow and issue securities abroad. As of January 1, 1976, Exxon's balance sheet showed $1.2 billion in long-term debt that was sold abroad. There is an active market in securities issued abroad by American firms, so foreigners have found these securities attractive. Such loans and bonds are frequently denominated in dollars instead of the foreign country's currency. Thus American firms have issued Eurodollar loans and Eurodollar bonds as a means to finance their foreign investments. Knowledge of these securities and their potential advantages further increases the specialized knowledge necessary for successful investing abroad, and large multinational firms have specialized staffs with this specialized knowledge to run their foreign operations.

A firm may borrow abroad

In summary, foreign investments have offered many American firms new markets and the opportunity for growth and expansion. Such investments, however, may significantly alter the risk complexion of the firm. Foreign investing requires specialized knowledge, ranging from local customs to tax laws to exchange rate hedging. The skills and knowledge necessary for successful investing abroad are numerous, but the opportunities for personal growth and advancement are plentiful. Financial managers who become skilled at international finance are truly valuable resources and are able to command top corporate salaries.

BANKRUPTCY AND REORGANIZATION

While some firms are able to achieve growth, others are not so fortunate. Actually, many firms fail every year, but most of these are relatively small firms. Failures by large companies are quite rare, but these failures can be spectacular, and they may receive a significant amount of publicity. The Penn Central collapse certainly received more publicity than the failure of many small operations, and it probably received more publicity than the success of Xerox, Johnson and Johnson, or IBM.

The cause of failure is usually the same for large and small firms—poor management. This cause, however, can cover a broad spectrum of errors, from failure to perceive changes in the indus-

Financial mismanagement is a frequent cause of failure

try or economy to fraud and embezzlement. One of the most frequent management errors is financial. Many companies fail because they are too financially leveraged (i.e., too much debt relative to equity) or because management did insufficient financial planning or lacked financial control. Thus poor financial management is frequently the cause of failure.

The inability to meet financial obligations as they come due

A firm must meet financial claims as they come due and meet the terms of its debt obligations. If the company fails to meet these financial claims, it is insolvent, and the debt goes into default. An insolvent firm, however, need not be bankrupt, for the creditors must decide on a course of action. Creditors will act in the manner that they believe is in their own best interest. Thus they may not press for payment or liquidation of the firm, for forcing payment through court proceedings may be expensive and perhaps even futile. Thus the creditors of many financially troubled real estate investment trusts that are currently or have been in default (e.g., Chase Manhattan Real Estate Investment Trust) are accepting reorganization instead of pressing for payment through court action.

Firm may seek voluntary reorganization

In many cases the insolvent firm will itself solicit a voluntary reorganization with its creditors. Such voluntary reorganizations seek to restructure the firm's obligations. For example, creditors may extend the maturity of the debt or waive some of the restrictive covenants. Long-term debt obligations may be converted into equity in a new, reorganized firm. Why would creditors be willing to agree voluntarily to such changes? The question really is, "Are the creditors better off with the firm operating or closed?" If the creditors seek to have the firm liquidated, they probably will not receive the full value of their claims. Instead they may receive a mere fraction of what they are owed. If they permit the firm to continue to operate, profitable operations may be established and the creditors may receive the full value of what they are owed. Obviously these profits cannot occur until some time in the future. Thus the creditors are faced with a typical financial question: which is greater, the present liquidation value of their claims or the present value of their claims if the firm is permitted to continue to operate?

The order of claims

How individual creditors answer this question will depend in part on their position in the pecking order in which claims are met. Not all claims are equal. Some are subordinate to others and the superior claims are paid first. If the firm is liquidated, the order of payment is

(1) the cost of the liquidation (i.e., court expense)
(2) unpaid labor expense
(3) taxes
(4) secured debt
(5) unsecured debt

This list points out the tenuous position of the unsecured debt and the perhaps tenuous position of the secured debt. If the firm's assets have deteriorated in value or have to be sold at bargain basement prices through a forced liquidation, even the secured creditors may receive only a fraction of their claims. Hence these creditors realize that they may profit through a voluntary reorganization which avoids formal bankruptcy proceedings, and thus they agree to accept reorganization.

If the firm is unable to work out an arrangement with its creditors, it may be forced into bankruptcy. Bankruptcy is as much a legal as a financial question. The firm may seek bankruptcy voluntarily (called a Chapter XI bankruptcy), in which case the court protects the firm from its creditors while the firm and the creditors work out a reorganization. The firm may be involuntarily thrown into bankruptcy (called Chapter X bankruptcy) by a creditor seeking payment. In Chapter X bankruptcy the court appoints a trustee for the debtor's property. The trustee will continue to operate the business, examine the debtor's books for fraud, and initiate a plan for reorganization. The emphasis is usually on reorganization and not on liquidation, but liquidation may be the final result. The final plan for reorganization must be acceptable to two thirds of the creditors. Then the court will accept the plan if it believes that the plan meets the statutory requirements of being feasible, fair, and equitable. Once the plan has been accepted, the firm is released from bankruptcy.

Chapter XI and Chapter X bankruptcies

After the firm is reorganized, the old debtors may become the new stockholders. The old stock is erased and the previous stockholders receive no stock in the new firm. For example, this type of reorganization has frequently been used in railroad reorganizations. Railroads are subject to regulation by the Interstate Commerce Commission, which does not usually permit the sale of railroad property to meet creditors' claims. Instead, a new railroad is organized with the old creditors becoming the new stockholders, and the old stockholders are wiped out. Since the reorganized firm no longer has the burden of the fixed claims (i.e., the debt) and has a new equity base, it now has borrowing capacity which it can use to acquire working capital. Also the management of the firm is usually changed. Thus, with new management, new working capital, and less fixed obligations, the firm has a new lease on life and may become a thriving, profitable operation. Therefore, while the creditors no longer have their old claims, they now have an investment in a new firm that has a chance of success. If the new firm does succeed, then the value of the creditors' investment (i.e., the new stock) should rise. They may even be able to sell their shares for substantial profits if the firm becomes sufficiently profitable.

The reorganized firm may have former creditors as owners

Two Case Studies: W. T. Grant and Elcor Corporation

W. T. Grant is an excellent case study in bankruptcy. The firm was a large operator of variety stores with a sales mix includ-

W. T. Grant: a case of liquidation

ing apparel, home furnishings, and housewares. In 1973 sales peaked at $1.8 billion. However, soon thereafter the firm was bankrupt and subsequently liquidated. This deterioration did not occur overnight but over a series of years, as the following selected financial information indicates:

	1970	1971	1972	1973	1974
Sales (in billions)	$1.25	1.37	1.64	1.85	1.76
Profits (in millions)	$39.6	35.2	37.8	8.4	(177.3)
Profit Margin	3.1%	2.6	2.3	.5	—

From 1970 to 1972 the company's sales grew, but its earnings were stable (i.e., the earnings were "flat"). Profit margins thus had to be deteriorating. This deterioration sped up in 1973 when the firm earned only .5 per cent on sales. Calamity hit in 1974 when the firm lost over $175 million (or about 10 cents on every $1 of sales).

What caused this substantial loss? Part of the answer may be seen in the firm's current assets and liabilities (i.e., its current position) (Table 27–2). There was a significant decline in the current position from 1973 as current debt (primarily bank loans) rose over $140 million and current assets declined by almost $200 million. The primary cause for this decline was a large write-off of uncollectable accounts receivable.

Grant's problems were primarily deteriorating profit margins, poor management of accounts receivable, and excessive short-term financing. Such a situation is grim because the first two problems make meeting the short-term obligations difficult. If W. T. Grant could have converted short-term debt to long-term debt, that would have bought time to solve the other problems. But who would be willing to lend the firm long-term money (i.e., buy bonds issued by W. T. Grant) or invest in a new issue of stock? Such securities would be very risky.

TABLE 27–2 Current Assets and Liabilities of W. T. Grant

	1972	1973	1974
Cash	$ 31(in millions)	$ 46	$ 80
Receivables	543	599	430
Inventory	400	451	407
Total current assets	974	1096	917
Payables	79	73	50
Debt due within a year	390	453	601
Other current liabilities	164	164	99
Total current liabilities	633	690	750
Current ratio	1.5:1	1.6:1	1.2:1

Initially the firm and creditors attempted to reorganize the firm. The company closed many unprofitable stores, and the banks accepted a restructuring of the debt that included a reduced rate of interest, a waiver of certain installment payments, and a lengthening of the maturity of $540 million in debt. The reorganization proved to be insufficient and the creditors pressed for liquidation, which the court ordered in February, 1976.

This analysis of the W. T. Grant bankruptcy points out the value of financial analysis. Rarely does bankruptcy occur quickly but is the result of many events. Since financial statements present financial transactions, studying such statements should give forewarning of financial difficulty. Of course, there is always the exception, like the massive recall of canned vichyssoise soup by Bon Vivant. The company never recovered from this recall. This type of random event rarely explains bankruptcy. Instead it is the steady deterioration of management, and especially financial management, that is the primary cause of failure.

Studying accounting statements is a means to protect oneself from financial difficulty. This is one reason that a firm's management, creditors, and owners should continually monitor the firm's financial position. Early detection by management may permit corrective courses of action, and early detection by creditors and owners may give them justification for coercing changes that may save the firm. In general, all three parties should be able to perceive problems before they occur. However, corrective action may be difficult, or there may be insufficient time for the action to correct the problem. In such cases the firm becomes insolvent and unable to meet its obligations. This forces managers and creditors to decide upon a course of action—voluntary or involuntary reorganization. Smoothing this process and protecting individual interest is the purpose of bankruptcy laws.

While W. T. Grant was liquidated, many bankrupt firms are successfully reorganized. For example, Elcor Corporation went bankrupt and was subsequently reorganized into a successful firm. Elcor's problems came from two sources. First, the firm had a new method to recover sulfur, but the recovery plant was very costly. Second, it was financed by a large amount of debt, which, of course, required substantial interest payments. While the plant was being built, sulfur prices declined, and then the firm experienced problems getting the plant on line. These operational problems plus the debt service caused the firm to become insolvent and go bankrupt. However, unlike W. T. Grant, the creditors and the firm, through the courts, worked out a successful reorganization.

Elcor Corporation: a successful reorganization

In the reorganization the company disposed of most of its operating property, and the sulfur recovery facility ceased operations. The commercial banks' loans were sold to a small group of private investors, and intermediate term notes and subordinate debt were exchanged for the company's stock. This reorganization removed several burdens by closing unprofitable operations and significantly reducing interest expense.

Why were the creditors willing to accept reorganization? In 1971 the firm had $11 million in assets and $33 million in debt. If the firm had been liquidated, it is doubtful that creditors (especially subordinate creditors) would have received 10 cents on $1.00 of claims. By accepting reorganization, these creditors had a chance to recoup their investment.

How have the creditors fared? Today Elcor Corporation is a profitable firm as may be seen in the following selected financial information:

	1975	1974	1973
Earnings per share	$2.40	.25	.20
Current ratio	1.8:1	1.4:1	1.2:1
Return on equity	26%	4.6%	4.8%

While the company may not have regained the lustre it had in 1968 (when the stock traded as high as 79¾), it appears now to be a viable operation. The firm even started to pay cash dividends to its stockholders in 1976. The subordinate bond holders, who exchanged $1000 face value of debt for 100 shares, have stock that traded as high as 9⅛ in 1976. While their investment was virtually worthless in 1971, these creditors held stock worth $700 at the end of 1976.

The case of Elcor Corporation illustrates that not every bankruptcy ends in liquidation and massive losses for stockholders and creditors. There have been many successful reorganizations that have proved to be very monetarily rewarding to those individuals willing to take the time and risk necessary to convert a failing operation into a profitable firm.

SUMMARY

This chapter has considered mergers, international operations, and bankruptcies. All three of these topics may be complex, and the business student could devote much more time to each of these subjects than is possible in an introductory survey.

There is a basic similarity to all three topics covered in this chapter. Earlier it was suggested that management will make investment decisions that maximize the value of the firm. The decision to merge, to enter foreign markets, or to reorganize all affect the value of the firm. These situations may be analyzed by the capital budgeting techniques presented in Chapter 23. In each case the potential benefits are weighed by the cost of the investment and alternative uses of the funds necessary to make the investment. Management should seek mergers or enter foreign markets when such decisions will increase the value of the firm. Creditors and courts may also view business failures and reorganizations in the same light, for successful reorganizations may be more beneficial to owners and creditors alike than forced liquidations.

_____ KEY WORDS AND TERMS

synergism
horizontal merger
vertical merger
conglomerate merger
pooling
purchase accounting
goodwill
multinational firm
joint ventures

spot price
futures price
hedging
Eurodollar bonds
Chapter X bankruptcy
Chapter XI bankruptcy
reorganization
liquidation

QUESTIONS AND PROBLEMS FOR THOUGHT
_____ AND DISCUSSION

1. How would the following mergers be classified?
   (a) American Motors and Chrysler.
   (b) Ethyl (a maker of gasoline additives) and Exxon.
   (c) MGM and Avon.

2. A firm has investments in a foreign country. If that country's currency declines in value, why may this reduce the firm's earnings? How may the firm protect itself from this reduction?

3. If a firm supplies a foreign firm located in a country that has a persistent balance of payments trade, what terms of trade credit should it offer? If an acceleration in these collections is not possible, what might the firm do with these accounts receivable? (If necessary, reread the material in Chapter 18 on managing accounts receivable.)

4. Penn Central went bankrupt but has not been liquidated. The rail operations are now run by a special government corporation, Conrail. The remaining operations of Penn Central are being reorganized into a new firm in which the creditors will become major stockholders. Why are these creditors willing to accept this reorganization?

5. Two firms with the following balance sheets merge through a

swapping of stocks. What will the new balance sheet be if the merger is treated as a pooling of interests?

A

Cash	$100	Accounts payable	$500
Accounts receivable	$1000	Equity	$4500
Inventory	$3900		

B

Accounts receivable	$500	Accounts payable	$300
Plant and		Long term debt	$1700
equipment	$2500	Equity	$1000

If firm A issued stock worth $5000 to acquire firm B and treated the merger as a purchase, will goodwill arise? What are the implications of goodwill on a firm's earnings and taxes?

Chapter 28

OVERVIEW OF FINANCIAL MANAGEMENT

Review Objectives

- Restate the role of the financial manager.

- Restate the criterion for judging a firm's performance.

- Explain the possible impact that monetary and fiscal policy may have on a firm.

- Contemplate why you took the course and ask yourself the following:

    (a) Was my conception of the world of finance too narrow?

    (b) Do I understand why finance is crucial for successful management of a firm?

    (c) Do I realize how this material will aid me in making financial decisions?

"They cannot see the forest for the trees."

Christoph Martin Wieland

Management's performance in general and the financial manager's performance in particular must ultimately be judged. In finance the criterion used to judge performance is the value of the firm. Management should take those actions that increase this value. Of course, many of these decisions involve nonfinancial aspects of a firm's operations, but the ultimate criterion still remains value. A course of action should only be taken if it is management's belief that the action is in the best interest of the owners of the firm. In the modern corporate world many firms are owned by investors (i.e., stockholders) who do not in reality participate in management decisions. Management is employed by these stockholders, and it is the value of these owners' investments that management should seek to maximize. It is the effect on this value that is the ultimate judge of the financial manager's performance. Successful financial management will lead to a higher value being placed on the firm. The tools, concepts, and facts presented in this text are a means to achieve this goal.

Value: the criterion for judging performance

THE ROLE OF THE FINANCIAL MANAGER
REVISITED

The role of the financial manager has been described in the preceding chapters. It is a complex job that must be performed by someone in the firm. For small proprietorships, the job will probably fall in the hands of the sole proprietor, the owner. Along with other roles, such as manager, salesman, purchaser, and bookkeeper, the owner will have to perform the many roles of the financial manager. With so many varied duties that must be performed, is it any wonder that many small firms fail? Large corporations may have staffs reporting to a vice president in charge of finance to perform the financial manager's job, but even these staffs do not guarantee that the job will be adequately performed.

What is the financial manager's job description again? First, the financial manager must assure that the firm has sufficient

Liquidity versus profitability

liquidity to meet its financial obligations as they come due. Perhaps this is individually the most important facet of the financial manager's job, for the firm must survive day to day. If the firm cannot meet these current cash needs, then there will be no tomorrow. Thus it is crucial that the financial manager insure that the firm has cash coming in to meet its bills as they come due. Of course, having liquidity costs the firm, for liquid assets (i.e., cash and demand deposits) do not earn any income. Increased liquidity costs the firm profits; the financial manager must seek a balance between sufficient liquidity and the investing of excess short-term funds in income earning assets. Thus successful cash management requires not only knowledge of the firm's liquidity needs but also knowledge of the money market and the various short-term money market instruments in which excess cash may be invested.

The financial manager has a variety of tools available to help perform this task. These tools can help forecast the level of sales and the assets necessary to achieve the anticipated level. The per cent of sales technique of forecasting, regression analysis, and the cash budget are tools that may be used by the financial manager to plan for the firm's cash needs. They will help insure that the firm has sufficient cash to meet its liabilities as they come due by permitting the financial manager to plan the firm's anticipated sales and expenses and its anticipated level of assets and liabilities. Such planning permits the financial manager to know when cash will be coming in and when the firm will have to seek outside sources of short-term finance.

Besides these planning tools, the financial manager may use a variety of ratios to analyze the firm's performance and financial condition. These ratios may be employed not only to identify trends but also to compare the firm with other firms in the industry. Each ratio may be classified into one of four classes.

Liquidity ratios seek to give an indication of the firm's ability to meet its obligations as they come due. Activity ratios show how rapidly assets flow through the firm. Leverage ratios indicate the extent to which debt is used to finance the firm, and profitability ratios show the firm's performance. The financial manager should realize that there are a large number of ratios which may be computed. However, some ratios will give similar information and hence may be redundant. Thus the financial manager (or any user of ratio analysis) should select those ratios most pertinent to the situation being analyzed.

Besides assuring that the firm has sufficient liquidity and that excess cash is invested in income earning assets, the financial manager plays a role in managing all assets. First, investments must be chosen from the many alternative uses of the firm's resources. Obviously the firm cannot make every possible investment but must select among the alternatives. There are several methods of capital budgeting, ranging from the simple payback method to net present value and internal rate of return approaches. These latter techniques can be made very complex, as an investment is analyzed under different hypotheses concerning risk and possible outcomes. Even after the decision to acquire a particular long-term asset has been made, these assets must still be managed. Long-term assets are depreciated and eventually must be replaced. The financial manager must also help determine the method for depreciating an asset and forecasting when it should be replaced.

Capital budgeting

Investments are made in the present, but the returns accrue in the future. The future is not certain; the financial manager works in a world of uncertainty and risk. Risk in the world of finance emanates from two sources. First, there is the risk associated with the nature of the business. For example, some industries require substantial amounts of fixed assets (i.e., they have a high degree of operating leverage). Fluctuations in the industry's sales will mean that firms in the industry are inherently more risky than firms in industries with more stable sales or that require few fixed assets. Other sources of business risk include technological change and change in consumer tastes. The speed with which technological change occurs, thus making equipment obsolete, and the rapid manner in which consumers alter their preferences make some businesses more risky. For example, many a small firm in the computer field found itself in serious difficulty as newer and more advanced equipment made their products or services obsolete.

Business risk

The second source of risk pertains to a firm's financing. All assets must be financed, and there are two sources: the owner's funds or creditors' funds. When a firm (or anyone) uses creditors' funds, it is financially leveraged. The prime advantage to the firm of borrowing funds is the potential to make the creditors' funds generate sufficient revenue not only

Financial risk

to pay the interest charges but also to generate additional funds which accrue to the owner. By borrowing and successfully using financial leverage, the firm increases the return on the equity. The use of borrowed money commits the firm to several legal obligations that vary with such factors as the amount of the loan, the length of time the loan is outstanding, and the credit worthiness of the borrower. Every loan is an individual package of terms, and each loan may have some subtle clause that differentiates it from other loans. If the firm fails to meet these terms, the creditors can take the firm to court to enforce the obligations. Such legal obligations may increase the element of risk. Thus the financing of a firm influences not only the potential return to the owner but also the degree of risk.

Optimal capital structure

One important role of the financial manager is to determine the firm's optimal combination of debt and equity financing. This optimal capital structure takes advantage of debt financing but does not unduly increase the element of financial risk. By determining the optimal capital structure, the financial manager minimizes the cost of capital. This minimum cost of capital is extremely important, for it is the criterion by which all potential investments must be judged. A firm's cost of capital is a measure of what the funds could earn if placed in alternative investments. Hence the firm must earn at least the cost of its capital to justify using these funds. This cost of capital is thus one of the important elements in the capital budgeting technique.

To determine the optimal capital structure which minimizes the cost of capital, the financial manager must know the varied sources of finance and their respective costs. A firm may borrow from a variety of sources, including commercial banks, insurance companies, trade creditors, and the general public. Securities may be privately placed with financial institutions, sold to the general public through intermediaries, or sold to current owners. The financial manager must be aware of all the potential sources of funds and know when the utilization of a particular source is the best alternative for raising funds.

Matching assets with the source of finance

To some extent the nature of the assets being financed influences the type of finance. In general, long-term assets should be financed only with long-term sources—namely, long-term debt or equity. Such permanent sources of funds are more suitable than short-term sources because the latter must continuously be refinanced. Should the firm be unable to roll over its short-term obligations, then it may be unable to pay them off. The use of short-term debt to finance long-term assets may subject the firm to liquidity problems if the firm has to sell the assets to meet its debt obligations. While it is desirable that a firm match the type of finance with the asset being financed, the very nature of some businesses violates this important financial principle. Perhaps the most striking example of this violation is the banking industry, which receives the majority of its funds by borrowing short-term (from depositors) and then lending the funds. Of course, commercial banks seek to protect themselves by stressing short-term and quality loans, but in general they do violate the principle of matching the suitability of assets and the sources used to finance the assets.

THE IMPACT OF NATIONAL ECONOMIC POLICY

No firm operates in a vacuum. Besides the force of competition and legal constraints, the firm is affected by national economic policy. This policy emanates from two sources: the fiscal policy of the Federal Government and the monetary policy of the Federal Reserve. Fiscal policy concerns expenditures and taxation and management of the national debt. Federal Government expenditures may affect the firm directly if it is a government supplier or indirectly by the Federal Government's effect on other firms and households. Federal Government taxation at both the corporate and individual levels affects virtually every firm. All taxes are a transfer of resources from the private sector to the public sector. Changes in taxation then must affect the firm, since they alter the resources which firms and households have to use.

Monetary policy is concerned with changes in the supply of money and the capacity of commercial banks to lend. Thus it primarily affects firms by altering the cost of funds and the availability of credit. To the extent that monetary policy affects aggregate spending, it will also alter the demand for a particular firm's output. This policy is carried out by the Federal Reserve, which is the nation's central bank. While the Federal Reserve is owned by private interests (i.e., the member banks), it operates as a quasi-governmental organization. It is independent of both its owners and the Federal Government but pursues economic goals that are national in scope, such as price stability. To carry out its goals, the Federal Reserve has several tools of monetary policy. Of the various tools, the following three are the most important: the reserve requirement, the discount rate, and open market operations. These three tools are used to affect the reserves of commercial banks, which in turn alters their ability to lend.

By far the most important of these tools is open market operations. The Federal Reserve may continuously and in any desired volume purchase or sell U.S. government securities. By buying these securities, the Federal Reserve is able to expand the money supply and the reserves of commercial banks, thereby increasing the supply of credit in the nation. The opposite is true when the Federal Reserve sells securities, which absorbs commercial banks' reserves and decreases the supply of money.

Monetary policy and capacity of commercial banks to lend

While the effect of monetary policy is to alter the available supply of credit and the cost of capital of all firms, the impact is felt more by firms in particular industries. For example, utilities need large amounts of capital to finance expansion of plant and equipment. Nuclear generating facilities require a substantial investment, which necessitates the selling of both debt and equity securities to the general public. Tight money and higher cost of capital significantly increase the expense associated with financing such generating facilities. Of all industries, perhaps the hardest hit by tight credit is construction. Buildings are primarily financed by mortgages, and hence a reduction in the supply of credit means a reduction in available mortgage money. Even if potential buyers are willing to pay higher interest charges, they may still be unable to find mortgage money. Thus the inability to secure finance results in a reduction in the demand for the industry's product.

The ability to anticipate policy

The financial manager needs to be aware of this financial environment. Both fiscal and monetary policies can have a major impact on the firm's financial health by altering both the cash flow from investments and the cost of funds. To some extent the financial manager may be able to anticipate particular actions by the Federal Government and the Federal Reserve and take steps to insulate the firm from the effects. For example, cost of funds does vary over time, and the firm may seek to obtain funds during periods of lower interest rates. The firm may issue long-term debt securities and invest the funds in short-term assets such as Treasury bills. The bills can then be converted into cash as the funds are needed. If the firm instead chose to issue these securities later, the interest cost may be higher. Thus, if the financial manager anticipates future increases in the cost of credit, it may be desirable to issue securities now, for such an action will lock in the lower interest charges.

The financial manager may anticipate some policy actions emanating from Washington but cannot be expected to foresee all policy changes that may be forthcoming. Some changes in policy may be swift and abrupt. For example, the sudden change on August 15, 1971, in President Nixon's stand from favoring moderate fiscal and monetary restraint to a wage-price freeze to fight inflation vividly illustrates how rapidly government policy may change. Many firms found themselves with frozen higher costs but were unable to raise prices to maintain profit margins. If these firms had anticipated such a change in policy, they may have been able to raise prices prior to the wage-price freeze. Of course, the sudden change in policy was designed to freeze all prices, since it would have been ineffective had the change been widely anticipated. Thus it is not surprising that financial managers were unable to anticipate the policy change.

While financial managers may be unable to insulate their firms from the effect of national economic policy, they certainly will react to these policies. Of course, much of this policy is designed to induce particular behavior. For example, accelerated depreciation and tax credits for investment spending are designed to induce spending on capital equipment by increasing the cash flow from the investment. High interest rates are designed to discourage investment spending by increasing the cost of capital. The financial managers will incorporate these policy changes into the analyses they perform and respond accordingly. If a financial manager fails to react to changes in national economic policy, this may significantly hurt the firm and reduce its value in the marketplace. Financial managers must work within the constraints of national economic policy. While they do not establish that policy and may have no impact on it, they can be well informed of current economic policy and how it affects their particular firms.

THE PURPOSE OF THE BOOK RESTATED

The student who has read the preceding chapters must be amazed by the complexity of the world of finance. But every firm and every individual make financial decisions. The role of the financial manager is not limited to firms but also applies to individuals who may use similar information and techniques in everyday financial decision making.

Of course, reading this text is only a beginning. Unfortunately for many students, an introductory course may be their only academic exposure to the discipline of finance. Many of these students may have to work and communicate with financial specialists. They need at least an elementary knowledge of finance. It is for these students that this text was designed, for the text briefly covered many facets and analytical tools used in the world of finance. No attempt was made to be exhaustive or to develop theoretical concepts fully.

This is only a beginning

The text has served as an introduction to the world of finance. A good introduction lays the foundations for further study, and any interested student may use the reading list for the financial manager that follows this chapter as a helpful guide. Of course, students desiring specialization in finance will encounter this material again at greater depth and at a higher level of sophistication in more advanced courses.

While many students may not continue in finance, it is hoped that this text has whetted the appetite of some non-finance students to do further work within the discipline. In many businessmen's minds, finance is the crucial element in a business. It is a necessary condition for a successful business operation, and poor financial management is frequently a major cause of business failure. Thus even for the non-specialist additional knowledge of finance may be extremely helpful for a successful career

Finance: (1) a crucial element of business

in business. This is well acknowledged, for example, by the accounting profession, for finance is part of the CMA certification, and financial topics and techniques appear on the CPA examination. Even people who work in the public sector (i.e., government) or with non-profit organizations (e.g., the church) make financial decisions. Thus knowledge of the world of finance is useful for virtually every type of career.

(2) An inescapable part of private life

Lastly, finance is a crucial component of one's private life. Financial leverage is frequently used by individuals as they borrow funds to finance purchases ranging from consumer goods to such durables as homes. Households must manage their cash in order to have money to pay bills as they come due. Many individuals are able to save and must decide the form in which to hold their savings, and there are numerous assets available to savers. The individual needs to be aware of the various assets so that the portfolio will match financial needs and goals. To function in modern society requires some knowledge and understanding of the world of finance.

A READING LIST FOR
THE FINANCIAL MANAGER

A next step for the student of financial management is to
develop the theoretical concepts and increase the
ability to use the tools of financial analysis. There are
several excellent advanced textbooks devoted to the
concepts and tools used in financial management,
including the following:

1. Van Horne, James C.: *Financial Management
   and Policy,* 3rd ed. Englewood Cliffs, New
   Jersey: Prentice Hall, Inc., 1974.
2. Weston, J. Fred, and Eugene F. Brigham: *Managerial
   Finance,* 5th ed. Hinsdale, Illinois: The Dryden
   Press, 1975.
3. Soldofsky, Robert M., and Garnet D. Olive:
   Financial Management. Cincinnati, Ohio:
   South-Western Publishing Co., 1974.

The difference among financial textbooks is substantial
and hence reading one does not exclude reading others.
For example, Van Horne has a more theoretical orientation,
while the Weston and Brigham text is more practical
and pragmatic. The Soldofsky and Olive text has a
more encyclopedic coverage.

In addition to textbooks, there are several excellent case
books in the area of finance. Cases seek to apply concepts
to situations which may be real or are simulations of
reality. Excellent casebooks that may be used in conjunction
with the above texts include:

4. Brigham, Eugene F. et al.: *Cases in Managerial
   Finance,* 2nd ed. Hinsdale, Illinois: The Dryden
   Press, 1974.
5. Cohan, Avery B., and Harold E. Wyman: *Cases in
   Financial Management.* Englewood Cliffs, New
   Jersey: Prentice Hall, Inc., 1972.

One text that includes both text and cases is:

    6. Hunt, Pearson, Charles M. Williams, and Gordon
       Donaldson: *Basic Business Text and Cases,*
       4th ed. Homewood, Illinois: Richard D. Irwin, Inc.,
       1971.

Further study of the financial environment with an
emphasis on the Federal Reserve System and monetary
and fiscal policy can be accomplished by reading textbooks
in money and banking. There are a large number of
excellent books in this area including:

    7. Ritter, Lawrence S., and William L.Silber:
       Principles of Money, Banking, and Financial Markets.
       New York: Basic Books, Inc., 1974.
    8. Chandler, Lester V.: *The Economics of Money and
       Banking,* 5th ed. New York: Harper and Row, 1969.
    9. Horvitz, Paul M.: *Monetary Policy and the Financial
       System,* 3rd ed. Englewood Cliffs, New Jersey:
       Prentice Hall, 1974.

The Chandler text includes a substantial amount of
banking history, while Ritter and Silber integrate various
economic theories of the effects of monetary policy. The
Horvitz text is perceptibly simpler than the other two
and may be preferred by students who find economics difficult.

Besides textbooks, the student of finance needs to be
aware of the vast and varied financial literature. This
literature may be divided (somewhat arbitrarily) into
academic and professionally oriented material. The most
important academic journal is:

    10. *Journal of Finance,* published by the American
       Finance Association.

Journals that combine articles oriented toward both the academic
and professional financial community include:

    11. *Financial Management,* published by Financial
       Management Association; and
    12. *Financial Analysts Journal,* published by Financial
       Analysts Federation.

The professional and popular press is varied and
includes such diverse publications as:

    13. *Business Week*
    14. *Forbes*
    15. *Fortune*
    16. *The Harvard Business Review*

The financial manager obviously will be unable to read all the material published on finance. One method to overcome this problem is to consult the:

17. *Journal of Economic Literature*

This gives abstracts of many articles appearing in financial and economic journals. Also the reading lists and bibliographies given in the Van Horne, Weston-Brigham, and Soldofsky-Olive texts provide excellent guides to this professional and academic literature. Since the student may consult these sources, it is not necessary to repeat here a repetitive list of readings from the literature.

Finding some of this literature may be difficult. However, the student may consult a book of readings which reprints important articles on specific areas of finance. Excellent books of readings include:

18. Brigham, Eugene F., ed.: *Readings in Managerial Finance*. New York: Holt, Rinehart and Winston, Inc., 1971.
19. Reilly, Frank K., ed.: *Readings and Issues in Investments*. Hinsdale, Illinois: The Dryden Press, 1975.
20. Ritter, Lawrence S., and William L. Silber, eds.: *Principles of Money, Banking, and Financial Markets*. New York: Basic Books, Inc., 1974.
21. Serraino, William J., Surendra S. Singhvi, and Robert M. Soldofsky, eds.: *Frontiers of Financial Management,* 2nd ed. Cincinnati, Ohio: South-Western Publishing Co., 1976.

The articles in these collections vary in difficulty, and there are books of readings that include substantially more difficult material. However, most of the material in the above reading books may be read in conjunction with a basic text in finance.

Besides the above literature, the financial manager may find the following books to be extremely useful reference material:

22. Samuelson, Paul A.: *Economics,* 10th ed. New York: McGraw-Hill, 1976. Perhaps the best introductory economics textbook ever written.
23. Graham, Benjamin, David L. Dodd, Sidney Cottle, and Charles Totham: *Security Analysis Principles and Techniques,* 4th ed. New York: McGraw-Hill, 1962. The classic, conservative book on investing in securities.

24. Cissell, Robert, and Helen Cissell: *Mathematics of Finance,* 4th ed. Boston, Massachusetts: Houghton-Mifflin Company, 1973. Provides useful mathematical formulations.

25. Hodges, John C., and Mary E. Whitten: *Harbrace College Handbook,* 7th ed. New York: Harcourt, Brace, Jovanovich, Inc., 1972. A classic handbook on English grammar.

The above items should keep the student of finance more than busy for many profitable hours. After sampling this varied literature, no doubt the student's knowledge of the world of finance will have grown and broadened, which should increase the potential for success in both advanced study and a career in finance.

GLOSSARY

AAA—highest credit rating awarded by credit rating agencies.

accelerated depreciation—depreciating a larger proportion of an asset's cost during the earlier years of its life.

acid test (quick ratio)—current assets excluding inventory divided by current liabilities.

aging schedule—table indicating length of time that accounts receivable have been outstanding.

annuity—series of equal payments.

arrearage—cumulative preferred stock dividends that have not been paid and have accumulated.

asset—items or property owned by a firm, household, or government and valued in monetary terms.

balance of payments—record of a country's receipts and disbursements with other nations.

balance of trade—summation of the current and capital accounts in the balance of payments.

balance sheet—listing of an economic unit's assets, liabilities, and net worth (equity).

bankruptcy—legal proceeding for the liquidation or reorganization of an insolvent firm.

barter—transfer of goods and services without the use of money.

beta coefficient—measure of the volatility of a stock's price relative to the market.

bid and ask—prices at which the market makers are willing to buy and sell a security.

Board of Governors—appointed by the President of the United States; the controlling body of the Federal Reserve.

bond—long-term debt instrument.

breakeven—level of output at which total expenses (costs) equals total revenues; neither profits nor losses.

breakeven analysis—determination of the level of output that produces neither losses nor profits.

broker—security dealer who buys and sells securities for customers' accounts.

budget—plan or forecast of receipts and disbursements.

business risk—risk associated with the nature of the enterprise.

call feature—the right of the issuer to repurchase and retire a debt issue before maturity.

capital budgeting—process of selecting among competing long-term investments.

capital gains—increase in the value of a capital asset.

cash budget—plan of anticipated cash receipts and disbursements.

cash flow—profits plus depreciation.

Chapter X bankruptcy—involuntary bankruptcy brought on by the firm's creditors.

Chapter XI bankruptcy—voluntary reorganization sought by a firm with court protection from the firm's creditors.

chartist—an investor who uses the technical approach to select securities.

closed-end investment company—investment company with a fixed number of shares.

collateral—assets used to secure debt.

commercial paper—short-term unsecured notes issued by the most credit-worthy corporations.

common stock—shares representing residual ownership in a corporation. Owners of common stock have the final claim on the firm's earnings and assets after the firm has met its obligations to its creditors and preferred stockholders.

compensating balance—funds a commercial bank requires be deposited in an account as part of a loan agreement.

compound interest—interest paid on the principal and interest accumulated in the previous periods.

conglomerate merger—merger of two firms in different industries.

consumer price index—aggregate measure of the prices of final goods and services.

convertible bond—bond that may be converted into stock at the option of the holder.

convertible preferred stock—preferred stock that may be converted into common stock at the option of the holder.

corporation—economic unit created by the state with the power to own assets, incur liabilities, and engage in specific activities.

cost of capital—the cost (or required rate of return) of a firm's sources of finance.

cost of equity—cost to a firm necessary to induce owners to invest funds.

coupon rate of interest—annual interest payments made by a bond.

coverage ratio—measure of the safety of debt; earnings available to pay interest divided by interest charges.

cumulative preferred stock—preferred stock whose dividends accumulate if not paid.

current asset—short-term assets that will (or are expected to) convert into cash during the fiscal year.

current liabilities—debts that must be paid during the fiscal year.

current yield—interest (or dividends) divided by the current price of the security.

debenture—an unsecured bond.

debt—a liability; a legal obligation.

debt ratio—total debt divided by total assets; measure of financial leverage.

default—not meeting the terms (i.e., the indenture) of a debt issue.

deficit spending—expenditures exceeding receipts.

degree of financial leverage—a measure of the responsiveness of earnings to changes in earnings before interest and taxes.

degree of operating leverage—measure of the responsiveness of earnings to changes in output.

demand deposit—a deposit that may be withdrawn on demand and transferred by check.

depreciation—the allocation of the cost of plant and equipment over its useful life.

devaluation—decrease in the price of one currency relative to other currencies.

dilution—reduction in earnings per share as the result of issuing more shares.

discount rate—the interest rate charged member banks for borrowing from the Federal Reserve.

discounted cash flow—future cash flows brought back to the present.

disintermediation—the process of withdrawing funds from financial intermediaries.

diversification—the spreading of risk by making investments in different industries.

dividend—distribution of cash or stock to stockholders.

dividend yield—cash dividends divided by the price of the stock.

Du Pont system—a measure of earning capacity that includes asset turnover and profitability.

earnings before interest and taxes—profit from operations.

earnings per share—total earnings after taxes divided by the number of shares outstanding.

economic order quantity (EOQ)—optimal size of an order of inventory.

effective interest rate—true (or simple) rate of interest.

equipment trust certificate—bonds issued by transportation companies that are secured by the equipment purchased with the proceeds.

equity—ownership in a firm; sum of stock, paid-in-capital, and retained earnings.

Eurodollar bonds—bonds issued abroad by American firms that are denominated in dollars instead of a foreign currency.

excess reserves—reserves in excess of a commercial bank's required reserves.

exchange rate—price of a foreign currency.

ex-dividend date—day after the day of record for a dividend payment.

exercise price—price at which rights may be exercised to buy new stock.

external finance—funds acquired through issuing debt and new stock.

external growth—growth through mergers and take-overs of other firms.

factoring—selling of accounts receivable.

Federal Deposit Insurance Corporation (FDIC)—Federal Government agency that supervises commercial banks and insures commercial bank deposits.

federal funds market—market in which commercial banks borrow and lend excess reserves.

Federal Reserve—central bank of the United States which controls the nation's supply of money.

federal reserve bank—one of twelve district banks of the Federal Reserve.

FIFO—method of valuation of inventory in which the First Inventory In is the First Inventory Out (i.e., sold).

financial intermediary—firm that transfers savings to borrowers by creating claims on itself.

financial leverage—use of another person's or firm's funds in return for agreeing to pay a fixed return on the funds; the use of debt and preferred stock financing.

financial risk—risk associated with the types of financing used to acquire assets.

fixed costs—those costs that do not vary with the level of output.

flexible exchange rates—currency prices that fluctuate with the supply and demand for each currency.

float—checks in process that are simultaneously counted as deposits in two commercial banks.

flotation costs—costs of issuing new securities.

foreign exchange market—market for foreign currencies.

fundamental approach—use of financial information concerning a firm to help select securities.

future value—amount to which a present dollar will grow compounded at some rate of interest.

futures price—price for future delivery of a commodity or currency.

general obligation bond—bond supported by the taxing power of the government that issued the bond.

gold certificate—warehouse receipt for gold held by the Treasury.

gold standard—monetary standard in which paper money is denominated and convertible into gold.

goodwill—accounting entry (intangible asset) that arises when the cost of an asset exceeds its value.

hedging—simultaneous purchases and sales designed to reduce risk of loss from commodity price or exchange rate fluctuations.

holding company—firm that acts as an umbrella by owning several firms.

horizontal merger—merger of two or more firms in the same industry.

hurdle rate—return necessary to justify making an investment.

income bonds—bonds secured only by the income generated by the investment financed by the proceeds of the sale of the bonds.

income statement—listing of a firm's revenues and expenses for the purpose of determining profit or loss.

indenture—document specifying the terms of a debt issue.

inflation—increase in the general level of prices.

insolvency—inability to meet debt as it comes due.

insolvent firm—firm that is unable to meet its financial obligations.

interest—payment for the use of money.

internal rate of return—rate of return that equates the present value and the present cost of an investment.

inventory cycle—period during which inventory is accumulated, sold, and subsequently replenished.

investment—(in economics) expenditure on plant, equipment, or inventory; (popular) purchase of a financial asset such as stock.

investment banker—middleman that brings together firms issuing new securities and buyers.

investment company—firm that primarily invests in secondhand securities.

joint project—investment undertaken by two firms or a firm and a government.

leasing—renting (as opposed to owning) plant or equipment.

LIFO—method of inventory valuation in which the Last Inventory In is the First Inventory Out (i.e., sold).

line of credit—right to borrow (at the option of the borrower) up to a specified amount from a commercial bank.

liquidation—sale of assets.

liquidity—ease of converting an asset into cash without loss.

long-term debt—debt that matures after one year.

M_1—demand deposits plus coins and currency.

M_2—demand deposits plus coins and currency plus savings accounts in commercial banks.

margin—minimum amount of funds an investor must put up to purchase securities; buying securities on credit.

marginal tax rate—tax rate paid on the last (marginal) dollar of income or profits.

market maker—firm or person willing to purchase or sell a security at a specified price.

market value—price at which a good or service may be sold or purchased.

maturity—time when a debt issue (i.e., the principal) must be retired.

merger—combining of two or more firms into a single firm.

money—anything that is generally accepted as means of payment.

money market—market for short-term securities (e.g., Treasury bills).

mortgage—long-term debt secured by property.

mortgage bonds—bonds secured by a claim on property.

multinational firm—firm with operations in several countries.

municipal bond—bond issued by a municipality whose interest is not subject to federal income taxation.

mutual fund—open-ended investment company that stands to issue and redeem its shares on demand.

NASDAQ—national system of security quotes (National Association of Security Dealers' Automatic Quotation system).

net present value—present value of future cash flows minus present cost.

net worth—difference between total assets and total liabilities; a firm's equity.

no load fund—mutual fund that does not charge a sales commission.

NOW account—special saving account against which negotiable orders of withdrawal may be drawn.

open-end investment company—firm that continually issues new shares and agrees to redeem these shares at the option of the stockholder.

open market operations—the buying and selling of securities by the Federal Reserve.

operating leverage—responsiveness of changes in earnings to changes in output.

opportunity cost—alternative use for funds.

optimal capital structure—combination of debt and equity financing that minimizes the average cost of capital.

over-the-counter market—unorganized security market in which transactions are between security dealers.

paper profit—unrealized profit.

par value—nominal value of stock used in accounting.

partnership—firm formed by two or more people, each of whom is liable for the firm's debts.

payback period—period of time necessary to recoup the cost of an investment.

payout ratio—ratio of cash dividends to earnings.

PE ratio—ratio of a stock's price to per-share earnings.

pooling of interest—method of accounting for mergers that combines the merged firms' balance sheets.

portfolio—collection of assets (primarily financial) designed to transfer purchasing power to the future.

preemptive right—right of stockholders to purchase any new issues of stock in order to maintain their proportionate ownership in the corporation.

preferred stock—certificates representing ownership in a corporation with a prior claim (before common stock) to the firm's earnings and assets (in case of liquidation).

present value—current value of a dollar to be received in the future.

prime rate—interest rate charged by commercial banks to their best customers.

principal—amount owed.

private placement—private sale of securities.

profit—revenues minus expenses.

profitability ratios—measures of performance.

progressive tax—a tax in which the tax rate increases as the tax base increases.

proportionate tax—a tax in which the tax rate stays the same as the tax base increases.

prospectus—document filed with the SEC describing new securities to be sold to the public.

purchase—method of accounting for a merger when a firm buys another firm.

quick ratio—alternative name for the acid test.

rate of return—percentage return earned on an investment.

recession—period of increased employment.

red herring—preliminary prospectus.

registered in street name—brokers holding stocks and bonds in their name for customers.

regression—a statistical technique that estimates an equation which summarizes a set of data.

regressive tax—a tax in which the tax rate decreases as the tax base increases.

Regulation Q—federal law that specifies maximum interest rates that commercial banks may pay on time and savings accounts.

required reserves—reserves commercial banks must hold against deposit liabilities.

reserves—non-income earning assets held by banks against their deposit liabilities.

retained earnings—earnings that have not been distributed.

revaluation—increase in the price of one currency relative to other currencies.

revenue bond—bond supported by revenues generated by the facility the bonds financed.

rights offering—offering of new stock to current stockholders.

risk—possibility of loss; degree of uncertainty.

safety stock—minimum desired level of inventory designed to protect against loss of sales due to being out of stock.

salvage value—any residual value in an asset after it has been depreciated.

SEC—Security and Exchange Commission; the Federal Government agency that enforces the federal security laws.

serial bond—bond issued in a series so that some of the issue periodically matures.

settlement date—date at which payment for the purchase of securities must be made.

short-term debt—debt that matures within a year.

simple interest—the true, annual rate of interest.

sinking fund—a fund established to retire periodically a debt issue.

slope—rate of change in a dependent variable relative to an independent variable.

sole proprietorship—firm with one owner.

specialist—market maker on the New York or American Stock Exchange.

spot price—current price of a commodity or currency.

spread—difference between the bid and ask prices.

stock—certificate representing share of ownership in a corporation.

stock dividend—dividend paid in additional shares of stock.

stock split—recapitalization achieved by changing the number of shares outstanding.

store of value—an asset that can transfer purchasing power from the present to the future.

subordinate debt—debt that has a lower claim on the assets and income of the firm.

syndicate—selling group formed to market a new issue of securities.

synergism—combining of two firms so that the combined firm is stronger than both firms by themselves.

systematic risk—the tendency for a security's price to move with the market.

tax credit—a direct reduction from one's tax liability.

tax exempt bonds—securities issued by state and local governments, the interest on which is exempt from federal income taxation.

technical approach—the use of security market data (e.g., volume of trading, price trends) to help select securities.

total return—the return on an investment in stock; dividends and capital gains.

total revenue—price times quantity sold.

trade credit—credit supplied by a wholesaler to its buyers.

trade discount—discount for prompt cash payment.

treasury bills—short-term U.S. Government securities.

trustee—representative of the rights of bondholders who enforces the terms of the indenture.

turnover—speed with which inventory is sold or accounts receivable are turned into cash.

underwriting—purchase of an issue of new securities for subsequent re-sale by investment bankers and their syndicate.

underwriting fee—commission charged firm for the sale of new securities.

value of money—its purchasing power.

variable costs—those costs that vary with the level of output.

vertical merger—a merger of a firm with a supplier or a distributor.

working capital—firm's short-term assets; cash, marketable securities, accounts receivable, inventory.

yield curve—relationship between time and interest rates for debt in the same risk classification.

yield to maturity—the return that includes current interest and any discount or premium paid for the bond; internal rate of return on a bond.

INDEX

Numbers in *italics* indicate an illustration; (t) indicates a table.